THE
PHILIPPINE
ECONOMY

THE PHILIPPINE ECONOMY

No Longer the East Asian Exception?

EDITED BY

RAMON L. CLARETE
EMMANUEL F. ESGUERRA
HAL HILL

ISEAS YUSOF ISHAK
INSTITUTE

First published in Singapore in 2018 by
ISEAS Publishing
30 Heng Mui Keng Terrace
Singapore 119614

Email: publish@iseas.edu.sg
Website: bookshop.iseas.edu.sg

The responsibility for facts and opinions in this publication rests exclusively with the authors and their interpretations do not necessarily reflect the views or the policy of the publisher or its supporters.

ISEAS Library Cataloguing-in-Publication Data

The Philippine Economy : No Longer the East Asian Exception? / edited by Ramon L. Clarete, Emmanuel F. Esguerra and Hal Hill.
1. Philippines—Economic conditions—1946-1986.
2. Philippines—Economic conditions—1986-
3. Poverty—Philippines.
4. Infrastructure (Economics)—Philippines.
5. Urbanization—Philippines.
6. Education—Philippines.
7. Public health—Philippines.
8. Philippines—Environmental conditions.
9. Energy security—Philippines.
10. Investments—Philippines.
11. Philippines—Politics and government—1986-
I. Clarete, Ramon L., editor.
II. Esguerra, Emmanuel F., editor.
III. Hill, Hal, 1948-, editor.
HC455 P568   2018

ISBN 978-981-4786-50-8 (soft cover)
ISBN 978-981-4786-62-1 (e-book, PDF)

Typeset by International Typesetters Pte Ltd
Printed in Singapore by Mainland Press Pte Ltd

Contents

Figures

Tables

Foreword

It gives me great pleasure and honour to provide the introductory message for this rather impressive volume on the Philippine economy. Authored by renowned Filipino scholars and serious observers of the Philippine economy, the volume is arguably the most comprehensive reference work on the economy since at least the global financial crisis in 2008–9 and will likely shape the thinking and practice of Philippine development policy in the years ahead.

This volume had its beginning, albeit accidental, during my stint as Socioeconomic Planning Secretary and, concurrently, Director-General of the National Economic and Development Authority under the administration of President Benigno S. Aquino III. At that time, in early 2014, I got hold of the ADB Report entitled *Asia 2050: Realizing the Asian Century*, and it caught my interest. The report talked about how Asia is in the middle of a historic transformation. To quote the report: "If it continues to follow its recent trajectory, by 2050 its per capita income could rise six-fold in purchasing power parity (PPP) terms to reach Europe's levels today. It would make some 3 billion additional Asians affluent by current standards. By nearly doubling its share of global gross domestic product (GDP) to 52 percent by 2050, Asia would regain the dominant economic position it held some 300 years ago, before the industrial revolution."

It was an exciting prospect for Asia, except for the Philippines. In the Report, the Philippines was a slow- or modest-growth aspiring country, lumped in the same group as Afghanistan, Bangladesh, North Korea, Laos, Myanmar, Nepal, Pakistan, and many of the Pacific Island countries. Even the Report's epic video-production did not make any reference to or show any significant Philippine landmark. That was, of course, understandable, given the country's poor-growth record in the three decades before 2010, which was the report's database for its extrapolation of the future. In contrast, since at least 2010, the country's economic performance has been quite stellar, impressively even earning the title "the rising tiger of Asia", among other accolades bestowed upon the Philippine economy by various global development observers, e.g., the World Bank and HSBC.

Both pride and necessity prodded me and my colleagues at NEDA, including one of the editors of this volume, Emmanuel Esguerra, to help change the narrative on the Philippine economy and society. The conditions were ripe for such a change. We could not allow ourselves to be left behind, to remain a laggard in an otherwise highly dynamic, rapidly growing and prospering region. We needed to reshape our future, to become part of the Asian Century. We needed to have a positive long-term vision for the country.

Meanwhile, even before my stint as NEDA chief, there were already discussions in different fora and media pushing for the creation of a long-term development plan, apart from the medium-term development plan of each administration. Private sector and civil society organizations, even some members of Congress, had been clamouring for a long-term development plan that transcends the fixed six-year term of political administrations.

But then we also considered political realities. We were aware of the fixed six-year term of a president and the tendency of each new administration to abandon even good plans and programmes of its predecessor to signify change and create a new "brand". A long-term plan crafted under one presidency runs the risk of discontinuity under the successor presidency.

Given all these, we thought that the best and the first thing to do was to have a common vision for ourselves over the long term. We need to define our long-term goals as a nation and unite around them such that medium-term plans of each administration will be guided by this set of goals — or our long-term vision — based on the standard of living that Filipinos want to have in twenty-five years or so. While people may differ on short- and medium-term objectives, as well as on approaches or strategies to achieve these goals, we believe it is important and possible to reach a consensus on a long-term vision.

The long-term vision exercise involved several activities intended to make it widely participatory, methodologically robust, and evidence-based. We conducted several public consultations through focus group discussions and a national household survey to ensure that the long-term vision we arrived at would be truly representative of the aspirations of the Filipino people. Moreover, as part of the exercise, we commissioned research and technical studies on various thematic areas that are widely known to be key factors affecting a country's economic development. These include growth and poverty, health, education, demography, innovation, infrastructure, environment, energy, finance, governance, and the global economy. A select set of the technical papers constitutes the chapters in this volume. Finally, we launched a communication plan to generate public awareness on the long-term vision, now dubbed *Ambisyon Natin 2040* — a play of English and Filipino words "The Vision" and "Our Ambition".

It was thus gratifying, to say the least, when the administration of the newly elected President Rodrigo Duterte embraced the long-term vision as the anchor for its socio-economic development agenda. Through Executive Order No. 5, President Duterte adopted the *Ambisyon Natin 2040* as the long-term vision for the Philippines, enjoining all government offices and instrumentalities to develop and implement their plans consistent with the long-term vision. The order resonates in the administration's recently crafted medium-term development blueprint, the *Philippine Development Plan 2017–2022*.

Let me now turn to another possible reason why I was given the honour to provide a foreword to this volume. My previous appointment as Socioeconomic Planning Secretary in the Aquino administration gave me a front-row seat to the country's transformation in recent years, the highs and lows of high-level policymaking, as well as the transition of power from President Aquino to President Duterte. In keeping with the theme of this volume, let me humbly share some of my own observations and reflections on where the Philippines has been, and some ideas on where it might be headed under this new administration.

As I noted earlier, the Philippines has enjoyed a surge of growth and macroeconomic stability in recent years. The country's economic growth rate averaged 6.3 per cent from 2010 to 2016 — the highest seven-year average growth since the late 1970s. This makes the Philippines one of the fastest-growing major emerging economies in the world today. The economy's structure is also changing, with signs of investment spending and resurgence in the industrial sector, though the economy is still very much consumption- and service-oriented. Such stellar economic performance has also been accompanied by strong macroeconomic fundamentals, an unprecedented level of confidence among players in the domestic and international business communities, improved competitiveness rankings, and a much stronger external position owing to the resilience of remittances and income from growth areas like business process outsourcing (BPO) activities and tourism, notwithstanding recent developments in the global political economy (e.g., Brexit, Trump's "America First" populism). These, along with many other positive indicators, have led many to think that the Philippines has, finally, shed its moniker as the "Sick Man of Asia", and is transforming into one of the region's brightest economic hubs.

Such a transformation, of course, has had its fair share of hiccups along the way. One of the major challenges faced by the previous administration — and one that is also likely to be faced by the current one — is how to make such growth more inclusive; i.e., how to translate economic gains into a faster reduction of poverty and inequality in access to opportunities. To be sure, part of the challenge is that, globally, economic growth today has become less able to reduce poverty compared to two or three decades ago. For one, economic growth has become less employment-intensive than before. The widespread growth of information and communication technology (ICT), a labour-saving technology, and globalization has also tended to widen the gap between skilled and unskilled segments of the global workforce.

In the Philippines, attaining inclusivity and poverty reduction has been made even more difficult by a number of natural challenges, such as the onset of major earthquakes in the Visayas and Typhoon Haiyan in 2013 (considered one of the strongest typhoons in recorded history). More importantly, there were also a number of institutional and governmental bottlenecks that weakened the translation of growth to poverty reduction. For instance, food policy experienced several wrinkles that kept basic food prices, particularly rice prices, much higher than what they would have been if international trade on food was less restrictive. A number of industries have also experienced increasing education–skills mismatches, contributing to the persistently high underemployment rate, even among college graduates. The country's low level of physical capital formation was addressed by instituting public–private partnerships and reforms in budget spending, but various implementation and coordination failures prevented many projects from proceeding at a much faster pace.

The election of President Duterte into office offers a golden opportunity to implement reforms towards greater inclusivity, while at the same time continuing and maintaining the previous administration's macroeconomic policies, including fiscal, monetary, and trade policies. For instance, there is now a deep-seated commitment to proceed at a more decisive and quicker pace when it comes to implementing projects and programmes and addressing bottlenecks, especially those on infrastructure. Many tax reforms aimed at improving tax administration and the progressivity of the tax regime are also in the pipeline. Peace and order, especially wars on drugs and crime, have also come to the fore of the development agenda.

But ensuring poverty reduction and greater inclusivity in the future requires nothing less than an acceleration of structural transformation — a shift of employment from low-productivity to high-productivity sectors, not only across agriculture, industry, and services, but also within each of these sectors. Evidence based on country experiences around the world in the past fifty years indicate that at the heart of the system driving poverty reduction is a structural economic transformation guided by efficiency-promoting policies and institutions. That is certainly the case in the country's neighbours — in China, Vietnam, Thailand and Indonesia, where structural transformation was key to their dramatic success in reducing poverty in the past three decades.

One of the key components of the overall strategy to make economic growth more enduring and more inclusive is the Philippine Competition Act, which became effective in August 2015. This legislation seeks to deepen efficiency-enhancing competitive practices so that economic growth becomes more enduring and more inclusive, thereby fostering public welfare both in the short and long run. It aims to create a policy environment that promotes a fair and competitive market — a level playing field — by regulating business practices that unreasonably restrain competition.

We see this legislation as a game-changer for the economy. The law is meant to address the very restrictive economic policies and anti-competitive business practices that have been too costly to the Philippine economy and public welfare. As evident in this volume, the economy had a comparatively poor performance over the last four decades. The highly unequal distribution of opportunities has perpetuated a condition of widespread poverty coexisting with growing affluence and prosperity in certain enclaves of Philippine society. Small and medium enterprises have found it extremely difficult to thrive and prosper in an economic environment where a level playing field is more of an exception than the norm, hindering the growth of employment opportunities. As is also evident in this volume, various anti-competitive business practices have their roots in certain laws, policies, regulations, and administrative issuances. Part of the reform effort has to involve deeply reforming governance to reinforce competitive market outcomes while achieving other societal goals, such as equity and health security.

All in all, the Philippines' reform story is far from complete. Moving forward, crafting and honing the reform agenda will require the collective effort of policymakers, advocates, and academics not only in the Philippines but also colleagues and friends from abroad. This volume plays a crucial role in deepening the understanding and collaboration between Filipino and non-Filipino scholars by way of thoughtful and structured policy research and analysis.

Arsenio M. Balisacan
Chairperson, Philippine Competition Commission
Secretary of Socioeconomic Planning and Director General of
NEDA, 2012–16

Manila, 15 March 2017

Preface

It is a pleasure to thank the many people and institutions who contributed generously to this volume, and without whom it would not have seen the light of day.

First and foremost, we would like to express our deep gratitude to our good friend and colleague, Arsenio M. Balisacan, and his staff, for initiating this project during his term as Secretary of Socioeconomic Planning and Director General of the National Economic and Development Authority (NEDA) in the Government of the Philippines from 2012 to 2016. As he explains in the Foreword written for this volume, he and his senior colleagues in government oversaw a period of strong economic growth. But they were also conscious of the importance of maintaining the momentum. To this end, they set to work on crafting a forward-looking agenda, *Ambisyon Natin 2040*, which articulated a vision for an inclusive and prosperous Philippines. Some of the works commissioned for this endeavor provided the germ for the analytical papers that fed into this volume.

The Asian Development Bank (ADB) played a crucial supporting role in facilitating work on this project, including a workshop at which draft papers were presented and discussed. We are most grateful to the staff of the Bank's Philippine Country Office, headed by Richard Bolt, for their enthusiastic support and wise counsel.

While thankful to NEDA and the ADB, we do wish to emphasize that the views and assessments in this volume are those of the contributors and editors alone, and should not be attributed to these two supporting institutions.

We are most grateful to our contributors for taking time out from their busy schedules to write stimulating papers, and to cheerfully endure the protracted editorial processes leading up to publication.

We thank Mr Ng Kok Kiong, Mr Stephen Logan and the ISEAS publishing team for their interest in our work, and an anonymous referee for very helpful and constructive comments on an earlier draft.

The current period is arguably one of the most significant in Philippine history. The country is frequently in the international news headlines, perhaps more than it would like to be. Behind these headlines is the question of whether the momentum of recent economic growth in the country can be sustained and its dividends enjoyed by more of the population. We hope this volume might be able to make some small contribution to the development policy debates directed at how to ensure continued socio-economic dynamism at this historic juncture in Philippine society.

The Editors
Manila and Canberra
September 2017

About the Contributors

Arsenio M. Balisacan is the first Chairman and CEO of the Philippine Competition Commission. Previously, he served as the Socioeconomic Planning Secretary in the Cabinet of President Benigno S. Aquino III and, concurrently, the Director-General of the National Economic and Development Authority (NEDA). Prior to his appointment in NEDA, he was the Dean and Professor of the University of the Philippines (UP) School of Economics and Director-Chief Executive of the Southeast Asian Regional Centre for Graduate Study and Research in Agriculture (SEARCA). Before joining the UP faculty, he was a Research Fellow at the East-West Center in Honolulu and Economist at the World Bank in Washington, D.C. He holds a PhD in Economics from the University of Hawaii and an MS degree in Agricultural Economics from the University of the Philippines Los Baños.

Ramon L. Clarete is a Professor and a former Dean of the University of the Philippines School of Economics in Diliman, Quezon City. His research interests are on trade, agriculture and food policies. For several years he managed the delivery of technical assistance programmes of the USAID/Philippines to the Philippine government, primarily on trade capacity building, and he has provided policy advice to the government and business support organizations in the Philippines. Under the Asian Development Bank (ADB), he led a team of experts who conducted the background studies for the National Economic Development Authority's long-term vision of the Philippine economy. The ADB had engaged him to give advice to and conduct training on food and trade policy to the members of the ASEAN Food Security Reserve Board. He currently is in the Advisory Board of the

Asian Rice Bowl Index (RBI) and until just recently in the Board of Advisors of the WTO Chairs Programme. He has published several papers on food policy, the latest being on "Deepening ASEAN Rice Trade".

Emmanuel F. Esguerra is Professor of Economics at the University of the Philippines School of Economics (UPSE). A member of the UPSE faculty since 1993, he was seconded to the National Economic and Development Authority (NEDA) in July 2012 where he served as Deputy Director-General for Policy and Planning and subsequently as Director-General and Secretary of Socioeconomic Planning from February to June 2016. Prior to his secondment at NEDA, he was chair of the Department of Economics at UPSE. He obtained his PhD in 1993 from the Ohio State University in Columbus, Ohio, USA. His research interests include labour economics and development microeconomics.

Hal Hill is the H.W. Arndt Professor Emeritus of Southeast Asian Economies at the Australian National University. His research interests focus on various aspects of the economic development and political economy of the Southeast Asian countries. He is the author or editor of eighteen books and has written about 150 academic papers and book chapters. He is an occasional op-ed contributor to Australian and Asian newspapers, magazines and websites, and a radio/TV commentator. He has worked as a consultant for the Australian Government, the Indonesian Government, the World Bank, the Asian Development Bank, and several United Nations agencies. He has held visiting academic appointments at institutions in ten countries, including the University of the Philippines. He is a Fellow of the Academy of Social Sciences of Australia, and has been an official guest of Indonesia as a "Presidential Friend of Indonesia".

Ruperto P. Alonzo was a Professor at the University of the Philippines School of Economics and had been with the faculty since 1968. He was also a Research Fellow at the Energy Policy and Development Program. He served as a Deputy Director-General of the National Economic and Development Authority from 1998 to 2001. He was also the Vice-President for Development for the University of the

Philippines System and a Commissioner for the UNESCO National Commission of the Philippines. He graduated magna cum laude from the Ateneo de Manila University with the AB degree in Humanities. He took his MA in Economics at the University of the Philippines and did doctoral studies at the University of Chicago. His fields of research interests were in Public Economics (Project Evaluation, Investment Programming, Public Expenditure Management), Human Resources Economics (Education, Health), and Development Economics (Informal Sector, Impact Assessment, Decentralization Studies).

Clarisa Joy A. Arellano is a research assistant at the World Bank Philippine Office under the Macroeconomics and Fiscal Management Global Practice. She is currently part of the team preparing the Bank's next flagship report, the "Mindanao Jobs Report". Prior to joining the World Bank she was part of the Energy Policy and Development Program research team, where she learned more about energy and environment issues and helped in writing the Filipino 2040 study on the environment, climate change and disaster resiliency. Issa is a graduate student at the UP School of Economics and is completing her masters' thesis on the effects of the IT-BPM industry on the Philippine labour markets. Her research interests include development economics, labour, trade and environmental economics.

Eduardo Banzon MD, MSc is Principal Health Specialist of the Sustainable Development and Climate Change Department of the Asian Development Bank (ADB). Dr Banzon champions Universal Health Coverage and has long provided technical support to countries in Asia and the Pacific in their pursuit of this goal. Before joining ADB he was President and CEO of the Philippine Health Insurance Corporation, a World Health Organization (WHO) regional adviser for health financing in the Eastern Mediterranean region, World Bank senior health specialist, WHO-Bangladesh health economist, and a faculty member of the University of the Philippines' College of Medicine, Ateneo Graduate School of Business, Ateneo School of Government and Asian Institute of Management. He holds a Doctor of Medicine degree from the University of the Philippines and an MSc in Health Policy Planning and Financing from the London School of Economics and the London School of Hygiene and Tropical Medicine.

Arturo G. Corpuz is an Urban-Regional Planner involved in private practice and public planning and policy studies. He received his baccalaureate from the University of the Philippines and his master's and doctoral degrees in urban and regional planning from Cornell University, where he was a recipient of an APA-AICP Award, a Sage Graduate Fellowship, and a John D. and Catherine T. MacArthur Foundation Grant. He also served as Lecturer at the Department of City and Regional Planning of the same university. He received an award from the Philippine Regulations Commission as Most Outstanding Environmental Planner, and from the University of the Philippines School of Urban and Regional Planning as Most Outstanding Teacher. He is a former President of the Philippine Economic Society; a Fellow of the Foundation for Economic Freedom and the Philippine Institute of Environmental Planning; a Member of the American Planning Association and the Philippine National Historical Society.

Rolando A. Danao is Professor Emeritus at the University of the Philippines School of Economics and a Research Fellow at the Energy Policy and Development Program. He has written various papers and books, particularly in the field of mathematical economics and econometrics. He graduated BS Geodetic Engineering and MS Mathematics from the University of the Philippines Diliman. He obtained his MA in Mathematics and PhD in Mathematics from the University of California at Berkeley and completed his Postdoctoral Studies in Econometrics at the University of Pennsylvania. His research interests are in Mathematical Economics, Operations Research, and Econometrics.

Raul V. Fabella is one of the Philippines' National Scientists and is a Professor Emeritus of the University of the Philippines School of Economics. He is also a Research Fellow at the Energy Policy and Development Program. He obtained his PhD in Economics at Yale University. He took his Master's Degree in Economics at the University of the Philippines, where he served as Dean from 1998 to 2007. He has written articles in both theoretical and applied fields: political economy and rent-seeking, the theory of teams; regulation; international economics; and mathematical economics. Notable concepts associated with him are the "Olson ratio" in rent-seeking, egalitarian Nash bargaining solutions, and the debt-adjusted real effective exchange rate. His current fields of interest are economic theory, agricultural economics and international economics.

Beverly Lorraine Ho MD MPH is Chief of the Health Research Division of the Philippine Department of Health's Health Policy Development and Planning Bureau. Prior to this, she was a consultant for the Asian Development Bank's Health Sector Group working on health financing, health security and health impact assessment in the Greater Mekong sub-region. Dr Ho teaches health policy in the Ateneo de Manila University, co-founded the Alliance for Improving Health Outcomes, and actively works with Bagumbayani Initiative, a loose collaboration of young civil servants. She has worked for the Philippine Health Insurance Corporation (PhilHealth) and Qualimed Health Network; conducted research on health informatics and maternal and child health; and provided technical assistance to the Philippine government through WHO and UNICEF. She holds a Doctor of Medicine degree from the University of the Philippines and a Master of Public Health in Health Policy and Management from the Harvard T.H. Chan School of Public Health.

Karl Robert L. Jandoc is an Assistant Professor at the University of the Philippines School of Economics. He earned his PhD in economics at the University of Hawaii at Manoa in 2016 and his MA in Economics and BS Economics at the School of Economics, University of the Philippines. His research interests are in microeconomic theory, resource and energy economics. Apart from his academic position, he has also engaged in consultancy work for the Asian Development Bank, World Bank and the Energy Policy and Development Program.

Gilberto Llanto was President of the Philippine Institute for Development Studies. He is Regional Coordinator of the East Asian Development Network, a network of East Asian research institutes conducting policy research and capacity building; Country Coordinator for the Philippines of the Network of East Asian Think Tanks (NEAT);

Lead Convenor of the Philippine APEC Study Center Network; Associate Editor of the *Philippine Review of Economics*; Chairman of the Editorial Board of the *Philippine Journal of Development*; Member of the Academic Steering Committee on Financial Inclusion of the International Cooperative and Mutual Insurance Federation (ICMIF United Kingdom); and Member of the Advisory Council, Microfinance Council of the Philippines, Inc. (MCPI). He was formerly Deputy Director-General of the National Economic and Development Authority, and President of the Philippine Economic Society. He has a PhD in Economics from the School of Economics, University of the Philippines. He has a Master's Degree in Economics and a Bachelor's Degree in Philosophy. His research interests include public economics, growth economics, financial inclusion, microfinance, regional integration and infrastructure regulation. His most recent publication is "Philippine Infrastructure and Connectivity: Challenges and Reform", *Asian Economic Policy Review* 11, no. 2, July 2016.

Dennis S. Mapa is the Dean and Professor in Statistics at the School of Statistics, University of the Philippines in Diliman. He also serves as an Affiliate Professor in Economics at the UP School of Economics, and Research Fellow at the Social Weather Stations (SWS). He is also a Research Fellow at the Energy Policy and Development Program. He was a visiting scholar at the International Centre for the Study of East Asian Development (ICSEAD) in Kitakyushu, Japan. A multi-awarded researcher, Dr Mapa is the SEARCA Regional Professorial Chair holder for 2015 and a University of the Philippines Scientist for 2012–14. In 2008 he received the Outstanding Young Scientist (OYS) Award from the National Academy of Science and Technology (NAST) for his research contribution in the areas of Econometric and Financial Time Series Analysis, Empirical Economic Growth, Poverty Analysis and Impact Evaluation. He obtained his PhD in Economics at the UP School of Economics and holds a Master's Degree both in Statistics and Economics from the same university.

Ronald U. Mendoza, PhD is Dean and Associate Professor at the Ateneo School of Government. From 2011 to 2015, he was an Associate Professor of Economics at the Asian Institute of Management (AIM), and the Executive Director of the AIM Rizalino S. Navarro Policy Center for Competitiveness. Prior to that, he was a Senior Economist with the United Nations in New York. His research background includes work with UNICEF, UNDP, the Federal Reserve Bank of Boston, the Economist Intelligence Unit (EIU), and several Manila-based non-governmental organizations. His work has appeared in various peer-reviewed economics and policy journals; and he has also published several books on international development, public finance and international cooperation. His work includes *Providing Global Public Goods: Managing Globalization* (2003), *The New Public Finance: Responding to Global Challenges* (2006), *Children in Crisis: Protecting the Vulnerable and Promoting Recovery for All* (2012) and *Building Inclusive Democracies in ASEAN* (2015; and Winner of the NAST Outstanding Book Award for 2016). Mendoza obtained his Bachelor's Degree in Economics (Honors Program) from the Ateneo de Manila University in the Philippines, his Masters in Public Administration and International Development (MPA-ID) from the John F. Kennedy School of Government, Harvard University, and his MA and PhD in Economics from Fordham University. He is a recipient of various awards, including the 2012 National Academy of Science and Technology's Ten Outstanding Young Scientists (OYS) in the Philippines (in Economics), the World Economic Forum's Young Global Leaders in 2013, and Devex 40 Under 40 Development Leader in 2013.

Rosechin Olfindo is consultant in the World Bank and non-resident research fellow in the Ateneo School of Government. In the World Bank, she is involved in analytical work on social protection, labour regulations, employment programmes, and education. In the Ateneo School of Government, she participates in research on governance, social protection, and housing. She was also non-resident research fellow in the Asian Institute of Management, consultant to the Asian Development Bank, and a staff member of the Philippines' National Economic and Development Authority. She holds a master's degree in public administration in international development from Harvard University and a master's degree in economics from the University of the Philippines.

Majah-Leah V. Ravago is Assistant Professor at the University of the Philippines School of Economics (UPSE). She is also the Program Director of the USAID grant – Energy Policy and Development Program (EPDP) at the UPecon Foundation. Her research interests include resource economics, development economics, energy economics, and economics of natural disasters. She has published papers on resource management and sustainability, climate change, agriculture, and experimental games. She has received research grants from the University of the Philippines, East-West Center, and the Metrobank Foundation. She is a Board Member and Secretary of the Philippine Economic Society (PES). In July 2016 she received the National Academy of Science and Technology (NAST) Outstanding Young Scientist (OYS) Award in the field of Economics. She obtained her BS in Business Economics and MA in Economics degrees from the University of the Philippines. Her PhD in Economics is from the University of Hawaii (UH) under the East-West Center (EWC) Graduate Degree Fellowship Program.

James A. Roumasset is a Professor of Economics at the University of Hawaii Manoa, where he has been on the Economics faculty since 1976. He received his PhD in economics from the University of Wisconsin-Madison in 1973 and also has economics degrees from the University of Hawaii (MA) and the University of California-Berkeley (BA). He has taught and conducted research at the University of California-Davis, University of the Philippines (both Diliman and Los Baños), Australian National University, Yale University, University of Maryland, International Rice Research Institute, and World Bank. From 1978 to 1979, he led the Agricultural Development Council, Philippines programme. He is a member of the Board of Directors of the Western Economic Association International and a member of the American Economic Association, American Agricultural Economics Association, Association of Environmental and Resource Economists, and International Society for New Institutional Economics. He has published widely on agricultural development, environmental and natural resource economics, transaction cost economics, risk and decision-making, and the nature, causes, and consequences of public policy.

Winfred M. Villamil is an Associate Professorial Lecturer at the De La Salle University School of Economics. He earned his bachelor's degree at the Ateneo de Manila University and his MA and PhD degrees in Economics at the University of the Philippines School of Economics. He has published locally and internationally in the fields of human resource economics and regional development.

1

The Philippine Economy:
An Overview

Ramon L. Clarete, Emmanuel F. Esguerra and
Hal Hill

1. Introduction

The Philippines has long been viewed as the "East Asian exception".
Although suffering massive wartime destruction, in the 1950s and
1960s its economic prospects were considered to be favourable. While
very poor, its per capita income was somewhat higher than most of
its neighbours. In the post-colonial era it neither closed off from the
global economy — as China, Indonesia and Myanmar did — nor
was it overwhelmed by the conflict that engulfed Indochina. Its civil
society and polity appeared to be among the most robust in developing
East Asia. And it retained close commercial and political ties with
the undisputed global super power of that era, the United States. As
a vote of confidence, Manila was selected to be the headquarters of
the Asia Pacific's premier development finance institution, the Asian
Development Bank, in 1966.[1]

However, these early high expectations were not realized. From
the late 1960s the Philippines increasingly parted company with its

neighbours, as first the four Asian NIEs, then the ASEAN four (i.e., Indonesia, Malaysia, Thailand, together with Singapore) and, most important of all, China began to register exceptionally high rates of economic growth. By contrast, Philippine economic growth began to falter, especially from the late 1970s, and particularly during the country's deep economic and political crisis in the mid-1980s. The collapse of the two-decade Marcos rule in early 1986 was accompanied by the sharpest economic contraction in the country's economic history as an independent nation state. The economy was in free fall, with GDP declining by about 15 per cent in the years 1984–86 and poverty incidence rising sharply.[2] Thereafter, a fragile political system was gradually constructed, punctuated by periodic political instability and extended debt negotiations. This was the country's lost decade, as most of East Asia boomed, fuelled by a newly dynamic China and the relocation of labour-intensive manufacturing from Northeast to Southeast Asia. At the turn of the century, Philippine per capita income (PCI) had not progressed beyond that achieved in 1980.

Comparative surveys of Asian economic development have highlighted, and puzzled over, the country's divergent economic path. A leading contributor to the literature on growth empirics speculated that the country was "a democratic dud" (Pritchett 2003). The landmark World Bank (1993) "Asian miracle" study focused on the exceptionally strong performance of seven East Asian economies, which are the four NIEs and the four ASEAN countries (Singapore being a member of both groups). Perkins (2013) drew attention to the comparative record by estimating by how many multiples PCI had risen in the East Asian economies for the half century 1960–2010. The conclusion was a stark one: whereas the most successful economies increased their PCI by 12- to 15-fold, and most of the major ASEAN economies by a still-impressive 6-fold or more, the Philippines managed to only double its PCI. The World Bank's Growth Commission report (2008) highlighted a similar trend. We return to these empirical patterns in section 3 below.

The good news for the Philippines is that these "exceptional" observations are no longer being made. Since the early 1990s the country's growth performance, while not stellar, has not diverged noticeably from the ASEAN norm. The country avoided the worst of the 1997–98 Asian financial crisis (AFC) that so severely affected

Indonesia, Malaysia and Thailand. As Noland (2000) colourfully observed, the "sick man avoided pneumonia". During the global financial crisis (GFC) of 2008–9, the country's growth remained surprisingly robust, again in contrast to the traditionally dynamic export-oriented economies — Malaysia, Singapore and Thailand. And since 2010 the Philippines has registered historically strong growth, of about 6 per cent per annum, that has placed it alongside China and India as one of Asia's fastest growing economies. It has now recorded a historically unprecedented twenty-four quarters of continuously positive economic growth. Moreover, in spite of the new administration still finding its bearings, and for all the complexities of governance in a nascent democracy, the political system embodied in the 1987 Constitution appears to be maturing, with peaceful regime change at six-year intervals commencing in 1992.

This renewed economic dynamism, its sustainability, and the socio-economic challenges the country faces in graduating to the ranks of the upper-middle-income group of developing economies are the central themes of this volume. The contributors look backwards and forwards: backwards in surveying the development record and the salient lessons learnt from it, and forward to the manifold policy challenges to sustain the recent growth. A notional target to graduate to the high-income group was embodied in the "Filipino 2040" (*AmBisyon Natin 2040*) document prepared by the outgoing Aquino administration. This chapter introduces these key issues and provides an analytical survey of the historical and institutional context. As part of the Filipino 2040 study, and in addition to a broad survey of the Philippine economy by Ramon L. Clarete in chapter 2, seven core issues are identified for analysis. These are energy, the environment, urbanization and infrastructure, education, health, financing development, and governance and institutions.

Our organization is as follows. By way of background, section 2 briefly articulates ten stylized facts that characterize Philippine development. Section 3 reviews development outcomes since the 1960s in comparative context. Section 4 summarizes the contents of this volume. Section 5 concludes by returning to our key themes as well as providing an early look at the development priorities and outcomes of the Duterte administration.

2. The Philippine Economy: Ten Stylized Facts

In this section we identify ten "stylized facts" that characterize some salient features of the Philippine economy, its history and its institutions. These facts reflect both the continuities and the changes that are a feature of the country's development trajectory. To illustrate both the continuities and the changes, if this volume was being written in the early 1980s, the dominant themes would surely have been how to reinvigorate the economy, how to strengthen macroeconomic management, how to achieve trade liberalization, how to overcome the country's entrenched inequality, and how to break out of the authoritarian politics of the Marcos regime.

It is a reminder of the country's progress that some — but by no means all — of these challenges are in the process of being addressed. That is, the economy is now growing quite strongly, macroeconomic management (especially monetary policy) is much improved, the country's trade regime has been significantly liberalized, and a functioning democracy restored. A major continuity is, of course, the high inequality and the frustratingly slow pace of poverty reduction. Meanwhile, new challenges, such as those analysed in this volume, have emerged as major development priorities.

I. Highly Episodic Development Outcomes

Philippine growth has been episodic over the past half century, with three main sub-periods evident. The first was moderate economic growth through to around 1980. Growth was somewhat slower than most neighbouring countries, and generally also more volatile owing to periodic balance of payments crises. But the record was still respectable by global standards. The second was the 1980s decade, dominated by the deep economic crisis in 1984–86, followed by a hesitant recovery. This was the period when Philippine economic development departed significantly from the East Asian mainstream of rapid growth, structural adjustment, and reform.[3] The third period, commencing around 1990, saw a return to moderate growth. Since then the Philippines has generally grown somewhat more slowly than the region's high-performing economies, but the difference has narrowed, and all but disappeared since 2008. Philippine growth has also become less volatile, as the earlier boom and bust pattern had been mitigated by the macroeconomic reforms discussed below.

Outcomes in these three sub-periods were of course interconnected. The adventurous macroeconomic policies of the 1970s — the large increase in foreign debt, combined with an appreciating real exchange rate and proliferating "crony capitalism"[4] — laid the foundations for the mid-1980s crisis, accentuated as it was by regime collapse and transition. The painful lessons of the crisis in turn paved the way for far-reaching economic reforms, especially in the conduct of monetary policy, and hence improved economic performance.

II. Unusual Sectoral Growth Patterns

Agriculture performed well during the 1960s and 1970s (David 2003) but, consistent with the theory of economic development, its share of output and employment has fallen since the 1960s (Clarete, chapter 2). In other respects, however, the country's sectoral drivers of growth have been unusual. In particular, manufacturing growth has been anaemic for much of the period since 1980, and its share of GDP has actually declined.

The Philippines was the first Southeast Asian country to embark on a comprehensive import substitution strategy. But, as it approached the limits inherent in such a policy regime, it struggled to switch to export orientation, a problem compounded by the 1980s economic crisis (Medalla et al. 1995/96). Eventually, a reasonably comprehensive trade liberalization programme was introduced, but supply-side factors — infrastructure, labour market regulations, restrictions on foreign investment — have continued to hold back manufacturing. Like India, the Philippines has not achieved the large-scale, export-oriented, labour-intensive industrialization that has been such an important driver of growth, and poverty reduction, in the successful East Asian economies.[5]

In addition, in spite of considerable mineral prospectivity, this sector has been relatively unimportant. A considerable proportion of the country's mineral deposits are in conflict-affected areas, especially Mindanao, and this has obviously deterred potential investors. But, more important, the mining industry and its critics have struggled to develop a "compact" that provides the basis for efficient operations to the benefit of all parties. The critics have included environmental groups, who worry about weak enforceability of safeguards, local communities whose livelihoods are disrupted with little compensation, and tax administrators who are concerned about the corruption of fiscal and regulatory arrangements. Elements of the Catholic Church have also been vocal. During the periods of authoritarian government, these critics were largely pushed aside. However, in the democratic era they have been a powerful and often effective voice.[6]

The failure to achieve comprehensive export-oriented industrialization has had two implications for growth patterns and drivers. First, the share of the services sector is unusually high for a country at current Philippine income levels.[7] This is a highly heterogeneous sector in terms of enterprise scale, factor proportions, geographic location, and international orientation. It ranges from the modern sector of the country's business process outsourcing (BPO), as well as finance, education and health, through to "last resort" activities such as petty trading and a vast informal sector. The major explanation for the size of the services sector is the lack of industrial and agricultural dynamism. But the strong growth of some service sectors has also been a factor, particularly BPO, in which the Philippines is emerging as a major international player, second in the developing world only to India.

Second, Philippine export patterns are unusual compared to most of its neighbours. Services constitute a relatively high proportion of the country's total exports. In 2015, for example, remittances totalled about $27 billion, while BPO earned about $22 billion. These two items alone were not far short of merchandise (goods) exports of some $58 billion that year.[8] The prominence of remittances and BPO reflect the Philippines' comparative advantage in semi-skilled and unskilled labour-intensive activities, both abroad in the former case and at home in the latter. The failure to achieve similar export success in manufactures reflects key policy weaknesses, particularly in logistics, business, and labour regulation. We return to this issue below.

III. Major Macroeconomic Reforms

In important respects, the single most significant and durable economic policy reform since the 1960s was the establishment of a high quality, independent central bank, the Bangko Sentral ng Pilipinas, BSP, in 1993 (Gochoco-Bautista and Canlas 2003). Prior to this the country suffered periodic balance of payments crises. These were "textbook" macroeconomic crises that so many developing countries have experienced. That is, they originated in fiscal deficits, often in election years, that were in turn monetized by an accommodating central bank. This triggered higher inflation, but the central bank hung on to a fixed nominal exchange rate, out of fear of the inflationary consequences of a devaluation or the increased value of the debt in peso terms, or simply for reasons of national pride. In any case, the inevitable consequence was an appreciation of the peso in real terms. Moreover, the government frequently invested this deficit spending in uneconomic projects. Hence, competitiveness was adversely affected by both the misaligned exchange rate and uneconomic investment, resulting in a debt and/or balance of payments crisis.

The reconstituted Philippine central bank has navigated effectively through a period of great volatility, with occasionally severe external and domestic shocks. In effect, the exchange rate has operated as a "shock absorber", enabling the economy to adjust to these shocks. Although not widely appreciated in the broader community, central bank reform is the key to understanding why the Philippines has not experienced a serious economic crisis since the early 1990s, and indeed hardly a year of negative economic growth. In addition, financial sector supervision has been greatly improved, in turn easing the monetary policy tasks of the BSP.

IV. Gradual but Partial Economic Liberalization

The strident nationalism of President Duterte, and the evident support his rhetoric receives from much of the community, is testimony to the country's ambivalence towards globalization. In spite of gradual but partial reforms over the past three decades, the country still remains less open to trade and investment than most of its neighbours.

The Philippines was the first Southeast Asian economy to deliberately turn inwards. The "temporary" protectionist measures introduced in response to a balance of payments crisis in the late 1940s became embedded in the country's political economy (Power and Sicat 1971) and were largely resistant to reform in the ensuing four decades. The trade regime that was constructed over this period resulted in a bias against agriculture, employment and exports, thereby contributing to the slower and more unequal growth. It also corrupted the political system through the proliferation of rent-seeking opportunities in the complex trade and foreign exchange regimes. In spite of partial liberalizations in the 1970s, the country therefore missed out on much of the East Asian export-oriented boom that took hold in the region from the late 1960s.

Eventually the reformers were in the ascendancy, and significant trade liberalization was implemented from the late 1980s. There was a confluence of factors at work (Bautista and Tecson 2003; Bernardo and Tang 2008): first, the decades of analytical work by professional economists, based mainly at the University of the Philippines; second, the demonstrated success of liberalizing reforms in neighbouring economies, including even reform laggards such as Indonesia; third, a weak peso from the early 1980s, removing any pressure for compensating "exchange rate protection"; fourth, largely bipartisan political support, with the Ramos administration of 1992–98 particularly reform-oriented; and fifth, low-key analytical support from international agencies, mainly the World Bank.

Trade reform resulted in some export success, including the country's increased participation in the then emerging global production networks (GPNs) centred on electronics. But the results were arguably less than might have been expected, for several reasons. First, as noted, the Philippines missed out on the first major wave of industrial relocation from Japan and the NIEs during the 1980s, while in the 1990s China was attracting the lion's share of labour-intensive FDI. Second, the reforms were incomplete, in the sense that the FDI regime remained quite restrictive, while labour regulations introduced after 1987 deterred some investors. Infrastructure and logistics remained problematic. Third, the reform momentum began to falter, and political instability rise, under the Estrada administration of 1998–2001, just as the GPNs entered a new growth phase.

The Philippines has a clear stake in unfettered access to international markets for service exports, as is illustrated by its success with BPO and labour exports. But it has been rather slow to liberalize its services policy regime. It is a huge labour exporter, but its policies towards labour inflows are more restrictive than those of Singapore, Malaysia and Thailand. Its constitutional provisions that place a ceiling on the share of foreign investment in most sectors continue to limit the country's access to international equity markets, and the attendant sources of capital, technology and export market access (Sicat 2014).[9]

V. An Infrastructure Deficit

As documented by Arturo Corpuz in chapter 3 (see also Llanto 2016), the Philippines has one of the lowest levels of infrastructure investment and performance in East Asia. According to almost every comparative indicator, it ranks poorly, whether for urban traffic congestion, rural infrastructure provision, the speed and quality of logistics at international nodes (both ports and airports), electricity costs and reliability, and even e-commerce facilities (the latter notwithstanding the BPO success). This underperformance really matters. On efficiency grounds, it limits the country's participation in global production networks, where seamless best-practice logistics are essential. On equity grounds, poor infrastructure (e.g., badly maintained rural roads) restricts employment opportunities for the poor and increases the cost of marketing farm produce. Poor infrastructure also reduces environmental quality; for example, traffic congestion contributes to high air pollution levels in Manila and other major cities. Not surprisingly, therefore, infrastructure is a very high priority of the current and recent administrations. From very low levels, and as economic growth has rebounded, public and private infrastructure investments have been picking up in recent years.

Infrastructure is a subset of the general investment climate, and thus the factors that explain low investment in general also apply to infrastructure. But infrastructure also has several unique characteristics. First, it has long time horizons, spanning presidential administrations in the case of the Philippines, and therefore perceptions of uncertainty (for example, major policy reversals) will deter investors. Second, the government will inevitably be heavily involved — as direct investor in many projects, and regulator in others. Therefore the health of public finances and the quality of regulatory capacities are critical variables. Third, and related to this, there is a widespread public perception that large infrastructure projects are a major source of corruption (both personally and to secure political support), and thus there needs to be special safeguards to protect the public interest and ensure transparency. Fourth, and also related, for most infrastructure projects there is no ready "market" for the service, in terms of competitive supply alternatives and price benchmarks, and thus benchmarks for competitive evaluation. Fifth, the responsibility for infrastructure provision extends across multiple jurisdictions, and as noted below the country has sometimes struggled to coordinate the activities of central and local governments.

All these factors are relevant in understanding Philippine outcomes. Stronger public finances are essential to fund more infrastructure projects. But Philippine public finances were battered for at least a decade in the wake of the 1980s crisis, while for several years during the decade 2000–2010 congressional logjams and political uncertainty stymied the ability of the government to raise revenue. To attract more private investment, including foreign investors, there need to be assurances, from both the executive and the legislature, that the policy settings will be stable. The country has a history of occasional high profile, protracted and costly legal disputes with major foreign infrastructure suppliers. The quality of the national government's main departments and the associated regulatory agencies is therefore of paramount importance. In particular, high quality regulatory capacity is required for the many cases of infrastructure investment that have natural monopoly characteristics (e.g., major toll roads, power generation and transmission). With regard to private finance, the domestic capital market is sometimes too small to meet the requirements of scale and payoff periods.[10] Therefore, foreign investment is needed, and is available if the investment climate is attractive, secure and open. As noted, the Philippines currently meets only some of these prerequisites (Llanto, chapter 8).

In addition, given the country's archipelagic geography and regional socio-economic disparities, much of the infrastructure deficit is in the regions, especially the poorer ones. Local governments (the LGUs) play a critical role in local infrastructure provision, especially the rural road network. Most LGUs have arguably underinvested in infrastructure, and there is therefore a role for the national government to provide a framework of incentives — and penalties — to induce them to play a larger role. Improving inter-jurisdictional coordination, among the LGUs and between them and the national government, is also needed.

VI. A Continuing but Shrinking Educational Advantage

In the early post-colonial period, the Philippines enjoyed a head start in education compared to almost all its neighbours. This education advantage is central to an understanding of the country's development record. Combined with widespread English-language fluency, it laid the foundations for the country's strong comparative advantage in semi-skilled activities. In turn it explains why, when technological change accelerated the internationalization of business services, the country quickly became a leader in BPO, without the need for significant government assistance. It also explains why, as the economy slowed and international employment opportunities expanded, the Philippines became one of the largest remittance-recipients in the developing world, typically ranking fourth after only China, India and Mexico. And the high levels of literacy were surely a factor in the country's successful return to a functioning democracy after 1986.

However, as Winfred Villamil emphasizes in chapter 4, the country's earlier education advantages are eroding. While the country performs strongly in niche private sector segments, the backbone of the system — reasonably effective universal public education at the primary and secondary levels — has failed to keep pace, while other countries are catching up through stronger public investments in education. Given the country's entrenched high levels of inequality, education is the single most important policy tool to redress deep-seated inequities. Uneven educational outcomes also have a geographic dimension, in that poorer regions typically also register weaker schooling outcomes. In conflict-prone areas, the gap is particularly evident. Conversely, one traditional strength of the system remains largely intact; namely, that gender inequalities are among the lowest in East Asia.

International experience clearly shows that, on both efficiency and equity grounds, public education funds are best directed towards ensuring a high quality, universal system of primary and secondary education. The Philippines already has a well-established system of public education, and therefore it has the absorptive capacity to spend additional funding, including better physical facilities, more attractive remuneration for teachers, and enhanced IT provision for open learning. An unusual feature of the country's 1991 Local Government Code is that education has remained a national government responsibility. However, this administrative feature can be employed effectively to ensure that minimum national standards are met throughout the country.

Given its earlier education advantages, the Philippines could have become a major regional centre for the rapidly internationalizing higher education sector. However, Malaysia has assumed that role in Southeast Asia (apart from Singapore at the very top end). This missed opportunity was the result of restrictions on the operations of foreign educational institutions (another illustration of the cost of the restrictive approach to FDI) and political-security uncertainty as the internationalization process took root.

VII. Narrow Growth

Reflecting its colonial and agrarian origins, the Philippines has always had high levels of inequality, with little long-term change in the various measures of inequality since they were first estimated comprehensively in the early post-colonial period.[11] Poverty has therefore been less responsive to economic growth; combined with the generally slower growth, this explains why poverty incidence has fallen more slowly than in most neighbouring countries (Clarete, chapter 2). In spite of the egalitarian rhetoric, most administrations have failed to introduce broad-based measures to overcome the historical legacy. First, the lack of agricultural dynamism since the 1980s has meant that the sector in which the majority of the poor works does not provide dynamic income-earning opportunities. (Although, as noted, agriculture performed quite well in the 1960s and 1970s.) Second, the Philippines has not experienced export-oriented, labour-intensive industrialization on a mass scale, East Asian style. Thus, the growth of non-agricultural employment in the formal sector has been correspondingly slow, resulting in the country's inability to reach the "turning point" in economic development commonly characterized as the end of labour surplus, when there is a broad-based increase in real wages. Third, in the post-1986 democratic era, labour regulations — in particular high minimum wages relative to the country's per capita income — have discouraged formal sector employment growth. Fourth, as documented in chapters 4 and 5 of this volume, there has been insufficient public investment in targeted high-quality, universal primary and secondary education, or in public health, to equip the poor to productively enter the labour market. Fifth, there have been very few explicitly redistributive policy measures of any significance. The Comprehensive Agrarian Reform Program (CARP) is generally regarded as having had rather limited beneficial impact at an aggregate level, although no doubt there have been individual beneficiaries.[12] There is little, if any, progressivity in the tax system. The recently introduced conditional cash transfer programme arguably constitutes the first serious redistributive programme, means testing the payments and making them conditional on continuing school attendance.[13]

There are also gender, regional and business dimensions to these poverty and inequality outcomes. As noted, gender inequality is relatively modest by East Asian standards, especially with respect to education outcomes. However, female-headed households are proportionately over-represented in poverty incidence, while there are pronounced labour market and earnings differentials among higher income groups.

Spatial inequality continues to be very high. In this, the world's second-largest archipelagic state, the data show that poverty incidence in the poorest regions, such as the Autonomous Region of Muslim Mindanao (ARMM), is many multiples of that of the National Capital Region and the areas surrounding Manila (see Clarete, chapter 2). As best as can be documented given the changes in administrative boundaries, the level of spatial inequality has hardly changed during the past half century. In fact, it has probably worsened during the frequent periods when conflict has intensified in Mindanao and other regions.[14]

The Philippine business sector is frequently characterized as highly concentrated, reflecting the country's unequal wealth distribution. A small number of "oligarchs", in the form of rich families, is alleged to dominate the country's business and politics. The business–politics connections are emphasized, consistent with the notion of "crony capitalism". Such a pattern is said to be reinforced by limited regulatory constraints on collusive behaviour, and by restrictions on the entry of foreign capital that might otherwise increase competitive pressures.[15]

In this vein, one of the most knowledgeable academic observers of the Philippines concludes pessimistically as follows:

> [The] persistence of oligarchic firms in the Philippines comes with some marked costs.... The country's ... recurring crises [have arisen] arguably from a fusion of political power and rent seeking, reducing both opportunity and prosperity. For the foreseeable future, it seems unlikely that the Philippines will undertake the 'broad institutional reforms and shifts in oligarchic control' that would allow it to move beyond the [country's] 'corruption, poor legal protections and perverse state institutions'. (McCoy 2015, p. 185)[16]

While there can be no doubting the high levels of business concentration, precise documentation of both levels and trends remains elusive. In a widely cited paper, Claessens et al. (2000) found that in 1996 the Philippines had the highest share of family control of corporate assets among nine East Asian economies, as measured by the shares of the top family and the top five families, and the second-highest shares for the top ten and fifteen families. However, the authors' analysis is confined mainly to publicly listed companies, a limitation they seek to rectify with a more detailed analysis of the country's premier business group, the Ayala family. Another crude indicator of business concentration is billionaire wealth relative to GDP, and the concentration of the very rich in "crony sectors". A survey by *The Economist* (15 March 2014) found the Philippines ranked sixth highest out of twenty-three countries on this indicator, with a high proportion of business wealth in what it termed "crony sectors". However, these data need to be interpreted with caution: three dynamic East Asian economies — Hong Kong, Malaysia and Singapore — ranked higher still according to these criteria.

Notwithstanding the persistence of very wealthy and influential families, there is arguably more social and occupational mobility than is sometimes portrayed. For one thing, there are dynamic new entrants on to the business scene. The best known of these, the fast food business Jollibee, which now has a global reach, is a little more than forty years old. The Gokongwei business empire had its origins somewhat earlier, in the late colonial period, but most of its growth occurred in the post-independence era. In addition, the public education system has at least allowed a steady flow of able students from families of modest means to progress through to higher education and beyond. Overseas remittances constitute another source of socio-economic mobility, however limited.

VIII. Institutions: Progress and Complexity

The Philippines has an unusually complex set of institutional and governance characteristics, which are analysed in chapter 9 by Ronald U. Mendoza and Rosechin Olfindo, who also provide a comprehensive reform agenda.

Since the mid-1980s, political reform in the Philippines has proceeded faster than other forms of institutional reform (De Dios and Hutchcroft 2003). The country has held presidential elections on a regular six-year timetable, together with more frequent congressional and local government elections. The Philippines has a vigorous and largely free media.[17] The country also successfully implemented major governance reform through decentralization of administrative and financial resources to local governments, beginning in 1992.

Nevertheless, there has been limited "deep" institutional reform of the system of governance, including the bureaucracy, the legal system and the police. In fact, for a country that, on current trajectories, will reach upper-middle-income developing status within a decade or so, it is striking how little serious bureaucratic reform has occurred over the past three decades of democracy.[18] In spite of their limitations, the comparative governance indicators presented in the next section do portray the key features of the current system; notably, that the country performs considerably better on indicators of democracy and accountability than it does on government effectiveness, control of corruption, and business regulation.

Three additional factors are relevant to any understanding of the Philippine system of governance. First, the one-term presidential limit creates very short political time horizons, compounded by the fact that each new administration appoints its own senior executive, not just at the secretary level but often reaching down two or more levels. This power of presidential appointments inhibits the ability of the country to develop a strong and competent civil service culture that can attract able young graduates to its ranks. It also tends to undermine the development of institutional memory. Moreover, since some of these appointments may not necessarily be based on merit and open competitive selection processes, quality may be problematic unless there is a far-sighted and powerful occupant of Malacanang. These comments apply at the national level, but they operate with additional force at the local level.

Second, although as noted the term "oligarchs" is somewhat overused in the Philippine context, particularly with pejorative connotations, there can be no doubting the immense political power and influence of the country's most wealthy families. While at the national level this power is moderated by the larger pool of competitors (including the emergence of new commercial players) and a more diverse media, at the local level powerful clans frequently maintain a strong grip on government across generations (De Dios 2007).

Third, generalizations concerning bureaucratic quality obviously need to be cognizant of the considerable variation in governance quality across departments and tiers of government. Within the bureaucracy, for example, there are ample examples of diligent and professional staff who are poorly remunerated alongside egregious cases of corruption and job buying. But the "islands of excellence" found throughout the country, involving agencies with greater autonomy and the ability to offer adequate remuneration packages to their staff, are testimony to the proposition that there is a large reform dividend in effecting broad-based institutional change. At the national level, as noted, the BSP is a highly regarded institution. Specialized agencies such as the Philippine Export Zone Authority also perform effectively.

These two examples illustrate that a package of clear assignment of objectives, managerial autonomy, transparency and performance-based incentives produce beneficial results. A similar observation applies at the local level, given the uneven quality of LGUs.

IX. Armed Conflict

Although the Philippines had a relatively smooth transition to independence and it has not hosted a major theatre of war, it has in some respects struggled against lawlessness and violence, particularly in various parts of the country. The communist New People's Army has been able to operate low-level insurgencies in the countryside for decades. But the most serious conflict has been the decades-long insurgency between the government and disparate opposition groups, mainly Muslim-oriented, in the southern island of Mindanao. In spite of various peace accords and agreements, the conflict remains just as serious as ever, as illustrated most recently in the protracted warfare in and around the city of Marawi. The presence of private armed groups engaged in criminal activities (e.g., kidnap-for-ransom) in the area is a complicating factor. The human casualties have been extensive, with thousands of Filipinos in effect internally displaced refugees in their own country. There are also regional and international ramifications. Jihadist groups with battle experience in the Middle East and Afghanistan have found sanctuary in Mindanao, after being hounded out of Indonesia and Malaysia (Hutchcroft 2016).

At one level, and notwithstanding the shocking personal costs, the conflict could be said to be relatively minor. The conflict-affected areas are a small part of the national economy, their economies accounting for less than 5 per cent of national GDP. Life in the country's major cities elsewhere is little affected. Even within the main island of Mindanao there are quite dynamic regions in the northern and eastern regions. Moreover, unlike other countries with protracted conflicts (e.g., Pakistan), there has not been a major diversion of resources into the military.[19]

But there are costs, and not just for those Filipinos caught up in the conflict. The social indicators of the most affected region, the ARMM, are among the worst in Southeast Asia. Mindanao is a frontier, resource-rich region with great commercial potential and environmental significance if peace were to be achieved. It was these resources that historically attracted predominantly Christian migrants from the rest of the country in the first place, and that in turn laid the foundations for the present conflict. Governments (and foreign donors) have concentrated a disproportionate share of their resources in Mindanao to promote socio-economic development. When serious insurgencies occur, as they do on a fairly regular basis, the international media attention they attract has adverse national reputation effects, for investors, tourists and the country's image abroad. More generally, while to be sure this is a deeply complex problem with no easy solutions, the failure to reach a durable peace underlines the limits of the Philippine state, in both authoritarian and democratic eras.

X. Environmental Fragility

As documented by Roumasset and colleagues in chapter 6, most indicators of Philippine environmental amenity and quality point to a steady long-term deterioration.[20] Deforestation has been extensive, to the point that very little of the country's original forest resources still exist. Maritime resources have been overexploited, including the already fragile coastal ecology. Most inland water systems are heavily polluted. Air quality in the major urban centres is poor, critically so in some districts, and with serious health consequences (Banzon and Ho, chapter 5). Extreme weather events evidently occur with increased intensity and frequency, as illustrated with dramatic effect in the case of Typhoon Haiyan, which battered the country in November 2013. This was one of the most intense tropical cyclones ever recorded, with fatalities of over six thousand people and damage estimated to be in excess of $3 billion.

In some respects, this is a conventional story of the so-called "Environmental Kuznets Curve" at work. That is, countries grow first and then, beyond some income threshold, the environment is accorded a higher priority. Overexploitation of the forests and the marine resources occurs because of weak property rights, and the limited remit of institutions that are designed to protect them. Agricultural activities extend into fragile upland regions as farmers, lacking alternative income sources, seek to eke out a marginal existence. (Separately, as noted, there is a debate in the Philippines over whether agrarian reform programmes may have adversely affected the maintenance of agricultural lands owing to tenure uncertainty.) Elements of the mining industry have a questionable record of environmental management, whether due to weak regulatory design, poor enforcement capacity or just plain corruption with impunity. As noted, such outcomes explain much of the community's ambivalence towards this sector. Urban air quality suffers owing to lax transport emission standards, in turn a result in part of the pressure to maintain low fares. (As Corpuz notes in chapter 3, the underinvestment in cleaner forms of public transport, most notably rail, exacerbates the problem.) For similar reasons, factories are allowed to dump industrial waste in waterways. In addition to all these factors, the inexorable population growth places greater strain on the country's ecosystems.

There are no simple solutions to these and other complex issues. But the challenges are of such magnitude that the country cannot postpone addressing them until it is rich. Moreover, as Roumasset et al. (chapter 6) point out, there are "win win" strategies that can be implemented now. Stronger protection of maritime resources results in a sustainable fishing industry, as well as having beneficial tourism and other effects. An efficient mass transit system is both economically viable (especially at the very low real interest rates currently on offer, as Llanto emphasizes in chapter 8) and pro-poor. Moreover, as Ravago et al. (chapter 7) point out, the Philippines already obtains a relatively high proportion of its power generation from renewable energy sources, and it may well be able to exploit this factor in the ongoing international climate negotiations. In addition, climate change mitigation initiatives have a very high socio-economic payoff, and may also attract international support.

3. Philippines Development Dynamics[21]

This section reviews Philippine economic development since the 1960s, where data permit. It provides empirical support for some of the stylized facts articulated in the previous section, and as a prelude to the more detailed analysis that is summarized in the following section. We focus on the past half-century, since socio-economic development is a long-term process, while also drawing attention to the three major episodes identified above. In addition, we place the Philippine record in comparative international perspective. As comparators, we choose three neighbouring countries: Indonesia, Malaysia and Thailand. Thailand is arguably the most relevant given the similarities in geographic size and (earlier) in population. Indonesia shares the Philippines' archipelagic geography and, a decade apart, deep economic and political crises leading in turn to a sudden transition from authoritarian to democratic rule, and a significant decentralization of financial and administrative authority.

Economic growth: Figure 1.1 charts the growth record since 1960.[22] It shows the first phase, of moderate growth during the 1960s, a brief debt-driven growth spurt in the mid-1970s after the declaration of Martial Law, then a return to moderate growth for the rest of that decade. The economic decline from around 1980 marks the beginning of the second phase, with negative growth being registered in the wake of the public assassination of the leading opposition figure Senator Benigno Aquino, Jr. in August 1983. There followed the deep recession of 1984–85, of almost 10 per cent in per capita terms in each of these two years, and President Marcos' failed bid to recapture the political momentum through a snap election in February 1986. The election in turn led to the famous EDSA People's Power revolution later that month that ushered in the restoration of electoral democracy under President Corazon Aquino. Notwithstanding the signal achievement of democratic consolidation, the economic recovery was fragile for most of her term, which ended in negative growth. Complex debt negotiations, corporate and financial sector indebtedness, fluid politics and periodic military meddling held back economic growth.

Although it was not apparent at the time, with the benefit of hindsight the early 1990s marked a turning point in Philippine economic history, as it clearly marked the end of economic decline. The election of President Fidel Ramos in 1992 ushered in a period

FIGURE 1.1
Philippines, GDP Growth, 1960–2016

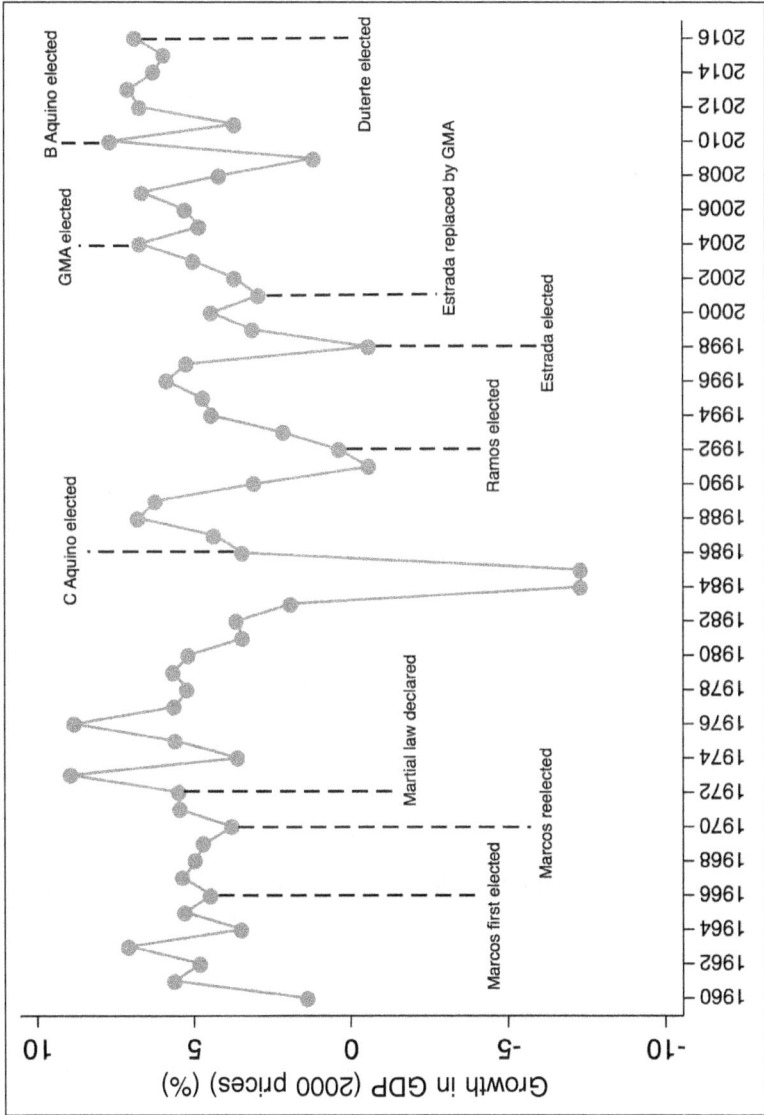

of reform, political stability and stronger growth. The economic momentum slowed only in the last year of his administration, and mainly due to external factors; namely the AFC, the effects of which were anyway comparatively mild. The brief Estrada presidency saw the return to moderate growth, punctuated by political uncertainty in 2001 with renewed political instability and the controversial ascension to power of President Gloria Macapagal-Arroyo. Although scarred by recurring challenges to her political legitimacy, arising from events in both 2001 and her formal election in 2004, Philippine economic growth averaged around 5 per cent during her nine-year term. As with the Ramos administration, her term also ended with slower growth, again owing mainly to external factors, in this case the GFC, which the Philippines navigated with little difficulty. Winning power in the wake of the GFC, the Benigno S. Aquino III presidency, 2010–16, saw the strongest economic growth of any six-year period in the country's history.

Structural change: As noted above, the process of structural change in the Philippines has been a mixture of the conventional and the unusual (Figure 1.2). Even though long-term economic growth has been slow, the share of agriculture in GDP has fallen substantially, from around 24 per cent in 1960 (and about 27 per cent in the mid-1970s) to just under 10 per cent in 2016. After quite strong growth in the 1960s and 1970s, mainly the result of effective adoption of high-yielding food crop varieties, especially in favoured irrigated areas, the share of agriculture has declined continuously since around 1980, more or less independently of the overall rate of economic growth. Six interrelated factors explain the decline. These are high population growth, progressively converting the Philippines from a moderately well-endowed economy to a resource-poor one; the exhaustion of frontier land expansion opportunities; the conflict in Mindanao, where what little of the frontier remains; the under-provision of public investment in aspects such as irrigation, rural roads and R&D; anaemic private investment, in part owing to tenure uncertainty in the wake of the agrarian reform programme; and policy distortions in the food market, principally through the operation of the National Food Authority.

FIGURE 1.2

Philippines, % of GDP from A, I, S Sectors, 1960–2016 (current prices)

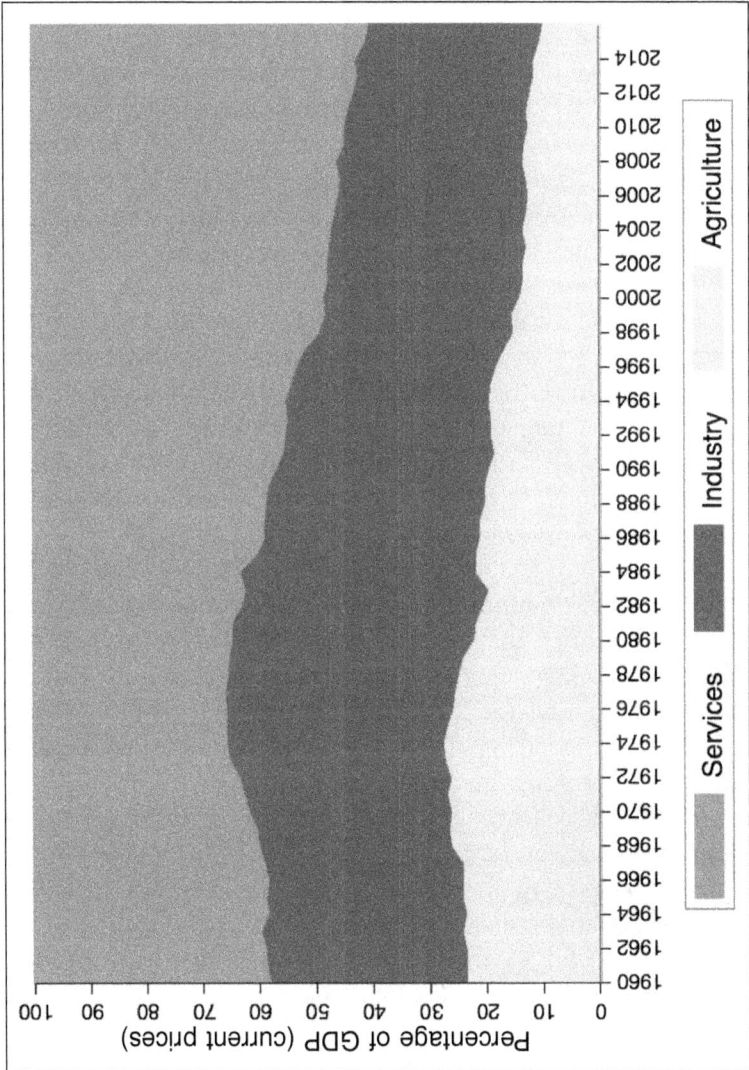

The unusual feature of Philippine structural change is that almost all the increase in GDP shares has occurred in the service sector. The current share of industry,[23] about 31 per cent, is similar to that prevailing in the early 1950s, and about 10 percentage points lower than that around 1980. Most of the decline has occurred in the major sub-sector, manufacturing, as the country failed to make the transition from import substitution to export orientation. The share of services has risen sharply since the 1970s, from about 35 per cent to almost 60 per cent. As noted, the rising services share is arguably more the result of slow growth in the goods sectors than of services dynamism, with the notable exception of BPO over the past decade.

Employment shares have followed these trends, with a lag. The very low relative labour productivity in agriculture is indicative of labour "trapped" in this sector. That is, agricultural labour productivity is about a third that of the economy-wide average, a figure that has been declining over time. Services labour productivity is similar to the economy-wide average, although this conceals large intra-sector variations, while that for industry continues to be by far the highest.

The changing composition of exports confirms these trends. Manufactures dominate Philippine merchandise exports, accounting for about 85 per cent of the total. The once important agricultural exports, including sugar and coconuts, now constitute little more than 5 per cent of the total. Mining exports are similarly unimportant. Within manufacturing, the share of electronics rose rapidly during the 1990s, peaking at 53 per cent of total exports in 2000 as the country successfully engaged with the rapidly growing global production network trade. However, policy and political uncertainty around the turn of the century deterred some key foreign investors and the country's share of this trade has since stagnated. Note that these data refer to merchandise exports and do not include the booming BPO exports. The latter explain the rapidly rising share of services in total exports, to about 21 per cent of the total, more than double that at the beginning of the century.[24] Recent work by, among others, Pasadilla and Wirjo (2017) and Serafica (2017) using OECD's Trade in Value Added (TiVA) database suggests, however, that the contribution of services to total Philippine exports is actually larger when services that are either embodied in merchandise exports or

FIGURE 1.3
Philippines, % of Employment from A, I, S Sectors, 1987–2016

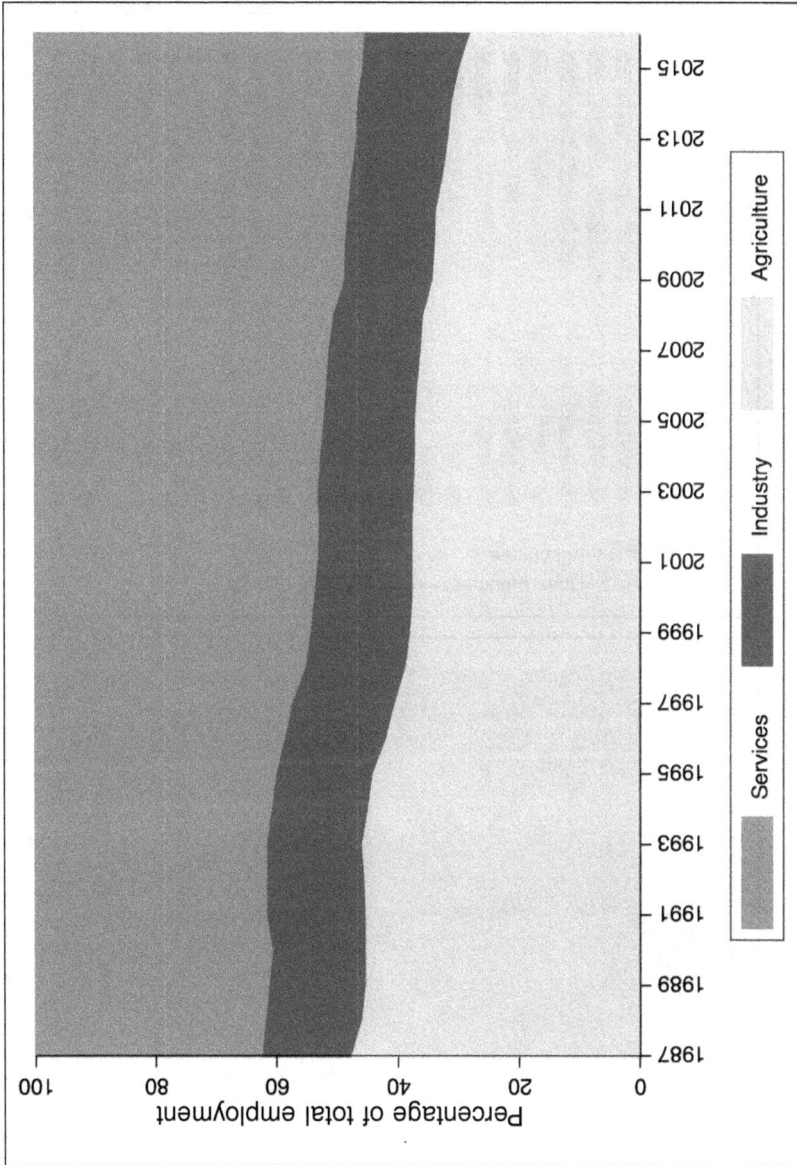

FIGURE 1.4
Philippines, Export Composition, 1960–2016 (% of total)

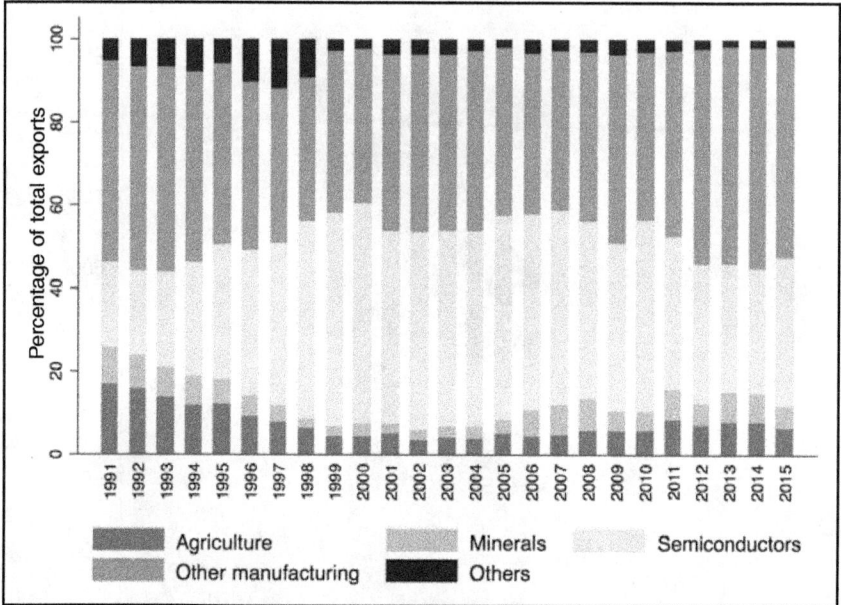

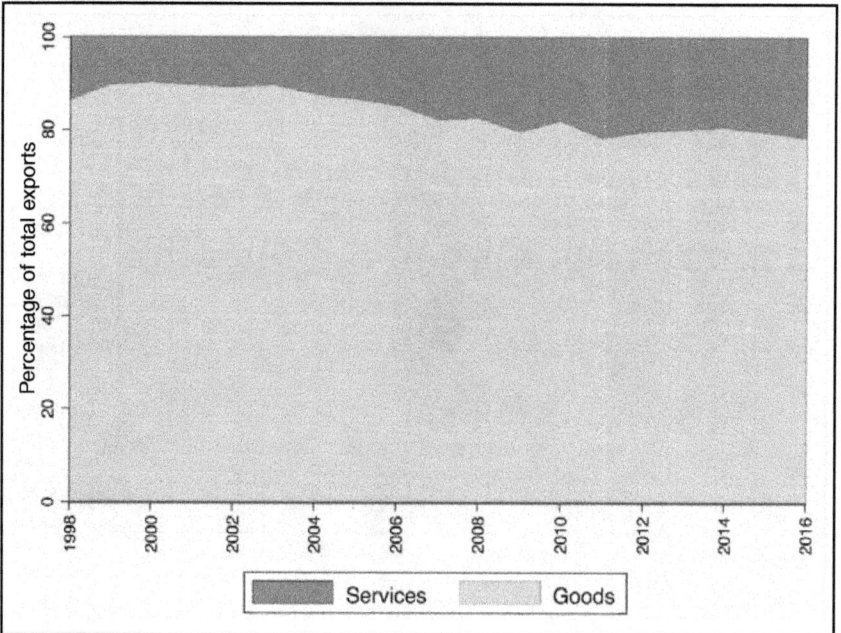

bundled with their sale are considered.

Macroeconomic management: Two key interrelated parameters aptly summarize Philippine macroeconomic management over this period. First, for reasons explained above, historically the country struggled to control inflation (Figure 1.5). There were several years of double-digit inflation in the 1970s and early 1980s, driven by fiscal deficits and the global oil shock. Then there was a major inflationary episode in the mid-1980s, triggered initially by the Marcos administration's attempts to spend its way out of the mounting political crisis, and subsequently by the sharp fall in the value of the peso. Inflation was a continuing challenge during most of the Cory Aquino administration. The reconstituted central bank, the BSP, marked a turning point, and the country has recorded inflation above 10 per cent just once in the past quarter century, and onlymarginally so (10.4 per cent in 1994). In recent years the low global inflation environment has facilitated this record, but it is important to emphasize that the achievement predated this development.

Figure 1.5 also illustrates the second outcome, the successful transition to inflation targeting and a flexible exchange rate regime. Through to the early 1980s, like many countries, the Philippines pegged its currency to the U.S. dollar within a narrow range and with occasional, albeit lagged, nominal depreciations that attempted to restore competitiveness. This regime collapsed around the time of the mid-1980s crisis, leading to a historically large nominal depreciation. The rate stabilized then for almost a decade, before declining further during the AFC. However, the decline was much less than for those of the crisis-affected neighbours. During this century the nominal rate has again stabilized, declining mainly during periods of political turbulence, such as the sudden regime change in 2001. It was little affected by the GFC, and in fact began to appreciate during the years of strong growth under President Benigno Aquino III.

Poverty and inequality: As documented in great detail by Clarete (chapter 2), the Philippines has struggled to reduce both poverty and inequality, even during periods of moderately strong growth. Figure 1.6, which is based on the periodic family income and

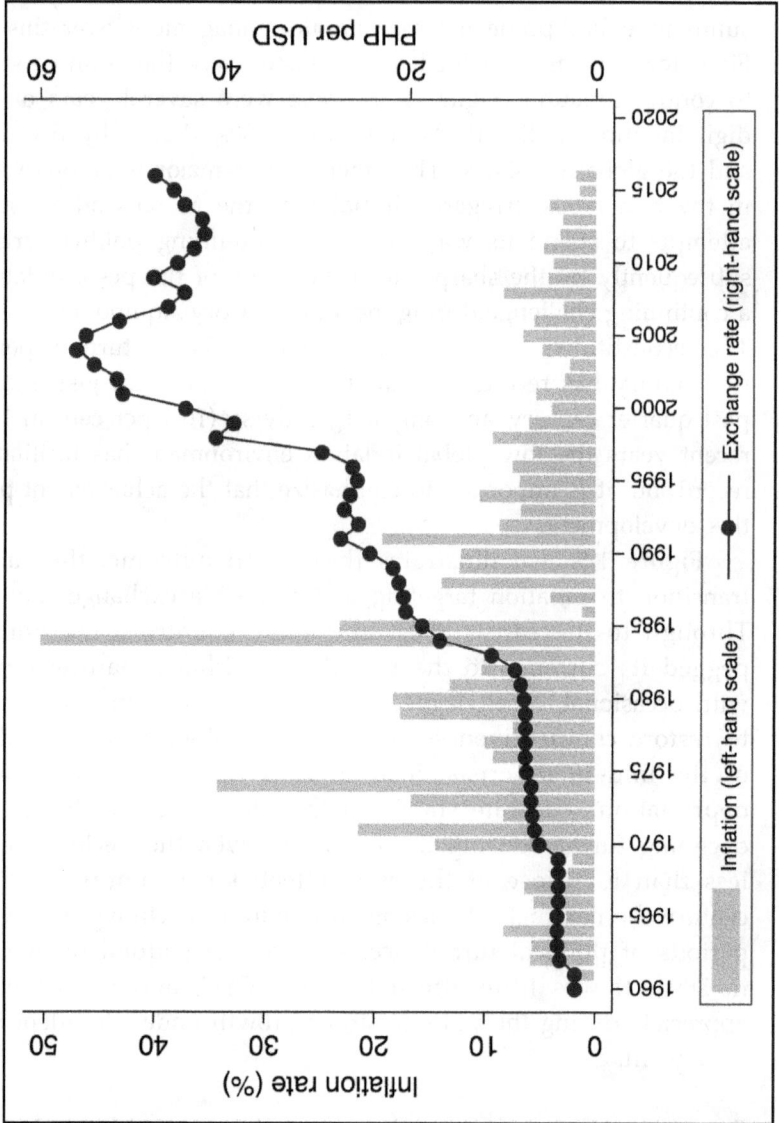

FIGURE 1.5
Philippines, Annual Inflation Rate and Peso/Dollar Exchange Rate, 1960–2015

FIGURE 1.6
Philippines, Poverty and Inequality

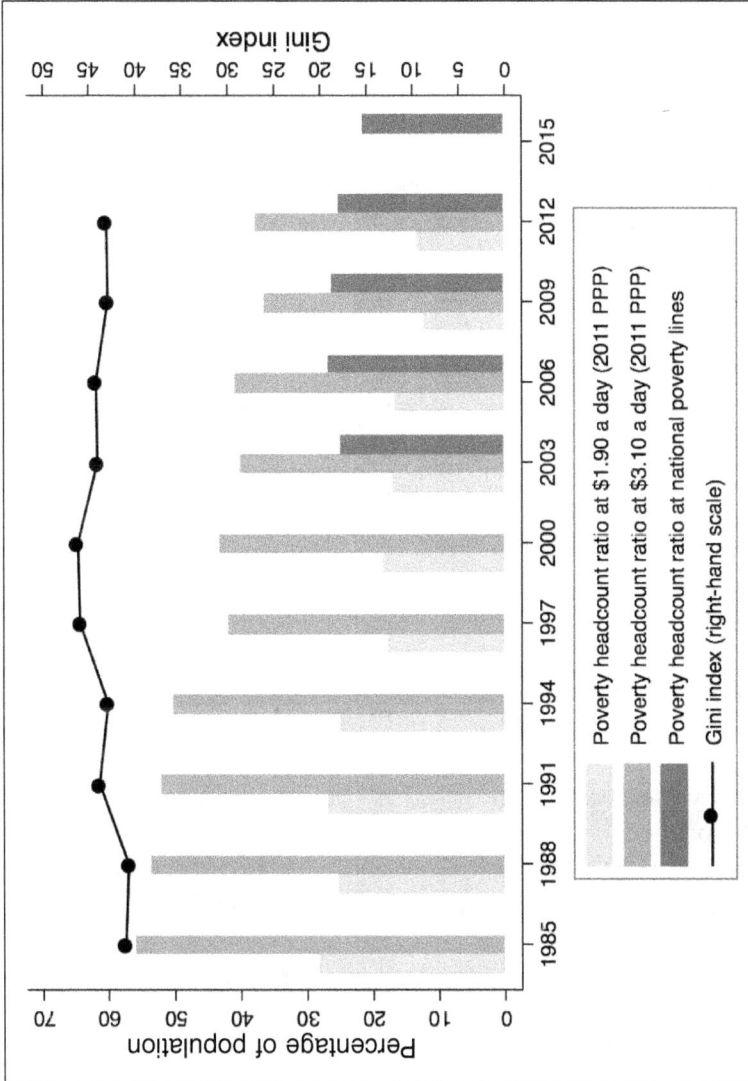

expenditure surveys (FIES), reports the trends since 1985, which have been computed on a comparable basis.[25] Five consistent head-count poverty estimates are shown, corresponding to the national poverty line (from 2003) and the international benchmarks of $1.90 and $3.10 per day. Inequality is measured by the gini ratio.

Inequality has been broadly stable throughout this period, with minor fluctuations caused mainly by external shocks such as the AFC and GFC. As noted, there have been no explicitly redistributive policies of any significance, except for the recently introduced CCT. As also noted, the decline in poverty incidence has been slower than for most neighbouring countries owing both to slower economic growth and to a lower poverty-growth elasticity. But contrary to much popular perception, poverty incidence has at least been declining.[26] Since 1985, the percentage of the population below the lower, "destitution" measure has halved. The percentage below the higher threshold has also declined, albeit more slowly. The fact that more than a fifth of the population remains below the latter threshold, with a very large number of people "precariously non-poor", illustrates the continuing magnitude of the Philippine poverty challenge.

Comparative indicators: So far we have focused on key Philippine socio-economic outcomes. What of the country's development record in comparative perspective, in this case compared to three of its Southeast Asian neighbours?

A useful first comparison is with reference to "initial conditions". As proxies, we select a range of socio-economic indicators for 1960. By then, all four countries were independent nation states and the quality of readily comparable international statistics had greatly improved.[27]

Around 1960, Philippine per capita income was almost double those of both Indonesia and Thailand, and not far short of Malaysia (Table 1.1). Its international orientation was similar to that of Thailand, less than Malaysia, and more than Indonesia (though the latter's statistic excludes its very large unrecorded trade at that time). The Philippines led the other three countries by a significant margin in its education indicators; the margin for Indonesia is particularly striking. Its health indicators were similar to Malaysia's and well ahead of the other two, again particularly Indonesia. Combined with other political

TABLE 1.1
Comparative Socio-economic Indicators: "Initial Conditions", ca. 1960

Country	GDP per capita (constant 2010 $)	Trade (% of GDP)	Years of schooling, for aged 15 and above	Years of schooling, for aged 25 and above	Life expectancy at birth (years)	Infant mortality (deaths per 1,000 lives)
Indonesia	577	11.6	1.57	1.11	47.0	166.7
Malaysia	1,408	85.7	2.83	2.26	57.9	81.1
Philippines	1,059	38.3	3.46	3.01	57.1	86.5
Thailand	571	34.9	2.55	2.07	53.3	108.9

and institutional indicators, the optimistic tone of the development literature of this period concerning Philippine prospects was therefore not surprising.

The same indicators for 2015 present a clear picture of comparative development dynamics (Table 1.2). The Philippines now had the lowest per capita income. The Philippine–Thai relativities were practically reversed: whereas the Philippines was almost double that of Thailand in 1960, fifty-five years later Thailand was more than double that of the Philippines. Indonesia had also overtaken the Philippines, in spite of its deep crisis in 1997–98, with a per capita income almost 50 per cent higher.[28] The gap in social indicators was less pronounced. The Philippines retained its educational advantage, at least over Indonesia and Thailand, but the gap had narrowed considerably. Philippine health indicators were similar to those of Indonesia, but lagged Malaysia and Thailand significantly.

The Philippine growth performance relative to its neighbours is further illustrated with reference to the changing PCI across various periods. Over the whole period 1960–2015, real Philippine per capita income rose just 2.5-fold, in contrast to 10.1 for Thailand, 7.7 for Malaysia and 6.6 for Indonesia. Taking 1980 as the base year, the gap is still large, with the increase in PCIs of the neighbours all at least double that of the Philippines, even though the other three economies were more seriously affected by the AFC. However, during the twenty-first century the gap disappears, as Philippine growth accelerated while those of its neighbours slowed. Thus, the Philippines was a clear outlier in the second half of the twentieth century, but it is no longer the "exception" this century.

A final set of comparative indicators relates to business and governance indicators (Table 1.4). Although generally subjective and arbitrary, they reinforce the observations elsewhere in this volume about the need for deep reform in the Philippines. The country receives the smallest value of foreign investment, as revealed by the stock of realized FDI relative to GDP; its business environment is perceived to be the most difficult to operate in; levels of corruption are among the highest; and its logistics efficiency performance is the weakest. These indicators are discussed in greater detail by Mendoza and Olfindo in chapter 9.

TABLE 1.2
Comparative Socio-economic Indicators: "Initial Conditions", 2015

Country	GDP per capita (constant 2010 $)	Trade (% of GDP)	Years of schooling, for aged 15 and above	Years of schooling, for aged 25 and above	Life expectancy at birth (years)	Infant mortality (deaths per 1,000 lives)
Indonesia	3,834	41.9	7.61	7.26	68.6	25.0
Malaysia	10,878	134.2	10.44	9.75	74.5	6.8
Philippines	2,640	63.0	8.43	8.18	68.0	23.2
Thailand	5,775	126.8	7.99	7.30	74.1	11.2

TABLE 1.3
Comparative Economic Growth

Country	2015 GDP per capita (constant 2010 US $)	2015 & 2000	2015 & 1980	2015 & 1960
Indonesia	3,834	1.8	3.5	6.6
Malaysia	10,878	1.6	3.3	7.7
Philippines	2,640	1.6	1.6	2.5
Thailand	5,775	1.7	4.1	10.1

TABLE 1.4
Comparative Institutional and Business Indicators

Country	Ease of doing business, 2016 (rankings: 1–190)	Stock of FDI, 2015 (% of GDP)	Corruption perceptions index, 2016 (rankings: 1–176)	Logistics performance index, 2016 (rankings: 1–160)
Indonesia	91	25.6	90	63
Malaysia	23	40.1	55	32
Philippines	99	19.9	101	71
Thailand	46	44.8	101	45

4. Major Themes and Findings

The eight chapters that follow provide comprehensive, analytical and policy-oriented accounts of the many complex issues facing the Philippines, looking both backwards and forwards.

In chapter 2, Ramon L. Clarete commences with the observation that the eradication of poverty and hunger and the availability of decent jobs should be the most important objectives of Philippine governments. His chapter examines the factors behind the Philippines' poverty problem and the recent economic growth performance. He asserts that increasing incomes would be more effective in reducing poverty if the issue of inequality is also addressed. His simulations show that poverty could be eliminated within fifteen years if per capita income grows annually by 8.3 per cent and the Gini index is reduced yearly by 3 per cent. However, if inequality is not reduced, it would take at least thirty-six years to eradicate poverty with the same growth in income. His policy analysis includes several pro-poor structural reforms that would potentially sustain high growth as well as addressing inequality and poverty.

Cities are engines of economic growth and venues of poverty reduction, supported by an infrastructure system that provides quality services and affordable housing. These form efficient and connected networks of sustainable settlements. However, Arturo G. Corpuz in chapter 3 argues that the state of infrastructure in the Philippines is way below existing requirements, even though the current urban growth trend (that is, slow growth of Metro Manila and rapid growth of regional centres) is consistent with the long-term vision of vibrant cities. To achieve accelerated infrastructure development, regional framework plans, including that for Mega Manila, are proposed to define urban expansion areas, integrate various infrastructure plans, incorporate disaster risk reduction and identify measures for higher quality planning and urban management.

Winfred M. Villamil frames chapter 4 around the proposition that the long-term economic success of a nation depends to a great extent on sustained increases in its endowment of human capital — the accumulated knowledge, skills and capacities of its workforce. The first section of his chapter commences with a brief discussion of the role of education and training in economic development. The next section provides a baseline assessment of education and training in the Philippines using indicators of educational *access*, *quality*, *achievement* and some indicators of workers' training. These are benchmarked against the performance of other ASEAN countries. The third section identifies the key issues that have to be addressed in the Philippines. Finally, he proposes strategic policy options that can influence the performance of education and training. Performance targets consistent with that of a middle-income economy like the Philippines are compared with the performance indicators associated with upper-middle and high-income economies.

In chapter 5, Eduardo Banzon and Beverly Lorraine Ho commence with a survey of the current health status and issues in the Philippines. They note the progress with regard to lowering the infant mortality rate, while stressing the slow progress and persistent inequalities across households. They also draw attention to the very limited financial coverage for healthcare provision and support. There has been a significant increase in public spending on health in the Philippines, albeit from a very low base and with indifferent efficiency. There is a shift towards a demand-driven system, but remnants of the earlier supply-driven system remain. They further argue that there is scope for strengthening the power and authority of the national health insurance programme, known as Philhealth, even while the Department of Health's regulatory functions continue to lag. Decentralized health delivery systems also need to be strengthened, and the private sector needs to be harnessed to better meet national goals.

Chapter 6 turns to environmental issues. James A. Roumasset, Majah-Leah V. Ravago, Karl Robert L. Jandoc and Clarisa Joy A. Arellano maintain that, while Filipinos aspire to improved living standards in vibrant and resilient communities, such an outcome will only be achieved if total environmental degradation and depletion of natural capital (TDD), partially estimated at 5 per cent of national income, will decline in the next twenty-five years. With improved environmental and resource management, TDD could shrink to as low as 0.6 per cent of national income by 2040. The authors then introduce the concept of comprehensive national income (CNI) to measure the country's well-being. Potential sources of CNI growth include effective environmental-resource conservation, disaster preparedness and removal of policy distortions. These are all relevant to attaining the Sustainable Development Goals (SDGs), a new global development agenda to be used by the government as a guide to improving Filipinos' future well-being.

In chapter 7 Majah-Leah V. Ravago, Raul V. Fabella, Ruperto P. Alonzo, Rolando A. Danao and Dennis S. Mapa examine electricity supply, pricing and regulation. They argue that this major industry bears heavily on every aspect of Philippine business and community life. By focusing on the generation sector, they present two possible scenarios for the next twenty-five years and illustrate how policy reforms on fuel mix can potentially reduce blended generation charges that make up 47 per cent of the total electric bill of households. The authors also provide an assessment of the power sector's performance and suggest key reforms and alternative pathways needed for the sector to contribute to the overall vision of strong economic growth and improved well-being.

Gilbert M. Llanto examines the financial resources needed to sustain the Philippine development momentum in chapter 8. He investigates three main sources of funds — households and firms, donors, and foreign investors. He assesses the long-term implications with reference to taxation, the overall financial system, public-private partnerships (PPPs), official development assistance (ODA), and remittances. Looking forward, he argues that it is imperative for the government to substantially raise tax revenues and rely more on domestic borrowing. ODA and PPPs should be used to strategically finance infrastructure needs and emerging regional public goods, respectively. Finally, financial reforms should be geared towards providing access to poor households and micro, small and medium-sized enterprises, as well as financial education for overseas Filipinos and their families, to widen their investment horizons.

Institutions determine the possibilities for effective governance and collective action. Both the state and the market need institutions to function well. Otherwise, market failures and governance failures could litter the landscape instead of properly provided public goods and services. In chapter 9, Ronald U. Mendoza and Rosechin Olfindo maintain that the success of the Philippines' overall development strategy is contingent on successful collective action over time, involving the elimination of governance and market failures through the formulation, implementation and institutionalization of key governance reforms. They assert that the challenge is not simply to eliminate corruption, but to provide public services and public goods much more efficiently and equitably. Their chapter maps the institutional development challenges of the Philippines and considers some of the possible pathways towards stronger and more sustained governance outcomes in the context of the country's ongoing institutional development. It outlines the main reform levers to build stronger institutions, including political and economic reforms and public finance reforms. The authors also argue that governance mechanisms need to be embedded in policy design in order to incentivize good governance outcomes.

5. Summing Up and Looking Forward

1. Summing Up

This is a crucial period in Philippine economic history. The country has long been considered the "sick man of Asia", a country that has failed to live up to its early promise. Yet, unusually, the Philippines has been one of the world's most dynamic economies in recent years, at par with China and India. The record of recent strong growth is all the more creditable given the sluggish and volatile state of the global economy. In fact, the bases of this historically unparalleled growth were established over the past quarter century: a functioning democracy, effective monetary policy, and a measure of trade liberalization. The country was able to weather both the Asian and global financial crises more effectively than most of its ASEAN neighbours. Moreover, once stable and credible government was established, the country was able to tap into global commercial opportunities, particularly in services trade.

The chapters that follow lay out key elements of a reform agenda that will be needed to maintain the recent development momentum. The agenda is a daunting but feasible one. As explained in these chapters, the agenda includes the following. First, how to overcome the deeply entrenched socio-economic and political inequality. Second, how to make cities both more liveable and more functional. Third, how to regain the educational advantage and to ensure better schooling outcomes regardless of socio-economic class. Fourth, how to improve health outcomes — and the efficiency of public spending — beyond the urban middle class. Fifth, how to address environmental fragilities without jeopardizing economic growth. Sixth, how to ensure energy availability and reliability at reasonable cost. Seventh, how to lift, and finance on a sustainable basis, the country's low level of private and public investment. And eighth, how to develop a system of governance and a set of institutions that underpin durably rapid and equitable economic growth.

2. Looking Forward: "Dutertenomics"

Rodrigo Duterte was elected President in May 2016 on the back of a promise to bring change to a nation impatient for relief from the daily inconvenience of poverty and the seeming inability of government to deal with urgent concerns — the worsening urban traffic, an inefficient public transport system, stalled post-disaster recovery, among others. With the reputation of a strongman[29] and a facility with populist rhetoric, Duterte tapped into a deep vein of discontent among the country's poor and middle classes, and even a segment of the affluent, to obtain a 39 per cent plurality of votes and win the presidency over four other aspirants.

Soon after assuming office, President Duterte launched an all-out war against the illegal drug trade, based on a narrative that the key to peace and progress is to rescue Philippine society from narco-politics. Invoking nationalism and independence in foreign policy, he has sought to distance his administration from the United States, a traditional development partner and military ally. He has also declined development assistance from the European Union. He has embraced China — the South China Sea dispute notwithstanding — expanded relations with Japan, and signalled greater openness to assistance from Russia.

Critical of the way development has favoured the national capital region ("imperial Manila"), the president has energized moves to shift from the current unitary structure towards a federal form of government. Early in his term he had called for the resumption of peace negotiations with the communist[30] and Muslim insurgents, even as he has expressed readiness to use force against armed extremist groups, particularly those operating in Mindanao. The president has also threatened to declare martial law, if necessary, to solve the drug problem, and denigrated human rights advocates as "criminal coddlers" for criticizing the brutality of his war on drugs.[31] In spite of his obvious authoritarian instincts, including attempts to disable critics and the free media and build support with the Marcoses and their constituency, his popularity, especially with the common people, remains high.[32]

In May of 2017, Duterte declared martial law in Mindanao following fighting that ensued between government forces and an armed group identifying itself with the Islamic State (IS) that had taken control of Marawi City. As the destruction continued and casualties on both sides mounted, the president obtained approval from both houses of Congress in July to extend martial law from sixty days until the end of the year.

At the time of writing, about a year into the Duterte presidency, it is too early to predict the likely course of events, much less pass judgment on the record to date, especially because the settling-in process for new administrations in the Philippines is extended not only by the need to obtain congressional approval for key appointments (e.g., in cabinet departments) but also by the steep learning curve faced by the political appointees and the people they bring onboard. Putting aside the various controversies, what can be said about the economic record? In particular, is there early reassurance that the economic momentum of recent years can be maintained? The Philippines has a history of nipping progress in the bud. Is the Duterte administration likely to be yet another example of this phenomenon?

It needs to be emphasized that predicting the future course of policy in the Philippines is exceptionally difficult because of institutional weakness and uncertainty. That is, from 1992 onwards, Philippine elections have in the main produced clear results. However, institutional reform has lagged behind political and economic progress. Thus, the prospects for each incoming administration are hard to predict because, in the absence of deeply embedded institutional strength, they depend more than anything else on the credibility of presidential leadership. The outcome of the last elections illustrates this proposition: the strong economic growth of recent years failed to translate into votes for the outgoing administration's candidate. Obviously for a considerable segment of the population the benefits of recent progress did not go deep enough to significantly improve their lives. What will the Duterte administration do differently to ensure that growth is in fact not only sustained but also truly inclusive?

Thus far the Duterte administration's economic policy pronounce-ments have been less controversial in nature. Through Executive Order No 5, series of 2016 (EO No. 5, s. 2016), it has accepted the work embodied in the previous administration's long-term development vision, as outlined in *AmBisyon Natin 2040*, as a guide for the latest Philippine Development Plan, 2017–22 (PDP). According to EO No. 5, moreover, *AmBisyon Natin 2040* shall provide the direction for succeeding PDPs through 2040, to ensure continuity.

Released in February 2017, the current PDP lays out the socio-economic programme and priorities of the administration until 2022.[33] It targets real GDP to grow annually by 7–8 per cent over the next five years, at which time the country is expected to reach upper-middle-income status with a per capita income of at least US$5,000 (in PPP), from US$3,550 in 2015. Poverty incidence is targeted to decline to 14 per cent by the end of the plan period; this is equivalent to six million Filipinos exiting poverty.

The plan also aims to cut unemployment to 5 per cent or less by 2022, particularly by bringing down youth unemployment from its current double-digit level; in areas outside the National Capital Region, reducing underemployment is the priority. The plan contains explicit targets for reducing inequalities in human development outcomes through interventions in health and nutrition, education, social protection, and disaster risk management.

The PDP 2017–22 is the programmatic translation of the administration's "0-10-point socio-economic agenda". Specific objectives include reforming taxation to achieve greater progressivity; accelerating infrastructure spending (towards "a golden age of infrastructure"); increasing competitiveness (including relaxing some of the more restrictive economic provisions of the Constitution); encouraging innovation (through enhanced support for science, technology and the creative arts); promoting rural development (through secure property rights, raising productivity and facilitating value chain linkages, among others); strengthening health and education systems, including social protection programmes; putting more teeth into the reproductive health policy; and pursuing the peace process. The last one is of particular significance under this, the country's first "Mindanao Presidency".

Looking forward, what are some of the key markers and parameters that are likely to shape economic progress in the medium term? At least four stand out.

First, early economic indicators: Indicators thus far suggest that the strong economic momentum is being maintained. For the first four quarters of the Duterte administration, real GDP growth averaged 6.7 per cent, albeit still reflecting investment decisions taken during the previous administration. However, with growth in the first half of 2017 at 6.5 per cent, the economy seems poised to attain its 6.5–7.5 per cent growth target for 2017, with expectations of more robust domestic spending and a resurgence of external demand. On the supply side, this depends on the absence of any major disruption in agricultural production, the diversification of the country's manufactured exports' destinations, and the steady growth of services supported by rising incomes, stable prices and the growth of external trade.

Since the beginning of 2017, the peso has continued to weaken, reaching a low not previously seen in the last decade. Higher outflows due to the strengthening of the dollar and prepayment of some of the country's foreign debt partly explain the recent depreciation. The government largely attributes this development to the economy's higher growth trajectory and the concomitantly greater demand for imports.[34] In this view the weak peso is a sign of better things to come, in addition to its immediate salutary effects on OFW remittances and exports. A less sanguine view points to a build-up of negative investor sentiment over the conduct of the war on drugs, the IS presence and martial law in Mindanao, and the lack of any palpable sign thus far that the "golden age of infrastructure" has finally dawned.[35] Investor confidence swings in any case, and can be turned around for better or worse depending upon what the incumbent administration chooses to do within the remaining years of its term. Meanwhile, the monetary authority assures that it has sufficient elbow room to deal with any adverse effect caused by sudden movements in the exchange rate.

The inflation rate bears watching, given its intimate association with poverty and the PDP's target of bringing poverty incidence down from 21.6 per cent in 2015 to 14 per cent by 2022. Early in 2017, headline inflation exceeded 3 per cent, from less than 2 per cent in the last two years, and peaked at 3.4 per cent in April. Not by coincidence, self-rated poverty rose to 50 per cent in the first quarter, from 44 per cent in the last quarter of 2016, before returning to the same level in the second quarter after inflation dropped back to below 3 per cent in June.[36] This calls attention to the careful management of inflation, especially as the peso depreciation, the proposed increases in consumption taxes (see below), and the additional demand spurred by income tax cuts (see below) and higher government spending are bound to create inflationary pressures going forward. A key variable, food price inflation, critically depends on whether the quantitative restriction on rice imports will finally be lifted and for good. But this requires legislative action.

Second, the cabinet team and other key presidential appointments: Philippine cabinets are appointed by the president and, although mediated by the need to balance a range of competing constituencies, they give an indication of presidential priorities and preferences. The Duterte cabinet is no exception, as it covers the spectrum of personal confidantes, individuals with conservative and leftist political orientation, regional power brokers, retired military and police officers, and technocrats. A reassuring feature of the three key economics appointments — in Finance, Budget and Management, and the National Economic and Development Authority (NEDA) — is their technical expertise. Two of the three appointees are economists. Two of the three have also held cabinet positions in previous administrations. The recent appointment of a career central banker to the post of BSP governor further provides reason for optimism on the matter of the country's macroeconomic management.

The president has so far deferred to the economic team on most matters of economic policy. It remains to be seen how long this situation will last, given the president's almost singular focus on law and order and his predilection for quick fixes. For now at least, it is safe to say that, with few exceptions, the economic team has been successful in moderating populist tendencies in the Duterte cabinet and containing their potentially adverse unintended results.[37]

Third, relations with the legislature: Philippine presidents need to secure congressional cooperation to get their bills passed, and even presidents whose parties have a majority in congress, such as Duterte, cannot take their party discipline and support for granted. When relations between the executive and legislative branches of government break down, key budget and other pieces of legislation can be blocked.

The first major economic policy challenge will be the financing of the administration's ambitious spending programme.[38] Congress has been debating a comprehensive tax reform proposal developed by the Department of Finance that would reduce the overall tax burden on the poor and middle classes and, at the same time, increase the government's fiscal space by raising additional revenue equivalent to about 1 per cent of GDP. Specific measures contained in the initial package[39] include: lowering personal income taxes as well as estate and donor taxes; increasing the excises on petroleum products, automobiles and sugar-sweetened beverages; broadening the value-added tax base;[40] and improving tax administration.[41] Compensating measures to protect the poor and vulnerable through highly targeted transfers are also envisaged.

At the time of writing, these proposals have passed the Lower House and are due for deliberation by the Senate. There is no telling what the final form of the tax law is going to be after it has gone through the legislative process. To be sure, it will be a product of much lobbying and negotiation. It is not unusual for lawmakers — especially those eyeing re-election — to support components of the bill that have a revenue-eroding effect while opposing those that would compensate for any lost revenue. This has prompted the secretary of finance to earlier recommend to the president that he veto any version of the tax reform bill that does not include the necessary revenue enhancing measures.

A second policy issue is the proposal to introduce a federal political system. Although a key platform in President Duterte's election campaign, the details have yet to be spelled out, and they would in any case require constitutional change. The Philippines has been a unitary state ever since independence. However, a major decentralization reform was introduced in 1992, and local governments have considerable expenditure responsibilities, funded mainly through automatic transfers from the national government under the Internal Revenue Allotment. Thus in some respects the system operates as a de facto federation. There is a strong case for revisiting and reforming the current arrangements, particularly given the very large vertical fiscal imbalances and the variable quality of local governance. Whether the adoption of a formal federal model is the solution is far from obvious, however. At this stage there are no proposals before Congress; neither has the Department of Finance undertaken any substantial preparatory work. The tax reform bill still pending in Congress assumes the status quo regarding the Philippine political system.

A third issue is developing a sustainable base and policy model for infrastructure financing, including the mix of sources — national and local government budgets, public–private partnerships (PPPs), private borrowing, and official development assistance (ODA) — and the accompanying regulatory arrangements. The objective of elevating infrastructure expenditure to 7 per cent of GDP from its previous level of less than 5 per cent is an ambitious one. The challenge is how to accelerate the approval and implementation processes without disregarding the due diligence requirements — complete staff work, in the lexicon of career-planning personnel — that are so critical to maintaining the integrity of government projects. A range of accompanying measures will need to be introduced, including improved bureaucratic capacity, especially for project preparation and development, more efficient procurement laws, and streamlined and transparent governmental procedures, not to mention major adjustments in traffic regulations. On the supply-side, the shortage of contractors will need to be addressed, in turn requiring a relaxation of foreign investment restrictions.

Failure to remove the institutional and administrative bottlenecks hindering infrastructure development could set back the public investment programme and reinforce private investors' uncertainties about the seriousness of government's efforts. This could also undermine future initiatives on tax reform, as higher revenues would only serve to magnify government underspending. At the same time, the expanded fiscal space offers fertile ground for more programmes promising quick relief to the marginalized and low-income segments of the population (e.g., free college education at state universities and colleges, free irrigation, free housing, among others) with little consideration for their distortive and longer-run effects.

Fourth, relations with the international community: Philippines foreign policy has tended to be ASEAN-centred, moderate and broadly U.S.-aligned. Will President Duterte's strident nationalist rhetoric change these settings? Among his first overseas trips were visits to the hemisphere's two dominant powers, China and Japan. He has sought to rejuvenate the critical Beijing relationship that was ruptured over the decision of the Permanent Court of Arbitration in The Hague in July 2016 to uphold the Philippines' exclusive sovereign rights over the West Philippine Sea and invalidate China's claim to resources in the area. This is a necessary step forward in order to ensure continuing access to Chinese investment and infrastructure financing. It remains unclear, however, what compromises the Philippines will have to make on its sea boundaries.

Meanwhile, while there is no evidence to date that the president's anti-American remarks have affected bilateral relations, President Trump's attacks on U.S. businesses that offshore their activities, and his proposed changes to the taxation of international income, may threaten the Philippine BPO industry. The United States is both the dominant market and foreign investor in this industry, accounting for at least 70 per cent of the total, and so any market disruption would have serious consequences. According to the Philippine Economic Zone Authority, the agency that administers the fiscal incentives and tariff-exemptions-granted BPO, approved investments declined in 2016. Foreign investment commitments in the information technology and transport and storage sectors similarly declined in the first quarter of 2017. The heightened nationalist rhetoric in both countries may have been a factor, but it is too early to be sure.

In summary, it remains to be seen whether the economic momentum thus far achieved in the last six years can carry forward to at least the next six and start delivering on the promise of a comfortable and secure life for the citizenry. While the prospects for attaining the growth targets seem favourable, as shown by recent economic performance, the risk of squandering opportunities is also very real. The hostility expressed towards long-standing development partners early on is a case in point. So is the preoccupation with congressional investigations of doubtful value in terms of legislation. In the meantime, attention is diverted from more urgent matters.[42]

How the economy has been able to keep the growth momentum despite the "noise" emanating from various quarters, including from the government itself, perhaps attests to its resilience and newfound dynamism. But then again, it may be asked if the negative international press the government received in the past year in connection with the country's human rights situation was not largely self-inflicted, and whether the nation could in fact be much further along the road to inclusive development without the controvesies.

As we have seen, the Philippines has generally underperformed in capital formation and equalizing opportunities, owing to regulatory impediments, poor infrastructure and perceived political instability. It would be a sad irony if the current administration is able to overcome the first two bottlenecks only to be undermined by the third by its own doing.

Notes

1. The most comprehensive recent treatise on Philippine economic history is that of Sicat (2014). Although ostensibly a biography (of one of the most

important economic policymakers in the modern Philippines), it is in fact a broad and nuanced analysis of the country's post-independence economic history.

2. The mid-1980s economic crisis has been dissected in detail in several excellent analyses by Philippine economists, especially those associated with the University of the Philippines School of Economics (UPSE). See, for example, de Dios et al. (1984) and Remolona, Mangahas, and Pante (1986) for analyses of the crisis and its aftermath.

3. Although the Philippine record resembled much of that in the rest of the developing world, as this was the decade of debt and stagnation in many developing countries.

4. A term that incidentally gained wide international currency from the Philippines during the Marcos era.

5. In path-breaking historical analysis, de Dios and Williamson (2013) investigate the record of Philippine industrialization, drawing attention both to its early start as the third Asian nation to record significant industrial growth (following Japan and China) and its "deviant behavior" from the 1980s as industrial growth slowed. They refer to a "perfect deindustrializing storm" and conjecture that the likely explanations included the 1980s political instability, a failure to exploit the Japanese industrial relocation to the region, institutional weaknesses, elements of the liberalizing policy package, a loss of skills from the large-scale outmigration, and Dutch Disease effects of the subsequent remittances.

6. As a recent illustration of the uneasy relationship, in February 2017 the country's environment secretary ordered the closure of the majority of the country's mines on grounds of alleged environmental violations. The secretary was subsequently removed from the cabinet.

7. This feature of Philippine development has been termed "development progeria" in a widely cited paper (Daway and Fabella 2015).

8. The remittance and BPO statistics are approximate, especially the remittances, which are a likely underestimate owing to unrecorded inflows.

9. One attempt to measure the openness of the services sector was the World Bank's 2011 Services Trade Restrictiveness Index that was developed on the basis of surveys of 103 economies for the period 2008–10. Among the eight developing East Asian economies surveyed (six from ASEAN), the Philippines was the most restrictive, more so even than Indonesia.

10. Although as Llanto notes in chapter 8, with reform, a bond market that taps into remittance flows could begin to play this role.

11. Scholars at the University of the Philippines School of Economics have investigated the country's poverty and inequality in great analytical detail. Mangahas and Barros (1979) analysed the record through to the mid-1980s,

while Balisacan (2003, 2015 and references cited therein) has written several seminal papers on the subject since the late 1980s.

12. The CARP continues to be a subject of continuing and spirited debate. See, for example, the recent exchanges between leading economists at the University of the Philippines (Fabella 2014; Monsod and Piza 2014).

13. Quimbo et al. (2015) provide an early and cautiously optimistic evaluation of the programme.

14. Detailed analyses of regional development are provided by Balisacan and Hill (2007) and Pernia et al. (1983). The most complex subnational development challenges are in Mindanao. These are extensively examined in the literature, most recently by Hutchcroft (2016).

15. The Philippines was a relative late starter in the establishment of a competition regulatory agency, with the Philippine Competition Commission being established in 2015 and commencing operations only in 2016. See the foreword to this volume.

16. The internal quotes are from Bennett (2014).

17. Nevertheless, the cornerstone of a free media, protection for journalists, remains problematic. The Philippines has one of the highest murder rates for journalists among non-conflict countries, according to statistics compiled by the international Committee to Protect Journalists (www.cpj.org).

18. In addition to chapter 9, see also De Dios (2009) and Fabella (2006) as leading political economy analyses of Philippine institutions.

19. In fact, Philippine defence expenditure is minuscule, at little more than 1 per cent of GDP, and the country's military has little modern hardware.

20. See Coxhead and Jayasuriya (2003) for an earlier stocktake and assessment.

21. We are grateful to Jan Carlo (JC) Punongbayan, a doctoral student at the University of the Philippines, for preparing the statistics on which this section is based.

22. Note that the growth data refer to GDP, not GDP per capita. Since around 1960, annual population growth has approximately halved, from just over 3 per cent to a little under 2 per cent per annum.

23. Note that "industry" here is defined in the national accounts sense to include the manufacturing, mining, construction, and utilities sectors.

24. Note also that, while overseas employment might be regarded as a "service export", for balance of payments purposes it is not recorded as such.

25. As noted above, Mangahas and Barros (1979) provide a comprehensive survey of the earlier period.

26. This trend is also confirmed in the more frequently reported self-rated poverty statistics. See Social Weather Stations (2017).

27. Economic historians would of course be quick to point out that "initial conditions" have much deeper and more complex origins than those

portrayed here. We recognize this point, but this deeper analysis is beyond the scope of this chapter. For a flavour of the literature, see Booth (2015) and Williamson (2015), companion chapters in the same volume. Note also that Indonesia and Malaysia have had international boundary changes since 1960, significantly so in the case of Malaysia.

28. Extending this comparison of the Philippine crisis in 1984–86 and Indonesia 1997–98, although the political transitions and the economic contractions were very similar, Indonesia took just seven years to return to its pre-crisis PCI, whereas the Philippines took almost twenty.

29. As mayor of Davao City in Mindanao for twenty-two years, Duterte built a reputation for quick and decisive action.

30. He has appointed a number of personalities associated with the militant Left to his cabinet.

31. At least 7,080 killings by the police or by unidentified assailants have been reported from 1 July 2016 to 31 January 2017 in connection with the government's campaign against illegal drugs, raising concerns about possible human rights violations from both domestic and international human rights groups. Independent groups have estimated the death toll to be around 13,000. Since January 2017, the police have also stopped reporting deaths from vigilante-style or unexplained killings; as of 26 July 2017, police data cite a figure of only 3,451 for people who have died in anti-drug operations.

32. This is reflected in the net satisfaction ratings reported by both the Social Weather Stations (www.sws.org.ph) and Pulse Asia Research, Inc. (www.pulseasia.ph) as of the first semester of 2017.

33. See www.pdp.neda.gov.ph.

34. After fifteen years of surplus, the current account sustained a deficit in the first quarter of 2017 and the BSP expects this to increase.

35. "Philippine Peso Slumps with no Sign of Infrastructure Push", *Financial Times*, 21 August 2017.

36. "Second Quarter 2016 Social Weather Survey: Families Self-Rated as Poor Decline to 44%; Food-Poor Families Decline to 32%", Social Weather Stations, 21 July 2017.

37. "Populism-proof", *The Economist*, 19–25 August 2017.

38. Early estimates from the Department of Finance put the figure at P366 billion a year until 2022 for incremental investments in infrastructure, education and training, health, and social protection, welfare and employment.

39. The proposed tax reforms are being introduced in phases, with other measures to reform corporate taxes and rationalize fiscal incentives, among others, to subsequently follow.

40. VAT exemptions are to be limited to only raw food and other items that can be justified by a strong economic rationale.
41. Measures here include fuel-marking, e-receipt, mandatory point-of-sale (POS) connection to the BIR, and relaxation of bank secrecy for criminal cases.
42. The peace process is one with serious implications on investor confidence. Another is the proposed amendment of the Public Service Act to liberalize rules on foreign investment in public utilities.

References

Athukorala, P.C., ed. *The Rise of Asia: Trade and Investment in Global Perspective*. London: Routledge, 2010.

Balisacan, A.M. "Poverty and Inequality". In *The Philippine Economy: Development, Policies and Challenges*, edited by A.M. Balisacan and H. Hill, pp. 311–41. New York: Oxford University Press, 2003.

———. 'The Growth-Poverty Nexus: Multidimensional Poverty in the Philippines". In *Sustainable Economic Development: Resources, Environment and Institutions*, edited by A.M. Balisacan, U. Chakravorty, and M.L.V. Ravago, pp. 445–68. Amsterdam: Elsevier, 2015.

Balisacan, A.M., and H. Hill, eds. *The Philippine Economy: Development, Policies and Challenges*. New York: Oxford University Press, 2003.

———, eds. *The Dynamics of Regional Development: The Philippines in East Asia*. Cheltenham: Elgar, 2007.

Bautista, R., and G. Tecson. "International Dimensions". In *The Philippine Economy: Development, Policies and Challenges*, edited by A.M. Balisacan and H. Hill, pp. 136–71. New York: Oxford University Press, 2003.

Bennett, R.J. *Entrepreneurship, Small Business and Public Policy: Evolution and Revolution*. London: Routledge, 2014.

Bernardo, R.L., and M.C. Tang. "The Political Economy of Reform during the Ramos Administration (1992–1998)". Working Paper No. 39, Commission on Growth and Development. Washington, DC: World Bank, 2008.

Booth, A. "A Century of Growth, Crisis, War and Recovery, 1870-1970". In *Routledge Handbook of Southeast Asian Economics*, edited by I. Coxhead, pp. 43–59. London: Routledge, 2015.

Capuno, J.J. "The Quality of Local Governance and Development under Decentralization". In *The Dynamics of Regional Development: The Philippines in East Asia*, edited by A.M. Balisacan and H. Hill, pp. 204–44. Cheltenham: Elgar, 2007.

Claessens, S., S. Djankov, L.H.P. Lang. "The Separation of Ownership and Control in East Asian Corporations". *Journal of Financial Economics* 58 (2000): 81–112.

Coxhead, I., ed. *Routledge Handbook of Southeast Asian Economics*. London: Routledge, 2015.

Coxhead, I., and S. Jayasuriya. "Environment and Natural Resources". In *The Philippine Economy: Development, Policies and Challenges*, edited by A.M. Balisacan and H. Hill, pp. 381–417. New York: Oxford University Press, 2003.

David, C.C. "Agriculture". In *The Philippine Economy: Development, Policies and Challenges*, edited by A.M. Balisacan and H. Hill, pp. 175–218. New York: Oxford University Press, 2003.

Daway, S.L.S., and R.V. Fabella. "Development Progeria". *Philippine Review of Economics* 52, no. 2 (2015): 84–99.

De Dios, E.S. "Local Politics and Local Economy". In *The Dynamics of Regional Development: The Philippines in East Asia*, edited by A.M. Balisacan and H. Hill, pp. 157–203. Cheltenham: Elgar, 2007.

———. "Governance, Institutions, and Political Economy". In *Diagnosing the Philippine Economy*, edited by D.B. Canlas, M.E. Khan, and J. Zhuang, pp. 295–336. London: Anthem, 2009.

De Dios, E.S., and P.D. Hutchcroft. "Political Economy". In *The Philippine Economy: Development, Policies and Challenges*, edited by A.M. Balisacan and H. Hill, pp. 45–73. New York: Oxford University Press, 2003.

De Dios, E.S., and J.G. Williamson. "Deviant Behavior: A Century of Philippine Industrialization". University of the Philippines School of Economics Discussion Paper 2013-03. 2013.

Fabella, R.V. "What Happens When Institutions Do Not Work: Jueteng, Crisis of Presidential Legitimacy and Electoral Failures in the Philippines. *Asian Economic Papers* 5, no. 3 (2006): 104–25.

———. "Comprehensive Agrarian Reform Program (CARP): Time to Let Go". *Philippine Review of Economics* 51, no. 1 (2014): 1–18.

Gochoco-Bautista, M.S., and D. Canlas. "Monetary and Exchange Rate Policy". In *The Philippine Economy: Development, Policies and Challenges*, edited by A.M. Balisacan and H. Hill, pp. 77–105. New York: Oxford University Press, 2003.

Hutchcroft, P., ed. *Mindanao: The Long Journey to Peace and Prosperity*. Manila: Anvil, 2016.

Llanto, G. "Philippine Infrastructure and Connectivity: Challenges and Reforms". *Asian Economic Policy Review* 11, no. 2 (2016): 243–61.

McCoy, A.W. "A Tale of Two Families: Generational Succession in Filipino and American Family Firms". *TRANS* 3, no. 2 (2015): 159–90.

Mangahas, M., and B. Barros. "The Distribution of Income and Wealth: A Survey of Philippine Research". Discussion Paper 7916, University of the Philippines School of Economics. 1979.

Medalla, E.M., G.R. Tecson, R.M. Bautista, J.H. Power and Associates. *Philippine Trade and Industrial Policies: Catching up with Asia's Tigers*, 2 vols. Makati: Philippine Institute for Development Studies, 1995/96.

Monsod, T.C., and S.A. Piza. "Time to Let Go of CARP? Not so Fast". *Philippine Review of Economics* 51, no. 1 (2004): 19–27.

Noland, M. "The Philippines in the Asian Financial Crisis: How the Sick Man Avoided Pneumonia". *Asian Survey* 40, no. 3 (2000): 401–12.

Perkins, D.H. *East Asian Development: Foundations and Strategies*. Cambridge: Harvard University Press, 2013.

Pernia, E.M., C.W. Paderanga, and V.P. Hermoso and Associates. *The Spatial and Urban Dimensions of Development in the Philippines*. Makati: Philippine Institute for Development Studies, 1983.

Power, J.H., and G.P. Sicat. *The Philippines: Industrialization and Trade Policies*. Oxford: Oxford University Press, 1971.

Pritchett, L. "A Toy Collection, a Socialist Star, and a Democratic Dud? Growth Theory, Vietnam and the Philippines". In *In Search of Prosperity: Analytical Narratives on Economic Growth*, edited by D. Rodrik, pp. 123–51. Princeton: Princeton University Press, 2003.

Quimbo, S., et al. "Where Does the Money Go? Assessing the Expenditure and Income Effects of the Philippines' Conditional Cash Transfer Program". University of the Philippines School of Economics Discussion Paper 2015-02. 2015.

Remolona, E.M., M. Mangahas, and F. Pante. "Foreign Debt, Balance of Payments and the Economic Crisis of the Philippines in 1983–84". *World Development* 14, no. 8 (1986): 993–1018.

Sicat, G.P. *Cesar Virata. Life and Times through Four Decades of Philippine Economic History*. Quezon City: University of the Philippines Press, 2014.

Vos, R., and J.T. Yap. *The Philippine Economy: East Asia's Stray Cat?* New York: St Martin's, 1996.

Williamson, J.G. "Trade, Growth and Distribution in Southeast Asia, 1500–1940". In *Routledge Handbook of Southeast Asian Economics*, edited by I. Coxhead, pp. 22–42. London: Routledge, 2015.

World Bank. *The East Asian Miracle*. New York: Oxford University Press, 1993.
——. *The Growth Report*. Washington, DC: Commission on Growth and Development, 2008.

2

Economic Growth and Poverty Reduction

Ramon L. Clarete

I. Introduction

The Philippine economy grew by 6.8 per cent in 2016, which is high by regional standards. The strong performance departs from its average growth of only 4.2 per cent since the 1960s. However, a quarter of the population remains poor, repeating its record in 2000, when it had as many poor despite a rate of growth of 6 per cent. Unlike its East Asian neighbours, the country has been weak in translating growth to lowering poverty (Balisacan and Fuwa 2004).

This chapter looks at the factors shaping growth and poverty in the Philippines. Studies have attributed significant gains in poverty eradication in East Asia to sustained robust growth (e.g., Dollar and Kraay 2002; World Bank 2006). The next section takes up the factors contributing to growth performance and examines how the current robust growth can be sustained. The third section focuses on the problem of the country's weak capacity of translating growth to poverty reduction. Apparently, high growth with less inequality reduces poverty faster (Bourguignon 2003; Fosu 2010). The chapter then tracks using an economy-wide model of the Philippines the per capita GDP and poverty trajectories of the country into the next twenty-five years under two growth and two income distribution scenarios. The last section states the study's key findings.

II. Factors Shaping Growth Performance

The Philippine economic growth in recent years has been robust by regional standards (Table 2.1): 6.8 per cent in 2016 and an average rate of 6.3 per cent from 2010 to 2016 (Figure 2.1). The performance departs significantly from its average of 4 per cent from 1961 to 2009. Since 2000 the average growth increased to 5.21 per cent per year, and could have been faster were it not for the global economic crisis in 2008.

Compared with selected East Asian countries (Table 2.1), the growth performance of the Philippines was markedly behind those of its neighbours in the 1980s and 1990s. In the 2000s, however, the country caught up with its Southeast Asian neighbours, and exceeded their growth in the last five years. The growth of the People's Republic of China (PRC), however, has remained the fastest since the 1980s.

TABLE 2.1
GDP Annual Growth Rates of Selected Asian Countries, 1961–2014 (%)

	PRC	Indonesia	Malaysia	Philippines	Thailand	Vietnam
1961–70	5.2	4.4	6.4	5.0	8.5	
1971–80	6.1	8.0	8.0	5.7	7.0	
1981–90	9.8	6.5	6.3	1.4	8.2	4.8
1991–2000	10.4	3.9	6.3	3.2	4.0	7.6
2001–10	10.6	5.5	5.1	4.9	4.2	6.6
2011–14	7.8	5.6	5.7	6.1	4.0	5.8
Average	8.3	5.6	6.4	4.2	6.0	6.4

Source: World Bank's World Development Indicators.

FIGURE 2.1
GDP Annual Growth Rate of the Philippines, 1961–2016 (%)

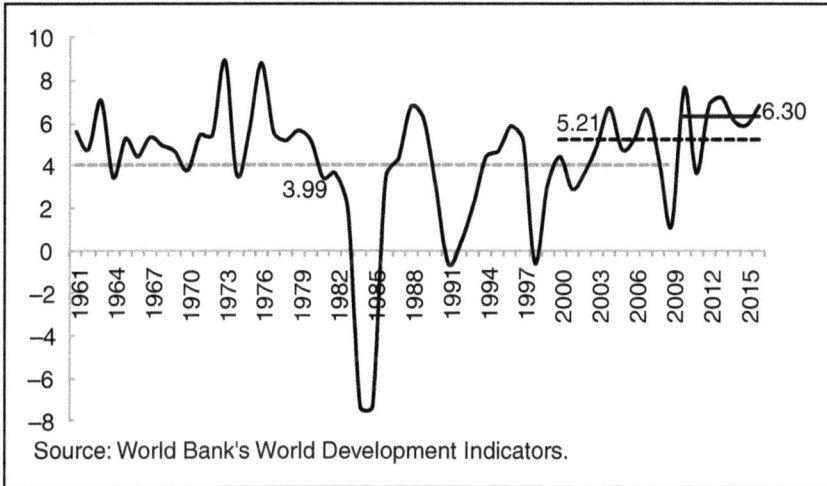

Source: World Bank's World Development Indicators.

The overriding challenge will be sustaining the recent high growth. In the past, growth has been relatively volatile. Bautista (2002) estimated the pattern as comprising three states of growth: low growth (2.12 per cent per year) with a duration of 1.5 years; moderate growth (5.16 per cent) lasting 5.7 years; and negative growth (−7.76 per cent), which transpired for 1.5 years. Structural problems such as a low domestic savings rate and weak tax collection may explain why these cycles persisted (de Dios 1998). Deeper policy reforms are needed to avoid reverting to the boom-and-bust growth pattern of the past.

A. Sources of Growth

In the following, the sources of growth are examined and compared with those in selected countries in East Asia.

Technical Progress

Technical progress contributed the largest to the country's GDP growth since 1993 (Bangko Sentral ng Pilipinas [BSP] 2014). The BSP showed that total factor productivity (TFP) has been rising, except in the earlier period from 1989 to 1992 (Table 2.2). TFP's positive contribution to GDP growth expanded to nearly half in the last period from 2010 to 2013. In a similar finding, Cororaton (2002) observed that while TFP declined in the middle of the 1980s (Cororaton and Cuenca 2001), its contribution to GDP growth from 1987 to 2000 was positive, at 0.93 per cent.

The picture was less encouraging before 1993. Cororaton (2002) observed that since the second half of the 1960s the number of industries with negative TFP growth increased. By 1992, sixteen of the twenty-three manufacturing industries covered by the study had negative TFP growth.

These findings connected well with the weakening of productivity growth in the Philippines. Williamson (1969) estimated a declining TFP from 55 per cent in the period 1947–55 to 15 per cent for 1955–65. Hooley (1985) found that TFP had declined by 0.15 per cent in the period 1956–80 and by negative 2 per cent each year from 1975 to 1980. Hooley observed that in the late 1950s, TFP growth consistently slowed down. After 1975, productivity had declined.

TABLE 2.2
Weighted Contribution of Factor Inputs to Potential GDP Growth,
1989–2013 (%)

Period	Potential GDP	Trend TFP	Capital	Trend Agricultural Labour	Trend Industry Labour	Trend Service Labour
1989–1992	2.63	−0.11	1.93	0.16	0.22	0.43
1993–2001	3.10	0.39	2.18	−0.27	0.12	0.68
2002–2007	4.79	2.02	1.91	0.16	0.08	0.62
2008–2009	4.40	1.66	1.93	0.08	0.11	0.61
2010–2013	5.79	2.50	2.25	−0.25	0.27	1.03

Source: Bangko Sentral ng Pilipinas (BSP) 2014.

Capital Accumulation and Employment

Capital accumulation accounted for nearly three fourths of output growth from 1989 to 2001, but its contribution to GDP growth had declined since then to nearly 39 per cent in the last period from 2010 to 2013. It lost to TFP its top driver role of growth in 2002, recovered it during the global economic crisis from 2008 to 2009, and lost it again to TFP in the last period.

Employment contributed the lowest to GDP growth. On average through the entire period, about a fifth of economic growth could be explained by increases in employment. In the period when TFP declined, the expansion of employment accounted for about a third of GDP growth. However, its share to GDP growth dropped to 18 per cent in the rest of the period. Agriculture labour employment contributed the least, while services labour contributed the most to GDP growth.

Comparative Performance

The top drivers of growth differ across countries in East Asia. For the PRC, Malaysia and Vietnam, the largest source of growth had been capital accumulation. For Indonesia, Thailand and the Philippines, TFP growth was the largest contributor to growth (Asian Productivity Organization [APO] 2014).

The Philippines has among the highest TFP growth rates and contribution to growth since 2005 (Table 2.3), with the former averaging 2.3 per cent from 2010 to 2012. This followed Indonesia's at 3.3 per cent. Over the past decade, both countries experienced more robust productivity growth, while Malaysia's TFP stagnated and those of the PRC, Thailand and Vietnam slowed down.

Before 2005, however, TFP in the Philippines expanded the slowest relative to other countries in the region. The slow technical progress largely explained why its GDP growth lagged behind those of its ASEAN neighbours and the PRC. However, the strong showing of TFP growth from 1.5 per cent in the 2000s to 2.3 per cent in 2010–12 may reflect the strong rebound of the country's manufacturing sector. Countries with rapid growth tended to have robust expansion of their TFPs.

TABLE 2.3
TFP Growth and Its Contribution to Output Growth in Selected Asian Countries, 1970–2012 (%)

Period	PRC		Indonesia		Malaysia		Philippines		Thailand		Vietnam	
	A	B	A	B	A	B	A	B	A	B	A	B
1970–1975	0.5	8	2.3	28	1.2	15	0.5	9	3.7	67	-0.4	-25
1975–1980	1.2	19	1.6	20	1.6	19	0.9	15	1	13	1.2	34
1980–1985	4.3	43	-1.7	-35	-2.5	-49	-6.0	447	2.3	44	1.7	28
1985–1990	0.9	12	2.2	29	2.2	31	3.2	65	4.2	42	1	23
1990–1995	7.1	61	3.1	41	1.8	20	-0.5	-18	2.3	29	3.9	48
1995–2000	3.1	38	-4.4	-594	-2.5	-52	0.9	19	-2.4	-341	3.8	52
2000–2005	3.9	42	1.8	39	1.3	27	0.9	19	3.2	60	3.8	47
2005–2010	4.2	39	1.3	23	1	21	2.1	44	1.3	37	-0.7	-11
2010–2012	2.1	26	3.3	53	1.5	29	2.3	45	1.9	50	1	17

A = average annual growth rate of total factor productivity; B = contribution share to output growth.
Source: Asian Productivity Organization (APO) 2014.

B. Structural Transformation

Since the second half of the 1970s, the share of services in GDP has risen, while agriculture's contribution steadily declined. Industry's share increased from 1974 to 1984, exceeding the respective contributions to GDP of services and agriculture, but has generally declined since 1985. The share of manufacturing, which makes up most of industry, has largely been unchanged, but starting 2000 began to fall. Since the middle of the 1980s, services has outpaced industry and agriculture, to become the largest contributor to GDP (Figure 2.2).

FIGURE 2.2
Sector Shares in Gross Domestic Product, 1961–2014 (%)

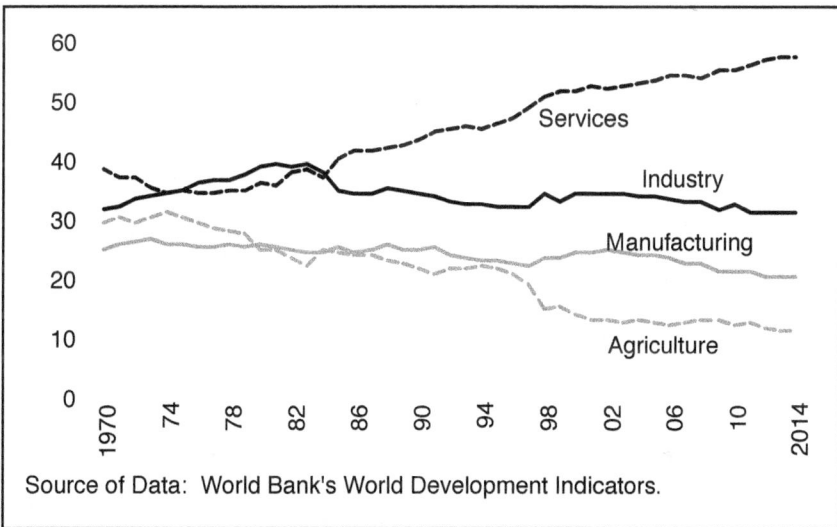

Source of Data: World Bank's World Development Indicators.

The country's structural transformation differed from the experiences of other developing countries in Asia. The contribution to GDP of the agriculture sectors in all the countries shown in Figure 2.3 had consistently fallen. In the Philippines, it dropped to 11.3 per cent in 2014 from 30.3 per cent in 1971. However, the respective shares of industry in GDP had increased for all countries except the Philippines. As portrayed in Figure 2.2, the value-added

FIGURE 2.3
Sectoral Composition of GDP in Selected Asian Countries (%)

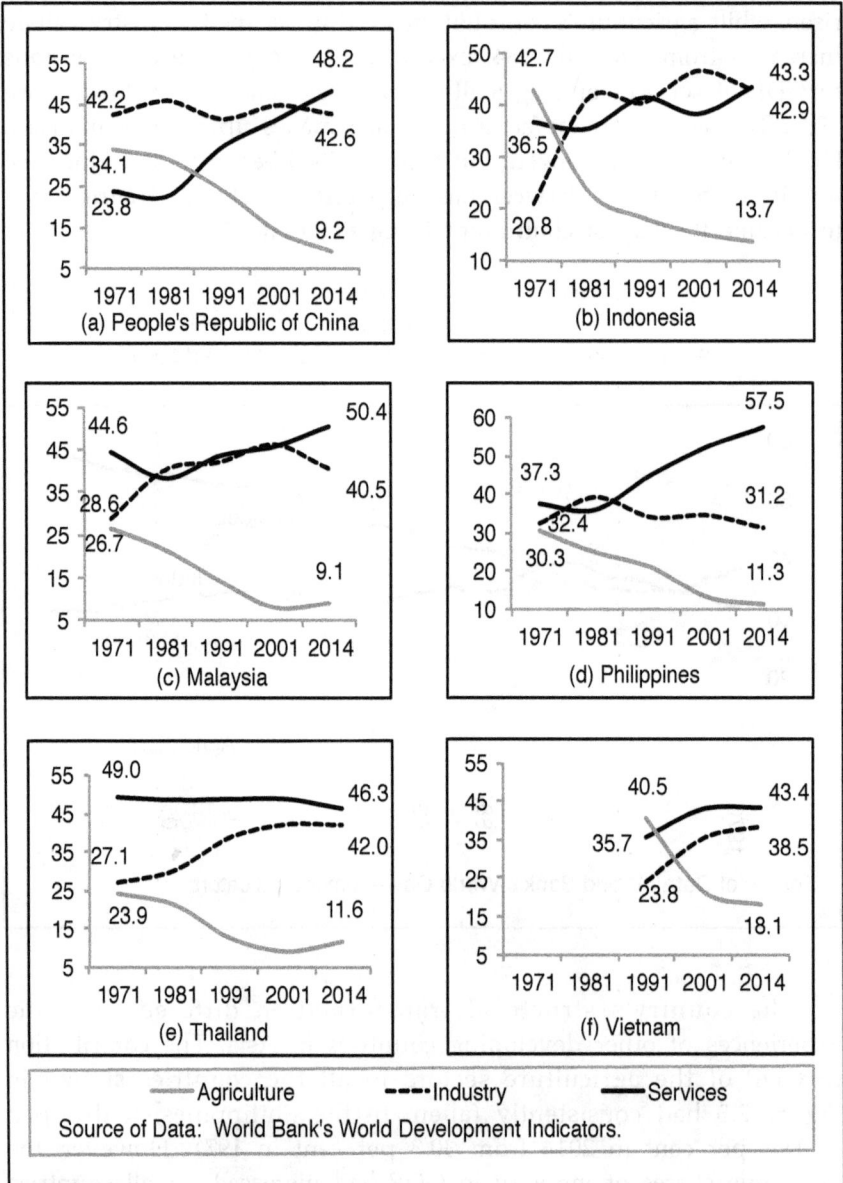

(a) People's Republic of China

(b) Indonesia

(c) Malaysia

(d) Philippines

(e) Thailand

(f) Vietnam

——— Agriculture   ----Industry   ———Services

Source of Data: World Bank's World Development Indicators.

share of the country's industries hardly changed through the years, while that of services steadily and sharply expanded, increasing from 37.3 per cent in 1971 to 57.5 per cent in 2014. In several countries the services' share exceeded that of industry, but, unlike in the Philippines, their industries increasingly contributed to their GDPs.

Fabella (2013) called the Philippines' pattern a "development progeria", a premature expression of a developed country feature. In industrialized countries, the services sector typically contributes the most to the country's GDP. However, in the case of the Philippines, the average labour productivity in services is substantially lower.

Daway and Fabella (2015) cited two possible factors to explain the pattern. One is Rodrik's hypothesis, which states that market and institutional distortions had disadvantaged tradable goods more than home goods. The other is an exchange rate policy favouring home goods. Clarete (2006) attributed high transaction costs for stakeholders in both the agriculture and industrial sectors, which slowed the movement of factors to exportable industries when the country liberalized its trade policies. Restrictions in agricultural land markets imposed by the government's agrarian reform programme and continuing restrictions on foreign direct investment (FDI) are among the factors preventing industry from absorbing the surplus labour from rural areas.

The typical structural transformation in other developing countries of East Asia is associated with faster income growth and poverty eradication. The PRC has been the world's largest eradicator of poverty — it moved 600 million people out of poverty.[1] The first phase of its structural transformation was purely based on agricultural growth, raising the returns of labour in rural areas. It is estimated that about 300 million people were liberated from poverty in this way. The second phase was the move from the farms to the factories, which happened in the middle of the 1990s when industry became the dominant sector of the economy. Another 300 million PRC citizens were moved out of poverty in this phase. In this period, when the economic growth of the PRC had slowed down, the expansion of industry decelerated, and in 2011 services started to be the dominant sector of the economy, which is typical for an industrialized country.

C. Employment and Productivity

With at least 50 per cent of GDP contributed by services, more than half of the country's work force is in this sector. This is a matter for concern, considering that the productivity of labour in this sector is lower compared to that of industry. While the sector has highly productive industries — including telecommunications, mobile phone services, business process outsourcing, and airline and tourism services — the number of workers they employ is low. The bulk of the workforce finds jobs in low-productive informal service industries. In a typical year, about 1.15 million Filipinos are looking for work: 650,000 of them will find low-paying jobs in the informal sector, and only 240,000 in the formal sector. The rest go abroad or join the unemployed (Vandenbrink 2016).

Since the 1970s, employment in the Philippines shifted from agriculture to services. Industry and manufacturing absorbed less labour from agriculture (Chua et al. 2013). Manufacturing's share in employment has declined over the past fifteen years, and these trends have persisted till today (Figure 2.4).

FIGURE 2.4
Employment Share by Sector, 2006–14 (%)

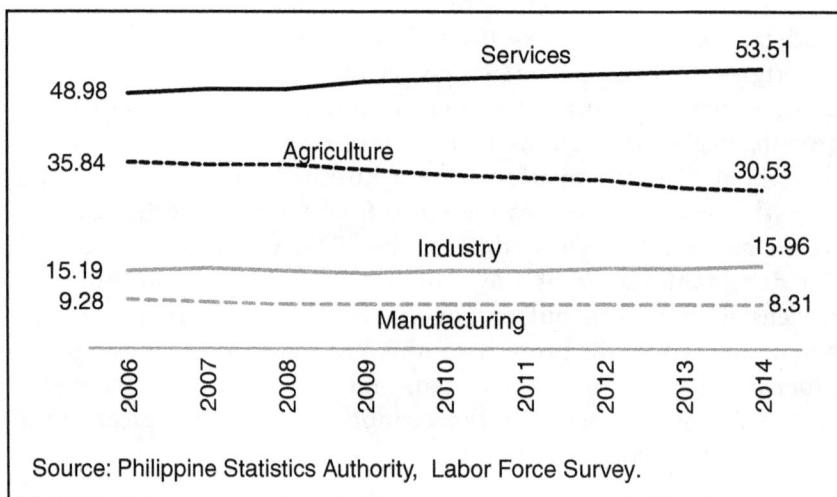

Source: Philippine Statistics Authority, Labor Force Survey.

With industry and manufacturing weak, the employment rate is affected. From 2006 to 2014, the unemployment rate averaged 7.3 per cent, despite high GDP growth of nearly 6 per cent (Figure 2.5). With high unemployment, underemployment is also a problem; it was 19.3 per cent in the high growth period from 2011 to 2013. One out of five workers and those partially employed still sought additional employment opportunities, indicating low labour productivity and compensation in available jobs. On a positive note, the unemployment rate slightly fell from 7.1 per cent in 2013 to 6.8 per cent in 2014, while underemployment also declined modestly from 20 per cent in 2012 to 19.3 per cent in 2013. These gains were associated with the rebound of the manufacturing sector of the country in that year.

FIGURE 2.5
Labour Unemployment and Underemployment, Philippines, 2006–14 (%)

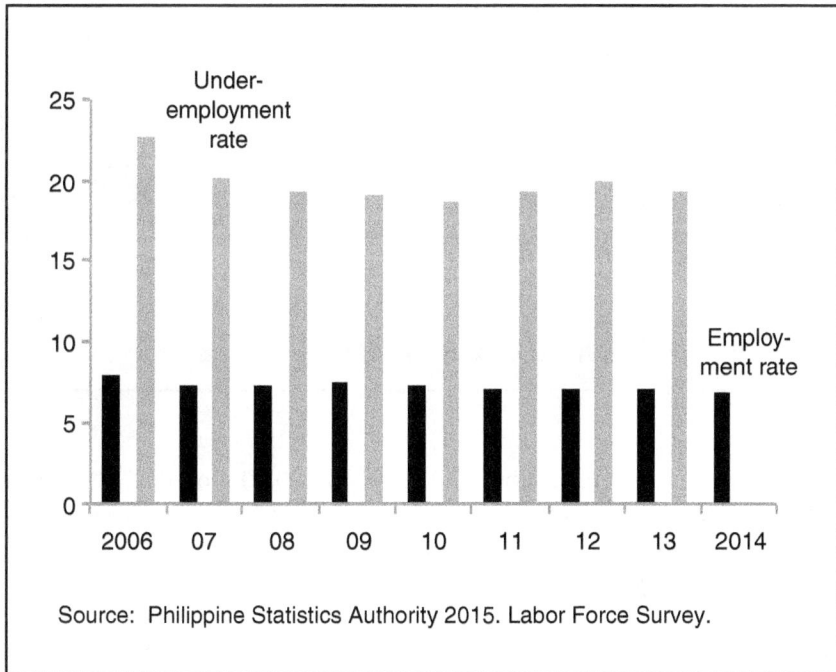

Source: Philippine Statistics Authority 2015. Labor Force Survey.

Labour Productivity

Labour has increasingly been absorbed by the services sector, the productivity of which is lower (Figure 2.6), and growing at a lower pace compared to industry. Agriculture had the lowest per worker output from 2010 to 2014, over sixfold below that of industry. While the productivity of labour in services exceeded that of agriculture, it was still about half that of industry. Moreover, the growth of labour productivity from 1999 to 2014 was 2.6 per cent in industry, 2 per cent in agriculture, and 1.9 in services, respectively.

FIGURE 2.6
Average Labour Productivity in the Philippines by Sector, 2010–14
('000 Pesos)

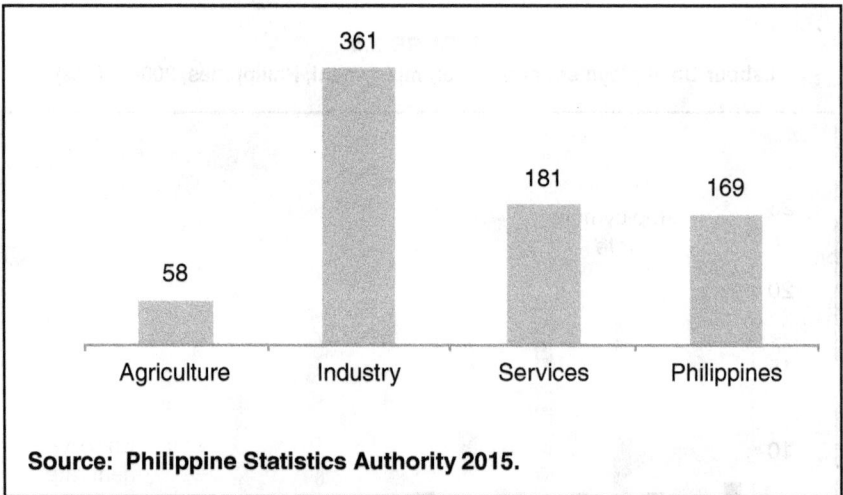

Source: Philippine Statistics Authority 2015.

In the 1980s, 1990s and 2000s, Usui (2011) noted that labour productivity in all three sectors in the economy failed to boost overall labour productivity (Figure 2.7). The respective outputs per worker in industry and agriculture declined, and did not increase in services. Considering that the latter absorbed over half of the country's employed workers, the flat growth of labour productivity in services has been an important concern.

FIGURE 2.7
Average Annual Aggregate Labour Productivity Growth and Decomposition in
Selected ASEAN Countries, 1980–2007

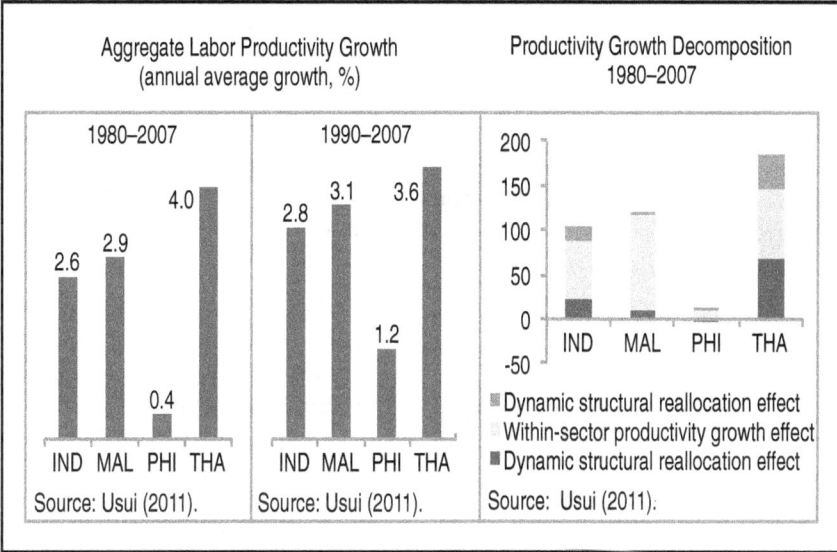

Aggregate Labor Productivity Growth
(annual average growth, %)

Productivity Growth Decomposition
1980–2007

1980–2007

1990–2007

Source: Usui (2011).

Source: Usui (2011).

Source: Usui (2011).

IND MAL PHI THA

IND MAL PHI THA

IND MAL PHI THA

■ Dynamic structural reallocation effect
Within-sector productivity growth effect
■ Dynamic structural reallocation effect

Labour productivity growth of the country was lowest in the
region in the same period. Usui (2011) reported that the country's
labour productivity increased at the rate of 0.4 per cent a year, or
10 per cent for the entire duration from 1980 to 2007, lower by
at least half compared to its ASEAN neighbours (Figure 2.7). In
East Asia, the country's labour productivity growth — 0.33 per cent
per year in the 1990s — also ranked lowest (Figure 2.8). In contrast,
China had nearly 7.6 per cent, and the other ASEAN countries in the
figure had an average growth of 3.2 per cent.

Usui (2011) noted that the country had not performed well in all
three components of aggregate labour productivity: productivity gains
arising from increased shares in employment of industries; within
industry productivity growth; and dynamic structural reallocation
effect, which captures how well the movements of workers across
industries are responsive to high productivity.

D. Work Force, Population and the Demographic Dividend

The country's labour force is fast growing by Asian standards. From 1991 to 2014, it increased at an average rate of 2.52 per cent per year, outdone only by Malaysia among the countries included in Table 2.4. Over the last quarter of a century, that growth slowed from a average of 3.16 per cent per year for 1991–95 to 2.30 per cent in 2011–14. Nonetheless, it remains fast growing in comparison to global rates. Lower-middle-income countries — which includes the Philippines — had an average labour force growth of 2.01 per cent in the same period.

The relationship between population and economic growth is not straightforward. Among the countries in Table 2.4, the Philippines has the fourth-largest population. Vietnam's population is 91 per cent of and Thailand's is two-thirds of the Philippines' population, yet these two countries have had significantly stronger economic growth through the years. Yet, the growth of Thailand's work force was only 0.91 per cent, while Vietnam's had about 2.1 per cent each year since 1991. The PRC, which is the most successful in East Asia in terms of GDP growth during these years, had only 0.98 per cent, and India 1.72 per cent growth.

The numbers convey that while population and thus work force growth are both considerations in accounting for the country's economic performance, effective labour force growth, i.e., the growth of the quantity and productivity of the country's workers, is a better determinant.

The Philippines has the lowest labour productivity growth among selected countries in East Asia (Figure 2.8). While Thailand's work force has been growing only relatively slowly, the productivity of its workers has expanded significantly faster, at 3.62 per cent, compared to the country's population growth of 0.33 per cent. The same pattern applies to the PRC.

Existing studies show that high population growth, far from being an asset, is a liability for economic growth if a country fails to exploit what is called the demographic dividend (Box 2.1). Mapa (2015) noted that the demographic transition accounted for about one-third of economic growth in East Asia during the period from 1965 to 1995.

TABLE 2.4
Labour Force Annual Growth, Selected Asian Countries, 1991–2014 (%)

Period	1991–1995	1996–2000	2001–2005	2006–2010	2011–2014	1991–2014
Philippines	3.16	2.19	2.33	2.59	2.30	2.52
Thailand	-0.14	1.65	1.62	0.72	0.66	0.91
Malaysia	3.06	3.30	2.23	2.15	2.42	2.64
Vietnam	2.13	2.51	2.29	1.90	1.58	2.10
PRC	1.40	1.30	0.89	0.48	0.80	0.98
Korea, Rep.	2.24	1.12	1.24	0.69	1.36	1.33
India	2.26	1.96	2.81	0.15	1.33	1.72
Indonesia	2.95	2.42	1.66	1.63	1.57	2.07

Source: World Bank's World Development Indicators.

FIGURE 2.8
Average Growth of Labour Productivity in Selected Countries, 1991–2000

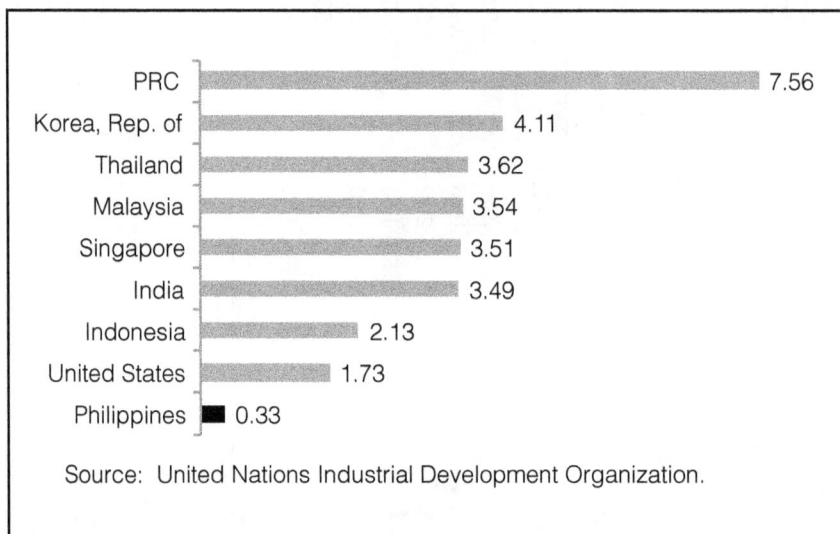

Source: United Nations Industrial Development Organization.

Box 2.1. The Demographic Dividend

As a country's population moves from a structure with high fertility to one with low fertility, it passes through what is called a *Goldilocks period*: a generation or two in which the fertility rate, of about 2.1, keeps the size of the population stable. The decline to replacement fertility rate is a unique opportunity for higher economic growth. A country that enters the Goldilocks period experiences sizable changes in the age structure of the population and, with the right policies, can enhance its economic growth. Studies (Mapa and Balisacan 2004; Mapa, Balisacan, and Briones 2006; and Mapa 2015) have documented that the Philippines has undergone this transition but failed to fully exploit it.

Source: Mapa (2015).

Mapa and Balisacan (2004) showed that because of its high population growth, the Philippines has not fully benefited from the demographic dividend. Looking at cross-country data from eighty countries over the period 1975 to 2000, population dynamics in the Philippines can be seen to have contributed an average of only about 1.06 percentage points per year to per capita GDP growth of the country, significantly below Thailand's 1.83 percentage points. The average per capita income growth could have risen by 0.63 percentage points per year had the country fully realized the demographic dividend (Mapa, Balisacan and Briones 2006).

E. Capital Formation and Foreign Direct Investment

The share of gross fixed capital formation in GDP hardly changed from 1991 to 2014. It was 20.2 per cent in 1991 and 19.7 per cent in 2014 (Figure 2.9), way below the 28.9 per cent average in the same period for four ASEAN countries (Indonesia, Malaysia, Thailand and Vietnam). Despite the Asian financial crisis in 1997, the average annual

FIGURE 2.9
Share of Capital Formation to GDP in Selected Countries, 1991–2014 (%)

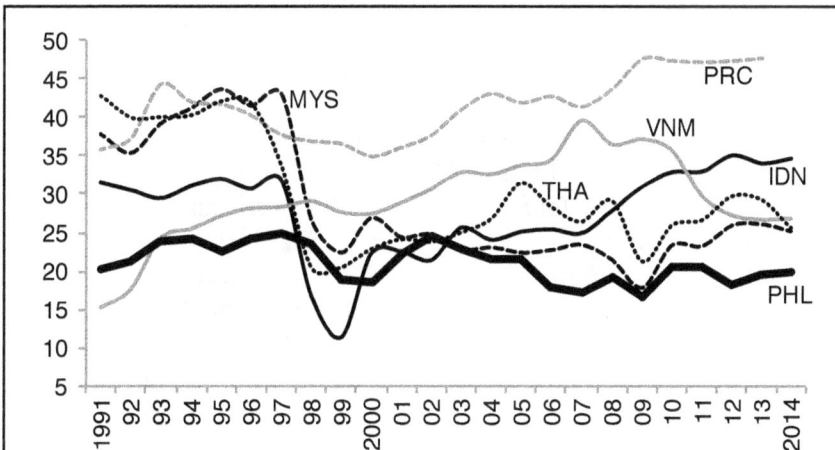

Source: World Bank's World Development Indicators.

growth of capital formation of the four ASEAN neighbours in the 1990s was 6.7 per cent, compared with 0.6 per cent for the Philippines (Table 2.5).

TABLE 2.5
Capital Accumulation Growth in Selected Countries, 1991–2014 (%)

Period	PRC	Indonesia	Malaysia	Philippines	Thailand	Vietnam
1991–1995	17.24	9.87	18.82	2.11	10.43	29.48
1996–2000	5.67	−6.71	−0.01	−0.82	−9.56	9.51
2001–2005	13.08	6.85	0.30	7.98	9.55	11.41
2006–2010	14.12	5.39	7.06	6.14	1.81	11.93
2011–2014	8.80	6.81	7.37	7.13	1.92	2.47
1991–2014	12.04	4.34	6.68	4.40	2.87	13.40

Source: World Bank's World Development Indicators.

The country's investment rate jumped to 4 per cent a year in the 2000s, closing in to the 6.67 per cent of the four ASEAN countries. This catching up continued and, from 2010, the Philippines surpassed its neighbours with a 12 per cent capital expansion growth, far higher than the 7.37 per cent of the four ASEAN member states. The PRC's rate was exceptional — 12 per cent from 1991 to 2014.

The problem of low investments is rooted in policies that restrict FDI. The Philippines' average net FDI inflows reached only 1.53 per cent of GDP, a rate that is exceeded by the average 3.59 per cent share of its four neighbours (Table 2.6). The country's total FDI inflows over the past four decades were just half those of Vietnam's, and around one-third of Indonesia's, Thailand's or Malaysia's (Figure 2.10). Annually, FDI inflows to the Philippines are low compared to those of other countries, and this gap has widened in recent years (Figure 2.11). During the 1990s up to the middle of the 2000s, Vietnam had relatively the same level of FDI inflows as the Philippines, but since 2005 it has outpaced the Philippines in attracting FDI.

TABLE 2.6
Share of Net FDI Inflows to GDP (%)

Period	PRC	Indonesia	Malaysia	Philippines	Thailand	Vietnam
1991–1995	4.18	1.41	6.98	1.68	1.51	7.25
1996–2000	4.06	0.11	4.42	2.15	3.62	6.58
2001–2005	3.56	0.32	2.49	1.02	3.78	3.48
2006–2010	4.32	1.54	3.43	1.34	3.40	7.20
2011–2014	3.86	2.52	4.04	1.43	2.84	5.35
1991–2014	4.01	1.13	4.29	1.53	3.04	6.03

Source: World Bank's World Development Indicators.

FIGURE 2.10
Accumulated Net FDI Inflows in Selected Countries, 1970–2013 ($ billion)

FIGURE 2.11
Annual FDI Inflows in Selected ASEAN Countries, 1990–2014 ($ billion)

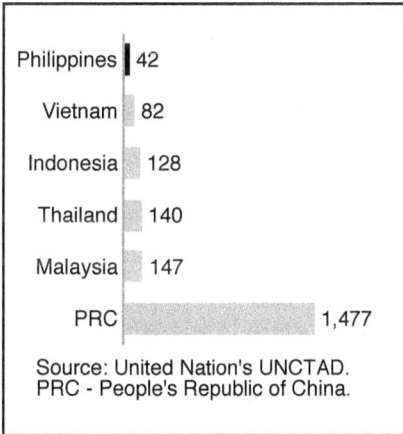

Philippines 42
Vietnam 82
Indonesia 128
Thailand 140
Malaysia 147
PRC 1,477

Source: United Nation's UNCTAD.
PRC - People's Republic of China.

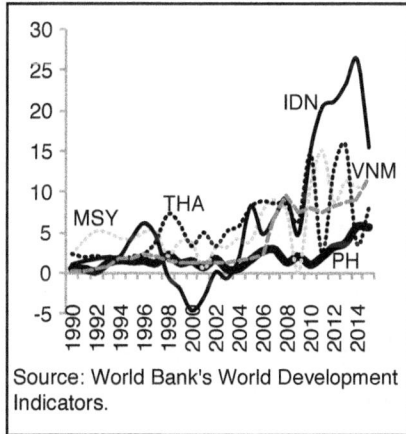

Source: World Bank's World Development Indicators.

FDI is an important driver of growth in developing countries. Besides adding to the capital availability in a host country, it promotes broad-based growth through the transfer and adoption of "best practices" of foreign multinationals (Klein et al. 2001). FDI undertakes tasks that local investors may find difficult to assume due to lack of financial or technical resources. The extraction of mineral resources illustrates this benefit, since it is highly capital intensive and requires world-class expertise in ensuring ecological integrity. FDI likewise provides competition, which is needed to deliver an even better product at a more affordable cost. Finally, it introduces local industries to new technologies. This allowed East Asia to rank among the top merchandise exporters in the 1990s after the introduction of efficient product assembly techniques and management practices.

To gain these benefits, restrictions on FDI entering the country have to be significantly reduced or lifted. The equity ceiling of FDI, particularly in utilities, telecommunications, retail and other services, is 40 per cent. Besides equity ceilings, other concerns of foreign investors include tax regimes that are implemented opaquely and discriminatingly against them; unclear information on and unstable investment requirements; and trust regulations that are unevenly enforced. These restrictions are not unique to the Philippines,[2] but somehow policymakers there seem less hospitable to foreign investors than other Asian countries, which has resulted in lower net FDI inflows to the country compared to its neighbours.

F. External Trade

Trade openness is positively correlated with economic growth (Edwards 1992; Krueger 1997). Rodriguez and Rodrik (2001) challenged the claim, observing that there was little evidence to support the idea that a liberal trade regime is correlated with growth. The trade openness indicators used were either inappropriate or correlated with other variables, which may well explain economic growth. They also noted that the mechanisms linking a liberal trade regime and economic growth are not well established. Several studies (Greenway et al. 2002; Winters et al. 2004) examined these criticisms and found that trade openness would more likely stimulate than reduce growth.

While the Philippines has been open to trade, it has not been as open as Malaysia, Thailand or Vietnam (Figure 2.12), which may help explain why in the 1980s and 1990s the country did not perform as well as these countries.

FIGURE 2.12
Trade Openness of Selected Asian Countries, 1991–2014 (% of GDP)

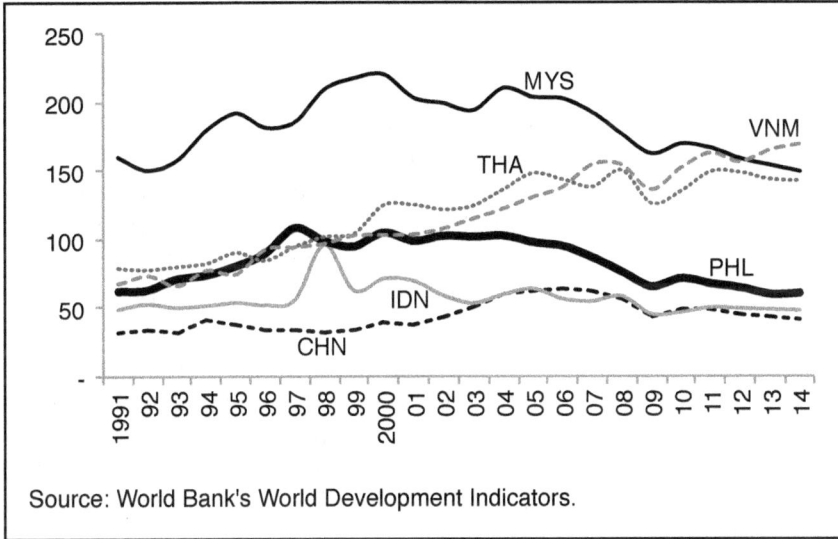

Source: World Bank's World Development Indicators.

The economy contracted in the middle of the 1980s and was compelled to avail of several structural assistance programmes from multilateral creditors. As a result of these the country unilaterally lowered tariff and non-tariff barriers and liberalized its exchange rate policy.

Several studies have noted the positive effects of a freer trade regime (Aldaba 2010; Austria 1998; Cororaton and Abdulla 1999; Balboa and Medalla 2006; Austria 2001; Austria and Medalla 1996). These have generally documented positive *ex post* effects of trade liberalization on economic performance indicators such as total factor productivity, growth, employment and wages, and income distribution.

Clarete (2006) observed that the country had failed to maximize its gains from a freer trade regime. Aggregate exports expanded by a factor of about 6.6 between 1980 and 2000. Machinery and transportation equipment explained the aggregate export performance in the 1990s. However, all the traditional major export performers, such as coconut oil, had lost export value over the two decades. On the other hand, imports in almost all the sectors responded positively to the lowering of import restrictions. Clarete attributed this performance to high transaction costs in the export sector.

Global Value Chains

The fairly good performance of machinery and transportation equipment can be traced to the country's participation in global value chains. Table 2.7 shows, however, that its capacity to transform imports into exports is relatively weak. In all the sub-periods, exports are less than imports, indicating a significant number of imported goods being destined for final rather than for intermediate use to be processed for exports.

Vietnam and Thailand were in a similar situation in earlier years. But, starting in the middle of the 1990s for Thailand and 2011 for Vietnam, they added more value to imports and exported more. The other ASEAN countries and the PRC throughout the period had positive net exports, as they were successful in transforming imports to exports.

Agricultural Trade

The agricultural industries tend to be among the more protected ones in the country, starting with rice. When the country joined the World Trade Organization (WTO) in 1995, the Philippines asked the WTO to postpone implementing its obligation to end the rice import monopoly of the National Food Authority, a state-owned enterprise, to prepare rice farmers for import competition, which the WTO granted. The WTO extended the privilege for another seven years, and then approved a subsequent request to waive this for a further three years until 30 June 2017.

Had the country not subscribed to special treatment in 1995, the country's agriculture is likely to be more diversified and competitive. Dawe (2016) noted how recent trade patterns in the 2000s involving ten food groups reflect changes towards crop and dietary diversification. The countries included in Table 2.8 have diversified their crop farming, except Malaysia, which concentrated in the oilseed complex. Accordingly, it has to import more food items. However,

TABLE 2.7
Trade Intensities in Selected Asian Countries, 1991–2014 (%)

Period	PRC	Indonesia	Malaysia	Philippines	Thailand	Vietnam
Exports as % of GDP						
1991–1995	18.30	26.65	83.19	32.05	38.32	32.24
1996–2000	18.64	36.63	108.35	46.22	54.24	45.75
2001–2005	26.61	33.70	110.78	46.93	68.00	54.53
2006–2010	30.44	27.75	100.52	38.76	72.63	68.71
2011–2014	23.90	24.66	84.52	29.96	75.13	82.36
Average	23.57	30.09	98.01	39.15	61.10	55.65
Imports as % of GDP						
1991–1995	17.48	25.17	84.78	38.15	43.60	39.54
1996–2000	15.72	31.14	94.63	53.05	47.80	52.27
2001–2005	24.32	27.55	91.44	53.81	63.26	61.39
2006–2010	24.92	24.70	80.27	40.21	66.15	78.44
2011–2014	21.09	24.52	72.77	33.25	71.05	81.16
Average	20.69	26.70	85.28	44.13	57.84	61.79

Source: World Bank's World Development Indicators.

TABLE 2.8
Net Trade for Various Food Groups, Averages A and B (US$ per capita)

Commodities	PRC		Indonesia		Malaysia		Philippines		Thailand		Vietnam	
	A	B	A	B	A	B	A	B	A	B	A	B
Rice	0	0	−4	−3	−9	−20	−3	−11	36	86	12	36
Wheat	0	−1	−3	−8	−10	−15	−7	−8	−3	−7	−2	−7
Maize	0	−1	−1	−2	−13	−27	−1	−1	0	2	0	−4
Oilseed complex	−4	−26	6	58	165	412	2	6	−11	−28	−4	−23
Fruit & Vegetables	2	7	1	−2	−12	−30	8	9	24	40	4	19
Meat	0	−2	0	−1	−9	−16	−2	−3	17	30	2	−12
Milk	−1	−2	−1	−3	−14	−15	−6	−6	−4	−5	−3	−5
Fish	2	5	9	11	−6	−1	5	5	68	74	22	53
Sugar	0	−1	−2	−5	−11	−23	0	1	13	39	0	−2
Food & Animals	−6	−1	−6	−18	−76	−136	−21	−36	88	196	22	35
Total	−1	−22	−1	27	5	129	−25	−44	228	427	53	90

Notes: Period A: 1999–2001; Period B: 2009–11.
The category *Food & Animals* does not equal the sum of the other nine food groups in the table, as those nine groups are not an exhaustive list.
Sources of raw data: FAO (2015) for trade and population data. IMF (2014) for US GDP deflator. Source: Dawe (2016).

over the last ten years Malaysia has succeeded in increasing its per capita net exports from $5 to $129. Its oilseed exports increased from $165 to $412 per person. The PRC has been most successful in crop diversification, even as it has remained largely a balanced participant in trade. Indonesia, Thailand and Vietnam have diversified their farming, increased both their exports and imports, and ended up increasing their net agricultural exports over the 2000s.

The Philippines was not as successful. Among the ASEAN countries in the table, its trade deficit in agricultural commodities expanded. In the 2000s it lost out significantly in vegetable oil exports, which increased marginally from $2 to $6 per person, compared to Malaysia's. Its net exports in fruits and vegetables, fish, and sugar expanded only very weakly. These gains were more than offset with increased per capita imports of the other food items that it had been importing. In the end, its net imports per person exceeded that of the PRC. While the respective areas harvested for fruits, vegetables and pulses, and oil crops had increased, the expansion was lower than that of rice, which had expanded significantly since the middle of the 1980s.

G. Rice Self Sufficiency and Land Market Restrictions

The agriculture sector can help arrest the flight of workers from farming into low-productivity service industries. A key idea is to raise agricultural productivity and keep food prices low to help stimulate renewed growth in the manufacturing industries. Getting more private sector investments in agriculture is required to correct the distortion in the country's structural transformation. However, there are at least two factors dampening private sector participation in agriculture: the rice self-sufficiency policy and restrictions on the sale or use of agricultural land imposed by the Comprehensive Agrarian Reform Program (CARP).

Rice Self Sufficiency

Self-sufficiency in rice has been the primary measure by which the performance of every administration of the Department of Agriculture

is informally evaluated. The latest policy on this front is the Food Self
Sufficiency Program of the Aquino government, primarily supported
by the import monopoly in rice of the National Food Authority. In
this plan the country was supposed to reach self-sufficiency by 2013,
or 2016. In both instances the government ended up not attaining the
goal. Clarete (2016) estimated that the Philippines had only a 5 per
cent likelihood of attaining self-sufficiency in 2013.

Dawe (2015) cited that island economies like the Philippines have
a natural disadvantage in attaining rice self-sufficiency, arguing that a
better measure of comparative advantage is per capita area harvested,
and not rice farm yield. Island economies, particularly Indonesia and
the Philippines, are at the bottom of the list in terms of this index.
Figure 2.13 reproduces the data and extends the average to 2013. In
turn, per capita area harvested is directly related to per capita water
supplies and the abundance of flat land. Countries in the Southeast
Asian mainland like Thailand, Vietnam and Myanmar have access to
dominant river deltas and have less varied landscapes, both of which
boost their per capita area harvested.

FIGURE 2.13
Rice Yield and Per Capita Rice Area Harvested, ASEAN Countries, 2000–13

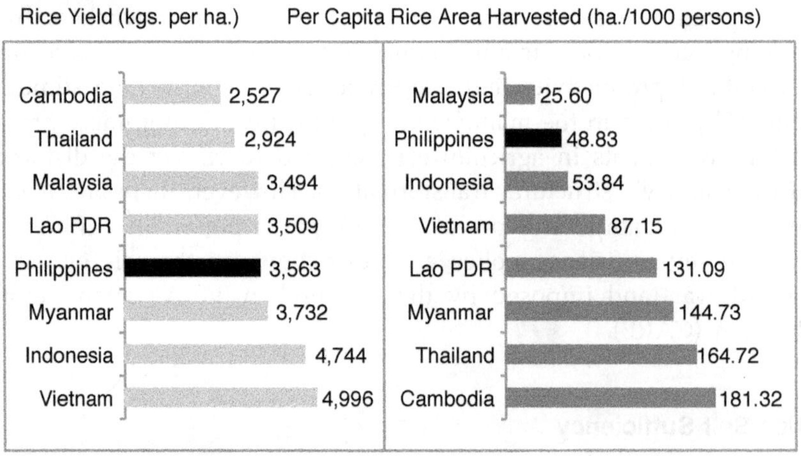

Rice Yield (kgs. per ha.)	Per Capita Rice Area Harvested (ha./1000 persons)
Cambodia 2,527	Malaysia 25.60
Thailand 2,924	Philippines 48.83
Malaysia 3,494	Indonesia 53.84
Lao PDR 3,509	Vietnam 87.15
Philippines 3,563	Lao PDR 131.09
Myanmar 3,732	Myanmar 144.73
Indonesia 4,744	Thailand 164.72
Vietnam 4,996	Cambodia 181.32

Source of basic data: United Nation's Food and Agricultural Organization.
Lao PDR - Lao People's Democratic Republic.

The high attention given to rice self-sufficiency has been at the expense of other crops and the livestock industries, which could return higher incomes to farmers. Figure 2.14 shows the crop diversification that had gone on since the 1960s in the Philippines. Following Dawe (2016), there are five commodity groups: rice, maize, fruits, vegetables and pulses, and oil crops. It is important to note how rice continues to displace or slow down the growth of other crops. The pattern apparently has gone on since the 1990s. Surprisingly, the expansion had become even sharper since the 2000s.

FIGURE 2.14
Crop Area Harvested in the Philippines, 1961–2013 (MH)

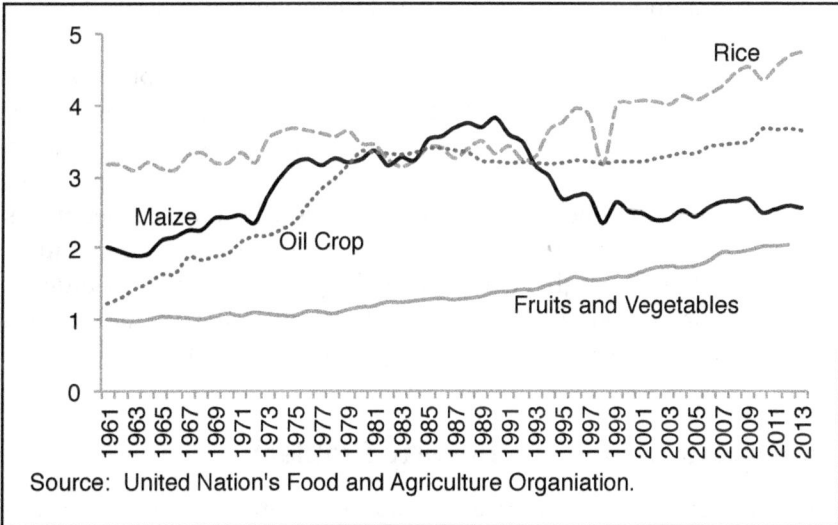

Source: United Nation's Food and Agriculture Organiation.

Rural Land Market Restrictions

The restrictions on lands covered by the CARP and the ensuing transaction costs can be summed up as follows:

- Collective Certificate of Land Ownership Awards (CLOAs), covering about 2.13 million hectares, have been awarded by the Department of Agrarian Reform, instead of individual

CLOAs (Adriano 2013). The CLOAs cannot be mortgaged or sold within ten years, and can only be sold to qualified beneficiaries with the approval of the Department of Agrarian Reform (DAR). These restrictions limit access to farmer-beneficiaries of credit from formal banking institutions. Moreover, for so long as their loan amortizations remain unpaid, the CLOAs are not released by the Land Bank of the Philippines, which then denies the CLOA owners access to formal credit sources.

- The leasing of CARP lands is not allowed, preventing their consolidation for scale farming. The current average farm size per beneficiary is around 1.72 hectares, but the smallest land size is about 1.2 hectares (Adriano 2013). These are too small for the introduction of more capital-intensive and efficient farming methods.

- Agribusiness processing plants do not have the option to own and control the sources of inputs and to not have to rely on small farmer households. Investments in agribusinesses are dampened by the problem of "pole vaulting", i.e., diverting contracted production to other buyers who offer higher prices. The inability of an agribusiness to consolidate farmland — whether through ownership or long-term lease — in order to ensure a continuous and reliable supply of farm output is a deterrent to investment in the agricultural sector.

III. Factors Behind the Poverty Problem

Despite higher growth in recent years, the country continues to have a poverty problem. Other countries succeeded in translating high growth to substantial gains in eradicating poverty (Balisacan and Fuwa 2004). When the East Asian region succeeded in reducing poverty from 31 to 12 per cent during 1990–2000, the Philippines only brought poverty down from 34 to 28 per cent (Balisacan and Fuwa 2007). Poverty-reduction elasticity to growth was lower compared to other countries in Southeast and East Asia.

This section will address the issues pertinent to untangling the enduring factor of poverty amidst growth. These include initial levels of development and inequality, income growth, and changes in income distribution (Fosu 2010). Not only does income growth matter, but so too does the sectoral composition of national income (Fuwa, Balisacan, and Bresciani 2015).

A. Poverty Problem

From the data on the number of the poor in 2012, 25.2 per cent of Filipinos live in poverty, which is ten percentage points lower than the 1991 level. In 2003 it dropped to 24.3 per cent, rose to 26.6 per cent in 2006, and subsequently declined, but only slightly, to 26.3 per cent in 2009, before settling at 25.2 per cent in 2012.[3]

Given the geographic diversity of the country, the poverty trend at the national level does not accurately reflect the problems of poverty across all regions. It is evident that while some regions have experienced rapid or slow declines in poverty, there are others, like Region 8, Region 12, and the Autonomous Region of Muslim Mindanao (ARMM), where poverty incidence has increased over time (Figure 2.15).

The disparities in poverty rates across regions are wide. For example, in 2012 the poverty incidence in Region 8 was 45.2 per cent, which is ten times higher than the rate for the National Capital Region (NCR), at 3.9 per cent. The NCR has consistently had the lowest rate of poverty incidence. The rates for the regions around the NCR — Regions 3 and 4A — have likewise been below the national poverty rate. Luzon generally, with the exceptions of Region 4B and Bicol, has rates of poverty below the national average. In contrast, the three regions in the Visayas have always had above average levels of poverty. Most of Mindanao, likewise, except in the earlier years of ARMM, has had greater than average levels of poverty. At the latest count it had the highest level of poverty. It is apparent that the level of productive activity in a given location is an important determinant in avoiding poverty. The NCR meets such a criterion with its significant share in the country's GDP, and, accordingly, engenders positive economy-activity linkages in the surrounding regions, at a diminishing rate to the distance from the centre.

FIGURE 2.15
Poverty Headcount Ratios by Region, 1991, 2006, 2009 and 2012

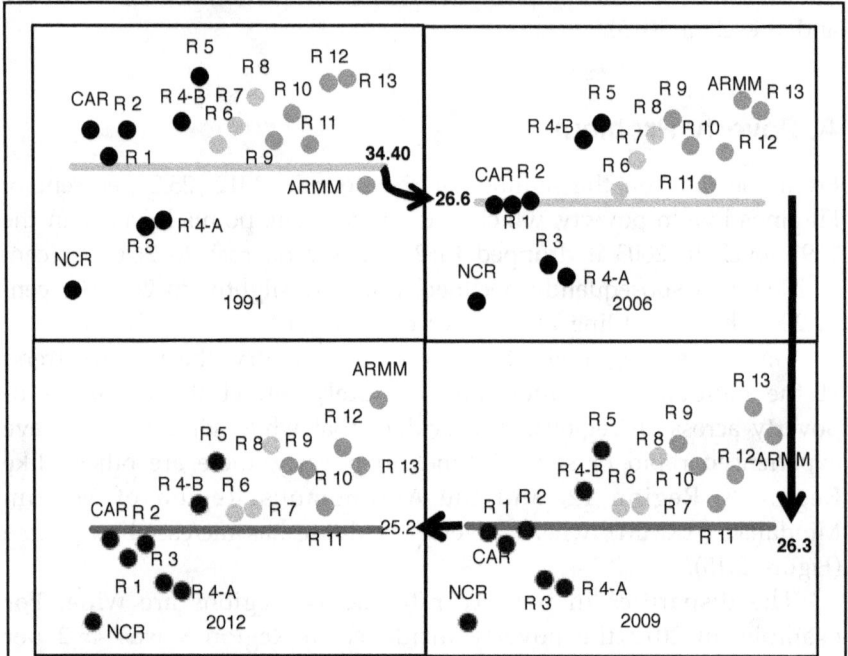

Source: Philippine Statistics Authority.

NCR: National capital region; CAR: Cordillera Autonomous Region; R 1: Region I - Ilocos;
R 2: Region II - Cagayan Valley; R 3: Region III - Central Luzon; R 4-A: Region IVA -
CALABARZON; R 4-B: Region IVB - MIMAROPA; R 5: Region V - Bicol; R 6: Region VI -
Western Visayas; R 7: Region VII - Central Visayas; R 8: Region VIII - Eastern Visayas;
R 9: Region IX - Zamboanga Peninsula; R 10: Region X - Northern Mindanao; R 11: Region XI
- Davao; R 12: Region XII - SOCCSKSARGEN; R 13: Region XIII - Caraga;
ARMM:Autonomous Region in Muslim Mindanao.

Fuwa et al. (2015), using a panel of provincial-level data from 1991 to 2006, noted that 62 of 73 provinces had reduced their respective poverty ratios. Of the 62 provinces, growth of non-agricultural income exceeded that of agricultural income in 58 provinces. It is more likely to observe headcount poverty going down with the faster growth of non-agricultural income than with agricultural income. This is likewise supported with three-year changes in incomes and the incidence of poverty.

Altogether, from 1991 to 2006, the authors observed a total of 365 three-year provincial income growth spells. Of these, 221 are correlated with falling poverty ratios. Furthermore, of the 221 cases, non-agricultural income growth was higher in 149 instances. The numbers indicate that non-agricultural income growth has a larger poverty-reduction contribution compared to agricultural growth in provinces with better initial conditions of access to infrastructure, human capital endowments, and intra-provincial inequality.

B. What Has Sustained Poverty?

Weak and Volatile Growth

Eliminating poverty in the Philippines has been slow due to its low and volatile growth record, particularly before the 2000s. The factors that dampened the growth performance of the country have been discussed in the preceding section. Higher growth rates were shown to be associated with deeper cuts in the incidence of headcount poverty (Ravallion and Chen 1997). Countries such as the PRC and Vietnam have significantly eradicated poverty over the past decades owing to their sustained impressive growth records (Lin 2003; Vandemoortele and Bird 2011). That the average income of the poor rises with overall average income implies that successful poverty eradication efforts may require policies to raise average incomes (Dollar and Kraay 2002).

High Population Growth

Population growth in the Philippines remains high, thus pulling down real per capita income. In 2016 the population growth rate stood at 1.68 per cent, higher than those of other countries in Asia (Table 2.9). A comparison of Thailand and the Philippines suggests that the higher population growth path of the Philippines resulted in foregone output growth for the country and a slower reduction in poverty incidence (Balisacan 2007).

TABLE 2.9
Population Growth in Selected Asian Countries, 1960–2014 (%)

Country	1960	1970	1980	1990	2000	2007	2014
PRC	1.8	2.8	1.3	1.5	0.8	0.5	0.5
Indonesia	2.4	2.6	2.3	1.8	1.4	1.4	1.2
Malaysia	3.2	2.5	2.4	2.8	2.3	1.8	1.6
Philippines	3.3	2.9	2.7	2.5	2.1	1.7	1.7
Thailand	3	2.9	2.1	1.3	1.2	0.3	0.3
Vietnam	1.6	2.3	2.1	1.9	1.3	1.1	1.1

Source: World Bank's World Development Indicators.

The country's total fertility rate (TFR) has been relatively high compared to some of its Asian neighbours (Table 2.10). Fertility rate reduction over the years has been slow. While the Philippines is currently in its demographic sweet spot, with more than half the population aged twenty-four and below (Philippine Statistics Authority 2012), the slow reduction in the fertility rate prevents the country from taking advantage of this window of opportunity that the demographic transition affords in enhancing growth potential (Mapa 2015).

TABLE 2.10
TFR in Selected Asian Countries, 1960–2013 (%)

	1960	1970	1980	1990	2000	2006	2013
PRC	5.8	5.5	2.7	2.5	1.5	1.6	1.7
Indonesia	5.7	5.5	4.4	3.1	2.5	2.5	2.3
Malaysia	6.2	4.9	3.8	3.5	2.8	2.1	2
Philippines	7	6.3	5.2	4.3	3.8	3.4	3
Thailand	6.1	5.6	3.4	2.1	1.7	1.5	1.4
Vietnam	6.3	6.5	5	3.6	2	1.9	1.7

Source: World Bank's World Development Indicators.

The poorest households (bottom quintile) and the poorest regions (ARMM and Bicol Region) have the highest TFR in the country, implying that these families are trapped in a vicious cycle of high fertility and poverty. In 2013, TFR for the poorest households was 5.2 (Table 2.11). For ARMM and Bicol Region, which represent the poorest regions in the country, the TFR was 4.2 and 4.1, respectively. These figures are higher than the Philippines' 2013 national average TFR, which was 3.0 (Table 2.12).

TABLE 2.11
TFR by Income Quintile, 2008 and 2013 Surveys (%)

Income Quintile	NDHS 2008 (Reference year: 2007)	NDHS 2013 (Reference year: 2012)
Bottom (Poorest)	5.2	5.2
Second	4.2	3.7
Third	3.3	3.1
Fourth	2.7	2.4
Highest (Richest)	1.9	1.7
Overall	3.3	3

Source: Mapa (2015) Compiled from the National Demographic and Health Survey (NDHS) 2008 and 2013, Philippine Statistics Authority (PSA).

TABLE 2.12
TFR by Region, Philippines, 1998–2013 (%)

Region	1998	2003	2008	2013
NCR	2.5	2.8	2.3	2.3
CAR	4.8	3.8	3.3	2.9
Region I - Ilocos	3.4	3.8	3.4	2.8
Region II - Cagayan Valley	3.6	3.4	4.1	3.2
Region III - Central Luzon	3.5	3.1	3	2.8
Region IVA - CALABARZON	3.7	3.2	3	2.7
Region IVB - MIMAROPA	...	5	4.3	3.7
Region V - Bicol	5.5	4.3	4.1	4.1
Region VI - Western Visayas	4	4	3.3	3.8
Region VII - Central Visayas	3.7	3.6	3.2	3.2
Region VIII - Eastern Visayas	5.9	4.6	4.3	3.5
Region IX - Zamboanga Peninsula	3.9	4.2	3.8	3.5
Region X - Northern Mindanao	4.8	3.8	3.3	3.5
Region XI - Davao	3.7	3.1	3.3	3.9
Region XII - SOCCSKSARGEN	4.2	4.2	3.6	3.2
Region XIII - Caraga	4.7	4.1	4.3	3.6
ARMM - Autonomous Region in Muslim Mindanao	4.6	4.2	4.3	4.2

Source: Philippine Statistics Authority.

Lack of Jobs and Good Quality Jobs

Job creation is needed to reduce poverty, since labour is likely the most important productive asset of the poor. The unemployment rate remained relatively unchanged at 7 per cent despite the higher growth rate of output, while the underemployment rate stood at 19.3 per cent.

Unemployment is highest among the youth (Figure 2.16). In 2013, unemployment of the youth (15–24 years old) stood at 16.1 per cent and accounted for half of the total unemployed population. The next age group (25–34 years old) also had high unemployment of around 8 per cent. Unemployment among the older age groups is lowest, at around 3 per cent.

FIGURE 2.16
Unemployment by Age and Poverty Incidence of Employed Persons, Philippines, 2006–13 (%)

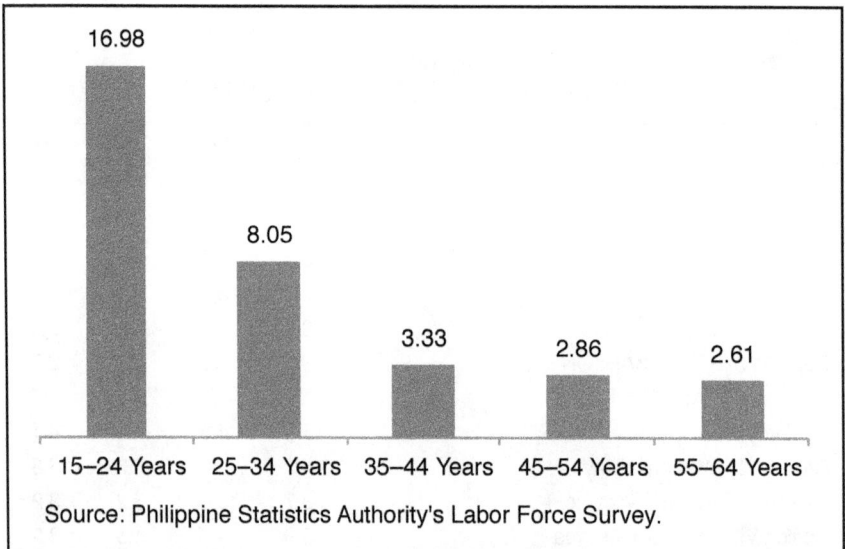

Source: Philippine Statistics Authority's Labor Force Survey.

Unemployment tends to be high among those with higher levels of education (Figure 2.17, left panel), which is unexpected. In 2013, unemployment among college students stood at 10.8 per cent, while that of college graduates was at 9.1 per cent. These figures suggest that either there is some skills mismatch or these groups might have higher reservation wages (Chua et al. 2013). On the other hand, underemployment is higher for people with lower levels of educational attainment (Figure 2.17, right panel). In the same year, underemployment for those who were not able to finish elementary school was 23.8 per cent. Since this group has lower levels of education, the average wage is substantially lower, thus inadequate to sustain the basic needs of households.

A significant proportion of the employed Filipinos remain poor (Figure 2.18). The quantity of jobs alone does not guarantee a way out of poverty. The quality of jobs matters as much. While data for the period from 2006 to 2012 is clearly indicative of a declining trend in the proportion of the employed living below the national poverty threshold, the poverty incidence of the employed nonetheless stood at 21.9 per cent.

FIGURE 2.17
Unemployed and Underemployed Persons, by Educational Attainment, Philippines, 2006–13 (%)

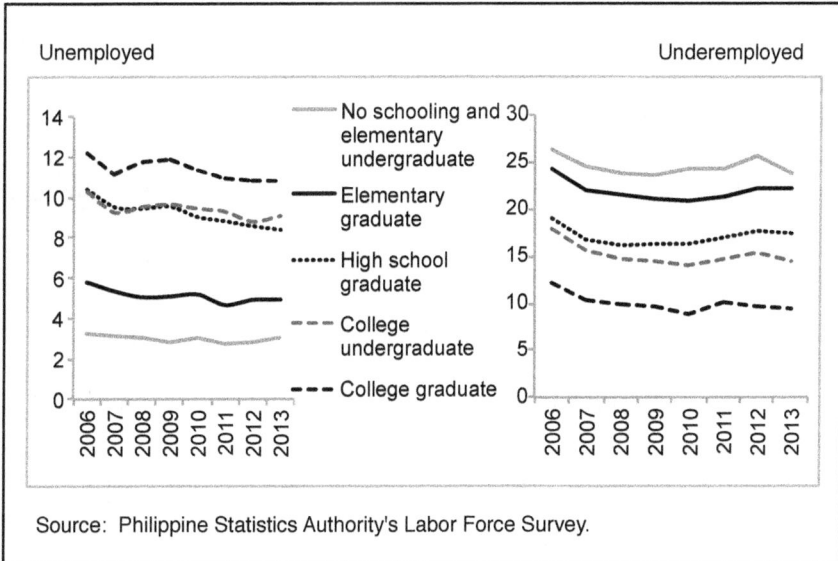

Source: Philippine Statistics Authority's Labor Force Survey.

FIGURE 2.18
Poverty Incidence of Employed Population, Philippines, 2006–12 (%)

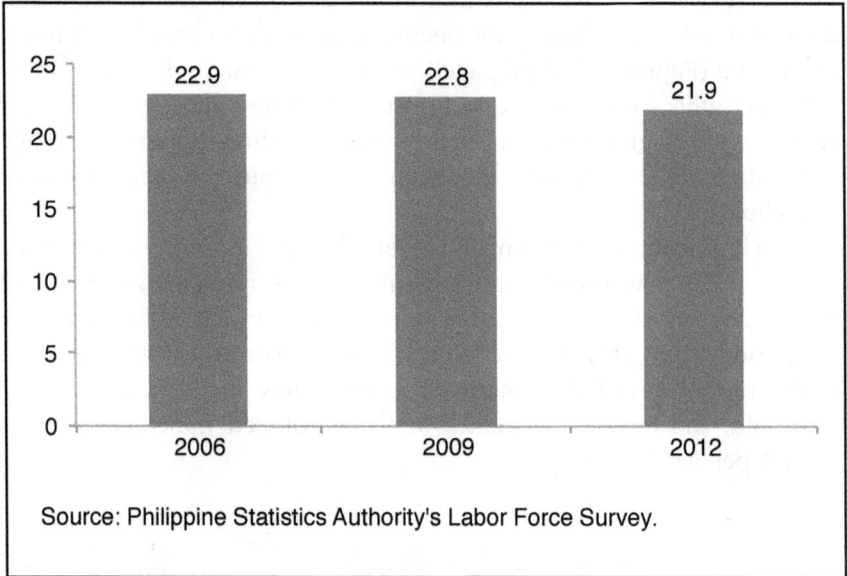

Source: Philippine Statistics Authority's Labor Force Survey.

High and Persistent Income Inequality

Income inequality, as measured by the Gini coefficient, stood at 0.4712 in 2012 (Figure 2.19). This had slightly declined from 0.4871 in 2003. Income inequality in urban areas had moderately decreased but had increased in rural areas. This is consistent with the fact that the lowest income quintile of the population received only 5 per cent of the total economic pie in 2012.

A recent work on economic inequality in the Philippines from 2000 to 2012 (Valenzuela et al. 2017) observed that urban and non-agricultural households are relatively better off. To the extent that there are more rural and agricultural households in the country, location and source of income help explain inequality. The same result applies to households whose heads are female or with higher educational attainment. The distribution of educational attainment is skewed towards those with less schooling. Younger Filipinos (aged thirty and under) are poorer than their older counterparts.

FIGURE 2.19
Gini Ratio by Area, 2003–12

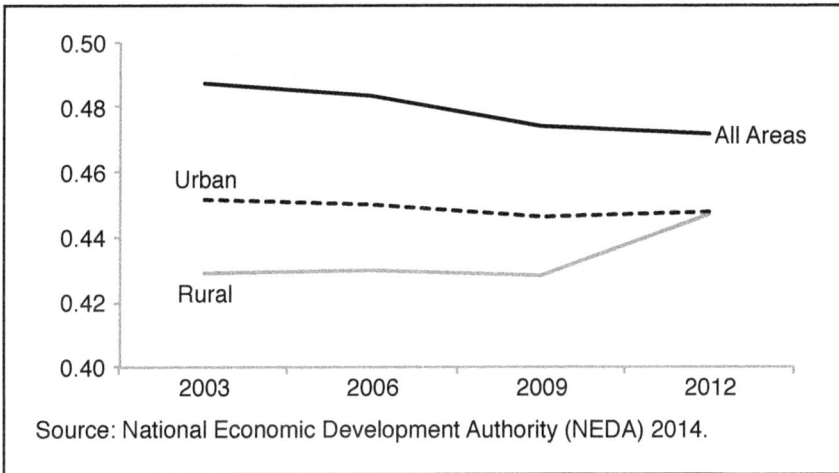

Source: National Economic Development Authority (NEDA) 2014.

Economic inequality is multidimensional. A recent report looks at processes within a country and among countries as contributors to income inequality (United Nations et al. 2017). The report addresses at least three structural dimensions, of marginalization, exclusion and inequality, whether within a country or between countries. First, while urbanization is correlated with higher incomes, it has increased inequality, exclusion and risk in Asia and the Pacific. It is therefore important to manage the process, as pointed out by Corpuz (chap. 3, this volume). Also, families in urban areas are more vulnerable to natural calamities, which reduces their incomes. Second, agriculture remains a challenge to policymakers. Its contribution to GDP is pulled down faster than expected by higher growth in industry and services in urban areas, low productivity of the sector, and faster rural to urban migration. This calls for modernization of the sector to increase productivity and raise rural incomes. This chapter explored above the important constraints to modernizing the agriculture sector. Thirdly, the integration of economies in the world today through global value chains, while increasing gains from trade, has left behind the small and medium enterprises, and certainly those in the informal sector. It is therefore important to assist the participation of SMEs in international trade. These companies face many challenges arising from their size, such as information about product standards, regulations, and others, needed to internationalize their businesses.

Compared to selected Asian countries, poverty and income inequality remains high in the Philippines. Using the poverty threshold of $1.51 per day, around 27 per cent of the country's population lived below the poverty line in 2010 (Table 2.13).[4] Only Indonesia had a higher poverty incidence, of 28 per cent. Malaysia, on the other hand, is close to achieving the complete eradication of extreme poverty.[5]

TABLE 2.13
Poverty and Inequality in Selected Asian Countries in Recent Years (%)

	Official Poverty Incidence (in 2012), %[a]	Share of population below $1.51 per day (in 2010), %[b]	Gini Ratio[c]
China	10.2	16.5	37.01
Indonesia	12	28	38.14
Malaysia	1.7	0.4	46.21
Philippines	25.2	26.9	43.03
Thailand	12.6	1.1	39.04
Vietnam	17.2	22.4	35.06

[a] 2014 ADB Key Indicators for China; World Development Indicators (WDI) for the rest.
[b] 2014 ADB Key Indicators.
[c] WDI; The latest available for China and Indonesia are from 2011, for Malaysia 2009, the Philippines and Vietnam 2012, and Thailand 2010.
Source: World Bank's World Development indicators.

The distribution of income in the Philippines is more unequal, as evidenced by the higher inequality indicator of 43.03 per cent in 2012 using data from the ADB (Table 2.13). Countries with higher initial levels of inequality experience slower rates of poverty reduction (Ravallion 1997), and this may help explain why the translation of growth to poverty eradication in the Philippines is weak, which is elaborated below.

C. Inequality, Income Growth, and Poverty Reduction

Several studies had observed that the gain from reducing poverty in several parts of the world has been impressive, with the PRC accounting for a major share of this accomplishment. Even excluding the PRC, poverty reduction in the rest of the developing world has been considerable (World Bank 2006; Ravallion and Chen 2008; Fosu 2010). These studies found that robust economic growth contributed significantly to accomplishing poverty reduction.

However, using an updated data set on poverty lines, Chen and Ravallon (2008) compared the growth and poverty-reduction performance of developing countries all over the world and reached a similar observation about "uneven progress" in poverty reduction despite satisfactory income growth.

As early as in the 1990s, several studies have looked into the contribution to poverty eradication of not just growth but of changes in the income distribution as well. Bourguignon (2003) showed how the poverty-reduction performance of developing countries is better explained if the empirical model used in the analysis included not just growth and income distribution changes but also the interaction of both variables as well.

Based on a mapping of poverty reduction and income growth in over eighty developing countries, Fosu (2010) noted that the response of poverty reduction to income growth in several countries, including the Philippines, was comparatively weak. Figure 2.20 shows that the two variables are inversely related to each other, such that countries with strong income growth spells from 1980 to 2007 had a stronger capacity for reducing their respective poverty. This is the usual observation that growth is important in reducing poverty.

However, to determine how inequality may affect the capability of transforming growth to poverty reduction, the data was partitioned into one group of countries that reduced their Gini inequality index and another group that increased the measure. Figure 2.21 still shows the inverse pattern between income and poverty growth. However, countries that reduced their inequality (Figure 2.21, Panel A) had poverty reduction twice as strong (−10.69 per cent) as those of developing countries, which experienced rising income inequality (−5.15 per cent), the Philippines being one of them. One may observe

FIGURE 2.20
Poverty and Income Growth, Eighty Developing Countries, 1980–2007

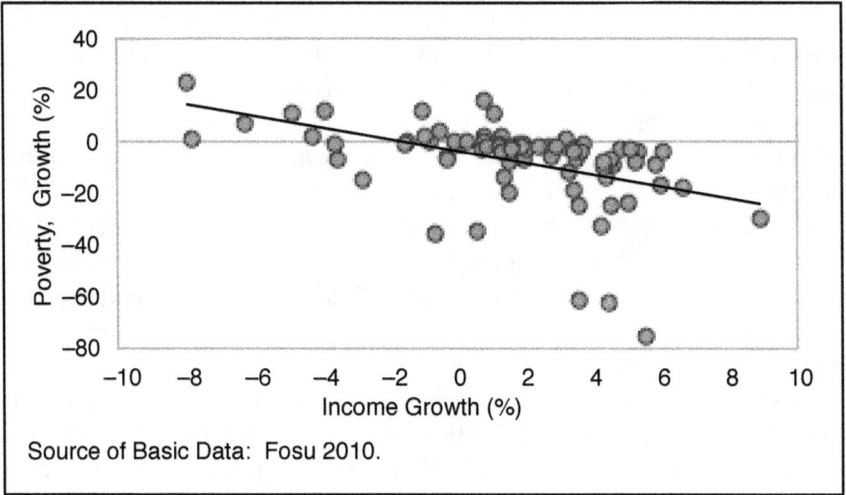

Source of Basic Data: Fosu 2010.

FIGURE 2.21
Poverty and Income Growth in Developing Countries That Reduced or Increased Income Inequality, 1980-2007

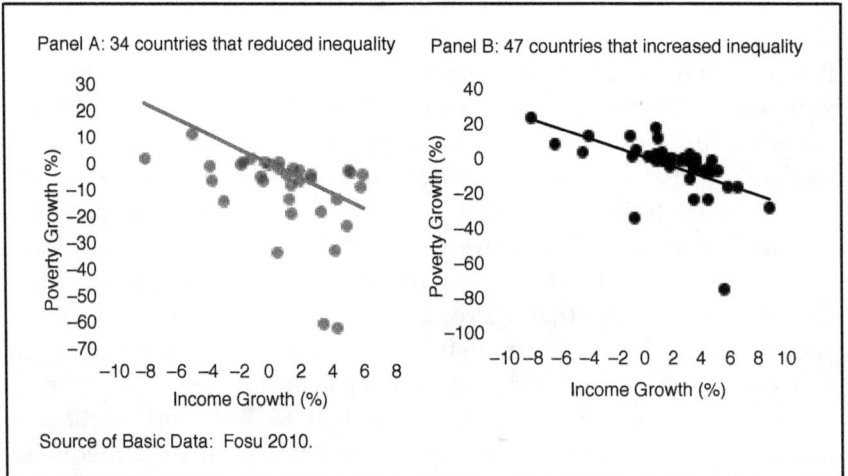

Panel A: 34 countries that reduced inequality   Panel B: 47 countries that increased inequality

Source of Basic Data: Fosu 2010.

in Figure 2.21 that countries in Panel A were able to reduce the numbers of their poor by much more compared to the countries in Panel B for the same amount of income growth.

The 1980s and 1990s were decades of low GDP growth for the Philippines, with average growth rates of 1.4 per cent and 3.2 per cent, respectively. Additionally, the country had relatively high population growth rates from 2.7 per cent to 2.1 per cent. Accordingly, the country's average per capita GDP annual growth was −0.9 per cent in the 1980s and 0.6 per cent in the 1990s, which pales in comparison with the corresponding data of its neighbours (Table 2.14).

TABLE 2.14
Per Capita GDP Growth Rates of Selected Countries, 1961–2014 (%)

Period	China	Indonesia	Malaysia	Philippines	Thailand	Vietnam
1961–1970	2.7	1.6	3.4	1.7	6.0	
1971–1980	4.4	5.3	5.3	3.0	4.2	
1981–1990	7.8	4.2	3.2	−0.9	6.0	2.3
1991–2000	9.3	2.8	4.6	0.6	3.6	5.9
2001–2010	9.9	3.8	2.7	2.9	3.7	5.4
2011–2014	7.5	4.4	3.7	4.1	2.2	4.6
Average	6.9	3.6	3.8	1.6	4.4	4.8

Source: World Bank's World Development Indicators.

Due to its poor growth performance in the 1980s and 1990s, the country would not have been in a position to significantly reduce poverty in those years. The country had a turnaround in the 2000s, but the global economic crisis in 2008 dampened such growth. The country's per capita GDP growth increased by 2.9 per cent, which is a significant departure from the pattern of hardly any growth in the preceding two decades. It further climbed to 4.1 per cent in the first half of the 2010s. Both GDP growth (6.27 per cent average for 2010 to 2014) and population growth (1.7 per cent, between 2007 and 2014) combined to give the turnaround figure of 4.1 per cent per capita GDP growth rate for the country.

4. Tracking the Economy over the Next Twenty-five Years

In the following, the per capita income, structural adjustment and poverty of the country are tracked using a recursive dynamic comput-able general equilibrium (CGE) model of the economy (Box 2.2). The possible trajectories over the next twenty-five years of key indicators are tracked under the strong and weak growth scenarios of the economy.

Box 2.2. Tracking the Growth Trajectory of the Economy

A computable general equilibrium (CGE) model of the Philippine economy, with twenty-seven sectors, two factors — labour and capital — and four types of consumers, representing the poor and non-poor households in rural and urban areas, is used. The structure of the model is adapted from Rutherford (1999). There are seven types of production activities: local products for the home market, Armington goods, imported products, foreign exchange, produced capital, household consumption, and government consumption. Households are endowed with exogenous supplies of labour and capital. Local production requires Armington products as intermediate inputs and the primary factors in producing two types of outputs, one for the home market and the other for export. Armington products are composite goods of local and imported goods. The final consumption of households and the government are of Armington products. Produced capital goods require Armington products.

The model's equilibrium is described by three sets of conditions. The first is the market clearing conditions, and there are nine types of market: local products, Armington goods, foreign exchange, primary factors, exported and imported goods, the composite final consumption good of households and government, and the produced capital good. The second are the zero profit conditions, one for each of the seven production activities. Third are the respective requirements that each agent spend exactly its

---

Box 2.2. (continued)

income, or Walras' law. There are four types of agent; namely, the representative households, government, financial intermediary, and the business sector.

The model is recursive dynamic. It is solved each year from 2015 to 2040, with the projected annual growth each year of the model's primary factor supplies acting as the model's shocks. The growth rates are projected outside the model. The labour growth rate is the sum of the respective expansion of the labour force and labour productivity growth. The resulting equilibrium values of the incomes of the consumers, government, representative business sector, and financial intermediary are added up to obtain the national income implied by the changes of factor endowments.

The model is numerically calibrated to replicate the base year equilibrium of the Philippines in 2015. It is solved using GAMS.

The annual increases of primary factor supplies in the model drive the changes of the model's income and other economic variables. Two scenarios of primary factor supply growth are considered and used in the simulations. First is the weak growth scenario, which incorporates changes of labour and capital supplies if economic policies are the way they had been set in the recent past.

The other scenario, the strong growth one, covers the expansion of supplies if the deeper policy reforms suggested by this study to enable the economy to sustain its recent high growth are adopted. These increase the capital and resource endowments of the model. Getting rid of restrictions to FDI, reducing transaction costs, and other related reforms open the economy to more investments. Government programmes in education and health and related policies increase the productivity of the labour force, effectively expanding the supplies of effective labour in the economy. Instead of calculating how much these policies may expand capital and labour supplies, the study uses a "catching up" approach, which is to look at the revealed growth of such factors in the country's more successful economies.

A. Resource Growth Scenarios

Gross Fixed Capital

Figure 2.22 (left panel) shows the average growth of the country's gross fixed capital formation (GFCF) from 1995 to 2014. With its GFCF growth at 4.64 per cent, the country's capacity to boost economic growth had been weak. Its investment growth compares well with those of Indonesia, Malaysia and Singapore. However, those of India, Vietnam and the PRC were at least 4 percentage points ahead of the country. The annual growth of Vietnam's GFCF averaged 9.23 per cent, while the PRC had 11.31 per cent.

FIGURE 2.22
Average Growth of GFCF, Selected Asian Countries, 1995–2014 and Observed Growth and Projected Growth Scenarios of GFCF, Philippines, 1995–2040 (%)

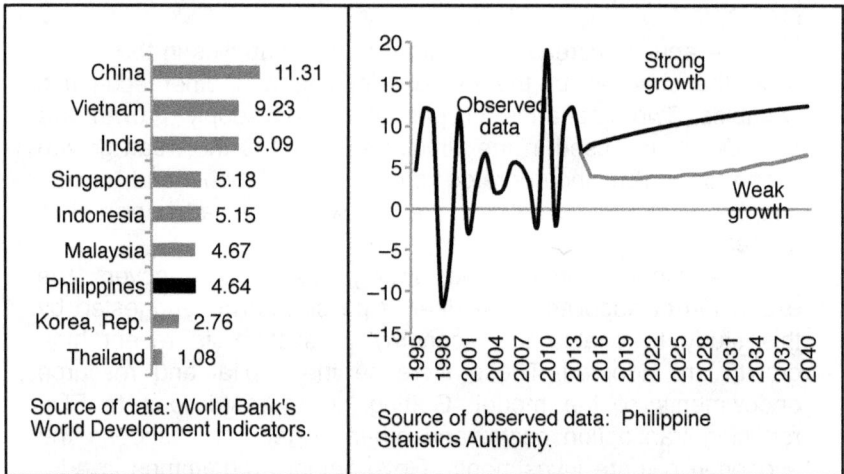

Source of data: World Bank's World Development Indicators.

Source of observed data: Philippine Statistics Authority.

The right panel of Figure 2.22 shows the observed growth of GFCF in the Philippines from 1995 to 2014 and its projected expansion under the two growth scenarios. The strong growth scenario requires GFCF to expand at an average rate of 9.9 per cent each year from 2015 to 2040, which is between that of Vietnam and the PRC's. The weak growth scenario ignores opening up the country to FDI, reducing transaction costs and the regulatory risk of investing in the economy, or implementing the related reforms that would bring down the cost of doing business in the country. Its business-as-usual investment growth is 4.64 per cent annually.

Effective Labour Resources

Since 1995 the labour force of the Philippines has grown at a rate of 2.35 per cent (Figure 2.23, left panel), second to Malaysia's 2.53 per cent. However, in terms of labour productivity growth the country

FIGURE 2.23
Average Growth of the Labour Force (1996–2014) and Labour Productivity (1990–2000) in Selected Countries (%)

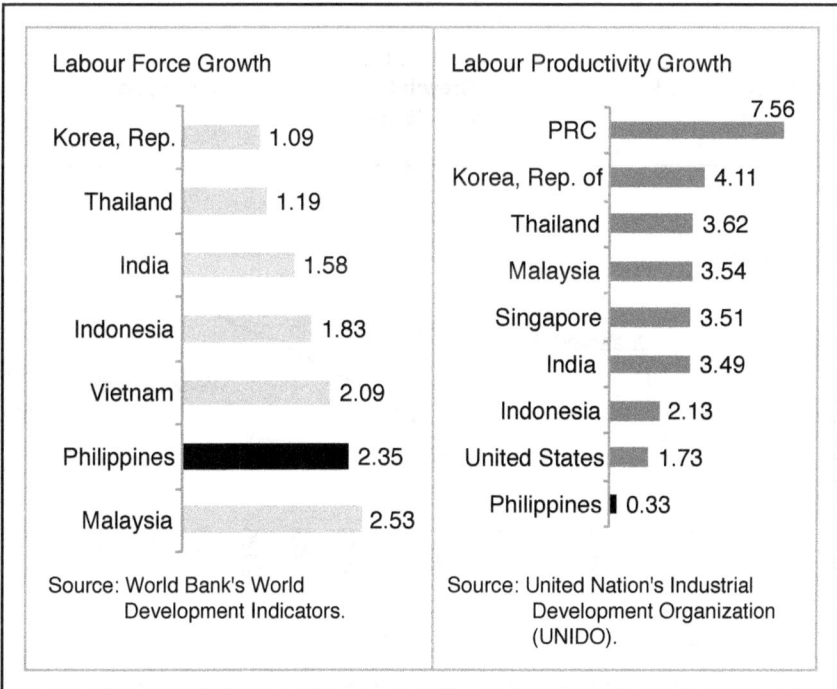

Labour Force Growth		Labour Productivity Growth	
Korea, Rep.	1.09	PRC	7.56
Thailand	1.19	Korea, Rep. of	4.11
India	1.58	Thailand	3.62
Indonesia	1.83	Malaysia	3.54
Vietnam	2.09	Singapore	3.51
Philippines	2.35	India	3.49
Malaysia	2.53	Indonesia	2.13
		United States	1.73
		Philippines	0.33

Source: World Bank's World Development Indicators.

Source: United Nation's Industrial Development Organization (UNIDO).

ranks at the bottom, with only 0.33 per cent growth per year from 1990 to 2000. In contrast, China had 7.56 per cent and the other ASEAN countries in the figure had 3.2 per cent. The proposed reforms in education and health, among others, and complementary reforms elsewhere, such as getting foreign investors to conduct business in the country, have the potential of raising the country's labour productivity growth.

The scenario for the higher effective growth rate of workers requires the country to perform to the level of its ASEAN neighbours, with their average productivity growth of 3.2 per cent. The effective labour resource growth, defined as the growth of the quantity and productivity of its work force, is 5.64 per cent; i.e., the sum of 3.2 and 2.44 per cent, the latter being the average of the Philippines and Malaysia's labour force growth. The weak growth scenario rate is three percentage points lower: 2.68 per cent; i.e., 2.35 plus 0.33. Figure 2.24 portrays these scenarios with the observed data.

FIGURE 2.24
Observed Growth and Projected Growth Scenarios of Effective Labour Force, Philippines, 1995–2040 (%)

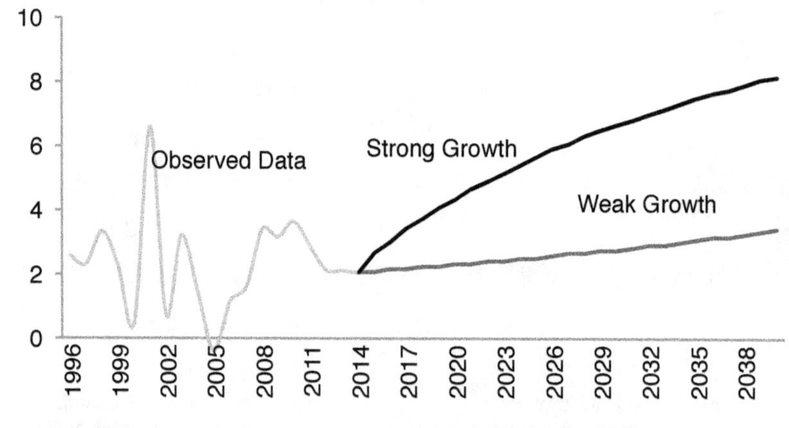

Source of observed data: World Bank's World Development Indicators.

Total Factor Productivity

Total factor productivity growth captures several enablers of growth. The introduction of improved technology is the usual contributor to such growth. However, the elimination of transaction costs or at least levelling the burden to those of its more successful neighbours would have the effect of raising the country's total factor productivity. Investments in infrastructure facilities and public utilities, including in information and communication technologies, and, more importantly, reducing the cost of doing business have the potential to stimulate more economic transactions. The country would have a greater chance of sustaining the recent high growth if it could maintain the same TFP growth rate as China, at 2.4 per cent annually (Figure 2.25, left panel). The weak growth scenario carries the average TFP growth of the country from 1991 to 2014 at 0.6 per cent. The right panel shows both scenarios of TFP growth.

FIGURE 2.25
Total Factor Productivity Growth Scenarios, Philippines, 1995–2040 (%)

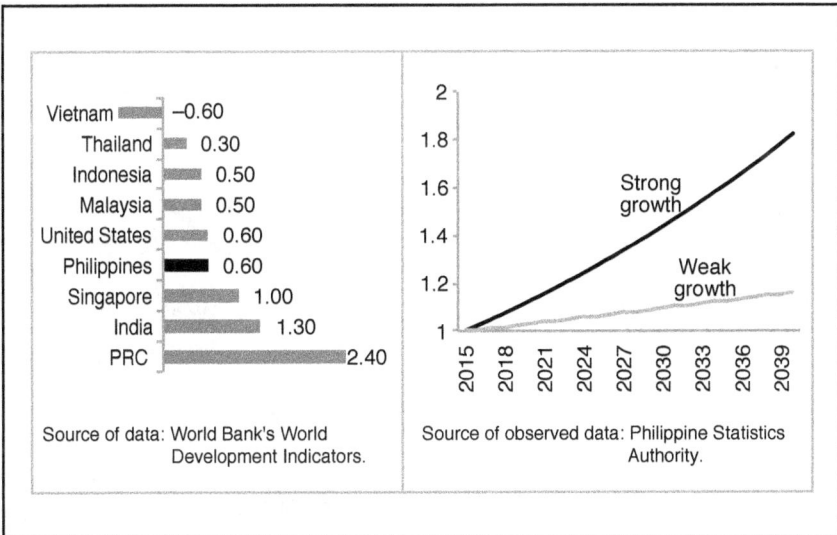

Source of data: World Bank's World Development Indicators.

Source of observed data: Philippine Statistics Authority.

D. Key Economic Indicators Tracked

Gross Domestic Product

In the base year of 2015, the GDP at 2000 prices stood at P7.164 trillion. Under the strong growth scenario, GDP increases by about 5.44 times over the quarter of a century, the average annual growth rate being about 7 per cent (Figure 2.26). The weak growth scenario has GDP rising to P20.987 trillion, 2.93 times its 2014 level, or about slightly over half of the strong growth GDP in 2040. The average growth rate is at 4 per cent each year, the low average that the country had when it was dubbed the "sick man of Asia". The simulated differential growth illustrates the beneficial effect of policy reforms that open up the country to more investments and the upgrading of labour skills through education and training programmes.

FIGURE 2.26
Observed and Simulated Growth Scenarios of GDP, Philippines, 1995–2040
(billion pesos at 2000 prices)

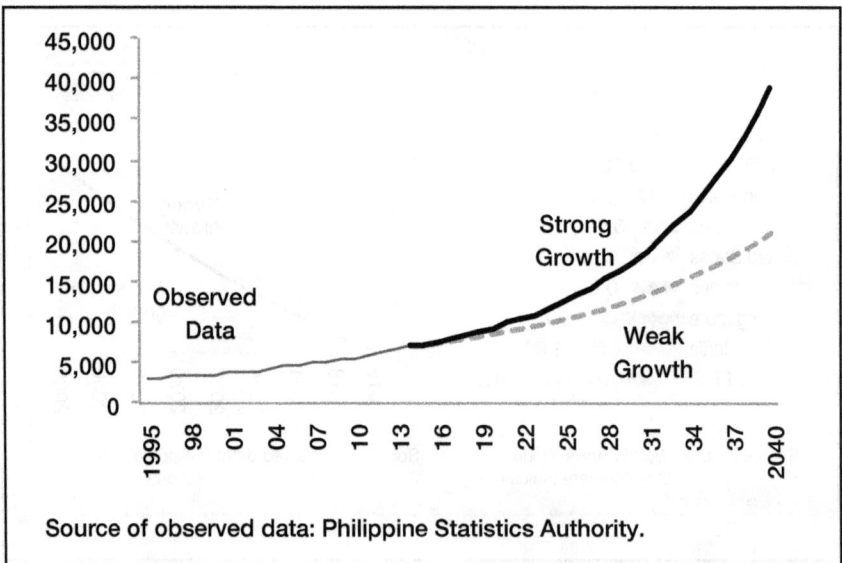

Source of observed data: Philippine Statistics Authority.

GDP Per Capita

The GDP per capita in 2014 was P70,538. Over the next twenty-five years this may rise to P299,539, 5.25 times its 2014 level (Figure 2.27). In contrast, GDP per capita in 2040 is projected at only P146,232 under the weak growth scenario, 2.07 times its 2014 level. The average yearly expansion rates are 2.92 per cent and 5.78 per cent, respectively, for the weak and strong growth scenarios. The numbers are roughly the difference between the GDP growth and population growth. Importantly, slowing down population growth is essential for attaining the expansion of GDP per capita. The projected population growth rates are 1.38 per cent and 0.99 per cent, respectively, for the weak and strong growth scenarios.

FIGURE 2.27
Observed and Simulated Growth Scenarios of Per Capita GDP, 1995–2040
(pesos)

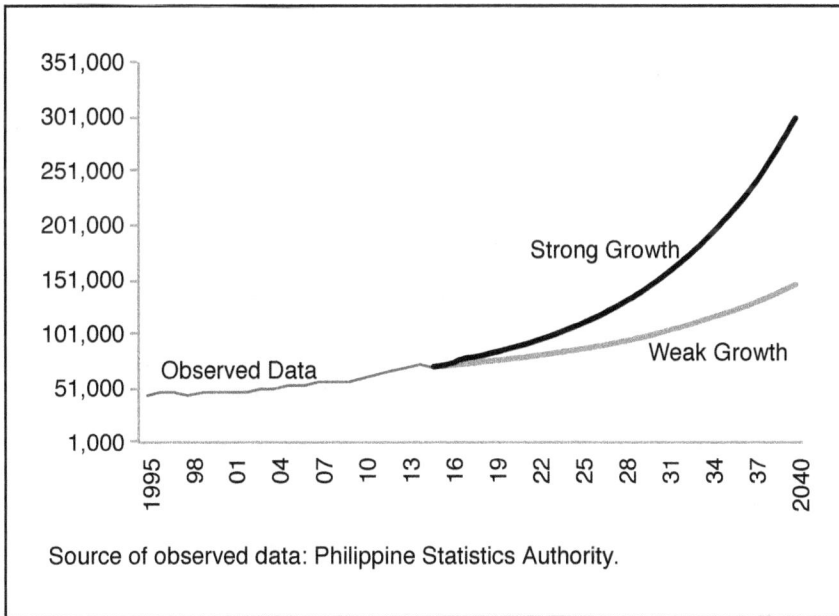

Source of observed data: Philippine Statistics Authority.

GNI Per Capita

The country is regarded to be a lower-middle-income country, with a per capita GNI of about $3,500 in 2014. Based on the World Bank's classification of countries, middle-income economies are those with a GNI per capita of more than $1,045 but less than $12,736. Lower-middle-income and upper-middle-income economies are separated at a GNI per capita of $4,125.

Under a weak growth scenario, the country may be upgraded to an upper-middle-income country by 2025, when its per capita GNI would have reached $4,215. Under the strong growth scenario such a development could be brought forward to as early as 2020, when the GNI per capita reaches $4,217.

By 2040 the country's GNI per capita is simulated to reach $14,615. Assuming the World Bank's threshold of $12,736 for a high-income country remains unchanged, this status is attainable by the country in 2039, when its GNI per capita is projected to reach $13,500. Under the weak growth scenario, however, the highest GNI per capita is $7,136.

Employment Shares

The employment shares of these sectors were computed through the years. The results are shown in Figure 2.28. Under the weak growth

FIGURE 2.28
Structural Transformation, Weak vs. Strong Growth Scenarios

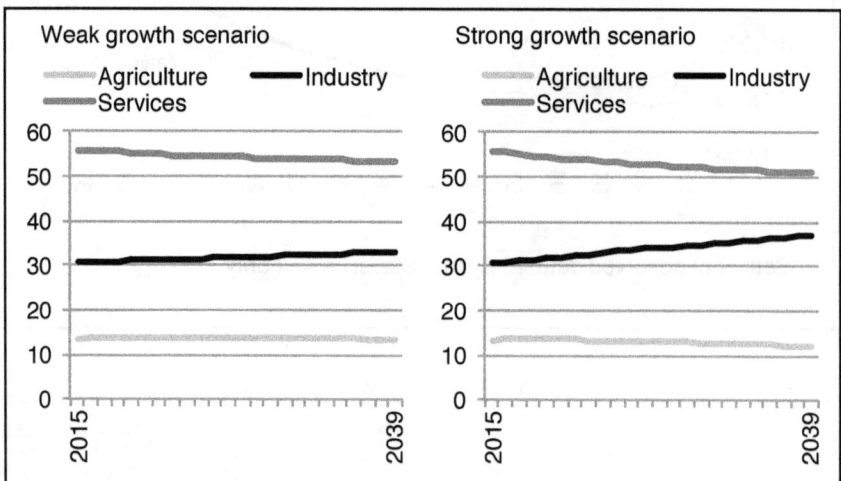

scenario there is hardly any change. However, under the strong growth scenario the distorted structural adjustment taken up above appears corrected. The share of services in employment falls, while that of industry rises. Agriculture's share continues to fall, but not as sharply as it had over the last twenty-five years.

E. Eradicating Poverty

Success in eradicating poverty over the next twenty-five years will depend on the robustness and level of income growth, as well as the distribution of income gains. Fuwa, Balisacan and Bresiciani (2015) pointed out that with a more even income distribution prevailing in the country, the transmission of the benefits of high growth flows proportionately more to the country's poor. However, the country's Gini index was high, at 47 per cent in 2014.

Growth Elasticities of Poverty

Fosu (2010) estimated the poverty, growth and inequality equation (Fosu 2003). Table 2.15 notes the estimated poverty elasticities to per capita income growth and inequality growth, which measure the responsiveness of the poverty situation to changes in the level of per capita income and in how it is distributed among the population. The elasticities are reported by poverty lines. For example, the second column shows poverty elasticities to per capita income growth, with the poverty headcount index at $1.25. The estimates range from –1.549 (Sub-Saharan Africa) to –3.994 (Eastern Europe and Central Asia). The Philippines has the weakest elasticity among ASEAN countries, and it bested only South Asia and sub-Saharan Africa.

A similar pattern applies to inequality, albeit the numbers are larger with positive signs (i.e., poverty worsens with higher income inequality). The estimates range from 1.681 (sub-Saharan Africa) to 6.377 (Eastern Europe and Central Asia). The Philippines' poverty inequality elasticity is the third weakest, at 3.216, with most countries and regions having stronger responses to poverty reduction to inequality growth. The elasticity indicates that for every percentage increase of the Gini index, the poverty headcount index (at $1.25 standard) tends to increase by 3.2 per cent.

TABLE 2.15
Estimated Poverty Elasticity to Per Capita Income and Inequality Growth (%)

Country	Poverty Elasticity to			
	Per Capita Income Growth $1.25	Inequality Growth $1.25	Per Capita Income Growth $2.50	Inequality Growth $2.50
China-Rur. ('05)	−2.339	3.065	−1.312	1.106
China-Urb. ('05)	−3.499	5.429	−2.116	2.38
Malaysia ('04)	−3.613	5.758	−2.166	2.634
Philippines ('06)	−2.301	3.216	−1.22	1.364
Thailand ('04)	−3.258	5.153	−1.887	2.397
Vietnam ('06)	−2.417	3.284	−1.349	1.271
East Asia and the Pacific	−2.485	3.434	−1.393	1.36
Eastern Europe and Central Asia	−3.994	6.377	−2.475	2.846
Latin America and the Carribean	−3.125	5.067	−1.74	2.494
Middle East and North Africa	−3.191	4.883	−1.879	2.149
South Asia	−2.036	2.453	−1.101	0.782
Sub-Saharan Africa	−1.549	1.681	−0.699	0.536

Source: Fosu 2010.

The other two sets of estimated elasticities for the $2.5 poverty standard resulted in similar relationships, but they tend to have weaker influences on poverty compared to those for the $1.25 poverty standard.

What will it take for the Philippines to eliminate poverty in fifteen years, starting with the current US$1.25 standard poverty headcount index of 25 per cent? It would entail a poverty-reduction rate per year of about 25 per cent, which is not overly optimistic. In Fosu's (2010) assessment of actual poverty-reduction rates, the highest observed rate reached 75 per cent for Latvia. Countries such as Poland, Belarus, Jamaica and Mexico had cut their poverty index at a rate per year of between 24 and 29 per cent. Thailand, as reported above, cut its poverty index at a rate of 19.4 per cent. It is possible, but not likely, for the Philippines with a much lower poverty growth rate per year of −1.8 per cent from the 1990s to 2000s.

But suppose the country raised its growth performance, what per capita GDP growth does getting rid of poverty in fifteen years entail, given the income and inequality elasticities of poverty of the country? If we take inequality as growing at the same rate as observed for the country between the 1900s and 2000s, 0.22 per cent, then this would require a per capita GDP growth of 12 per cent.[6] Assuming a population growth rate of 1.7 per cent annually, then the annual GDP growth rate would need to be 13.7 per cent, which is unlikely.

Assuming a more workable annual GDP growth rate of 7 per cent (which would obviously require fundamental structural reform), and given the same assumptions as above, poverty reduction would proceed at an average rate of 10.5 per cent per year, which would mean it would require about thirty-one years to eliminate poverty in the country.

Thus, it is important to consider a policy reform package that will create strong growth but is at the same time pro-poor. In Fosu's (2010) assessment, the decline of the Gini index among several countries ranges from as deep as 7.31 per cent in the case of Azerbaijan to just about zero in the case of Burundi. Malaysia had a Gini index at the rate of 2.742 per cent. Suppose the Philippines, in addition to having per capita GDP growth of 5.7844 per cent, could also reduce its Gini index by 3 per cent each year; its poverty index could fall at the rate of 20.4 per cent annually. If it could take thirty-one years to eliminate poverty with the feasible but nonetheless challenging GDP growth rate of 7 per cent, making such growth pro-poor (as indicated by the reduction of the Gini index at the rate of 3 per cent each year) would mean it would only take about sixteen years to eliminate poverty (Figure 2.29).

Figure 2.29 shows the results of simulating the eradication of poverty using Fosu's equation with the estimated parameters for the Philippines. The topmost line in the figure shows that, under weak growth combined with rising inequality, the country would require more than a quarter of a century to eliminate its poverty problem. By 2040 the poverty headcount ratio would still be at 6 per cent. On the other hand, if the country's Gini index declines at a rate of 3 per cent annually, as in Malaysia (Fosu 2010), poverty cuts would

FIGURE 2.29
Scenarios of Eradicating Poverty, Philippines, 2015–40

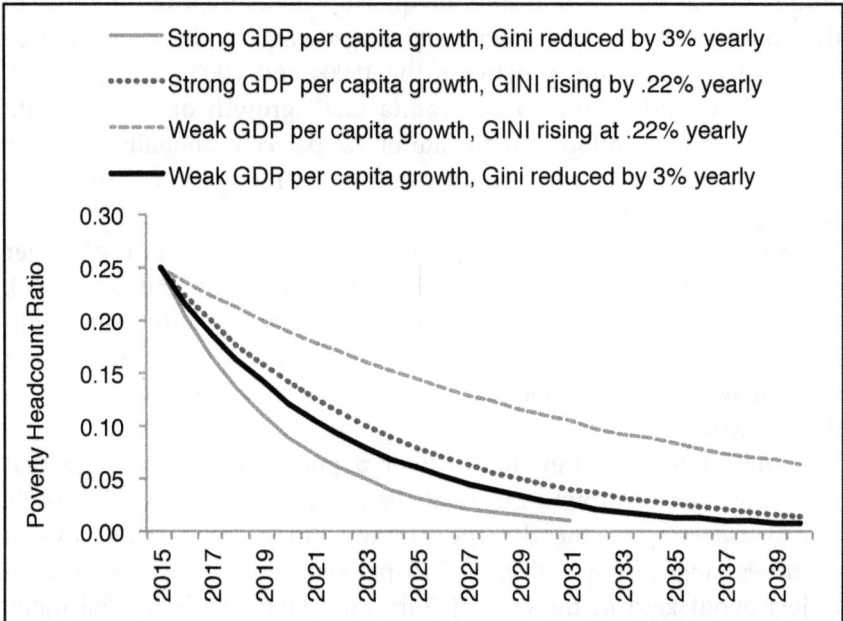

be deeper, and thus the process of eradicating poverty shorter (second line). That is, even with weak growth, poverty is eradicated in twenty-five years, which in this simulation is regarded as a poverty ratio equal to 0.01.

Sensitivity Analysis

The elasticities play an important role in the pace of poverty eradication. In the above simulation, the elasticity of poverty to income growth used was 2.089. Fuwa, Balisacan and Bresciani (2015) estimated this parameter using a panel of provincial household data. The authors had two parameters. The first is the elasticity of poverty to per capita non-agricultural income growth, and the second is with respect to that of per hectare agricultural income. The estimate for the former is −1.67, while for the latter it is −0.23.

The computations were redone using −1.67 instead of −2.089 for the poverty-to-income-growth elasticity. Hardly any change was observed. It will still take twenty-five years to bring down the poverty headcount ratio to about 0.01 in a weak growth scenario that is pro-poor, as well as in the strong growth scenario that is not pro-poor. The country would still face a 7 per cent poverty problem in 2040 employing a business-as-usual exclusive growth scenario. Finally, the strong growth, pro-poor scenario has the promise of eradicating poverty by 2031. It would appear that because of the moderate difference between the two elasticities (−1.67 versus −2.08), the results of the simulation conducted in this study to eradicate poverty are holding up both in the extent and direction of change.

Notes

1. Estimates were obtained from Vandenbrink (2016).
2. Neuman (2014) wrote that Asia has the largest number of restrictions to FDI, citing World Bank data. The average equity ceiling in Asia is 77 per cent, compared to 92 per cent in Latin America and sub-Saharan Africa.
3. The NEDA director general announced in 2016 that the poverty headcount ratio is now at 21.6 per cent based on the 2015 Family Income and Expenditure Survey.
4. The Asian Development Bank (ADB) recently estimated a regional poverty line to enable an appropriate comparison of the poverty situation across Asian countries. This regional poverty line, below which would mean extreme poverty, was determined to be $1.51 per day. In its *Key Indicators for Asia and the Pacific 2014* it was noted that one concern with the World Bank's $1.25 per day absolute poverty line is that it does not accurately reflect national poverty lines in Asian countries. The figure of $1.25 per day is a substantial underestimation of the national poverty lines of several countries, as these nations raised their poverty lines for relevant policymaking.
5. Eradication of extreme poverty in this case is in the absolute sense. OECD countries measure poverty in relative terms, with the poor identified as those earning below 50 per cent of the country's per capita income or expenditure. In relative terms, extreme poverty cannot be driven down to zero.
6. That is, $24.5\% \approx -2.089*12\% + 2.759*0.22\%$.

References

ADB (Asian Development Bank). "Key Indicators for Asia and the Pacific 2014". 2014 <http://www.adb.org/publications/key-indicators-asia-and-pacific-2014/>.

Adriano, Fermin. "Sustaining the Momentum of Inclusive Growth in the Post-CARP Scenario". Integrative Report submitted to the Inter-Agency Committee on Institutional Arrangements for Land Management and Rural Development. 2013.

Aldaba, R. "Does Trade Protection Improve Firm Productivity? Evidence from Philippines Micro Data". PIDS Discussion Paper Series no. 2010-32. 2010.

APO (Asian Productivity Organization). *APO Productivity Databook 2014*. Tokyo: Keio University Press, 2014.

Austria, M. "Liberalization and Regional Integration: The Philippines' Strategy to Global Competitiveness". PIDS Discussion Paper Series no. 2001-09. 2001.

Austria, M.S. "Productivity Growth in the Philippines after the Industrial Reforms". PIDS Discussion Paper Series no. 98-26. 1998.

Austria, M., and E.M. Medalla. "A Study on the Trade and Investment Policies of Developing Countries: The Case of the Philippines". PIDS Discussion Paper Series no. 96-03. 1996.

Austria, M., and W. Martin. "Macroeconomic Instability and Growth in the Philippines: A Dynamic Approach". Economics Division Working Papers, Research School of Pacific Studies, Australian National University, 1992.

Balboa, J., and E.M. Medalla. "State of Trade and Investments in the Philippines". PIDS Discussion Paper Series no. 2006-15. 2006.

Balisacan, A.M. "Why Does Poverty Persist in the Philippines? Facts, Fancies and Policies". In *Whither the Philippines in the 21st Century?* edited by R.C. Severino and L.C. Salazar, pp. 202–21. Singapore: Institute of Southeast Asian Studies, 2007.

Balisacan, A.M., and Nobuhiko Fuwa. "Going beyond Cross-country Averages: Growth, Inequality, and Poverty in the Philippines". *World Development* 32, no. 11 (2004): 1891–1907

———., eds. "Reasserting the Rural Development Agenda: Lessons Learned and Emerging Challenges in Asia". Los Baños/Singapore: Southeast Asian Regional Center for Graduate Study and Research in Agriculture (SEARCA)/ Institute of Southeast Asian Studies, 2007.

Bautista, C. "Boom-Bust Cycles and Crisis Periods in the Philippines: A Regime-Switching Analysis". *Philippine Review of Economics* 39, no. 1 (2002): 20–37.

Bautista, Romeo M., and John H. Power and Associates. *Industrial Promotion Policies in the Philippines*. Makati: Philippine Institute for Development Studies, 1979.

BSP (Bangko Sentral ng Pilipinas). "Inflation Report: First Quarter 2014". 2014 <http://www.bsp.gov.ph/downloads/Publications/2014/IR1qtr_2014.pdf>.

Chua, K.K., N. Mylenko, N. Chaudhury, C. Figueroa-Geron, M. Hayakawa, and M. Enerva. "Philippine Development Report: Creating More and Better Jobs". 2013 <http://documents.worldbank.org/curated/en/2013/09/18741265/philippine-development-report-creating-more-better-jobs>.

Clarete, R. "Ex-post Effects of Trade Liberalization in the Philippines". In *Coping with Trade Reforms: A Developing-Country Perspective on the WTO Industrial Tariff Negotiations*, edited by S. Laird and S. Fernando de Cordoba. New York: Palgrave Macmillan, 2006.

———. "Philipine Rice Self-Sufficiency Program: Pitfalls and Remedies". In *Sustainable Economic Development – Resources, Environment and Institutions*, edited by A. Balisacan, U. Chakravorty, and M. Ravago. Oxford: Elsevier, 2016.

Cororaton, C.B. "Total Factor Productivity in the Philippines". PIDS Discussion Paper Series no. 2002-01. 2002.

Cororaton, C., and R. Abdula. "Productivity of Philippine Manufacturing". PIDS Discussion Paper Series no. 99-21. 1999.

Cororaton, C., and J.S. Cuenca. "Estimates of Total Factor Productivity in the Philippines". PIDS Discussion Paper Series no. 2001-02. 2001.

Cororaton, C., Benjamin Endriga, Derrick Ornedo, and Consolacion Chua. "Estimation of Total Factor Productivity of Philippine Manufacturing Industries: The Estimates". PIDS Discussion Paper Series no. 95-32. 1995.

Daway, S., and R. Fabella. "Development Progeria: The Role of Institutions and the Exchange Rate". *Philippine Review of Economics* 52, no. 2 (2015).

Dawe, D. "Geographic Determinants of Rice Self-sufficiency in Southeast Asia". Agricultural and Development Economics Division (ESA) Working Paper no. 13-03. 2015.

———."Agricultural Transformation of Middle-income Asian Economies: Diversification, Farm size and Mechanization". Unpublished paper, 2016.

de Dios, E. "Philippine Economic Growth: Can it Last?" In *The Philippines: New Directions in Domestic Policy and Foreign Relations*, edited by D. Timberman. USA: Asia Society, 1998.

de Silva, M.A.A. *Measuring Total Factor Productivity: The Philippines*. Tokyo: Asian Productivity Organization, 2001.

Dollar, D., and A. Kraay. "Growth is Good for the Poor". *Journal of Economic Growth* 7, no. 3 (2002): 195–225.

Edwards, S. "Trade Orientation, Distortions and Growth in Developing Countries". *Journal of Development Economics* 39, no. 1 (1992): 31–57.

Fabella, R. "Sustainability of the 1994 Economic Recovery: Portents from the Past". In *Towards Sustained Growth*, edited by R. Fabella and H. Sakai. Tokyo: Institute of Developing Economies, 1995.

———. "Development Progeria: Genesis and Healing". Paper presented at the Second BSP UP Professorial Lecture, Philippines, 2013.

Fosu, A.K. "Growth, Inequality and Poverty Reduction in Developing Countries: Recent Global Evidence". Background paper for Global Development Outlook 2010, OECD Development Centre, Paris <https://www.oecd.org/dev/pgd/44773119.pdf>.

Fuwa, Nobuhiko, A.M. Balisacan, and F. Bresciani. "In Search of a Strategy for Making Growth More Pro-Poor in the Philippines". *Asian Economic Papers* 14, no. 1 (2015): 202–26.

Greenaway, D., W. Morgan, and P. Wright. "Trade Liberalization and Growth in Developing Countries". *Journal of Development Economics* 67, no. 1 (2002): 229–44.

Hooley, R. *Productivity Growth in Philippine Manufacturing: Retrospect and Future Prospects*. PIDS Monograph Series, 1985.

Klein, M., C. Aaron, and B. Hadjimichael. "Foreign Direct Investment and Poverty Reduction". World Bank Policy Research Working Paper Series no. 2613. 2001.

Krueger, A. "Trade Policy and Economic Development: How We Learn. *American Economic Review* 87, no. 1 (1997): 1–22.

Lin, B.Q. "Economic Growth, Income Inequality, and Poverty Reduction in People's Republic of China". *Asian Development Review* 20, no. 2 (2003): 105–24.

Mapa, D.S. "Demographic Sweet Spot and Dividend in the Philippines: The Window of Opportunity is Closing Fast". UNDP-supported report submitted to the National Economic Development Authority (NEDA), 2015.

Mapa, D.S., and A.M. Balisacan. "Quantifying the Impact of Population on Economic Growth and Poverty: The Philippines in an East Asian Context". In *Population and Development in the Philippines: The Ties That Bind*, edited by L.A. Sevilla. Makati City: AIM Policy Center, 2004.

Mapa, D.S., A.M. Balisacan, and K.J. Briones. "Robust Determinants of Income Growth in the Philippines". *Philippine Journal of Development* 33, nos. 1–2 (2006): 1–32.

NEDA (National Economic Development Authority). *Fifth Progress Report – Millennium Development Goals*. Pasig City: NEDA, 2014.

Neuman, F. "Opening Asia to Foreign Direct Investment". *Asian Wall Street Journal*, 23 September 2014 <http://www.wsj.com/articles/frederic-neumann-opening-asia-to-foreign-direct-investment-1411487589>.

Patalinhug, E. "Labour Quality and Growth Accounting: The Philippines". *Philippine Review of Economics and Business* 21, nos. 3–4 (1984): 201–17.

PSA (Philippine Statistics Authority). "The Age and Sex Structure of the Philippine Population (Facts from the 2010 Census)". 2012 <https://psa.gov.ph/content/age-and-sex-structure-philippine-population-facts-2010-census>.

Ravallion, M. "Can High Inequality Developing Countries Escape Absolute Poverty?" *Economics Letters* 56 (1997): 51–57.

Ravallion, M., and S.H. Chen. "What Can New Survey Data Tell Us about Recent Changes in Distribution and Poverty?" *World Bank Economic Review* 11, no. 2 (1997): 357–82.

Rodriguez, F., and D. Rodrik. "Trade Policy and Economic Growth: A Sceptic's Guide to the Cross-national Evidence". In *Macroeconomics Annual 2000*, edited by B. Bernanke and K.S. Rogoff. Cambridge, MA: MIT Press for NBER, 2001.

Rutherford, T. "Applied General Equilibrium Modeling with MPSGE as a GAMS Subsystem: An Overview of the Modeling Framework and Syntax". *Computational Economics* 14, nos. 1–2 (1999): 1-46.

United Nations, Asian Development Bank, and United Nations Development Programme. "Eradicating Poverty and Promoting Prosperity in a Changing Asia-Pacific". March 2017 <http://sdgasiapacific.net/download/Asia%20Pacific%20Annual%20Thematic%20Report%202017_FINAL_e%20Version.pdf>.

Usui, N. "Transforming the Philippine Economy: 'Walking on Two Legs'". ADB Economics Working Paper Series no. 252. 2011.

Valenzuela, M., Wing-Keung Wong, and Zhu Zhen Zhen. "Income and Consumption Inequality in the Philippines: A Stochastic Dominance Analysis of Household Unit Records". Asian Development Bank Institute, Working Paper no. 662. February 2017.

Vandemoortele, M., and K. Bird. *Viet Nam's Progress on Economic Growth and Poverty Reduction: Impressive Improvements*. London: Overseas Development Institute, 2011.

Vandenbrink, R. "The Challenge of Inclusive Growth: Selected Policy Notes for the Next Administration". Presented at the BSP Conference on Gearing Up for External Competitiveness, Iloilo City, 24 May 2016.

Williamson, J. "Dimensions of Postwar Philippine Economic Progress". *Quarterly Journal of Economics* 83, no. 1 (1969): 93–109.

Winters, L., N. McCulloch, and A. McKay. "Trade Liberalization and Poverty: The Evidence So Far". *Journal of Economic Literature* 42, no. 1 (2004): 72–115.

3

Infrastructure and Urbanization

Arturo G. Corpuz

Infrastructure is a driver of growth. It provides energy, water and other production inputs. It connects products with markets, and labour with jobs. Infrastructure enables access to education, healthcare, housing and other services that let communities thrive and be more resilient.

Investments in infrastructure promote economic activities that generate employment, increase household incomes and reduce poverty. According to an estimate of the World Economic Forum (WEF), every dollar spent on a capital project (in utilities, energy, transport, waste management, flood prevention, telecommunications) generates a 5–25 per cent economic return. Clearly, the lack of infrastructure is a constraint to growth and poverty reduction (Llanto 2015).

Ideally, infrastructure keeps pace with demand even as demand itself is catalysed by infrastructure in a virtuous spiral of growth. Not surprisingly, the biggest demand for infrastructure is in urban areas, where population and activities are concentrated. With scale and agglomeration economies, these areas are often associated with innovation and productivity, economic growth, employment generation and higher (than rural) family incomes. This is consistent with the Philippine experience, as the largest urban centre, Metro Manila, is the primary venue for poverty reduction in the country. It is useful, therefore, to view infrastructure in the context of the country's network of settlements, keeping in mind that rural areas are inextricable elements of this network (e.g., as agricultural productivity rises, surplus labour migrates to urban-based industries and services which, in turn, are fuelled by rising worker incomes as industrial productivity also rises).

Based on public consultations on the aspirations of Filipinos, a 2040 vision for the state of infrastructure and urban development may be stated as follows:

> Cities are working as engines of economic growth and venues of poverty reduction, with infrastructure that provides quality services and affordable housing, and forms efficient and connected networks of sustainable communities.

This chapter looks at infrastructure (including housing) in the Philippines as it relates to the vision from two analytical perspectives. The first is a summary of how the infrastructure sector has performed. It covers both the national and local (metro/region) dimensions. Performance indicators, benchmarks and targets are identified. The second is a complementary and broader analysis of infrastructure from the perspective of urbanization, or, broadly speaking, the settlements network. It looks at how population is distributed throughout the country and how this affects the location of infrastructure, as well as overall urban and regional development.

The rest of the chapter begins with a description of current infrastructure conditions, urban growth trends, and the identification of benchmarks and targets towards the vision. This is followed by a discussion of key issues and constraints. Next is the identification of possible pathways by which development targets can be attained. The chapter ends with a concluding summary with key messages.

I. Baseline Assessment of Performance and Benchmarks

As a whole, the country's severe infrastructure deficits pose a serious threat to the growth momentum it has been experiencing in recent years (Whaley 2014; Guinto 2014; Saclag 2015). These deficits may be characterized as insufficient capacity relative to demand, poor connectivity, and low quality, particularly in comparison to most regional neighbours. While there have been significant improvements in some areas (e.g., Metro Manila's water supply, acceleration of public works, adoption of various infrastructure roadmaps and a pipeline of key projects), transportation and telecommunication infrastructure, availability of affordable housing, delivery of other services, environmental quality and disaster preparedness remain sub-par compared to many other countries and accepted standards.

The Philippines is experiencing severe infrastructure deficits brought about by decades of underinvestment — less than 3 per cent of gross domestic product (GDP) compared to the 5–9 per cent average of its Asian neighbours (*Economist* 2014). Practically all of the country's transportation modes, as well as housing, lag significantly behind demand requirements. These deficits are felt most severely in Metro Manila, which has the highest concentration of infrastructure and housing demand in the country, but they are no less worrisome in other cities. Although there have been improvements in recent years, the Philippines still ranks lowest among six countries of the Association of Southeast Asian Nations (ASEAN) in terms of infrastructure competitiveness (see Table 3.1).

TABLE 3.1
Global Infrastructure Competitiveness Ranking of Selected Southeast Asian Countries, 2015–16

Indicator	Philippines	Singapore	Malaysia	Thailand	Indonesia	Vietnam
Quality of Roads	97	3	15	51	80	93
Quality of Railroads	84	8	13	78	43	48
Quality of Ports	103	2	16	52	82	76
Quality of Airports	98	1	21	38	66	75
Quality of Electric Supply	89	3	36	56	86	87
Fixed Telephone Connectivity	108	29	73	88	80	100
Mobile Telephone Connectivity	76	14	24	31	49	28
Overall	106	4	16	71	81	99

Source: WEF 2015.

A. Road and Rail

Metro Manila's traffic congestion affects 2.2 million vehicles daily and costs the country P876 billion a year in lost productivity and wasted energy. This amounts to about 8 per cent of total economic production (Whaley 2014).

In terms of level of service, Metro Manila's roads have already been rated lowest (rating of F; see Table 3.2), which means that the volume of vehicles exceeds road capacity, resulting in forced flow, stop-and-go congestion. Average travel speed hovered at the 15–20 kilometre per hour mark as of 2000. It has worsened since then, especially with a 10–20 per cent compound annual growth rate (CAGR) in vehicle sales since 2002 and minimal additional road and transit facilities.

Part of the problem lies with the relatively high modal share of private vehicles (30 per cent), inefficient public utility vehicles and the low level (6 per cent) of rail transit compared to benchmark Asian countries (25, 19 and 48 per cent in Hong Kong, Singapore and Tokyo, respectively). Light rail ridership has also been declining since 2012 (an 18 per cent drop for mass rail transit), suggesting a deterioration of facilities and increased congestion. Metro Manila pioneered light rail in the region, but it is now among the lowest in terms of rail service per capita — 12.1 kilometres per million persons, compared to the Hong Kong benchmark of 30.4 (see Table 3.3), and higher only than Ho Chi Minh City.

In the rest of the country, while the paved road density is at par with some countries, quality is low compared to ASEAN and neighbouring countries.

The quality of the country's rail infrastructure is rated lowest in the region. Rail density is at the bottom of regional rankings, with 0.42 km/1000 km^2, compared with the Republic of Korea (37.66), Thailand (10.43), and Vietnam (7.57). Indonesia, which shares an archipelagic constraint to rail network construction, is much higher, at 2.59. The Philippines used to operate about 1,100 kilometres of rail; today the network is down to about 85 kilometres (Corpuz 1999).

Rebuilding the rail network and recovering existing rights of ways will significantly expand rail coverage in the country. These include the main lines to La Union, Batangas and Albay. Ideally, the network should be expanded to other parts of Luzon (i.e., Cagayan Valley, Ilocos) and integrated into an interregional strategy that defines the expansion of metropolitan areas, enhances connections among regional

TABLE 3.2
Key Indicators for Road Infrastructure

Indicator	Benchmark	Target
Urban		
Level of Service (LOS) = F	LOS = D	LOS = D
Volume/Capacity Ratio > 1	Optimal use of urban roads	0.71–0.85
Average Travel Speed = 10 kph	Jakarta, Kuala Lumpur, Bangkok = 15–25 kph	20–25 kph
(i) Private = 30% (ii) Public = 64% (iii) Rail = 6% (iv) Cycle = 0% (v) Walk, Others = 0%	(i) Hong Kong = 11%; Singapore = 29%; Tokyo = 12% (ii) Hong Kong = 63%; Singapore = 29%; Tokyo = 3% (iii) Hong Kong = 25%; Singapore = 19%; Tokyo = 48% (iv) Hong Kong = 0%; Singapore = 1%; Tokyo = 14% (v) Hong Kong = 1%; Singapore = 22%; Tokyo = 23%	Increase rail/bus rapid transit, cycle, walk shares; reduce or at least maintain 30% private transport share.
National		
Paved Road Density = 452 km/ 1,000 km	Vietnam, Thailand and Malaysia = 350–860 km/ 1,000 km	...
World Economic Forum: Quality of Road Infrastructure Rating = 3.3 (range = 1–7)	Singapore = 6.2; Hong Kong = 6.2	6
km of Paved Road/Total Road Length = 77%	Thailand = 97%	90%

Sources: Di 2013; ALMEC 2014; WEF 2015.

TABLE 3.3
Key Indicators for Rail Infrastructure

Indicator	Benchmark	Target
Urban		
Rail Length = 12.1 km/million persons	Hong Kong = 30.4 km/million persons	30 km/million persons
National		
Rail Density = 0.42 km/1,000 km^2	Malaysia = 6.85 km/1,000 km^2	5 km/1,000 km^2 (Integrate into regional strategy, rebuild Luzon 1,000+ km coverage and expand to include Ilocos provinces, Cagayan Valley, Batangas; reinforce nautical highways; enhance disaster risk reduction).
	Vietnam = 7.57 km/1,000 km^2	
	Thailand = 10.43 km/1,000 km^2	
	Republic of Korea = 37.66 km/1,000 km^2	
World Economic Forum: Quality of Rail Infrastructure Rating = 2.2 (range = 1–7)	Japan = 6.7; Republic of Korea = 5.6; Malaysia = 5.1	5

Source: WEF 2015; World Bank 2013.

centres, reinforces inter-island nautical highways, increases passenger and cargo transport capacity, and provides redundancy for disaster risk reduction.

In rural areas, roads are vital to increasing agricultural productivity and, thus, to incomes and poverty reduction. They connect rural areas with growing markets and reduce input and transaction costs (Llanto 2012; Schneider and Gugerty 2011). Approximately 48,350 kilometres of farm-to-market roads are needed, and, of these, 34,477 (71 per cent) have already been built. The balance of 13,873 kilometres is programmed to be built by 2017 (Rodriguez 2014).

B. Ports

The Philippines has 114 major ports distributed across the country (Luzon 45 per cent, Visayas 33 per cent, Mindanao 22 per cent). Container traffic has been increasing (by 15 per cent in 2012–14), consistent with the overall economic growth trend, with the bulk (71 per cent) being handled by the Manila/North Luzon ports (PPA 2012).

Port congestion is a major problem, with utilization of Manila South Harbor exceeding capacity (108 per cent; ALMEC 2014). Other ports, including Cebu and Davao, also experience congestion related to inadequate road infrastructure, regulatory restrictions that cause delays, and inadequate equipment. The 2014 truck ban that was triggered by an attempt to curb traffic congestion in Manila caused a 40 per cent drop in containers handled in the Port of Manila, causing significant build-up and inefficiency, and disruption of supply chains. The Port of Manila has ranked lowest in terms of quality among its Asian neighbours (Oxford 2015; WEF 2015). See Table 3.4.

Investments in port upgrades, improved road infrastructure and the construction of new ports and port facilities (similar to the International Container Terminal Services expansion project) will be required to handle increased traffic due to economic growth. Manila ranks among the lowest (36) in world port rankings based on TEU (twenty-foot equivalent unit) traffic — lower than Ho Chi Minh (24), Thailand's Laem Chabang (22), Kelang of Malaysia (13), Hong Kong, China (4), Singapore (2) and Shanghai (1) (World Shipping Council 2012).

TABLE 3.4
Key Indicators for Port Infrastructure

Indicator	Benchmark	Target
Urban		
Port Utilization: (i) Manila International Container Terminal = 62% (ii) South Harbor = 108% (iii) Batangas = 2% (iv) Subic = 6%	...	80% (increase Batangas and Subic utilization; improve intermodal connectivity)
World Port Ranking (2013) = 36	Singapore = 2; Hong Kong, China = 4; Republic of Korea = 5; Malaysia = 13; Thailand = 22	...
World Economic Forum: Quality of Port Infrastructure Rating = 3.2 (Range = 1-7)	Singapore = 6.7; Hong Kong = 6.4, China = 4.5; Republic of Korea = 5.2; Malaysia = 5.6; Thailand = 4.5	6
Twenty-Foot Equivalent Traffic ('000) = 3,779 for Manila	Shanghai = 33,617; Singapore = 32,240; Hong Kong = 22,352; Busan = 17,686; Kelang (Malaysia) = 10,350; L Chabang (Thailand) = 6.031	...
National		
Incomplete and Disjoint Nautical Highway/Roll On-Roll Off Network	...	Seamless and Complete Network

Source: ALMEC 2014; WEF 2015; World Shipping Council 2012.

Although Manila South Harbor is congested, the ports of Subic and Batangas, intended as alternates and expansion ports to Manila, remain underutilized (at 2 and 6 per cent, respectively, prior to the truck ban). Increasing utilization of these ports will require placing a cap on Manila port use, improving regional road connections and increasing manufacturing activities to improve demand for port locations north and south of Manila. Notably, utilization at Subic and Batangas increased during and since the truck ban that plagued the Port of Manila (Oxford 2015).

Further improvement of the country's ports, especially ro-ro (roll-on roll-off) ports along designated Nautical Highways, is also needed to improve intermodal connectivity, enhance tourism, and increase redundancy as part of efforts to reduce disaster-related risks. It has been estimated that the use of ro-ro leads to a reduction of travel time of twelve hours between Mindanao and Luzon, and 30 and 40 per cent cost reductions for freight and passenger transport, respectively (Oxford 2015).

Serving as points of passenger and cargo transfer, ports play important regional roles, especially in an archipelago where intermodal connectivity is even more critical. Ports also serve as nodes of economic concentration — transport breaks that evolve to become large cities and even global metropolitan centres. Thus, ports define (not just connect) land transportation networks. They should not be viewed in isolation; rather, they should be integral elements of broader regional development strategies and plans.

C. Airports

Of the country's 215 airports, 84 are owned and controlled by the Civil Aviation Authority of the Philippines, with the balance owned by the private sector. Eleven of the 84 are designated as international airports, with the Ninoy Aquino International Airport (NAIA) the busiest, with over 35 million passengers annually, followed by Mactan Cebu and Clark International.

Primarily because of runway limitations, NAIA airplane movements are capped at 36 per hour. This is significantly lower than the 50–60 movements per hour of other airports in the region (Bangkok, Hong Kong, Kuala Lumpur, Jakarta), as shown in Table 3.5. All other airports in the Philippines have about half or less than half of NAIA's capacity.

TABLE 3.5
Key Indicators for Airport Infrastructure

Indicator	Benchmark	Target
Urban		
NAIA demand exceeds runway capacity of 36 planes/hour	Bangkok = 60 planes/hour; Hong Kong = 50 planes/hour; Kuala Lumpur = 50 planes/hour; Taipei = 50 planes/hour	50–60 planes/hour (to increase capacity: build new airport with larger facilities and more runways; or build additional runway)
World Economic Forum: Quality of Airport Infrastructure Rating = 3.7 (range = 1–7)	Hong Kong = 6.6; Kuala Lumpur = 5.7; Bangkok = 5.1	6
National/Regional		
Access Road Congestion	...	Improve intermodal connectivity; integrate into local and regional development strategies

Source: JICA 2011; Senggutuyan 2006; WEF 2015.

Since 2010, the increase in the number of low-cost carriers, combined with a rise in disposable incomes, have increased demand for air travel, resulting in aircraft movements reaching the airport threshold (ALMEC 2014). This has led to congestion and flight delays. Demand is expected to increase further as tourism and other arrivals rise, fuelled by aviation rating upgrades, the lifting of bans on Philippine-based carriers, and new air service agreements. Unfortunately, no new major capacity increases are likely in the near future; this will require the construction of a new airport (in Sangley, if the recommendation of Japan International Cooperation Agency is followed), the construction of an additional runway in NAIA, or splitting air traffic between NAIA and Clark.

Continuous upgrading and construction of new regional airports similar to Mactan may alleviate NAIA congestion if direct international flights from these airports are allowed. Institutional constraints, primarily related to immigration and customs operations, along with the lack of intermodal (mostly road) connectivity remain.

Similar to the other transportation modes, the country's competitiveness rating of 3.7 for its gateway airport lags behind its higher-capacity Asian neighbours of 5.1–6.8 (WEF 2015).

Like ports, airports define as well as connect transportation networks. Traditionally relegated to the urban fringe because of their need for vast tracts of land, the potential of airports as anchors of urban development (e.g., aerotropolis) is increasingly being recognized (Kasarda and Lindsay 2011). This potential should be tapped in local and regional development strategies.

D. Telecommunications

Telecommunications has been an important component of the recent growth of the Philippine economy, especially the rapidly expanding business-process outsourcing sector. But, like the rest of the country's infrastructure, a lot more can be done to improve productivity and competitiveness.

Similar to many developing countries, the Philippines leapfrogged from fixed to mobile telephone services. This started during the 1990s when submarine cables were put in place and as the Philippine Long

Distance Telephone monopoly was dismantled. The new carriers focused on the mobile market, and by 2014 mobile penetration had soared to 105 per cent (an average of more than one account per person) with a unique penetration rate of about 80 per cent. By this time, fixed phone subscriptions were still less than 3 per cent (Oxford 2015).

The initial growth of mobile phone use was anchored on text messaging. Dubbed the text capital of the world, the Philippines accounted for 10 per cent of global short message service (SMS) traffic, with about two billion text messages being sent every day in the country.

Future growth, however, is being driven by smartphone use. Although the Philippines had one of the lowest smartphone penetrations (15 per cent) in East Asia in 2014, its year-on-year growth was a phenomenal 75 per cent, compared to the flat to low-teens rate in Malaysia, Thailand, Vietnam, Indonesia and Singapore. Smartphone use is growing rapidly because of the availability of cheap smartphones in the market, including local brands that sell for less than 10 per cent of the cost of premium phones. Smartphone popularity is also increasing as more applications become part of routine, work and non-work related activities — mobile banking (which has a large potential for overseas Filipinos), education, dining, entertainment, travel, and others (Oxford 2015).

With respect to the use of smartphones, and online use in general, the biggest constraint to further growth has been the low efficiency of Internet service in the country, as shown in Table 3.6. This is a critical issue because of the potential high impact of the Internet, not just on smartphone use but on employment generation and economic growth as a whole (McKinsey Global Institute 2011).

Since the 1990s it had already been recognized that the Internet increased the availability and exchange of labour market information, helping to match job seekers with potential employers. Likewise, it gave access to resources and offered new business opportunities (Green, de Hoyos and Yuxin 2012). In developing countries there is increasing evidence of the positive impact of the Internet on mobile phone use, employment, farm gate prices, and the production of processed goods (Burga and Barreto 2014). It has also been observed that the Internet drastically reduced the costs of entrepreneurship,

TABLE 3.6
Key Indicators for Internet and Broadband Use in Selected Asian Countries

Indicator	Philippines	Singapore	Malaysia	Thailand	Indonesia	Vietnam
Rating for Internet Access in Schools (1=none; 7=widespread)	4.5 (58)	6.3 (2)	5.5 (26)	4.6 (54)	4.8 (43)	4.6 (57)
Internet Users (% of individuals)	39.7 (89)	82 (24)	67.5 (45)	34.9 (93)	17.1 (113)	48.3 (73)
Fixed broadband in Internet subscriptions (per 100 population)	23.2 (37)	27.8 (23)	10.1 (68)	8.2 (73)	1.2 (106)	6.5 (79)
Internet Bandwidth kbs/user)	27.7 (76)	616.5 (4)	27.2 (77)	46.8 (55)	6.2 (111)	20.7 (86)
Mobile broadband subscriptions (per 100 population)	28 (92)	156.1 (1)	58.3 (48)	79.9 (23)	34.7 (76)	31 (83)

Note: Numbers in parentheses are the countries' respective Global Competitiveness rank.
Source: WEF 2015.

through online education, open source software, crowdsourcing and cloud computing (Layton 2014). As noted by the World Bank, information and communications technology is "creating new job opportunities and making labour markets more innovative, inclusive and global" (World Bank 2013).

But, realizing the Internet's growth potential in the Philippines is constrained by its significantly slow speed (3.7 Mbps, the slowest in Southeast Asia; Table 3.7). This has been attributed to relatively higher costs and barriers to putting in place required infrastructure — because of the archipelagic geography of the country and informal government requirements, especially at the local level — and the absence of Internet peering (the free exchange of traffic among the telecommunication companies that results in faster connections).

The cost of Internet services in the country is also among the highest in the world, with two Mbps costing a thousand pesos a month, an amount that can buy six to seven times more Mbps in Thailand and Singapore, for example (Oxford 2015).

TABLE 3.7
Average Internet Download Speed in Selected Countries (Mbps)

Country	Average Internet Download Speed
Philippines	3.7
Myanmar	5.1
Laos	5.6
Indonesia	7.45
Malaysia	7.56
Cambodia	9.42
Vietnam	18.5
Thailand	29.63
China	30.5
USA	73.3
Japan	103.2
Singapore	133.1
Global average	24.2

Source: dela Paz 2015.

More investments are needed to improve the country's broadband infrastructure. It has been estimated that an additional P800 billion worth of investments will be required, but only P60–70 billion a year is spent (by the private sector). The use of unused television white space is also being considered in order to increase capacity and Internet speed. As a strategic target, Internet speed should exceed the global average (24.2 Mbps in 2014).

E. Water Supply

Water security is a concern, as the population and demand for water continue to rise. In the Metro Manila area, demand is projected to exceed the supply capacity of 4,000 million litres per day (MLD) by 2020 (4,500 MLD) and further by 2030 (5,100 MLD), as presented in Table 3.8

TABLE 3.8
Key Indicators for Water Supply Infrastructure

Indicator	Benchmark	Target
Urban (Metro Manila)		
Current supply of 4,000 MLD cannot serve future demand	Demand by 2020 = 4,500 MLD;	Develop new supply sources: Sumag river diversion (188 MLD), Balingtingon dam (1,300 MLD), Bayabas dam (330 MLD), Maasim dam (130 MLD), Wawa dam (50 MLD), Laiban dam (1,900 MLD), Kanan 2 dam (3,300 MLD), Kaliwa low dam (550 MLD), Agos dam (3,000 MLD, Laguna Lake bulk (200 MLD)
	Demand by 2030 = 5,100 MLD	
National		
Level 2 and 3 Water Supply (% of population) (i) Urban = 93% (ii) Rural = 91%	Japan = 100%; Malaysia = 100%; Republic of Korea = 100%	100% (increase resilience of water supply sources and distribution networks; reduce disaster risk)

Source: World Bank 2012.

(World Bank 2012). New supply sources will be required. And while various water supply projects have been identified, the larger-capacity projects capable of addressing demand will not be completed by 2020. In the interim, smaller supply projects along with demand-management measures will have to be undertaken.

In the rest of the country, full access to water supply (level 2 and 3) remains to be accomplished. As of 2012, 9 per cent of the rural population and 7 per cent of the urban population did not have access to water (World Bank 2012).

Dams and other water supply sources and distribution networks need to be made more resilient to potential disasters.

F. Housing

The following are various estimates on the country's housing needs (see Table 3.9):

(i)   The country's housing backlog is about 3.9 million units and is projected to increase to about 6.5 million units by 2030, even accounting for a high estimate production capacity of 200,000 units per year (SHDA 2012).

(ii) Based on the 2010 census, the total number of families living in shanties (less than 19 m^2) is 7.32 million families, or about 33 million people. For Metro Manila, the numbers are 763,400 families, or about 3.5 million people (Tan 2015).

(iii) Data from the National Housing Authority (NHA) list the total number of informal settler families in the country, as of 2011, at 1.5 million, with 39 per cent (584,000 families) in Metro Manila; about 61 per cent of informal settlers are in Mega Manila (Metro Manila plus the Central Luzon and Calabarzon regions). Of the 1.5 million informal settler families, about 51 per cent are in danger zones (ICF 2014).

Addressing the housing backlog can have a major impact on growth and poverty reduction because housing construction contributes to economic output, generates employment for both skilled and unskilled workers, and creates demand for housing materials and related services. Further, it raises the living standards of occupants, mostly through improved access to water and sanitation (Doling, Vandenberg and Tolentino 2013).

TABLE 3.9
Key Indicators for Housing

Indicator	Target
National	
Current Backlog = 3,919,566 units	Zero backlog, including housing of informal settlers in areas that are reasonably accessible to and from places of employment, with priority given to those in danger zones.
New Housing Need for 2012–30 = 6,226,540 units (345,941 units per year)	Integration of housing projects into local and regional development plans (e.g., transportation infrastructure); medium-rise and higher density housing; rental housing; expanded private sector participation.
Housing Production Capacity for 2012–30 = 3,600,000 units (200,000 units per year)	
2030 Backlog given Production Capacity = 6,546,106 units	

Source: SHDA 2012.

Zero backlog is the only acceptable target. This includes addressing the housing needs of all informal settlers through on-site, in-city or off-city relocation, while maintaining reasonable access to places of employment. Priority should be given to informal settlers in danger zones (e.g., riverbanks prone to flooding, slopes susceptible to erosion and landslides, fault lines).

Attaining zero backlog will require unprecedented funding. According to the National Informal Settlements Upgrading Strategy of the Philippines, the investment requirements to address the backlog and the housing needs of informal settlers range from a low of P507 billion to a high estimate of P1.05 trillion over the 2014–25 period. This includes the construction of between 400,000 and 700,000 new housing units and the relocation/upgrading of between 1 million and 1.5 million informal settler families. It requires an annual production of about 120,000 units (new construction plus relocation/upgrading), which is about three to four times current production (ICF 2014).

Other elements that need to be in place in order to achieve zero backlog include the provision of sufficient land for housing development. This will require financial subsidies, especially for on-site or in-city locations, along with transportation and other service infrastructure if housing sites are further away. Housing projects should be integrated into local and regional development plans. Medium-rise and higher density housing will also have to be the norm in urban sites, and the development of a much larger rental housing market should be provided as an option. Finally, private sector participation in financing and housing production has to be expanded.

G. Urbanization

As mentioned earlier, cities and urbanization are associated with economic growth and poverty reduction (see Figures 3.1 and 3.2). In the Philippines, not only are urban areas performing much better than rural areas from a production point of view, but they also exhibit lower poverty incidence, infant-neonatal-child mortality rates, underemployment, as well as higher functional literacy. Unemployment tends to be higher in cities because of continuous in-migration that expands the labour pool, but the low urban underemployment rate

FIGURE 3.1
Relationship between GDP per Capita and Urban Population Size in Selected Asian Countries

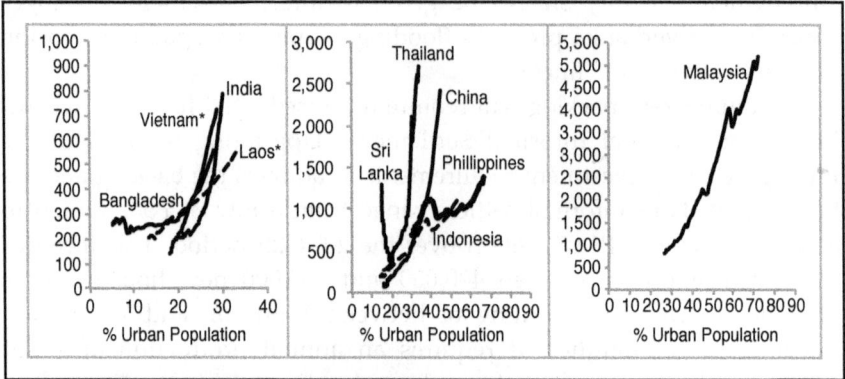

Source: Corpuz 2013 (prepared with the assistance of R. Clarete).

FIGURE 3.2
Relationship between GDP per Capita and Urban Population Size in Selected Asian Countries, with Japan, USA and Republic of Korea

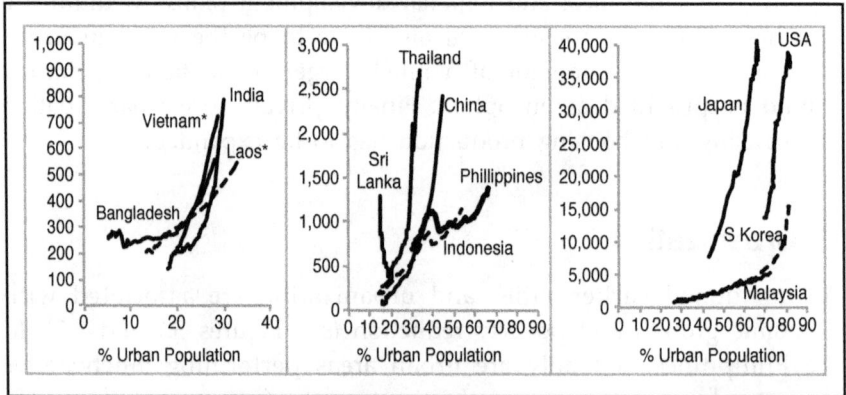

Note: The data for Malaysia, South Korea, the USA and Japan are read from the secondary vertical axis.
Source: Corpuz 2013 (prepared with the assistance of R. Clarete).

suggests that cities continue to attract and provide migrants with much needed (although clearly insufficient) part-time or informal work.

Compared to other countries, however, it appears that Metro Manila and other urban areas of the country have been under-performing. Poverty reduction has been slow in the Philippines compared to Indonesia, Thailand, Malaysia and Vietnam (see Figure 3.3; see also Clarete, chap. 2).

FIGURE 3.3
Poverty Incidence in Selected ASEAN Countries, Selected Periods (%)

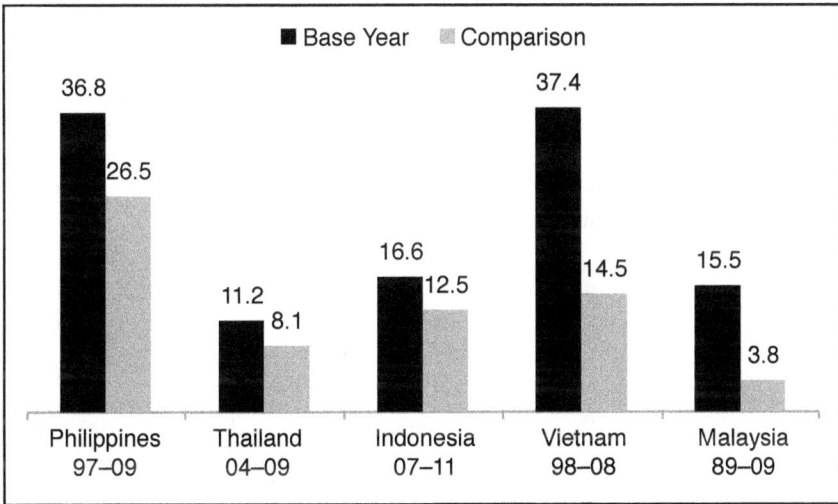

And yet, Philippine cities share similar growth trends with these and other countries:

(i)   The country's settlement network, like virtually all settlement networks in the world, is hierarchically distributed. Its most obvious feature is the primacy of Metro Manila, which accounts for 0.2 per cent of the country's land area, 13 per cent of total population and 37 per cent of GDP. Many other metropolitan centres of other countries are similarly dominant.

(ii) The country's urban population continues to increase its share of total population. This is a long-term trend, with the urban share of population rising from 30 per cent in 1960 to 67 per cent in 2010. This trend is consistent with most countries in Asia, as well as other developed countries such as the United States and Japan. In the Philippines, the largest cities are increasing their shares of the country's population (e.g., the top twenty-five settlements increased their population share from 19.9 per cent in 1970 to 25.5 per cent in 2010).

(iii) Metro Manila's share of population is decreasing. It has been declining since the 1990 census, while the shares of the rest of the country's largest cities — Cebu City, Davao City, Zamboanga City, Cagayan de Oro, Dasmarinas, General Santos, Bacoor, Bacolod, San Jose del Monte, Iloilo, Calamba, Angeles, etc. — have increased. Metro Manila's declining share is similar to the experiences of many large metropolitan centres of the world.

(iv) Although its population share is declining, Metro Manila's economic influence is expanding as it continues to annex parts of its surrounding regions into its direct, day-to-day orbit of activities. The functional boundaries of Metro Manila now include corridors of municipalities in the neighbouring provinces of Bulacan, Pampanga, Laguna, Batangas, Cavite and Rizal.

(v) Urban growth is taking place using more land area per capita (implying less efficient land use). This is based on a global study of urban expansion, including Metro Manila (Angel, Sheppard and Civco 2005; Corpuz 2013).

The reasons for the underperformance of Philippine cities are not easily identified or understood, because cities are spatial entities that cut across various sectors, each with its own set of drivers and constraints. But the lack of and poor quality of infrastructure — resulting in inefficiencies in the delivery of services and increased costs of production and distribution — is at least in part responsible.

Lack of infrastructure also discourages investments, which further compromises urban competitiveness. In a 2015 global survey it was cited as second to inefficient government bureaucracy as a "problematic factor" in doing business in the Philippines (WEF 2015).

Notwithstanding this, it is important to keep in mind that overall urban growth patterns in the Philippines are consistent with the underlying characteristics that allow cities throughout the world to be engines of growth and venues of poverty reduction — economies of scale and agglomeration. Thus, while the large size of Metro Manila — and, to some extent, other regional cities — may make it more difficult to provide the services and facilities required by the expanding population, it is not necessarily a constraint to growth and poverty reduction, and, in principle, it should even be an advantage. As we have seen, other countries with similarly large cities (e.g., the metropolitan areas of Jakarta, Shanghai, Tokyo, Seoul, Bangkok) have performed much better.

II. Key Issues

The various issues surrounding the country's lack of infrastructure, low quality urban environments and overall underperformance in terms of growth and poverty reduction may be organized according to three elements which need to be in place in order for the government to get things done: (i) a plan, and mandate to implement the plan; (ii) sufficient funding resources; and (iii) a capable bureaucracy.

A. Mandate and Plan

Various infrastructure studies and plans have already been prepared, and components of these plans are in various stages of approval, project development and implementation (e.g., Dream Plan, High Standard Highway Plan, Mega Cebu Public Transport Master Plan, Davao Sustainable Urban Transport Project, North South Commuter Railway, Gateway to Airport Roadmap to 2040, Salintubig Program, National Informal Settlements Upgrading Strategy). Many projects are listed as part of programmes of the Department of Public Works and Highways (DPWH), Department of Transportation and Communications, Department of Energy, Department of Tourism, Department of Agriculture, NHA and other housing agencies that cover transportation, telecommunications, flood control, water supply, energy supply, housing, etc. By and large, mandates and plans are in place.

Some critical planning initiatives need to be pursued, including:

(i) Geographical convergence of projects (i.e., integration of road, port/airport and housing projects in local and national/regional strategies and plans);

(ii Intersectoral coordination and accurate up-to-date monitoring (because plans and mandates are scattered throughout various agencies); and

(iii) Enhancement of the catalytic effect of strategic infrastructure by not dissipating resources across locations and on low-impact projects, even as basic "spatially blind" social service projects are implemented throughout the country (NEDA 2014).

There is also a need to align infrastructure plans and implementation responsibilities between local government units (LGU) and national agencies. Ideally, national agency and concerned LGU plans should be consistent with each other, so that projects are implemented without delays or operational conflicts (arising from, for example, unanticipated imposition of local taxes or non-issuance of local permits). Problems typically arise from differences in timing priorities (long-term infrastructure requirements are not consistent with the short-term, three-year single-term horizon of local officials) and turf issues (e.g., when dealing with vote-rich informal settler communities).

LGUs also don't have much incentive to support metropolitan–regional development plans, because these are viewed as impositions on local autonomy. (For example, Metro Manila Development Plans formulated after the Local Government Code was enacted never became operational to the extent that planning standards and local plans were established and infrastructure projects were implemented during the Marcos years.) Further, these plans are essentially toothless because of the absence of metropolitan or regional governments. Individual projects have a better chance of being implemented if they are packaged as part of a sector plan (attributed to a single agency), which are less threatening to local autonomy compared to a multi-sector, and thus more encompassing, metropolitan or regional plan.

The propensity for local–national conflicts is a serious concern because an increasing number of development issues (e.g., transportation, pollution, flooding) are inter-local in nature and are therefore likely to involve national agencies.

Finally, so much needs to be done to bridge the wide service gaps across many infrastructure subsectors, and therefore rigid prioritization is not as important as implementing whatever can be implemented as soon as possible.

The mandate for urban development is less clear. Primary responsibility lies with the Housing and Urban Development Coordinating Council; although, as its name implies, only in a coordinating capacity. It has an Urban Development and Housing Framework that is updated once in a while, but the mandate and budget for implementing specific projects are with other sector agencies. This means that there is no single agency below the Office of the President that has sufficient institutional and budget clout to push inter-sector or urban and regional development policies (including inter-LGU issues) and programmes. It is unlikely, however, under the current political economy, that any single agency can be given direct responsibility for the multi-sector planning and implementation required by metropolitan–regional development plans, and therefore this responsibility will have to be shouldered, if ever, by the president.

As far as actual plan preparation is concerned, there is room for improving technical planning capability, especially at the local level. But even at the national and regional levels there is a need to push the fundamental objective of equalizing opportunities and not outcomes, and thus to dispel the still popular idea of allocating resources evenly across regions with the intent of reducing social disparities (NEDA 2014). In fact, there is no congruence between social and spatial equity, and therefore attempts to achieve interregional equity do not necessarily translate, and may even be counterproductive to efficiency and public welfare (Gore 1984). This does not mean that interregional equity should not be pursued; but, rather, such an initiative should be recognized on its political merit.

B. Funding Resources

Not only has the Philippines been spending a smaller percentage of its GDP for infrastructure, but the growth of its GDP has also not kept pace with its Asian neighbours. During the 1980–2007 period, right before the global financial crisis, Philippine GDP growth averaged only

3.1 per cent, compared to 6.1 per cent for the ASEAN-5 (Indonesia, Malaysia, Thailand, Singapore and Vietnam) and 10.1 per cent for China. Moreover, the economy has consistently gone through boom and bust cycles (featuring moderate, low and crisis states; Bautista 2002) that have prevented sustained investments required by many large, multi-phase infrastructure programmes.

Key fiscal and sectoral reforms and the country's impressive growth performance since 2008 have improved the government's financial position and allowed it to catch up with its infrastructure spending. Further, private sector participation in infrastructure projects in the short and medium term is promising, given robust corporate incomes, low interest rates and limited overseas options in a lacklustre global investment environment.

For infrastructure, the government target is to spend at least 5 per cent of GDP starting 2016. This translates to about P4.75 trillion for 2016–30. Not included in the 5 per cent GDP spending, but considered part of the available pool of funding, is the projected P6.58 trillion private sector investments in public-private partnership (PPP) projects for 2013–30. Of this amount, P3 trillion is expected to be spent for transportation projects, 1.3 trillion for social infrastructure, a trillion for water resources, 847 billion for energy resources, and P89 billion for information and communications technology (Marasigan 2015). As of 2015, nine infrastructure projects amounting to P256 billion have been awarded, excluding school and orthopedic building projects (PPP Center 2015). Included in the projects to be implemented, whether directly by government or through PPP, are those in the P2.61 trillion Dream Plan (ALMEC 2014), which are intended to relieve the congestion and address the land transport requirements of the Mega Manila region, which includes Central Luzon and Calabarzon (dela Paz 2014).

Spending 5 per cent of GDP for infrastructure is an optimistic but doable projection of the trajectory of infrastructure spending of recent years: 1.98 per cent of GDP in 2013, 2.08 per cent in 2014, and 2.6 per cent (estimate) for 2015. The budget allocation of DPWH follows this trend, with P191 billion in 2014, P273 billion in 2015 and a projected P391 billion for 2016 (Llanto 2015; *Interaksyon* 2015).

Currently, funding constraints exist; but, as a whole, sourcing funds from the public and private sectors does not appear to be a major problem as far as infrastructure development is concerned. In the future, more long-term financing may be available from the bond and equity markets as these mature (see Llanto, chap. 8.)

Still, there is a need to allow and encourage foreign investments in infrastructure beyond what is currently allowed in order to (i) expand the pool of funding sources, given the limited number of domestic conglomerate–investors; (ii) augment funding in cases of an economic downturn that reduces local sources; and (iii) increase competition during the bidding process and improve efficiency in bid preparation, project design and execution. But these will also require addressing deterrents to foreign infrastructure investments, such as the recent history of contractual disputes (e.g., MWSS–Manila Water concession agreement, NAIA Terminal 3–Fraport/PIATCO contract), recalled biddings, and regulatory inconsistencies that take place, especially as administrations change.

Unlike infrastructure, funding to address the housing backlog is a serious concern. Based on the National Informal Settlements Upgrading Strategy, an annual budget of P42.2 billion (low estimate) is needed to address a backlog of 1.5 million housing units by 2025. The housing production and relocation budget for 2015, however, is only P11 billion (Official Gazette 2015).

In general, low-income housing is a problem of low income and not of housing. There is a direct correlation between slum housing and poverty/low GDP. And therefore, the solution requires economic growth that increases income and improves affordability — that is, inclusive growth. But, enabling conditions such as enforcement of property rights, tenure security, and functional land and finance markets are also needed. For example, there is a lot of room for increasing access to mortgage finance; using the ratio of mortgage debt (outstanding) to GDP as an indicator, the ratio for developed countries is over 50 per cent; it is approaching 45 per cent in emerging Asian countries such as Singapore and China; and less than 20 per cent for most Asian countries. In the Philippines, the ratio is less than 5 per cent (Doling, Vandenberg and Tolentino 2013).

Ultimately, the key to the problem is affordability, which means that without significant increases in household income, government subsidies will be required if the majority of the low-income groups are to benefit from current housing programmes. These can be in the form of targeted financing (non-regressive), land that is reasonably priced and accessible to places of employment, support transport and other service infrastructure, and affordable rental housing programmes. Above all, these have to be done in a transparent and accountable manner.

C. Bureaucracy and Institutional Capacity

A more serious issue than funding, at least currently, is the ability of government agencies to absorb large budget increases and, in the case of metropolitan areas, the capacity to withstand further congestion while projects are being implemented. This has been acknowledged by government, which has tried to improve public spending capacity (e.g., the formation of a subcommittee of the Development Budget Coordinating Committee to evaluate project proposals costing less than a billion pesos, and the issuance of Administrative Order 46, which creates full-time delivery units in all government agencies) (dela Peña 2015; de Vera 2015).

But more will have to be done, considering that the government has fallen short of its percentage-of-GDP target spending for infrastructure in the past decade. Among others, obligation-to-allotment ratios (an indicator of fund utilization) must increase from the 70–75 per cent level of 2014, not only to improve public spending but also to attract even more funding (dela Cruz 2014; Montecillo 2015).

Improving the ability of the bureaucracy to deliver infrastructure projects is not simple or easy. As noted by former Socioeconomic Planning Secretary Gerardo Sicat (2002), it requires a purposeful and extended programme of capacity building among the project planning and management agencies of government — from design to financing, implementation, coordination and monitoring — involving training and working experience with local and international technical agencies. If successful, it results in a culture of project development within government that extends to the regional and local levels.

As a whole, the country's institutional capacity to update and integrate plans and to implement and manage a much larger number of projects remains to be amply demonstrated.

III. Pathways

For infrastructure, the default pathway to the vision is anchored on the government's plan to spend at least 5 per cent of GDP for infrastructure starting in 2016. This pathway assumes that the private sector does its part through PPP and its commitments to address specific sector targets (e.g., broadband infrastructure). It also requires, as noted earlier, that the government will have the capacity to further accelerate infrastructure spending.

Spending at least 5 per cent of GDP means that infrastructure gaps can be covered earlier, enabling faster growth to take place. According to one estimate, every additional 1 per cent of GDP invested in transportation and communication on a sustained basis increases the GDP per capita growth rate by 0.6 per cent (PwC 2014).

Reverting to the 2–3 per cent spending range of past decades will put downward pressure on growth, service delivery, housing availability, and connectivity by 2040. In the case of the Dream Plan (ALMEC 2014), for example, its intended benefits — economic savings of P1.2 trillion per year starting 2030; public transport savings of P18 per person per day; travel time reduction by 49 minutes per person per trip; and additional toll and fare revenues of P119 billion per year — will be compromised (dela Peña 2015).

To some extent, increasing private sector investments in infrastructure projects can offset government underspending. This can be enhanced by legislative reforms (e.g., amending the Build–Operate–Transfer Law) that remove disincentives or prohibitions to foreign investments in public utilities, land and other components of infrastructure projects. Other constraints to project identification, procurement, financing, operations and maintenance should also be addressed.

In the absence of significant subsidies, private sector investments in infrastructure will tend to favour projects in large metropolitan centres where market feasibility is more likely. (Already, of the total project cost of PPP contracts awarded by 2015, 87 per cent were allocated to projects in the Mega Manila region.) This contrasts with the current practice of the DPWH where Mindanao receives the largest share of its budget at 27 per cent, followed by North Luzon (23 per cent), South Luzon (20 per cent), Visayas (18 per cent) and, lastly, Metro Manila at 12 per cent (DPWH 2012, 2014, 2015).

With respect to urbanization, pathways to the vision may be defined by how population will be distributed among the country's settlements; in particular, whether it will be biased towards existing large cities or towards smaller and new settlements. This will affect the way infrastructure investments will be distributed, as well as the overall urban environment where an increasing proportion of Filipinos will be living.

Three scenarios are considered: (i) *Trend scenario;* (ii) *No Growth in Metro Manila scenario,* where all growth is absorbed by the rest of the hierarchy of settlements; and (iii) *No New Settlements scenario,* where all growth is absorbed by existing settlements.

The latter two scenarios are hypothetical, because we know that Metro Manila will continue to grow and that new settlements will be formed as growth takes place. They are presented to frame the Trend scenario and illustrate the extreme impacts of two opposing but popular policies: (i) preventing further growth in Metro Manila, based on the argument that it has reached capacity limits; and (ii) preventing new settlements from forming, with the intent of curbing expansion into agricultural land (Corpuz 2013).

All scenarios are based on a linear estimate of the country's hierarchy of settlements, defined by the structure (slope) of the hierarchy and the size of the largest settlement (Metro Manila). All use the Philippine Statistics Authority medium assumption of a population of 142 million for the country by 2040. It should be kept in mind that the scenarios are not intended to provide detailed quantitative estimates and forecasts, although numbers will be cited for illustrative and directional purposes. Rather, they provide context and order-of-magnitude conditions to appreciate corresponding policy implications.

The following are the results of the scenario simulations, which are also shown in Table 3.10:

(i) The Trend scenario shows that the total number of settlements and the amount of built-up land increase by 13 per cent and 44 per cent, respectively, to accommodate future growth. Further, 5 per cent of total agricultural land is converted to built-up land. Metro Manila and its surrounding areas (Mega Manila) double in population; other large regional metro centres (Metro Pampanga, Metro Cebu, Metro Davao) also almost double their populations.

TABLE 3.10
Scenarios of Future Growth, 2040

Scenario	Total Population (million)	Total Number of Settlements	Total Built-Up Land (km²)	Built-Up over Total Land (%)	Total Agricultural Land (km²)	Mega Manila Growth Multiple
Base 2010	92.4	1,513	10,936	3.7	97,270	0
Trend (based on PSA medium assumption)	142	1,715 13.30%	15,768 44.20%	5.3	92,438 (−5.0%)	2
No Growth in Metro Manila	142	2,733 80.60%	20,072 83.50%	6.8	88,134 (−9.4%)	1
No New Settlements	142	1,513 0.00%	14,966 36.90%	5.1	93,240 (−4.1%)	2.3

Note: PSA = Philippine Statistics Authority; Percentages are per cent changes from Base 2010 scenario.

(ii) The No Growth in Metro Manila scenario, as defined, does not allow any growth in Metro Manila. In order to accommodate the same amount of total growth, the number of settlements balloon by 80 per cent and built-up land increases by 84 per cent, requiring 10 per cent of total agricultural land to be converted.

(iii) The No New Settlements scenario confines all growth to existing settlements, although this still requires conversion of agricultural land (4 per cent) as existing settlements expand their peripheries to accommodate growth. Built-up land increases by 37 per cent and Mega Manila's population increases by 230 per cent.

Although hypothetical, the No Growth in Metro Manila and No New Settlements scenarios illustrate the trade-offs as we deviate substantially from the trend. These trade-offs exist because changes in one part of the settlement network affects the other parts. The more Metro Manila's growth is curtailed, the more growth takes place in other settlements (existing and new). And since densities are lower in smaller and newer settlements, then a greater amount of built-up area, and thus agricultural land conversion, is needed.

Preventing the growth of the largest cities could ease some of the environmental pressures being experienced in Metro Manila and other regional centres. But this also means that infrastructure has to be dispersed throughout more settlements. This is likely to be more expensive, especially if it involves the construction of new cities. Typically, the material, social (e.g., relocating population and employment areas) and environmental costs of building new cities, as opposed to increasing capacities and improving efficiencies of existing metropolitan centres, are much higher. To illustrate the high cost of building a new city, an estimate of the construction cost of the core of Brasilia, the capital of Brazil built starting in 1950, in current value terms and excluding private sector spending, displacement and other social costs, is US$83 billion — equivalent to P3.9 trillion, or about eighteen times the 2014 budget of the DPWH (Blemya 2012).

Alternatively, the more growth is confined to existing settlements, the greater the tendency for large cities (the regional centres) to grow even larger. Appropriate infrastructure investments will be required to prevent further congestion and service inefficiencies. But it also means a potential for greater economies of scale and agglomeration, and thus increased opportunities for employment and investments to expand and improve services. For example, once a city's population approaches 200,000 to 250,000, larger scale medical, accommodation, retail and travel services, including rudimentary business process outsourcing, begin to become feasible, extending beyond the local market and involving more specialized business and logistic requirements (Corpuz 2013).

In the case of Metro Manila, the prospect of further population increase can be daunting, given existing congestion conditions. These conditions, however, are products not just of its large population and high density but also of the lack of infrastructure. Other large urban areas of the world have densities higher than Metro Manila, but because of extensive infrastructure and more efficient urban planning and management, services are more effective, and overall quality of life is higher. The population density of Hong Kong (urban), for example, is more than double that of Metro Manila, but congestion, among others, is much worse in the latter (ALMEC 2014; Hong Kong Transport Advisory Committee 2014).

Congestion and other service inefficiencies are products of supply and demand — of the amount of population to be served and the extent of infrastructure and facilities in service. Just because Metro Manila has a large population does not mean that it has to be inefficient. Viewed in this manner, the large scale of Metro Manila's labour, services and commodity markets should be treated as a key asset that needs to be made more productive — not ignored or wasted by underinvesting in the metropolitan area — by improving the quality of density through infrastructure and effective urban management. The objective, in this case, is to increase productivity and global competitiveness and to further drive growth across the country. In addition to global-standard international linkages, this also requires efficient domestic connectivity (across urban and rural areas), in order for the rest of the country to benefit from the scale and agglomeration economies of Metro Manila and other metropolitan centres.

The high cost of modernizing Metro Manila's infrastructure is sometimes cited as its own deterrent, but the cost of inaction and allowing Metro Manila to become even more inefficient and uncompetitive may even be much higher.

Another potential benefit of population growth biased towards the regional centres is less land conversion compared to growth favouring smaller settlements and new cities, because in the former, more of the growth will be accommodated in existing urban areas. This has positive implications on food production as well as on the reduction of disaster risks caused by encroachment on agricultural land and forests.

The Trend scenario appears to be consistent with the 2040 vision. Under this scenario, Metro Manila grows at a much slower pace, reaching a population of 13.8 million, with a density of about 22,400 persons/km^2 (up from 19,200 persons/km^2) by 2040; and Mega Manila grows to 30.1 million, with an overall density of 11,800 persons/km^2. These numbers are high compared to the rest of the country, but globally they are not unprecedented. They translate to an annual growth rate of only 0.5 per cent for Metro Manila and 1.6 per cent for Mega Manila as a whole. The rest of Mega Manila (the adjacent provinces of Bulacan, Rizal, Cavite, Laguna) grows at a much faster pace of 2.8 per cent, but its density remains relatively low at 8,400 persons/km^2. Overall, the scenario follows the basic strategy of having the rest of the Mega Manila region absorb a large part of future population growth while building up the infrastructure and service facilities of Metro Manila to catch up with demand.

It is useful to keep in mind that the fundamental characteristics of the Trend scenario — the slow growth of Metro Manila and the rapid growth of the rest of Mega Manila — are already taking place. Implementation, therefore, requires guidance and not a drastic change in the existing growth trajectory.

The Trend scenario may be translated into a Mega Manila regional framework plan that includes the following objectives:

(i)   Define urban expansion areas (e.g., eastern side of North Luzon Expressway), including new townships, where the housing backlog and industrial expansion can be accommodated and supported by necessary infrastructure;

(ii) Integrate various infrastructure plans (e.g., Dream Plan) with urban expansion plans;

(iii) Incorporate disaster risk reduction, including strengthening lifeline systems, creating redundancy, watershed/river basin planning, etc.; and

(iv) Identify measures to introduce much higher quality planning and urban management capability given the unprecedented scale of urbanization and infrastructure for the Philippines. An effective governance mechanism for Metro Manila that addresses the difficulties of its fragmented local structure (which can be a model for regional metropolitan centres) will be of particular importance. As mentioned earlier, effective urban management, including the ability to create and implement a pipeline of infrastructure projects, is crucial for the attainment of the vision.

Two additional points are worth mentioning. First, the proposed Mega Manila plan should be a framework that allows flexibility at the design and implementation levels, especially to account for local inputs. But the driving parameters (e.g., target markets or service areas) of proposed projects should be clear, so that changes are guided and not arbitrary.

Second, similar framework plans for other regional centres may also be prepared. These are not the same as the regional physical framework plans prepared for the administrative regions; rather, each plan is anchored on a metropolitan centre, and the plan's boundaries are determined by the extent of metropolitan functional influence. The basic objectives — accommodating future growth, infrastructure integration, connectivity, disaster risk reduction, implementation strategy — and many key elements should be similar. Many other plans have been prepared, but most of these, unlike the proposed framework, do not account for, or only superficially account for, the demand side.

IV. Concluding Summary

Infrastructure is a driver of growth. It allows inputs to production and the distribution of goods, as well as access to education, healthcare and other basic services. It provides mobility to labour, which is critical to employment and poverty reduction. It is an essential ingredient towards attaining the vision of cities working as engines of economic growth, providing quality services and affordable housing, and forming connected networks of sustainable communities.

The Philippines is plagued with deficits in infrastructure and low-income housing as a result of decades of underinvestment and inefficiencies in the processes of planning–investment and programming–budgeting–implementation. The nature of the deficits may be characterized as (i) low and inadequate capacity relative to demand, (ii) poor connectivity, and (iii) low quality. Because of these, the country's infrastructure ranks the lowest or close to the lowest in East Asia.

Still, current urban growth trends are consistent with the long-term vision. This is an opportunity that should not be missed, particularly with respect to the relatively rapid growth of regional centres and the existing large markets in and around Metro Manila. These can increase the feasibility of service infrastructure, drive demand for domestic (including rural) production, reduce encroachments into agricultural areas, and help establish transportation networks that extend hierarchically across the country.

Clearly, a lot of work needs to be done in order to put in place the plans, funds, and organizational capacity needed to provide the infrastructure and housing requirements of the 2040 vision. The priority tasks are as follows:

(i) Ensure consistency, connectivity and geographical conver-
     gence among infrastructure projects by integrating them into
     metropolitan–regional plans that:

     (a) Provide for urban expansion and disaster risk reduction, and
         incorporate new housing areas;

     (b) Maximize the catalytic effect of infrastructure by not dis-
         sipating resources across locations and low-impact projects,
         even as basic "spatially blind" social service projects
         are pursued. Allocating infrastructure resources evenly
         across regions will not necessarily reduce social welfare
         disparities, because social equity does not follow spatial
         equity, and the latter may even be counterproductive to
         public welfare; and

(c) Enhance physical and digital connectivity throughout the network of settlements;

(ii) Increase public infrastructure spending on a sustained basis to 5–8 per cent of GDP:

(a) Expand the pool of funding sources (e.g., by increasing foreign infrastructure investment limits) to augment domestic sources and to increase efficiency through competition; and

(b) Re-establish government capability to create and implement a pipeline of infrastructure projects;

(iii) Maximize the opportunities provided by the large labour, service and commodity markets of regional and metropolitan centres to improve productivity, increase competitiveness, drive growth and reduce poverty. Improve the quality of density of these centres, especially Metro Manila, through strategic infrastructure investments and reliable service delivery;

(iv) Establish effective urban–metropolitan management, especially for the rapidly growing regional centres, and substantially upgrade the quality and discipline of public service. Inter-local governance will be critical, as unprecedented growth takes place in the country's regional and metropolitan centres; and

(v) Increase funding and production capacity for low-income housing in order to attain zero backlog:

(a) Provide subsidies in the form of targeted financing (non-regressive), land that is reasonably priced, support transport and other service infrastructure, and affordable rental housing programmes; and

(b) Incorporate new housing in urban expansion areas identified in metropolitan–regional plans, with sufficient access to and from places of employment. Among informal settler beneficiaries, priority should be given to those in danger zones.

References

ALMEC. "Roadmap for Infrastructure Development for Metro Manila and Its Surrounding Areas". Report submitted to Japan International Cooperation Agency (JICA) and National Economic and Development Authority (NEDA), March 2014.

Angel, S., S. Sheppard, and D. Civco. "The Dynamics of Global Urban Expansion". World Bank working paper, September 2005.

Blemya. "Brasilia a Huge Capital Built in a Nightshift". 2012 <http://www.blemya.com/2012/04/brasilia-huge-capital-built-in.html>.

Burga, P., and M. Barreto. "The Effect of Internet and Cell Phones on Employment and Agricultural Production in Rural Villages in Peru". University of Piura working paper, February 2014 <http://udep.edu.pe/cceeee/files/2014/07/3B_2_RitterGUERRERO.pdf>.

Camus, M. "Government Rolls Out P171B Railway Project". *Philippine Daily Inquirer*, 16 July 2015 <http://business.inquirer.net/195368/govt-rolls-out-p171-b-railway-project#ixzz3hBMRnUs4>.

Corpuz, A. *The Colonial Iron Horse: Railroads and Regional Development in the Philippines, 1872–1935*. Quezon City, Philippines: UP Press, 1999.

──────. "National Spatial Strategy". Paper submitted to NEDA and ADB, 2013.

de Vera, B. "Government Spending Plays Catch Up in Second Half". *Philippine Daily Inquirer*, 12 October 2015.

dela Cruz, J.M. "Mindanao to Get Lion's Share in 2015 Public Works Budget—Singson". *Business Mirror*, 13 August 2014 <http://businessmirror.com.ph/index.php/en/news/regions/37004-mindanao-to-get-lion-s-share-in-2015-public-works-budget-singson>.

dela Paz, C. "New Internet Speed Minimum Throwback to 90s?" *Rappler*, 18 August 2015 <http://www.rappler.com/business/industries/172-telecommunications-media/99482-philippines-internet-speed-woes>.

──────. "NCR Solution to Need Half of Outlay for Infrastructure". *Business World*, 25 September 2014 <http://www.bworldonline.com/content.php?section=TopStory&title=ncr-solution-to-need-half-of-outlay-for-infrastructure&id=95013>.

dela Peña, Z. "Public Spending for Infra, Capital Outlay up 40% in April". *Philippine Star*, 1 July 2015 <http://www.philstar.com/business/2015/07/01/1471819/public-spending-infra-capital-outlay-40-april>.

Di, P. "Key Transport Statistics of World Cities". In *Journeys: Sharing Urban Transport Solutions*, edited by George Sun, Evan Gwee, Foo Jong Ai, and Augustine Low, pp. 105–12. Singapore: Land Transport Authority, 2013.

Doling, J., P. Vandenberg, and J. Tolentino. "Housing and Housing Finance: A Review of the Links to Economic Development and Poverty Reduction". ADB economics working paper series 362. 2013.

DPWH (Department of Public Works and Highways). "Strategic Infrastructure Policies and Programs". 2012

———. Strategic Infrastructure Policies and Programs". 5 August 2014.

———. Investment Opportunities in the Philippines". 12 May 2015.

The Economist. "Bridge to Somewhere". 19 July 2014.

Gore, C. *Regions in Question: Space, Development Theory and Regional Policy.* London: Methuen, 2014.

Green, A., M. de Hoyos, and Yuxin Li. "Employment and the Internet". Nominet Trust State of the Art Reviews. 2012.

Guinto, J. "Urban Decay Threatens Hot Philippine Economy". *Yahoo! News,* 11 October 2014 <http://news.yahoo.com/urban-decay-threatens-hot-philippine-economy-001404882.html?soc_src=mediacontentsharebuttons&soc_trk=ma>.

ICF International. "Developing a National Informal Settlements Upgrading Strategy for the Philippines: Final Report". Report submitted to Housing and Urban Development Coordinating Council (HUDCC), July 2014.

Interaksyon. "Philippines on Track to Hitting Infra Spending Target by 2016, Says DPWH Official". 23 July 2015 <http://www.interaksyon.com/business/114714/phl-on-track-hitting-5-of-gdp-infra-spending-by-2016>.

Kasarda, J., and G. Lindsay. *Aerotropolis: The Way We'll Live Next.* New York: Farrar, Strauss and Giroux, 2011.

Layton, R. "Does the Internet Create or Destroy Jobs? A Snapshot from the Global Debate on Digitally Enabled Employment". *TechPolicyDaily.com,* 29 December 2014 <http://techpolicydaily.com/internet/the-internet-create-destroy-jobs-snapshot-global-debate-digitally-enabled-employment>.

Llanto, G. "The Impact of Infrastructure on Agricultural Productivity". PIDS Discussion Paper Series 2012-12. 2012.

———. "Philippine Infrastructure and Connectivity: Challenges and Reforms". Unpublished draft, 20 September 2015.

Marasigan, L. "Will PPP, P6.58T Infra Binge End Pinoy's Transport Woes?" *Business Mirror,* 10 May 2015 <http://www.businessmirror.com.ph/will-ppp-p6-58-t-infra-binge-end-pinoys-transport-woes/>.

McKinsey Global Institute. "Internet Matters: The Net's Sweeping Impact on Growth, Jobs and Prosperity". 2011.

Montecillo, P. "Bureaucratic Inefficiencies to Curb Spending". *Philippine Daily Inquirer,* 13 October 2015.

NEDA (National Economic Development Authority). *Philippine Development Plan: 2011–2016, Midterm Update with Revalidated Results Matrices.* Pasig City, Philippines: NEDA, 2014.

Official Gazette. "P11-B Housing Budget to Cover Vulnerable Communities". 16 February 2015 <http://www.officialgazette.gov.ph/2015/02/16/p11-b-housing-budget-to-cover-vulnerable-communities/>.

Oxford Business Group. "The report: The Philippines 2015". 2015.

PPA (Philippine Ports Authority). *2012 Annual Report.* New York: PPA, 2013.

PPP (Public Private Partnership) Center. "Status of PPP Projects (as of 21 September 2015)". 2015 <https://ppp.gov.ph/?page_id=26075>.

Rodriguez, F. "Farm to Market Roads: A Farmer's Journey". *Rappler*, 7 March 2014 <http://www.rappler.com/move-ph/issues/hunger/52218-farm-to-market-roads-food-security-livelihood>.

Saclag, D.E. "S&P Reminds Philippines Inadequate Infrastructure Still Prime Growth Risk". *BusinessWorld Online*, 21 May 2015 <http://www.bworldonline.com/content.php?section=TopStory&title=s&38p-reminds-Philippines-inadequate-infrastructure-still-prime-growth-risk&id=108393>.

Schneider, K., and M.K Gugerty. "Agricultural Production and Poverty Reduction: Linkages and Pathways". *Evans School Review* 1, no. 1 (2011).

Sicat, G. "Notes on Infrastructure: Then, Now and Tomorrow". UPSE Discussion Paper 0209. 2002.

SHDA (Subdivision & Housing Developers Association). "The Housing Industry Road Map of the Philippines: 2012–2030". Presentation to the Board of Investments, 2012.

Tan, E. "Solving the Slum Problem". *Philippine Daily Inquirer*, 16 August 2015.

WEF (World Economic Forum). *The Global Competitiveness Report 2015–2016.* Switzerland: WEF, 2015.

World Bank. "ICTs are Creating New Jobs and Making Labor Markets More Innovative, Inclusive, and Global". Press release, 10 September 2013 <http://www.worldbank.org/en/news/press-release/2013/09/10/icts-are-creating-new-jobs-and-making-labor-markets-more-innovative-inclusive-and-global-world-bank-study>.

Whaley, F. "Strained Infrastructure in Philippines Erodes the Nation's Growth Prospects". *New York Times*, 3 August 2014 <http://mobile.nytimes.com/2014/08/04/business/international/strained-infrastructure-in-philippines-erodes-the-nations-growth-prospects.html>.

World Shipping Council. "Top 50 World Container Ports". 2012.

4

Education and Training

Winfred Villamil

I. Introduction

The long-term economic success of a nation depends to a great extent on sustained increases in its endowment of human capital — the accumulated knowledge, skills and capacities of its workforce. This chapter focuses on the crucial role that investments in human capital, specifically in the education and training of the population, will play in maintaining the Philippine's development momentum.

The important role of education in development is well known. Nobel laureate Amartya Sen (2011) argued that "the elimination of ignorance, of illiteracy ... and of needless inequalities in opportunities [is] to be seen as objectives that are valued for their own sake. They expand our freedom to lead the lives we have reason to value, and these elementary capabilities are of importance on their own" (p. 240). Indeed, limited access to education, particularly of poor households, consistently emerged as a major concern in the recent focused group discussions conducted for Filipino 2040 (see David 2015).

Education is not only an end in itself; it is also a means to enhance well-being by increasing an individual's productivity and therefore earnings. Incontrovertible evidence suggests that people with greater education and training have better employment opportunities and higher earnings.[1]

Access to education can help lift poor households out of poverty by breaking the intergenerational cycle of poverty (HDN 2000). Poverty is perpetuated mainly because poorly educated parents, mired in low-paying occupations, lack the means to continue to send their children to school, effectively condemning them to low-productivity employment and, consequently, meagre earnings. To households earning subsistence incomes, the opportunity cost of sending their children to school — hence foregoing income from their children's labour — is too high. Studies have shown that dropout rates are higher in poor households where parents have low education.[2] The obvious way out of this poverty trap is for children to acquire an education that allows them entry into higher paying jobs. This can happen if private entities or the government subsidize the cost of education of the children of poor households.

The benefits of education extend well beyond the well-being of those who receive it. Society also gains from the positive externalities of an educated citizenry. People with more education are more likely to be more civic-minded, better able to understand social and political issues, vote more wisely, obey the law, and adhere to the basic rules of good manners and conduct. An educated citizenry is essential to good governance and social harmony, which in turn are necessary conditions for rapid economic growth.

Recent theories emphasize the key role played by technological progress in promoting productivity and economic growth over the long term.[3] Technological advances refer to the discovery of new and more productive inputs that raise production efficiency, introduce new products or improve the quality of existing outputs. Growth based solely on increases in the capital stock cannot be sustained in the long run, because of diminishing returns. However, growth based on technological change and innovation, which come from human knowledge and ideas and is therefore unlimited, allows society to achieve continuing growth in productivity and per capita incomes (Romer 1990). Countries with more human capital would be more adept in producing new knowledge and be more proficient in adapting to the local situation new technologies discovered elsewhere (Barro 2001). A highly educated population is therefore viewed by many economists as a prerequisite to technological progress and innovation, higher productivity and rapid economic growth.

The chapter is organized as follows. The second section provides a baseline assessment of education and training in the country using indicators of performance in formal education and workers' training. This will be benchmarked against that of ASEAN member states and other developing countries with the same level of per capita income. Philippine performance will also be compared with selected high-income and high-middle-income economies.

The third section gives an overview of the country's educational system at all three levels: basic, tertiary, and technical and vocational education. It analyses performance at each level and identifies the key issues that have to be addressed, focusing on access, quality and relevance.

The fourth section presents the specific vision for the sector in line with the overall vision and direction that policymakers can take to achieve it.

II. Comparative Performance of the Philippine Education and Training System

The impressive achievements of the Philippines in the education of its citizens are well known. Table 4.1 shows the educational attainment, measured as a percentage of the respective populations aged 25–54, of selected countries in East Asia. The proportion of the country's population with a primary education is 98.3 per cent. It is higher than India's (70.1 per cent), Indonesia's (97.8 per cent), Thailand's (95.8 per cent) and Malaysia's (95.9 per cent). Its secondary achievement rate at 75.9 per cent is better than those of India (48 per cent), Vietnam (38.2 per cent), Indonesia (61 per cent) and Thailand (51.9 per cent). Its tertiary achievement rate of 29.3 per cent exceeds that of Vietnam (6.2 per cent), India (10.7 per cent), Indonesia (11 per cent) and even economies with higher levels of development such as Thailand (20.5 per cent) and Malaysia (19 per cent).

However, the country's enrolment rates stagnated in the past decade and are presently low compared with its neighbours. As shown in Table 4.2, the gross or net enrolment rates at all levels (pre-school, primary, secondary and tertiary) in 2010 lagged behind those of many

TABLE 4.1
Educational Attainment Rates, Age 25–54, All Levels,
Selected Asian Countries (%)

Economy	Primary	Secondary	Tertiary
Cambodia	82.5	33.2	2.1
China	97.9	77.3	8.4
India	70.1	48	10.7
Indonesia	97.8	61.1	11.1
Korea, Rep. of	99.8	98.5	43.9
Laos	100	98.2	22.3
Malaysia	95.9	83.6	19
Philippines	98.3	75.9	29.3
Thailand	95.8	51.9	20.5
Vietnam	94.7	38.2	6.2

Source: World Economic Forum, *Human Capital Report 2015*.

TABLE 4.2
Enrolment Rates, Selected Asian Countries, 2010 and 2013 (%)

Economy	Pre-primary (Gross)		Primary (Net)		Secondary (Net)		Tertiary (Gross)	
	2010	2013	2010	2013	2010	2013	2010	2013
Cambodia	13	15	98	98[b]	38[d]	...	14	...
Laos	20	26	94	96	38	45	16	18
India	56	...	94	93[b]	...	...	18	25
Vietnam	69	82	90	99	...	...	22	25
Philippines	51[c]	...	88[c]	90	61[c]	65	29	34
Indonesia	40	51	95	92	68	76	25	32[b]
Thailand	108	119	96[c]	...	78	79[b]	50	51
China	56	74	...	...	...	...	23	30
Malaysia	78	84[b]	97[e]	...	66	69[b]	37	37[b]
Korea, Rep. of	...	93[a]	99	99	96	96	101	98
Hong Kong, China	101[d]	...	91	94	79	87	58	67

Notes: [a] 2014; [b] 2012; [c] 2009; [d] 2008; [e] 2005.
Source: World Bank, World Development Indicators.

of the countries in the table. In 2009, the pre-school enrolment rate of the Philippines was 51 per cent, which was below those of Vietnam, Thailand and Malaysia.[4]

A similar pattern can be observed with primary, secondary and tertiary enrolment rates. At 88 per cent, the net primary enrolment rate of the country in 2010 was the lowest among the countries in the table. The Philippine net secondary enrolment rate stood at 61 per cent. Indonesia, Thailand and Malaysia had higher rates than this. While surpassing most of its neighbours with the same level of development, its gross tertiary enrolment rate fell short of Thailand's, Malaysia's and Singapore's. Nonetheless, the country has apparently started to reverse this pattern. It managed to post significant improvements in enrolment rates at all levels from 2010 to 2013.

Table 4.3 may explain why enrolment rates failed to keep pace with those of other countries in the region. It is apparent from the data in the table that, unlike many other Asian countries, the

TABLE 4.3
Government Spending on Education, Selected Asian Countries, 2010 (%)

Economy	Total Government Spending (% of GDP)	Total Government Spending (% of Total Government Spending)	Government Spending per Student (% of per capita GDP)		
			Primary (2010)	Secondary	Tertiary
Cambodia	2.6	13.1	6.9	...	27.8
Laos	2.8	14	...	...	...
India	3.3	11.7	7.2	13.6	68.7
Vietnam	6.3	20.9	25.3	...	39.8
Philippines	2.7	13.2	9.0[b]	9.1[b]	10.5[a]
Indonesia	3	16.7	10.6	8.8	23.1
Thailand	3.8	16.5	19.4	14.8	17
Malaysia	5.1	18.4	14	18.6	47
Korea, Rep. of	4.7[a]	...	21.5[a]	22.0[a]	12.2[a]
Hong Kong, China	3.5	19.9	14.7	17.5	25.9

Notes: [a] 2009; [b] 2008.
Source: World Bank, World Development Indicators.

Philippines held back on government education spending in the previous decade.[5] By 2010, total public spending for education was 2.7 per cent of GDP, comparable to that of Cambodia (and Laos) but lower than those of India, Vietnam, Thailand and Malaysia by at least half a percentage point.

While education gets the largest budgetary allocation, which was 13.2 per cent of the total in 2010, it failed to get as much as in Vietnam, Thailand or Malaysia. These countries had, respectively, 20.9 per cent, 16.5 per cent and 18.4 per cent of their budgets earmarked for education in 2010. Compared to many of its neighbours, government spending per pupil for primary and secondary education was low.

It was in spending per pupil in tertiary education that the country ranked the lowest among many Asian countries. At 10.5 per cent of per capita GDP, this is not even half the corresponding numbers in other countries: 27.8 per cent for Cambodia, 68.7 per cent for India, 39.8 per cent for Vietnam, 23.1 per cent for Indonesia, and 47 per cent for Malaysia. Nevertheless, the country allocated more for tertiary education than it did for primary and secondary education. However, it is not buying quality tertiary education. Clearly, this heavy load has been manifested in the proliferation of heavily subsidized state universities and colleges and local government universities and colleges, instead of spending to deepen the quality of college and university education in the country.

Technical and Vocational Education and Training (TVET)

Apart from the education workers receive from formal schooling, additions to the country's stock of human capital come from the training provided by employers. After the desired level of formal education is completed, most of a person's accumulation of human capital will most likely come from on-the-job training. Firms invest in training their workers, particularly those from low-income households and who may have less education and fewer skills. TVET also assumes greater importance these days, even for skilled workers, because of increased trade openness and more intense international market competition, which compel firms to improve their competitiveness by, among other measures, constantly retraining their employees on new technologies and organizational structures.

On-the-job training has varied contents and takes many forms. At the very least, all firms need to orient new hires on the company's operating procedures and on the people they will need to deal with. Workers also acquire firm-specific practical skills that they do not learn from the education system. They are taught safety measures, how to operate machines and other equipment, and quality control practices. The training can be on-the-job and done under the guidance of supervisors or experienced co-workers. It can be formal, combining classroom lectures with practical applications in the workplace. The training can be conducted inside or outside the company premises, with trainers coming from within the firm or hired from outside. Or the firm can sponsor the training of workers in short, specialized courses offered by reputable training institutions.

Based on a survey of local executives, the Philippines seems to do better than many of its neighbours in the extent of training local companies provide their employees. The average rating given by the respondents to the question, "To what extent do companies in your country invest in training and employee development?" was 4.6 on a 1–7 scale, with 1 equivalent to "hardly at all" and 7 "to a great extent". From the survey responses, the country ranked 25th among the 144 countries covered, a ranking higher than many other countries, including those with higher levels of industrial development such as China (41st), Thailand (34th) and the Republic of Korea (47th). Malaysia, however, is doing much better, with a rating of 5.4, placing it at number 4 in the world rankings. The Philippines is also perceived to be doing well by the business community in terms of the availability of high quality specialized training services. It received an average rating of 4.4 from business leaders in response to the question, "In your country, to what extent are high quality specialized training services available?" (ranging from 1, "not at all", to 7, "widely available"). The rating for the country is close to that achieved by the Republic of Korea, a highly industrialized country.

TABLE 4.4
Training and Employee Development, Selected Asian Countries

| | Staff Training | | Specialized Training Service |
	Value*	Rank	Value**
Cambodia	3.9	92	3.56
Laos	4.3	40	3.92
India	3.94	70	4.21
Vietnam	3.88	76	3.34
Philippines	4.61	25	4.4
Indonesia	4.66	23	4.4
Thailand	4.41	34	4.17
China	4.29	41	4.35
Malaysia	5.35	4	5.44
Rep. of Korea	4.22	47	4.67

*Survey response on a scale of 1–7 (1 = hardly at all, 7 = to a great extent) to the question, "To what extent do companies in your country invest in training and employee development?"
** Survey response to the question, "In your country to what extent, are high quality specialized training services available?" (1 = not at all, 7 = widely available).
Source: World Economic Forum, *Human Capital Report 2015*.

Employment

Nearly a fifth of the Philippines' employed labour force work in jobs requiring only a primary education (see Table 4.5). The proportion is unusually high, especially compared to that of Indonesia (10.2 per cent), whose level of development is similar. On the other hand, the proportion of workers employed in jobs requiring a secondary education is low, at 27 per cent, compared, for instance, to Vietnam (37.3 per cent) and Indonesia (46.6 per cent). This may indicate that the country has still an inordinately large number of surplus workers with secondary education (semi-skilled workers) that are stuck in low skill, low productivity agriculture and the informal services sector, a consequence of the severe lack of employment opportunities for semi-skilled workers in the manufacturing sector.[6]

Nevertheless, compared to its neighbours the country has a larger proportion of its employed workers (12.6 per cent) in jobs that require a tertiary education. This can be explained by the fairly rapid growth in recent years of employment in high productivity services (information technology and business process outsourcing, tourism and other hospitality services, real estate, finance, etc.) that require skilled labour.

TABLE 4.5
Employment by Education Requirement, Selected Asian Countries (%)

Economy	Tertiary	Secondary	Primary	Others	Total
Philippines	12.6	27	19.2	0.3	59.1
Indonesia	5.6	46.6	10.2	0.3	62.7
Vietnam	7.6	37.3	31.1	0.2	76.2
Malaysia	16.1	40.7	8.2	0	65
Thailand	9.9	54.5	6.2	0.2	70.8
Korea, Rep. of	13.4	41	8	0	62.3
Japan	15.3	42.2	4.2	0	61.7

Source: World Economic Forum, *Human Capital Report 2015*.

III. The State of Philippine Education and Training: Key Issues

There are five basic issues in the education and training sector that may need to be addressed if the country is to sustain high growth and eliminate poverty. These are the need to exert greater effort in (1) equalizing opportunities by broadening access, especially of the poor, to education at all levels; (2) raising the quality of education at all levels to international standards; (3) making it more relevant to the needs of a rapidly changing globalizing economy; (4) transforming the education system into a more effective instrument for technological progress and innovation; and (5) increasing the demand for and the productive use of human capital resources.

Limited Access of the Poor to Education at All Levels.

The earnings of an individual or a family depend on their ownership
of productive assets such as land, labour and capital. For most of the
poor, labour is their only asset, and the only way out of poverty for
them is to raise the productivity of their labour through education.

Access of the poor and other disadvantaged groups to education is
a continuing concern for the country. Enrolment and completion rates
are particularly low for children in depressed rural communities, urban
slums and among indigenous peoples. In 2011, net enrolment rates in
secondary education for the poorest quintile was 35 percentage points
below that of the richest quintile (ADB 2014b).

Another frequently used indicator of access to education is the
cohort survival rate — the proportion of enrolees at the beginning
grade who reach the final grade on time. As shown in Table 4.6,
the country did not do substantially better than neighbours such
as Cambodia, Laos or India. Furthermore, its cohort survival rates
were way behind Malaysia, the Republic of Korea, Hong Kong and
Vietnam.

TABLE 4.6
Cohort Survival Rates, Elementary Schooling,
Selected Asian Countries (%)

Economy	Male	Female
Cambodia	64	69
Laos	72	74
India	60	64
Vietnam	94	95
Philippines	72	80
Indonesia	77	83
Malaysia	99	100
Korea, Rep. of	100	100
Hong Kong, China	99	99

Note: Based on the latest available data.
Source: World Bank World Development Indicators.

The converse of the cohort survival rate is the number of children who are out of school (OOSC). Table 4.7, which is computed using the Annual Poverty Indicators Survey (APIS) data set by David and Albert (2015), shows the OOSC as a proportion of the total number of children 5–15 years of age. In 2008, this was around 13.5 per cent, but dropped to just 5.2 per cent in 2013. The main reason for the sharp decline in the incidence of OOSC during the period was the passage in 2012 of the Kindergarten Act, which made kindergarten mandatory for entry into grade 1.[7] Another major factor was the incentive provided to parents to keep their children in school through the government's conditional cash transfer programme.

TABLE 4.7
Percentage of Out of School Children to Total Number of Children
Aged 5–15 Years, 2008 and 2013, by Region

Region	2008	2013
Region I – Ilocos	10.4	5.6
Region II – Cagayan Valley	13.9	4.1
Region III – Central Luzon	10	5.6
Region V – Bicol	15.6	5.3
Region VI – Western Visayas	12.6	2.5
Region VII – Central Visayas	14.3	4.9
Region VIII – Eastern Visayas	17.9	4.8
Region IX – Zamboanga Peninsula	20	5.7
Region X – Northern Mindanao	15.3	5
Region XI – Davao	17.3	4.3
Region XII – SOCCSKSARGEN	17.5	7.4
National Capital Region	8.6	3.6
Cordillera Administrative Region	10.2	7.7
Autonomous Region in Muslim Mindanao	25.1	16.7
Region XIII – Caraga	14	4.2
Region IVA – CALABARZON	9.2	3.5
Region IVB – MIMAROPA	14.6	5.5
Philippines	13.5	5.2

Source: David and Albert 2015.

As shown in the table, the incidence of OOSC varies considerably across the country's administrative regions. In most econometric analyses of OOSC, poverty stands out as a major determinant of the probability of being out of school.[8] For many poor households mired in a daily struggle for survival, the opportunity cost of going to school, which is the foregone income from child labour, is high.[9] Other studies also cite geographical barriers brought about by distance, poor road conditions and high transportation costs specifically in rural areas as factors affecting school drop-out rates. They also identify peace and security specifically in some areas in Mindanao such as the Autonomous Region of Muslim Mindanao (ARMM) as a major determinant of the decision to drop out of school (see UNESCO 2015).

The incidence of child labour in the Philippines is indeed high by regional standards, as shown in Table 4.8.

Extreme poverty is still the principal reason why children drop out of school and work. An analysis of the data from the 2011 APIS reveals that the rate of school leavers for children aged 6–11 was 4.6 per cent for children belonging to the poorest quintile, much higher than the 1.1 per cent for those belonging to the richest quintile (ADB 2014*b*). Moreover, the rate of school leavers for children aged 12–15 belonging to the poorest quintile was 14.2 per cent, compared to just 1.1 per cent for the richest quintile.

TABLE 4.8
Incidence of Child Labour (aged under 15), Selected Asian Countries

Economy	Value	Rank
Cambodia	18.3	87
Laos	10.1	72
India	11.8	76
Vietnam	6.9	60
Philippines	11.1	74
Indonesia	6.9	60
Thailand	8.3	64
Korea, Rep. of	1	3

Source: World Economic Forum, *Human Capital Report 2015*.

In a related study using the APIS panel data, Albert et al. (2012) report that the children of poor families that experience income shocks are more likely to have a higher number of OOSC. The result suggests that leaving school to find work is among the steps taken by poor households to cope with income shocks. The action applies particularly to children of secondary school age.[10] Because poor families have barely any savings, they are the ones who are most vulnerable to temporary income shocks such as from weather disturbances, economic recessions, and falling farm prices.

Data for the highest education grade completed by the population cohort 5 years old and over by income strata show that 35 per cent of children belonging to the lowest 30 per cent income class reported elementary undergraduate education as their highest attainment (Philippine Statistical Authority [PSA] 2013, using the APIS dataset for 2011), as shown in Table 4.9. In contrast, only 17 per cent of those belonging to the highest 70 per cent income class had an elementary

TABLE 4.9
Population 5 Years Old and Over by Highest Grade Completed by Income Stratum, Philippines, 2011

Highest Grade Completed	Income Stratum (% distribution)		
	Both Income Strata	Lowest 30%	Highest 70%
Philippines ('000)	86,806	31,477	55,330
Total	100	100	100
No Grade Completed	4.2	7.1	2.5
Pre-school	3.4	4.6	2.7
Elementary Undergraduate	23.7	35	17.3
Elementary Graduate	12.4	15.7	10.6
High School Undergraduate	15.2	17.1	14.1
High School Graduate	19.4	14.6	22.1
Post-Secondary	2.1	0.7	2.8
College Undergraduate	10.1	3.9	13.6
College Graduate or Higher	9.6	1.2	14.3

Source: Philippine Statistical Authority 2013, Results of the 2011 Annual Poverty Survey.

undergraduate education as their highest grade. On the other hand, only 5.8 per cent of individuals belonging to the lowest 30 per cent income stratum had an education beyond high school, compared to 30.7 per cent of those belonging to the highest 70 per cent income stratum that were able to complete an education beyond the secondary level.

A tertiary education is also beyond the reach of most poor families. Of individuals 16–24 years of age, only 5 per cent belonging to the lowest income decile would enrol in college or postgraduate studies compared to over 21 per cent for the highest decile. One reason for this is that among the poorest decile, about 50 per cent would not finish high school, compared to only 3 per cent for the richest decile (Tan 2011).

The Philippine government, especially in recent years, has been implementing various programmes to broaden access by the poor to education. The most noteworthy is the conditional cash transfer programme, otherwise known as the 4Ps (Pantawid Pamilyang Pilipino Program), which provides cash transfers to poor families on the condition that family members avail of health services on a regular basis and keep their children in school. At present, the cash subsidy is limited to families with children in elementary schools, but there are plans to extend the coverage up to completion of a high school education. The conditional cash transfer programme has been generally successful in increasing enrolment and reducing leavers among poor families, but issues remain regarding the targeting of poor families and inefficiencies in the transfers of funds.

The government has also been implementing the Education Service Contracting (ESC) programme, which aims to provide graduates of elementary schools access to quality high school education through a fixed tuition subsidy for those who wish to enrol in an accredited private high school.

Starting in 2016, the government is implementing a senior high school voucher programme. It is also providing a fixed tuition subsidy to graduates of public junior high schools to enable them to proceed to senior high in an accredited private school. These subsidies approximate the cost of public provision.

Since both the ESC and the voucher programme are open to all, regardless of means, it is apparent that the main objective is not necessarily to increase the access of poor families to quality education, but rather to reduce congestion and relieve pressure for school space and teaching resources in public schools. The problem has become more acute with the addition of three additional years (K to 12) to the basic education cycle. Since the subsidy is only partial, it is unlikely that children from poor families will be able to afford the remaining tuition and other costs of enrolling in a private school.

The Technical Education and Skills Development Authority (TESDA) also provides scholarships to help high school graduates from poor families pursue technical and vocational education under its Private Education Student Financial Assistance (PEFSA) programme. PESFA shoulders the cost of training and provides grantees a modest training and book allowance. TESDA also runs the Training for Work Scholarship Program (TWSP), which provides free training to grantees.

For higher education, the Commission on Higher Education (CHED) has a number of Student Financial Assistance Programs (STUFAPs), consisting of merit-based scholarships, need-based grants-in-aid and loans. Government support programmes to broaden access by the poor to tertiary education are beset by the same problems hindering access by the poor to basic education; namely, limited coverage and funding, weak targeting, and inefficient fund transfers.

Low Quality of Education at All Levels for the Poor

While many of the poor are deprived of an education even at the primary level, most that do succeed in getting an education have to make do with the low quality offered by the public school system. The inadequate learning they receive effectively bars them from entry into better paying jobs.

Table 4.10 shows the ranking of selected Asian countries (out of a total of 144 countries) in terms of the quality of education as perceived by their respective local business executives. The Philippines is ranked 61st in quality of primary education, 31st in overall quality of the education system, 67th in the quality of maths and science education, and 58th in Internet access in schools. These are significant improvements from the country's rankings in 2010–11: 99th for primary

Winfred Villamil

TABLE 4.10
Quality of Education, Selected Asian Countries

Economy	Quality of Primary Education		Quality of the Education System		Quality of Maths and Science Education		Internet Access in Schools	
	Value	Rank	Value	Rank	Value	Rank	Value	Rank
Cambodia	2.9	114	3.2	100	3.2	112	3.5	106
Laos	3.3	95	3.8	62	3.6	90	3.6	101
India	4.3	52	4.2	43	4.2	63	3.6	100
Vietnam	3.8	83	3.5	78	4.2	65	4.6	57
Philippines	4.1	61	4.5	31	4.1	67	4.5	58
Indonesia	4.2	57	4.3	41	4.4	52	4.8	43
Thailand	3.5	89	3.6	74	3.9	79	4.6	54
China	4.2	55	3.9	56	4.4	49	4.8	47
Malaysia	5.3	15	5.4	6	5.3	12	5.5	26
Rep. of Korea	4.7	36	3.7	66	4.8	30	5.8	19
Hong Kong, China	5	24	4.8	20	5.5	8	6	10

Source: World Economic Forum, Global Competitiveness Report, 2015–16.

education, 69th overall education system, 112th in maths and science, and 76th in Internet access. Nevertheless, the country ranked lower than India, Indonesia, China, Malaysia, South Korea and Hong Kong in the quality of primary education. It ranked lower than most of its neighbours in the quality of maths and science education and Internet access in schools. The country surpassed only Cambodia, Laos and Thailand in the former, and in Internet access Cambodia, Laos and India. The Philippines did relatively well in the ranking for overall quality of the education system, primarily because of the presence of a good number of reputable public and private higher education institutions, which have attracted students from all over the world.

Local and international perceptions regarding the quality of the education system in the country are generally mixed. This can be explained by glaring differences in the quality of schools, leading to a "hierarchy" catering to various income classes (see HDN 2000). On the one hand, there are a few high-quality schools at all levels with rigorous entry and retention standards where the children of better-off families go, not only because they can afford to but also because they are better prepared academically to qualify for entry. These consist of private schools run by religious orders or the Filipino-Chinese community, international schools that originally catered to the children of expatriates, government-funded science or laboratory schools at the secondary level, and one or two state universities.

On the other hand, the children of low-income families are relegated to the regular public school system, where the quality of education is low, or to private for-profit non-sectarian schools where costs are lower than that of the high-quality private schools but where standards are also low. Children of poor families cannot afford the cost of private elementary schools with high standards, and are forced to enrol in public elementary schools, most of which provide low-quality education. Because of their weak foundation in primary education, they fail to qualify for scholarships in private high schools or in public science or laboratory schools that offer better quality education. Ultimately, only a handful will ever qualify for higher education, even in a public university.

A good indication of the poor quality of public elementary and secondary schools is the average scores of students in National

Achievement Tests. While these have vastly improved in recent years, as shown in Table 4.11, average scores overall were 69 per cent for grade 6 students and 51 per cent for fourth-year high school students. This is still below the 75 per cent target of the government, especially at the secondary level, where apparently the quality of education is even poorer. Of greater concern are the low average achievement scores of high school students in mathematics, science and critical thinking, where the average scores were 47 per cent, 41 per cent and 39 per cent, respectively, as shown in Table 4.12.

TABLE 4.11
National Achievement Test, Mean Percentage Score,
Elementary and Secondary, SY 2005–6 to SY 2012–13

	2005–6	2006–7	2007–8	2008–9	2009–10	2010–11	2011–12	2012–13
Grade 6	54.5	60.2	64.8	65.6	68	68.1	66.8	68.9
Year 4	47	46.6	49.3	46.7	45.6	47.9	48.9	51.4

Source: UNESCO 2015.

TABLE 4.12
National Achievement Test, Mean Percentage Score,
by Subject, SY 2012–13

	Filipino	Math	English	Science	Hekasi Araling Panlipunan	Critical Thinking	Overall Test
Grade 6	72.4	69	67.1	65.7	70.1		68.9
Year 4	58	46.8	54	41.4	60.2	39.1	51.4

Source: UNESCO 2015.

The same can be observed of the quality of technical and vocational education institutions (TVEIs). Compared to other countries at similar levels of development, enrolment in TVEIs is fairly large for the Philippines. There are over 4,500 TVEIs in the country, 60 per cent of which are private. The delivery network consists of school-based public and private higher education institutions, industry-based training centres, NGO-based training centres, training centres of local government units, and training centres directly supervised by TESDA. Careful analysis reveals that the government continues to account for a significant source of funding for TVET (World Bank 2010).

The generally low quality of TVEIs is evident in the low employability of graduates (only 65 per cent in 2013). Dropout rates are high, particularly in medium and long-term courses. Only 60 per cent of assessed students eventually get TESDA certification for competency based on industry standards upon completion of their training (World Bank 2010). The low quality of training provided by TVEIs is more pronounced in private institutions and is associated with the lack of qualifications of trainers and the inadequacy of equipment and facilities (World Bank 2010). The relevance of technical and vocation education is encumbered by the limited or restricted range of course offerings and the use of outdated or low-quality equipment that is insufficient to familiarize students with new technologies used in the workplace.

The country has a sizable higher education system consisting of over 1800 higher education institutions, the majority of which are private institutions (88 per cent). The rest are public institutions funded by the national government, state universities and colleges, local government units, and local universities and colleges. Nevertheless, private institutes account for only 57 per cent of students, while the other 47 per cent are enrolled in public institutes of higher education. Most of these institutes, public or private, provide education of inferior quality. An indication of the poor quality of most institutes of higher education is the fact that only three are on the list of the top five hundred universities in the world (albeit with low rankings). Another gauge of quality is performance in professional licensure examinations, where the overall average passing rate is 35 per cent (UNESCO 2009). Poor quality is also evident in the persistently high unemployment of college graduates in the face of severe shortages of skilled workers reported by industry.

Quality is poor in many private colleges primarily because most students cannot afford quality education, which is expensive, so that the market responds by offering cheap but lower quality higher education. The poor quality of the basic education has also forced higher education institutes to lower standards. For private institutes, the lack of competition provides little incentive for schools to raise quality. On the other hand, the few good schools that offer quality education exercise so much market power that they have little incentive to lower tuition fees. To a large extent, the market power enjoyed by these schools arises from restrictions on the entry of foreign universities.

The proliferation of public institutes of education — 110 state universities/colleges and 77 local universities/colleges — which depend almost entirely on government subsidies for their operation, has been achieved at the cost of quality. Government colleges and universities were established to provide access for poor and other disadvantaged students to affordable high quality education, but their unbridled expansion spread resources thinly, resulting in lower per pupil spending and education of an inferior quality.

The Philippines has, in recent years, adopted key policy reforms to improve the quality of education. Each year, since 2010, it has been increasing the education budget to close input gaps in basic education. The DepEd has over the last four years effectively used its increased budgetary allocation to eliminate the perennial shortage of classrooms, textbooks and seats and to reduce pupil–teacher ratios to more acceptable levels. However, congestion remains a problem, particularly in cities with large populations such as the National Capital Region, where schools try to overcome shortages of classrooms and teachers by dividing class hours into two shifts (6 a.m. to noon and noon to 6 p.m.) and by converting corridors, libraries, laboratories and offices into classrooms. A more determined effort by DepEd to spend its budget allocation efficiently and quickly and improve its absorptive capacity could help alleviate the problem. However, heavy in-migration to large cities will continue to challenge government efforts to reduce congestion in the public school system.

The passage of the Enhanced Basic Education Act of 2013 (K to 12), which expanded the basic education cycle from 10 to 13 years (1 year of kindergarten, 6 years of primary school, 4 years of junior high school and 2 years of senior high school), together with reforms in the curriculum for grades 1 to 10, is expected to considerably improve the quality of basic education, raise it to international standards, and make graduates more globally competitive. However, the addition of three more years to the basic education cycle will exert tremendous pressure on the resources of government and consequently may undermine other interventions to raise quality.

To promote quality and relevance in the TVET subsector, TESDA adopted two basic approaches. First, all TVEIs are required to register their courses with TESDA to ensure compliance with minimum requirements in curricula, faculty and staff qualifications, facilities and equipment prior to accreditation to conduct the programme. TESDA also puts the programme through a compliance audit. These training regulations were promulgated in collaboration with industry. Secondly, TESDA develops competency standards for middle-level skills, which it uses to assess and certify the qualifications of workers. The assessment process seeks to determine whether a TVEI graduate meets predefined competency standards. These competency standards were developed with the participation of private sector stakeholders. There is a problem, however, with TESDA being the regulator and at the same time a provider of technical and vocational education. This situation distracts the agency from its main regulatory function and introduces a conflict of interest that may undermine efforts by TESDA to raise and strictly enforce standards to improve quality.

The principal strategy of CHED to promote quality is by accrediting programmes offered by each higher education institute and through incentive programmes such as the Center for Excellence and the Center for Development that reward departments and colleges, public and private, identified as models of excellence in particular disciplines. CHED has recently shifted its strategy from input-based accreditation to evaluations based primarily on learning outcomes or competencies. It is also shifting attention to improving the quality and relevance of state and local universities and colleges, with plans to limit their number and growth, closing programmes that are undersubscribed and duplicative, increasing support for the graduate studies of faculty, and by concentrating public resources in only a few public universities that have the potential to be globally competitive. The issue of quality remains also a challenge for many private institutes, however, and the continuing effort of CHED to control tuition fee increases may promote access by making a college education more affordable. But it may also severely constrain private initiatives to promote quality.

Education Less Responsive to Industry's Needs

Today's economies are becoming increasingly globalized, knowledge-based, technology driven and characterized by rapid change, so much so that it is almost impossible to predict what the jobs of tomorrow will look like (World Economic Forum 2015). The corresponding need to continuously retrain workers has shifted attention to the creation of a flexible workforce with the capacity for lifelong learning and the ability to quickly learn new ways of doing things. The new challenge faced by the education sector at all levels is to teach the future workforce how to learn. This means greater emphasis on developing skills associated with learning such as critical thinking and problem-solving skills, communication skills, research skills, and collaborative skills or the ability to work and learn together in teams. Rather than being learner-centred and transformative, with a focus on developing the ability of students to learn on their own, most educational institutions are still predominantly teacher-centred and rote-based; that is, students are trained to memorize information transmitted to them by teachers.

Employer surveys consistently point to the mismatch between the required qualifications and the competencies of Filipino graduates (World Bank 2010). Specifically, they complain of weaknesses in the non-cognitive, generic, or "life" skills of new hires consisting of critical and creative thinking, problem-solving and communication, organization and leadership skills. They have also identified the lack of job-specific skills of new hires as a major concern, an indication of the weak linkage between industry and academe during the period when students are still in the process of acquiring an education.

The demand for higher-level skills — that is, those requiring post-secondary education — has been growing over time to the extent that skill gaps in the Philippines have started to emerge (World Bank 2010). There are indications that the lack of skills might act as a constraint to rapid growth. Evidence of the growing skills gap is the increasing wage premiums for workers with tertiary education. This growing demand and shortage of skills, however, comes primarily from the service sector — in particular, tourism, transportation and communications, finance, insurance, real estate, and business services — all of which are experiencing concurrent increases in wage premiums and skill shares.

Technical and vocational education (TVE) also has the potential to address the issue of relevance of the education system to industry's needs. The K to 12 basic education programme will offer a tech-vocational track at the junior and senior high school levels to equip students with relevant skills that will make them employable. Implementing this is a formidable challenge, however, in terms of mustering the resources needed to provide the necessary tools, equipment, laboratories, workshops and qualified instructors for the technical and vocational subjects to be offered in all public high schools.

On the whole, despite significant changes in recent years, the TVE system in the country is still not completely effective in producing graduates with competencies aligned with the requirements of the labour market. This is due primarily to the weak linkages of TVE to industry and workplace training.

Education System Less Effective in Generating Technology and Innovation

With rising wages and rapid technological change, it has become imperative for the Philippines to move up the value chain in global production networks by absorbing and applying advances in global technology (ADB 2014c). This will require an economy where rising productivity is increasingly driven by the application of new knowledge and innovation in the production of goods and services. By becoming a knowledge-based economy, the country can overcome the so-called middle-income trap[11] and achieve higher rates of sustained economic growth into the future. Ideas and technical skills play an important role in the formation of a knowledge-based economy. Hence the presence of a highly educated and skilled workforce is critical.

Table 4.13 compares the country's ranking relative to selected Asian countries in the application of knowledge to the economy and the capacity for innovation based on the 2015–16 Global Competitiveness Report of the World Economic Forum. The country ranks higher than Cambodia, Laos, Vietnam and India in terms of the adoption of new technology and ICT usage. However, it is behind the other ASEAN

TABLE 4.13
Ranking of Selected Asian Countries in Technological Innovation

Economy	Technological Adoption	ICT Use	Capacity for Innovation	Quality of Scientific Research Institutions	University–Industry Collaboration in R&D	Availability of Scientists and Engineers
Cambodia	85	107	113	122	114	127
Laos	100	120	89	103	76	129
India	102	121	50	45	50	49
Vietnam	112	73	81	95	92	75
Philippines	57	74	33	69	55	67
Indonesia	51	95	30	41	30	34
Thailand	53	64	54	53	45	47
China	79	76	49	42	32	36
Malaysia	19	63	7	20	12	5
Rep. of Korea	37	22	24	27	26	40
Hong Kong, China	14	7	29	29	28	41

*Ranking among 140 Countries.
Source: World Economic Forum, Global Competitiveness Report, 2015–16.

member states and East Asian countries in these areas. It also ranked high in the capacity or potential for innovation. However, in the quality of its scientific research institutions, university–industry collaboration in research and development (R&D) and availability of scientists and engineers, the country was rated low, lower than India and Indonesia and way behind Thailand, China, Malaysia and the Republic of Korea. Only a handful of the country's universities are research-oriented and provide graduate-level education. With a few exceptions, academe–industry research collaboration is weak due to mistrust between them. Universities tend to view collaboration as having little to contribute in terms of publication, prestige or patents, while industry prefers less complicated options such as consultancy arrangements to direct collaborative relationships with universities, which tend to have competing priorities, unrealistic revenue expecta-tions and cumbersome administrative procedures (STRIDE 2014). The quality of many of the country's research institutions is not rated highly and the country has a very shallow pool of scientist and engineers with advanced degrees.

The dearth of science and technology (S&T) manpower is rooted in the poor quality of basic education, which hinders the development among students of an aptitude for the sciences and mathematics. As pointed out earlier, average scores in maths and science in the National Achievement Test are exceedingly low. According to the Department of Science and Technology, the majority of science teachers do not have the qualifications to teach these courses. These include 73 per cent of physics teachers and 66 per cent of chemistry teachers (ADB 2014a). The lack of qualified teachers is exacerbated by inadequacies in teaching materials, laboratory facilities and equipment. In particular, more resources will need to be directed to improve learning outcomes in mathematics and the sciences by addressing deficiencies in instruc-tional equipment and laboratories and the acute lack of qualified maths and science teachers. In school year 2012–13, around 27 per cent of DepEd junior high schools faced shortages of mathematics teachers, while almost 80 per cent lacked qualified instructors in biology, chemistry and physics (ADB 2014b).

Unless subsidized, science programmes are not popular choices among students entering college because they tend to be more costly, particularly in comparison with business and liberal arts programmes, and because future job prospects are uncertain given the perceived lack of domestic demand for science, technology, engineering and maths graduates. Lack of opportunities for better paying jobs in the local market is evidenced by the underemployment and continuing outmigration of many skilled workers. According to the Philippine Overseas Employment Administration, the number of scientists and engineers that left the country increased from 10,000 in 1998 to around 25,000 in 2009.

Another reason why the domestic supply of S&T graduates is low is because of a vicious cycle wherein the lack of high technology industries constrains the demand for skilled manpower, while the lack of skilled manpower in turn prevents the growth of high technology industries. In effect, S&T manpower and high technology industries are complementary goods — one cannot exist without the other — a situation that often leads to market failure. This cycle can be broken through government intervention in the form of much higher levels of government spending on R&D to jumpstart the growth in demand for S&T graduates. Once an adequate pool of S&T manpower is established, private investments in high technology industries are bound to increase. This, however, will also require serious efforts to eliminate restrictions and promote a favourable climate for foreign investment in the country.

Scientific research is often funded by government grants. Most of these grants are directed to state colleges and universities, and not necessarily to the most deserving, which includes some reputable research institutes based in private universities. This bias against allocating funds to private universities, which are perceived to be in a better position to generate their own funds, may work against efforts to improve research quality, by reducing the incentive of both public and private universities to compete for government funds by building a reputation for producing solid research.

Low Demand and Productive Use of Human Capital Resources

Because of weak domestic demand, the Philippines' endowment of human capital remains severely underutilized, with persistent unemployment rates higher for high school and college graduates than for those with only an elementary education, many of whom are able to secure jobs in primary occupations in agriculture and low-productivity services.

On the other hand, growth in the demand for skilled workers in the industry sector has been sluggish. A good indication of declining demand for semi-skilled workers is the declining wage premiums for those with secondary and post-secondary technical and vocational education in industry, particularly in manufacturing (World Bank 2010). This is due to the fact that manufacturing growth remained stagnant for three decades, although it has started to pick up recently. Furthermore, the country has only a few capital-intensive, high technology industries needing educated workers with middle-level and higher-level technical skills.

The resurgence of manufacturing growth is expected to continue with a more stable macroeconomic environment and the effort to reduce corruption and address critical infrastructure bottlenecks through public–private partnerships. Challenges remain, particularly in simplifying business regulations, attaining energy security, paring down the negative list for foreign direct investment (FDI) and in providing the manufacturing sector with a workforce armed with the appropriate skills. After all, the slow growth of the manufacturing sector in the past, which translated to weak demand for high-level skills, was due in part to the low quality of the workforce (World Bank 2014).

Labour market regulations may also have an adverse impact on investment and, consequently, on the demand for labour, whether skilled or unskilled. The increasing integration of local markets into the international economy and the intense competition that it entails has fuelled calls for greater labour flexibility through the liberalization of labour market regulations.[12] This is believed to enable firms to adjust to rapidly changing conditions in order to remain viable and competitive.

The World Economic Forum (2015) cites some of the other benefits from greater labour market flexibility. For one, flexible labour markets promote productivity by allowing the reallocation of labour to its most productive use. It allows workers to shift from declining to emerging industries. As technology advances, firms that would like to upgrade technologically will have to reduce their workforce. High firing and redundancy costs will discourage firms from adopting labour-saving innovations, which will slow down the adoption of new technologies. But restrictive labour laws in the country may also have a negative impact on training. In an analysis of firm-level data across several developing countries, Almeida and Aterido (2008) found that labour laws that impose higher firing costs to increase the protection of regular employees promote the adoption of temporary contracts, which in turn reduce the incentive of firms to invest in the human capital of their workers through training. Because of the temporary nature of employment, contractual employees are unlikely to be trained, because firms will not be able to recover the costs of the training.

Business perceptions of the international standing of the Philippines relative to its neighbours with regard to labour market flexibility are shown in Table 4.14. Business executives based in the Philippines considered restrictive labour regulations a major problem, ranking it 7th among the 16 most problematic factors for doing business in the country. This was significantly higher than the importance given this factor by executives of most of the other countries in the table, including the socialist countries of China and Vietnam, who ranked this concern 12th and 13th, respectively. On the other hand, the country scored better on cooperation in labour–employer relations. It was also considered to be more flexible with regard to wage determination and in terms of the alignment of pay with worker productivity. However, the information from the table also suggests that there is less flexibility in the hiring and firing of workers and that terminating redundant workers is considered to be quite costly in the country.

A World Bank (2013) study, based primarily on an enterprise survey, concludes that although Philippine labour regulations are not the principal impediment to economic growth and employment generation, they impose substantial costs on some firms, and have contributed to the decline of the manufacturing sector. The study finds that the country's high cost of hiring and firing relative to its neighbours is associated with lower FDI inflows. Large firms are most affected by restrictive labour regulations compared to MSMEs, many of which are unregistered, informal and better able to evade inspection. High informality is the consequence of the high cost of doing business, which, aside from corruption and red tape, includes

TABLE 4.14
Ranking by Labour Market Efficiency, Selected Asian Countries

Economy	Restrictive Labour Regulations*	Cooperation in Labour–Employer Relations	Flexibility of Wage Determination	Hiring and Firing Practices	Redundancy Costs	Pay and Productivity
Cambodia	15	76	107	22	87	57
Laos	10	38	30	50	132	16
India	13	86	120	25	70	47
Vietnam	13	71	67	44	108	45
Philippines	7	26	96	74	117	19
Indonesia	15	49	112	34	135	33
Thailand	12	34	111	23	129	53
China	12	62	73	17	117	20
Malaysia	11	11	31	6	107	5
Rep. of Korea	3	132	66	115	117	24
Hong Kong, China	5	12	3	1	14	2

Note: *Ranking of "restrictive labour regulations" among sixteen of the most problematic factors for doing business in the country.
Source: World Economic Forum, *Global Competitiveness Report, 2015–16.*

rigid labour regulations. The same study finds that minimum wages have resulted in lower employment in manufacturing. A 10 per cent increase in the real minimum wage reduces manufacturing employment by 3 per cent.

The big concern of many companies in the Philippines is the high costs associated with terminating an employee. Although the severance pay is not high by international standards, termination costs tend to be higher in practice because of the long and tedious process involved in dismissing an employee, especially when it is legally challenged by the latter. Under the Labor Code, termination for cause must be justified by the employer, but they must follow prescribed procedures and processes that are time-consuming and costly. The aim of these procedures is to promote job security. The result, however, is less job stability, as many employers try to get around the restrictions by avoiding regularizing their employees through subcontracting arrangements and the use of short-term fixed contracts in the employment relationship.

IV. Moving Forward in Education on a Faster Track

The reforms undertaken by the present administration in the education sector have laid the foundations for the building of a world-class education system. What is needed now is to sustain the momentum of reform and move it forward on a faster track in order for the country to realize its overall vision of inclusive prosperity under Filipino 2040 within the next twenty-five years.

The overall vision is underpinned by the specific vision for the education sector, which is:

> an education system that provides access to every Filipino, who so desires and qualifies, to quality education at all levels; one that equips them with the knowledge and skills that enable them to lead productive lives; and one that is able to produce the skilled and flexible manpower needed by the nation to promote innovation and the growth of high productivity industries that are globally competitive.

The main findings of the report and the vision for the education subsector point to the following policy options:

Broadening Access, Especially by the Poor to Quality Education at All Levels

- The main objective of the basic education sector is to make it more accessible, particularly to poor families, and ensure that every child completes at least a high school education. Special attention should be given to localities that are disadvantaged by natural disasters, geography, high transportation costs, and peace and order problems.
- The best way to expand the access of the poor to quality basic education is through a more focused effort to raise the quality of public basic education. This can be combined with a concerted effort at the local government level to enforce the child truancy law.
- The conditional cash transfer programme of the government has been generally successful in increasing enrolment and reducing leavers. Targeting should be improved, coverage expanded and implementation bottlenecks eliminated, not only for the conditional cash transfer programme but for the scholarship programmes of the government as well.
- Equitable access by the poor to education can be broadened by increasing the coverage of means-tested scholarships. The more extensive use of vouchers and education service contracts to allow beneficiaries to choose which private schools to go to can also help foster competition among private schools, promote quality and reduce congestion in the public school system. However, poverty reduction must continue to be the main goal of these programmes, and, consequently, poor families the principal beneficiaries.
- The implementation of socialized tuition schemes in a few state universities and colleges was quite successful and can be replicated in all public colleges and universities. Because of market failure in educational loans and because the private returns to investments in higher education tend to be large, the establishment of a more extensive government subsidized student loan programme for higher education can be a viable alternative to scholarship grants to poor families.

Enhancing the Quality of Education at All Levels and Making it More Relevant to the Needs of a Rapidly Changing Global Economy

- While the DepEd has effectively used its increased budgetary allocation to substantially reduce the shortage of teachers, classrooms, textbooks and seats, it may need to shift its attention to providing other inputs to enhance the quality of basic education. Greater effort should now be devoted to improving the quality of teaching, particularly in maths and science courses, and addressing shortfalls in equipment and laboratories for these courses.

- K to 12 has the potential of increasing the quality of basic education. On the other hand, the addition of three more years to the basic education cycle will exert tremendous pressure on the limited resources of government, which may undermine other interventions to raise quality. With K to 12, the government may have to give priority in its budgetary allocations to basic education for some time. The national government may also need to intensify efforts to get the private sector and local government units to increase their support for education in their localities and to address bottlenecks in the spending of funds that have already been allocated for education. It will be essential to mobilize existing and new financial resources, particularly from private and voluntary sources.

- Compared to its Asian neighbours, current spending on education by the country is relatively low, at 2.3 per cent of GDP. The Philippine government should consider increasing this to at least 6 per cent of GDP, a magnitude more at par with that of its more progressive neighbours and consistent with international benchmarks.

- A longer-term solution to the continued increase in the population of students and, consequently, the increased demand for education inputs at all levels is the promotion of the widespread use of ICTs in the delivery of education services, especially in public schools. ICTs are likely to be the most important instrument for improving the quality and relevance of education. Blended learning or the combination of classroom instruction with distance learning through multimedia and the Internet can help ease the demand for classroom space, teachers and instructional materials and make the practice of two class shifts per day in basic education a more viable option. Educational games and interactive learning materials will make pedagogy more effective and transformational. The universal provision of ICT and affordable high-speed broadband connectivity is essential to making this possible.

- By fostering competition, the elimination of existing restrictions on foreign investments in education services at all levels can help improve the quality of education in the country, particularly at the tertiary level.

- An effective and high-quality tertiary education system can only be achieved by improving the quality of education at the basic level, particularly at the secondary level. To promote relevance, the focus should be on developing generic or soft skills and aptitude for science and technology at the secondary level.

- Only a few tertiary educational institutions in the country participate in international accreditation and ranking activities. In the case of basic education, in recent years the Philippines has also stopped participating in TIMMS (Trends in International Mathematics and Science Study). There is a need for more international benchmarking of the country's education institutions at all levels through participation in international assessments that will enable it to compare the quality of its institutions, students and workers with those of other countries.

- Education quality can be substantially improved through greater government support for efforts to enhance the quality assurance (QA) system of Philippine higher education institutes and TVEIs where assessment, recognition and accreditation is based primarily on educational outcomes and learning competencies. These competencies should not only meet national and industry standards in specific disciplines and professions but international standards as well. The national QA system should be benchmarked against international/regional QA frameworks.

- Greater relevance in the education system can be promoted by putting more emphasis on developing generic skills and the ability and desire of individuals to learn on their own. Academe and industry collaboration in curriculum design should be promoted. More technical and vocational training programmes should be aligned with workplace training and undertaken in partnership with industry. TESDA should continue to strengthen its efforts to set standards in cooperation with or validated by industry.

- Aside from incorporating technical and vocational skills in the curriculum for basic education, the relevance of education can be promoted further through a more extensive internship and apprenticeship programme built into the curricula at the secondary and tertiary levels. A review and possible amendments to the Apprenticeship Law to encourage firms to provide training to their employees may be in order.

- TESDA must continue with the effort to transfer the administration of its training centres to other agencies, particularly to the private sector and local government units, and concentrate on its oversight functions. It must focus its attention to increasing the quality of TVEIs through the implementation of a more effective accreditation programme, quality assurance systems and a more rigorous competency assessment and certification of technical and vocational education graduates.

Transforming the Education System into a More Effective Instrument for Technological Progress and Innovation

- Technological change and innovation can be promoted through a highly developed research culture and infrastructure. This will require more government support for R&D, the promotion of research collaboration among government, industry and the academe, increasing the pool of research-oriented PhDs in science and engineering, the protection of intellectual property rights, and the establishment of more effective mechanisms to facilitate entrepreneurship and the commercialization of new discoveries.

- Compared to its Asian neighbours, spending on research and development in the Philippines is relatively low, at only 0.09 per cent of GDP. The country will need to increase the share of public spending on S&T research and development to at least 1.5 per cent of GDP, a level that approximates spending on R&D by the country's more progressive neighbours such as Japan, Singapore and the Republic of Korea when they were middle-income countries starting out on the path to becoming knowledge-based economies.

- The government should continue and expand its current efforts to encourage the young to choose a career in science and technology through educational subsidies, by increasing support for public science high schools and expanding scholarships for courses in science and technology at the tertiary level. Higher government spending in R&D and the consequent upsurge in research activity will increase the demand for and consequently enlarge the pool of highly skilled S&T graduates.

- Efforts and resources should concentrate on developing a core of higher education institutions and research centres — public and private — with the greatest potential for becoming world-class centres for excellence in science, technology and engineering research. Forging linkages with world leading universities and research institutes is a key strategy for boosting the quality of local research. To further promote quality research, the allocation of government grants for research and development should be competitive and based on proven competence or the track record of the institution in research.

- University–industry–government collaboration in R&D should be strengthened through the elimination of institutional bottlenecks for joint research, such as burdensome processes and administrative procedures, particularly in the case of public higher education and research institutions. The establishment of shared R&D facilities, science and engineering research hubs, and the co-location of public and corporate research institutions in industry clusters enabled countries such as Singapore to quickly transition to a knowledge-based economy (ADB 2014c). The protection of intellectual property should be resolutely pursued and enforced. Funding support should be made available for the acquisition of patents and the enforcement of intellectual property rights.

- Higher education institutes should not only have strong extension programmes and linkages with firms for the transfer of technology but should also be centres for the assimilation of rapidly growing global knowledge, their adaption to local needs and conditions, and the creation of new technology. More students should be sent abroad to earn advanced degrees in engineering and the sciences. Student and faculty mobility should be promoted and more foreign and Filipino experts working abroad should be encouraged to return to the country to share their expertise.

• Industrial policy, taking primarily the form of subsidies to R&D in specific high impact sectors, should play a crucial role, and can be justified by the failure of private firms to spend enough on R&D, because the spillover effects of their technological breakthroughs on other firms and industries is highly significant. Examples of technologies with high spillover effects are robotics, biotechnology, alternative energy and ICT.

Increasing the Demand and Productive Use of Human Capital Resources

• The country must continue to address the need to increase the utilization of its human capital through policies that promote the faster growth of investments, domestic and foreign, in labour-absorbing, high skill and high technology industries. More effort should be exerted to further simplify business regulations, achieve energy security, reduce the negative list for FDI, and provide the manufacturing sector with a workforce armed with the appropriate skills.

• More efforts should also be exerted to make the country's labour laws less restrictive and allow greater flexibility by companies to adjust to changing economic conditions. More importantly, appropriate steps can be taken to bring together labour and capital to agree on policies that enable firms to be viable and competitive while protecting workers. The principle that should govern the discussions is that it is the main responsibility of government, not private companies, to ensure that proper safety nets are in place to protect workers and their families from the vagaries of globalization.

Acknowledgements

This research was made possible through the guidance and support provided by the Asian Development Bank and the National Economic and Development Authority. It benefitted greatly from the comments and suggestions of the members of the working group tasked to draft the various background papers for "Vision 2040: The Filipino". I am particularly indebted to Ramon Clarete of the University of the Philippines School of Economics and Sona Shrestha of the ADB for their substantial contributions to the improvement of the draft. All errors and omissions are mine alone.

Notes

1. See, for instance, Psacharopoulos and Patrinos (2004).
2. The latest is by Rufino (2015), who estimates a multinomial logit model that shows a significant and negative relationship between the education of the household head and the likelihood that a child 5–17 years of age is in school and not working. Albert et al. (2012) estimated a logit model that shows that children with more educated mothers are less likely to be out of school (OOSC), while the low education of the mother increases the probability that a child will drop out of school.
3. This view, known as endogenous growth theory, was first put forward by Romer (1990) and elaborated by Grossman and Helpman (1991), Barro and Sala-i-Martin (2004), and Acemoglu (2009), among others.
4. This is expected to considerably improve with the passage in 2012 of the Kindergarten Education Act, which made kindergarten education free, mandatory and compulsory for all children entering grade 1.
5. To reign in a growing budget deficit, the government reduced spending in most sectors, including education, in the early 2000s, so that from a peak of 2.9 per cent of GDP in 1998, spending for education fell to a low of 1.9 per cent of GDP in 2005. In the context of a growing school-age population, the drop in spending led to significant shortages in teachers, classrooms, furniture, textbook and other inputs, with adverse consequences on enrolment rates (see Asian Development Bank 2014a).
6. Over three quarters of service sector employment consists of low skill, low paying jobs such as petty trading and public transport (World Bank 2013).
7. Prior to the passage of the Kindergarten Law, some households delayed enrolment of their children in grade 1 until they were 7 years old, instead of the 6 years of age required by law. This raised the proportion of

children 6–15 years of age that were considered out of school. Under the Kindergarten Act, children who have reached the age of 5 are required to enrol for kindergarten.

8. See, for instance, Albert et al. (2012).
9. Most studies on child labour, including research on the Philippines, point to poverty as a major determinant of child labour. See, for instance, Villamil (2002) and Rufino (2015).
10. This phenomenon is quite pervasive, especially in developing economies, and is known in the literature as the added-worker effect.
11. The "middle-income trap" refers to the phenomenon wherein countries which have attained middle-income status in terms of per capita GDP are unable to reach (converge to) the income levels of high-income countries within a prescribed period of time based on historical averages. See Im and Rosenblatt (2013) for a survey of the literature.
12. See, for instance, Sicat (2004).

References

Acemoglu, D. *Introduction to Modern Economic Growth*. Princeton. NJ: Princeton University Press, 2009.

Asian Development Bank (ADB). "Program Expenditure and Financing Assessment". *Senior High School Support Program: Report and Recommendation of the President*. 2014a <http://www.adb.org/sites/default/files/linked-documents/45089-002-pef.pdf>.

———. "Summary Sector Assessment: Education". *Senior High School Support Program: Report and Recommendation of the President*. 2014b <http://www.adb.org/sites/default/files/linked-documents/45089-002-ssa.pdf>.

———. *Innovative Asia: Advancing the Knowledge-Based Economy, the Next Policy Agenda*. 2014c <http://www.adb.org/sites/default/files/publication/41752/innovative-asia-knowledge-based-economy.pdf>.

Albert, J.R.G., F.M.A. Quimba, A.P.E. Ramos, and J.P. Almeda. "Profile of Out-of-School-Children in the Philippines". PIDS discussion paper series no. 2012-01. Makati City: Philippine Institute of Development Studies, 2012.

Almeida, R.K., and A. Reyes. "The Incentives to Invest in Job Training: Do Strict Labor Codes Influence the Decision?" In *Social Protection and Labor*, SP Discussion Paper No. 0832. Washington, DC: World Bank, 2008.

Barro, R.J. "Human Capital and Economic Growth". In "Papers and Proceedings of the Hundred Thirteenth Annual Meeting of the American Economic Association". *American Economic Review* 91, no. 2 (2001): 12–17.

Barro, R.J., and Xavier Sala-i-Martin. *Economic Growth*, 2nd ed. Cambridge, MA: MIT Press, 2004.

David, C.C., and J.R.G. Albert. "How Has Basic Education in the Philippines Fared and What Else Needs to be Done?" Policy Notes no. 2015-08. Philippine Institute for Development Studies, 2015.

Fernando, G., and D. Rosenblatt. *Middle-Income Traps: A Conceptual and Empirical Survey*. Policy research working paper no. WPS 6594. 2013 <http://documents.worldbank.org/curated/en/2013/09/18220959/middle-income-traps-conceptual-empirical-survey>.

Grossman, G.M., and E. Helpman. *Innovation and Growth in the Global Economy*. Cambridge, MA. MIT Press, 1991.

Human Development Network. *Philippine Human Development Report*. Quezon City: Human Development Network (HDN) and the United Nations Development Program (UNDP), 2000.

National Statistics Office. "Statistical Tables". 2011 <https://psa.gov.ph/sites/default/files/attachments/hsd/article/APIS%202011_Statistical%20Tables%201%20to%2035.pdf>.

Psacharopoulos, G., and H.A. Patrinos. "Returns to Investment in Education: A Further Update". *Education Economics* 12, no. 2 (2004), 111–34.

Romer, P.M. "Endogenous Technical Change". *Journal of Political Economy* 98, no. 5 (1990): S71–102.

Rufino, C. "Joint Estimation of Filipino Child's Participation in Schooling and Employment and New Stylized Facts on the Philippine Child Labor Situation". *DLSU Business and Economics Review* 25, no. 1 (2015): 119–42.

Sen, A. "Radical Needs and Moderate Reforms". In *Perspectives on Modern South Asia: A Reader in Culture, History, and Representation*, edited by K. Visweswaran. Wiley-Blackwell, 1997.

Sicat, G.P. *Reforming the Philippine Labor Market*. University of the Philippines School of Economics Discussion Paper No. 0404. Quezon City: University of the Philippines, 2004.

STRIDE. *Philippines Innovation Ecosystem Assessment: Executive Summary*. United States Agency for International Development (USAID). 2014 <http://www.stride.org.ph/Project/1_Website/Design/Main_Layout/images/other/Executive%20Summary.pdf>.

Tan, E.A. "What's Wrong with Philippine Higher Education?" *Philippine Review of Economics* 48, no. 1 (2011): 147–84.

UNESCO. *Education for All 2015 National Review Report: Philippines*. 2015 <http://unesdoc.unesco.org/images/0023/002303/230331e.pdf>.

World Bank. *Philippine Skills Report: Skills for the Labor Market in the Philippines*. 2010 <http://siteresources.worldbank.org/EASTASIAPACIFICEXT/Resources/226300-1279680449418/HigherEd_PhilippinesSkillsReport.pdf>.

———. *Philippine Development Report: Creating More and Better Jobs*. 2013 <http://www-wds.worldbank.org/external/default/WDSContentServer/WDSP/IB/2014/01/02/000461832_20140102180252/Rendered/PDF/ACS58420WP0P120Box0382112B00PUBLIC0.pdf>.

5

Universal Health Coverage, Health Security and Resilient Health Systems[1]

Eduardo Banzon and Beverly Lorraine Ho

No one wants to be sick. Yet, those who fall ill are punished with the high cost of accessing healthcare. While one cannot totally prevent it, conditions where an individual is born, grows, works, lives and ages contribute to the likelihood of falling ill. For example, population groups residing near development projects are unnecessarily exposed to hazards, thus increasing their vulnerability. Residents of disaster-prone areas cannot rely on their health system in the aftermath of a shock, even after a few years, for them to live the way they used to.

This chapter argues why the government should sustain its ongoing investments in health, and proposes where and how these investments should be channelled in order to ensure that (1) the system is designed as one which promotes health or makes it easy for people to *choose* the healthier option; (2) those who fall sick are not driven to impoverishment; and (3) the system remains dependable in the event of shocks/disasters.

Box 5.1. A Typical Case of a Filipino Family in 2016

Jose and Alicia, are minimum wage earners. They live in Cavite but work in a factory in Mandaluyong City, Metro Manila. Commuting to work means losing four hours daily to travel. Because they are home late and have to leave early the next day, they are unable to prepare lunch. They are *suki* (frequent patrons) to Aling Nene's ration consisting of one-fourth serving of viand and three-fourth serving of rice — food with little nutritional value and that is often salty. At work they are exposed to high heat, with the factory having little ventilation.

One day Jose had a bad case of diarrhoea requiring admission. They chose to go to the nearest government hospital. Since Jose, a PhilHealth insurance member, was confined in the "charity ward", where one nurse takes care of eighteen patients simultaneously, Alicia had to stay as a watcher to make sure all of Jose's needs were being met. Moreover, the attending physician tasked Alicia to purchase medicines in a drug outlet a few kilometres away, as the hospital pharmacy had run out of stock.

After three days in the hospital, both Jose and Alicia had lost three days of work and had spent most of their savings. Jose will also need to start allocating a portion of his salary for maintenance medications.

A vision for the state of Filipinos' health in the next twenty-five years may be articulated as follows:

By 2040, all Filipinos shall enjoy longer and healthier lives, with minimal socio-economic and geographic disparities in health status, comparable to residents of high-income countries. Filipinos are empowered and active participants in healthcare and are secure in the knowledge that accessing quality health services does not depend on one's capacity to pay and will not lead to impoverishment, that the system is designed to minimize vulnerabilities to communicable disease threats and lifestyle risks, and that the health system remains dependable in times of disaster.

The next sections build the case that health remains a sound investment for the country and provides a concise overview of the

Philippine health system. Health system performance is rated using three indicators. The chapter then summarizes the gains from recent reforms. The last section describes two possible scenarios for the health system — one simply the continuation of and incremental improvement to the status quo, and the other requiring system-wide structural reform.

I. Investing in Health

As countries move to sustain inclusive growth that reduces poverty and inequities, health is not only a cornerstone for which other reforms can be built on but is also a potential threat that can hold back economic development and inclusive growth.

Various studies substantiate the strong, positive relationship between health (measured in terms of increase in life expectancy, decrease in disease prevalence or malnutrition, or reduction in mortality) and economic growth (measured in terms of GDP per capita). Nobel laureate in economics Robert W. Fogel found that improvements in the population's food consumption accounted for between a third and a half of England's economic growth over the past two hundred years (Mexican Commission for Macroeconomics in Health 2004). Mayer (2001) concluded that health was responsible for approximately a third of long-term economic growth in Mexico from 1970 to 1995. For Latin America and the Caribbean, health, measured as the probability of surviving to the next age group, has a strong long-term relationship with growth. Cross-country macroeconomic studies have also shown the following:

1. An increase in life expectancy from 50 to 70 years would raise the economic growth rate by 1.4 percentage points per year (Barro 1996);
2. One extra year of life expectancy raises steady-state GDP per capita by about 4 per cent (Bloom et al. 2004);
3. A 10 per cent decrease in malaria is associated with increased annual growth of 0.3 per cent (Gallup and Sachs 2001); and
4. Malnutrition causes a decrease in the annual GDP per capita growth worldwide of between 0.23 per cent and 4.7 per cent (Arcand 2001).

There are several mechanisms linking population health with economic performance. First, better health means higher labour productivity (i.e., less absenteeism) (Bloom, Canning and Jamison 2004). Second, better health alters decision space for families and provides the incentive to save. Longer life spans make retirement a realistic prospect and fewer children an option, since people will have a high probability of reaching adulthood, thereby allowing them to invest more per child, or save (Jamison et al. 2006). Third, better health can lead to relative workforce size expansion, as longer life expectancies mean extended time in the workforce, while a decreasing infant mortality rate creates a "baby boom" cohort and contributes to future workforce size.

There is a growing body of evidence indicating that better health was both a precedent and catalyst for the sustained high rates of economic growth in East Asia from 1960 to 1990 (Bloom, Canning and Jamison 2004). Conversely, illnesses have adverse economic consequences. The severe acute respiratory syndrome (SARS) outbreak in 2003 hit the People's Republic of China's tourism sector and this resulted in GDP of 1–2 percentage points lower than had the outbreak not occurred (Hai et al. 2004). The Ebola outbreak is projected to have cost Sierra Leone and Liberia up to 8.9 per cent and 12 per cent of their GDPs, respectively, in 2015 (Bausch and Schwartz 2014). These outbreaks would likely lead to "destabilization, political unrest, civil disorder" (Price-Smith 2004), with the related economic costs.

At the individual level, a health system that relies on out-of-pocket payments (OOP) or direct payments (i.e., payments made at the point of service in exchange for services rendered, procedures done or medicines dispensed [World Health Report 2010]) with negligible safety nets can prevent the upward mobility of poor families and impoverish non-poor families. Moreover, OOPs deter and delay people from using health services, potentially causing heavier future financial strain from worsening health conditions, thus exacerbating inequities. A predominantly OOP-financed system is unable to capitalize on the purchasing power of prepayments pooled from a hundred million Filipinos to drive down costs and reduce inefficiencies.

II. Current Philippine Healthcare System

The passage of the Local Government Code of 1991 devolved and transferred the majority of the government health service delivery functions (i.e., implementing programmes and operating local government owned health facilities, such as provincial and municipal hospitals, rural health units and barangay health stations) to the local government units (LGUs). The Department of Health (DOH) retained control of specialized and regional hospitals and was mandated to focus on "organizing programs that will promote health, formulating solutions to emerging health situations, developing national plans, technical standards and guidelines on health, and regulating all health services and products" (Hartigan-Go, Valera, and Visperas 2013).

Two attached agencies help the DOH fulfil its primary function: the Food and Drug Administration (FDA) and Philippine Health Insurance Corporation (PhilHealth). The FDA regulates all health products/equipment (i.e., processed food, drugs, medical/radiation devices, cosmetics, household hazardous substances), while PhilHealth administers the National Health Insurance Program (NHIP). The establishment of PhilHealth signalled the start of the ongoing shift of the country's healthcare system from a budget-based, public service provision, supply-driven system (i.e., government money flows to healthcare facilities) to an output-oriented, demand-driven system (i.e., government money now following where the member goes) that is agnostic to the provider, whether public or private.

Currently, financing for health is mobilized through households and firms contributing through direct and indirect tax payments, health insurance premiums and OOP, complemented by government revenues from the lottery and casinos. Tax revenues then fund the budget of the DOH and other national agencies providing health services, LGU's Internal Revenue Allotments (IRA), or share of revenues from the national government, and national government subsidies for the health insurance coverage of the poor and other subsidized population. From the IRA, LGUs have the discretion to allot funds to health, thus contributing to significant variations in LGU health budgets. Health insurance premiums from households and firms and government subsidies are generally pooled in a publicly managed fund — PhilHealth — complemented and supplemented with smaller private funds such as private health insurance and health maintenance organizations (HMOs). See Figure 5.1.

FIGURE 5.1
Schematic Representation of Financial Flows

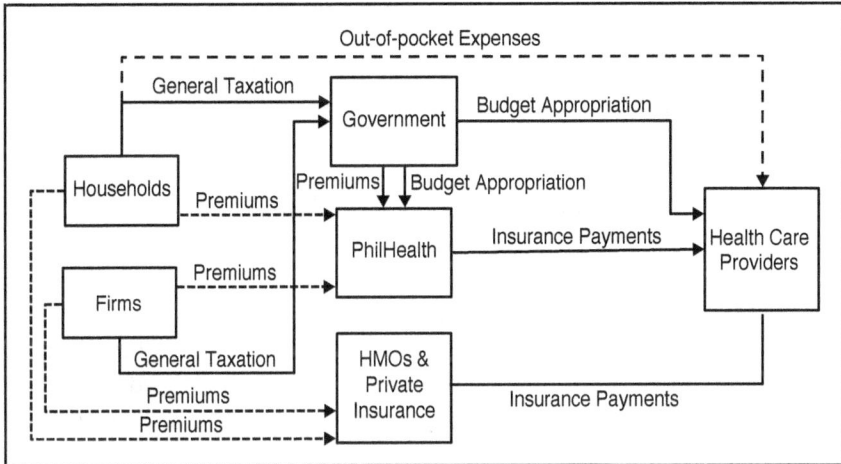

Source: Romualdez et al. 2011.

Private healthcare providers are compensated for their services through PhilHealth and private health insurance reimbursements, negotiated rates by HMOs and individual/household OOP, while government healthcare providers receive OOP, PhilHealth output-based reimbursements, and line item budgetary transfers from the DOH or LGU that pay for inputs that are not linked to outputs or performance.

Health insurance reimbursements are paid to healthcare providers through different mechanisms based on the service provided. For example, primary care services are paid at a per capita (household) rate, while inpatient, ambulatory surgery care and a number of outpatient services are paid in uniform case rates regardless of level of accommodation, healthcare provider skill or geographic location. The case rates are based on a fixed published fee schedule, with the remainder of the bill ("balance bill" or co-payment) traditionally uncapped or without a ceiling and expected to be shouldered by the patient, either through a supplementary health insurance or by OOP. Fortunately, since 2011, PhilHealth has mandated government hospitals to ensure "no balance billing or NBB" when providing care to government-subsidized poor PhilHealth members and dependents.

Healthcare services are delivered by a fragmented and mixed system of public and private providers, characterized by scarcity and inequitable distribution of healthcare capacities (Banzon et al. 2014). Patients can bypass primary care and directly seek secondary or tertiary level care. Coordination between the DOH and LGUs, and among LGUs, varies. Several municipalities continue to plan and function as isolated health systems. Market activity generally dictates where private facilities and professionals set up shop, especially since there is no clear national hospital/health facility distribution or zoning plan.

The poor oversight and weak regulation, as manifested by the absence of a hospital development plan, have resulted in business conglomerates buying out hospitals and pharmacies and consolidating them without clear government guidance as to how they contribute to national health objectives. This extends further to private medical clinics that only require LGU-issued business permits to operate. This has also contributed to confusion on the role of public hospitals, given the continued expansion of private rooms and wards, despite legal limitations to keep private beds at 10 per cent of total beds, thus raising some questions on resource allocation practices within public hospitals. Moreover, the majority of physicians in the private sector are independent free agents whom hospitals have difficulty regulating. These physicians manage their own outpatient clinics and own shares of or affiliate themselves with hospitals for higher-level care, thus creating an accountability gap wherein hospitals are unable to vouch for quality or implement professional fee ceilings. Meanwhile, salaried physicians in the public sector usually engage in dual practices, with the same private practice behaviour described above.

III. Health System Performance

The health system has many aspects; with health system performance often measured using several indicators. For the purpose of this chapter, macro-level indicators reflecting final outcomes of population health, financial protection, responsiveness and equity have been selected, with the intention of using them to track progress towards the vision for health by 2040. However, there is currently no available reliable baseline data for responsiveness. Indicators for clinical quality and appropriateness of care, effectiveness, productivity or efficiency are considered intermediate outcomes and will not be expounded further.

In measuring overall population health, gains in life expectancy have traditionally been cited as the leading indicator of improvement (NRC 2010). In recent years this has been replaced with Health or Disability

Adjusted Life Expectancy (HALE/DALE), a more comprehensive and nuanced indicator that measures both quantity and quality of life (WHO 2015). HALE/DALE is able to capture the current phenomenon where advances in healthcare allow people to live longer but are not able to restore people to full health and productivity. Studies have demonstrated a nearly perfect linear correlation between life expectancy and HALE/DALE, with an average difference of 7.1 years (WHO 2000). DALE estimates in 2013 show that the Philippines ranks poorly compared to its ASEAN counterparts, as shown in Table 5.1. Unfortunately, there are no disaggregated data based on income class in DALE.

From 1990 to 2010 there has been a gradual shift towards non-communicable or lifestyle diseases as the cause of the disability or disease burden. The overall top three risk factors are dietary risks, tobacco smoking, and high blood pressure (GBD 2013). Projections shown in Figure 5.2 illustrate that by 2040 the double burden of

TABLE 5.1
Disability-Adjusted Life Expectancy in Selected Countries, 1990 and 2013

Area/Country	1990		2013	
	Male population	Female population	Male population	Female population
Global	55.4	58.51	60.59	64.13
OECD	62.86	67.18	67.34	70.67
ASEAN	55.83	59.78	62.05	66.28
Brunei	65.11	67.12	68.8	70.97
Singapore	65.26	68.49	70.75	73.35
Cambodia	39.74	47.15	54.62	60.23
Indonesia	56.2	59.01	61.33	64.51
Laos	47.82	50.26	56.48	59.74
Malaysia	62.4	65.99	64.09	68.89
Myanmar	49.78	52.71	57.55	61.97
Philippines	54.96	62.28	58.76	64.59
Thailand	61.38	66.07	64.3	69.2
Vietnam	55.6	58.75	63.77	69.33

Note: OECD = Organization for Economic Co-operation and Development;
     ASEAN = Association of Southeast Asian Nations; Philippines ranks 8th of 10 ASEAN countries.
Source: Institute for Health Metrics and Evaluation, 2010.

FIGURE 5.2
Ranking of Burden of Disease, Selected Years

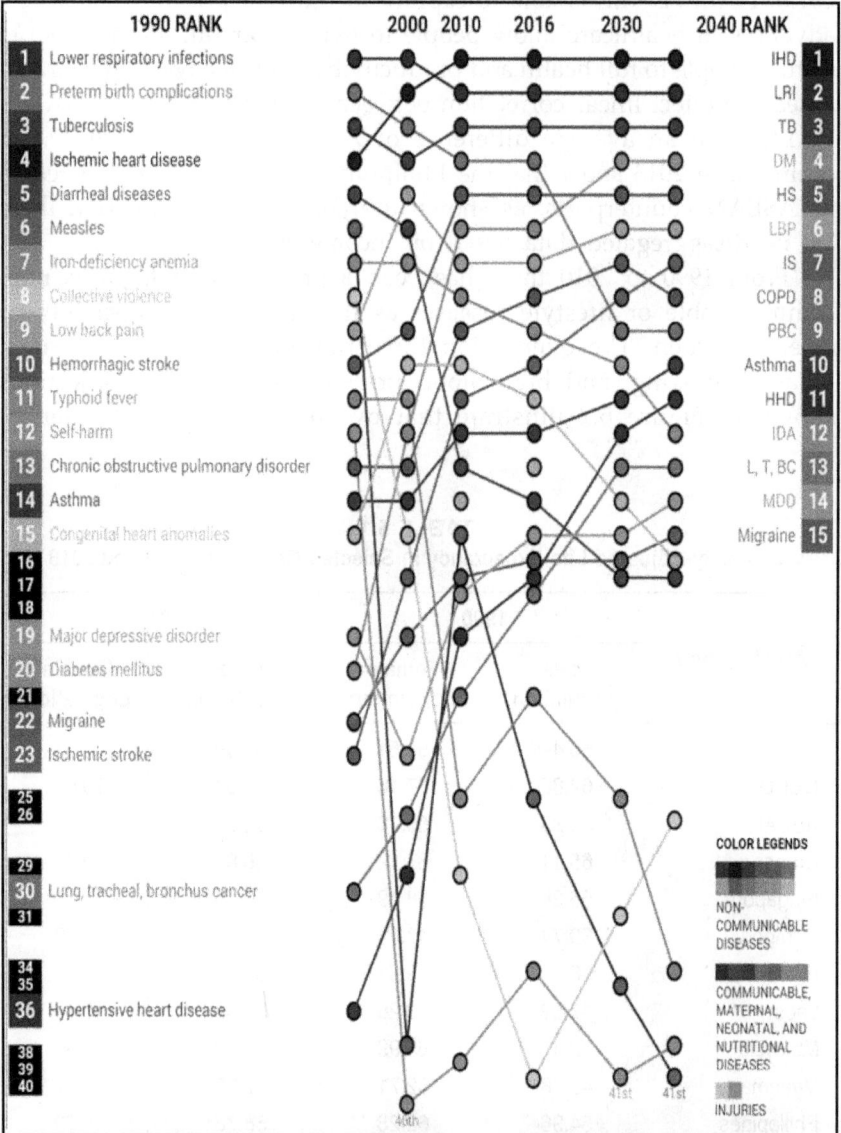

Notes: Data for 1990 and 2000 are from modelled point estimates by the Institute for Health Metrics and Evaluation (IHME), University of Washington. Data for 2016, 2030 and 2040 are based from 2013 IHME estimates, adjusted according to the age and sex structure of the Philippines during those years. Data for population projections are from the Philippine Statistics Authority and based on the 2010 Census of Population and Housing. Visualization by Nel Jason L. Haw.

communicable and non-communicable diseases will persist, but with the latter overtaking the former (Wong, Haw and Uy 2016).

Because of the complexity of collecting and processing data to arrive at a DALE estimate, the infant mortality rate (IMR), or the number of children for every thousand live births who die before their first birthday, would be an alternate indicator for population health. It is routinely collected but also regarded as a highly sensitive proxy measure of population health (Blaxter 1981; Robine 2003). High IMR is indicative of gaps in both access to and quality of maternal and child care, nutrition, water and sanitation — all determinants of child survival. From 1990 to 2015, significant progress has been made in reducing the IMR in the Philippines, but the rate of decline has been slow compared to ASEAN averages (see Figure 5.3).

Based on the national average of 23 per 1000 live births, the country currently ranks sixth best among ASEAN nations. Income, regional and rural–urban differences are glaring, with some approximating the levels found in high-income and others low-income countries (see Figure 5.4). This can, however, be taken to mean that the infrastructure and capacities are there, but not equitably distributed. More than half of these deaths occur in the neonatal period or the first twenty-eight days of life, suggesting the need for targeted and focused cost-effective antenatal and intrapartum interventions.

In terms of financial risk protection, keeping the share of private OOP low is important because financial catastrophe (i.e., paying more than 40 per cent of household income directly on healthcare after basic needs have been met) and impoverishment occur greatest in high OOP settings (Xu et al. 2003).

In the last decade, average OOP continued to increase (Figure 5.5), with medicines consistently the main driver despite increased central health government spending in absolute terms and on a per capita basis (Figure 5.6). Figure 5.7 shows that the incidence of catastrophic spending has increased from 2000 to 2012 for all income groups, translating roughly to 1.1 million people (Bredenkamp and Buisman 2015), but the number may even be an underestimate, as the poor, when sick, are not seeking care as much as the rich (see Figure 5.8). Using 2012 data, health OOP adds one percentage point to the poverty rate at the $1.25 poverty line, and 1.5 percentage points to the poverty rate at the $2 poverty line (Bredenkamp and Buisman 2015). When compared to other Asian countries, the country performs rather poorly (see Table 5.2).

FIGURE 5.3
Mortality Rate for the Philippines, ASEAN and OECD Countries, 2003, 2008 and 2013

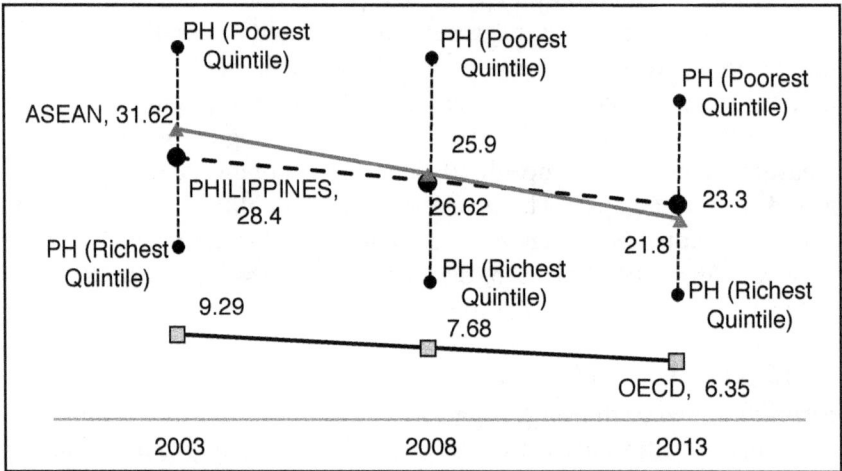

Note: ASEAN = Association of Southeast Asian Nations; OECD = Organisation for Economic Co-operation and Development.
Source: World Bank's World Development Indicators; and National Demographic and Health Survey, 2003.

FIGURE 5.4
Infant Mortality Rate by Region and Income Quintile in Selected Countries, 2013

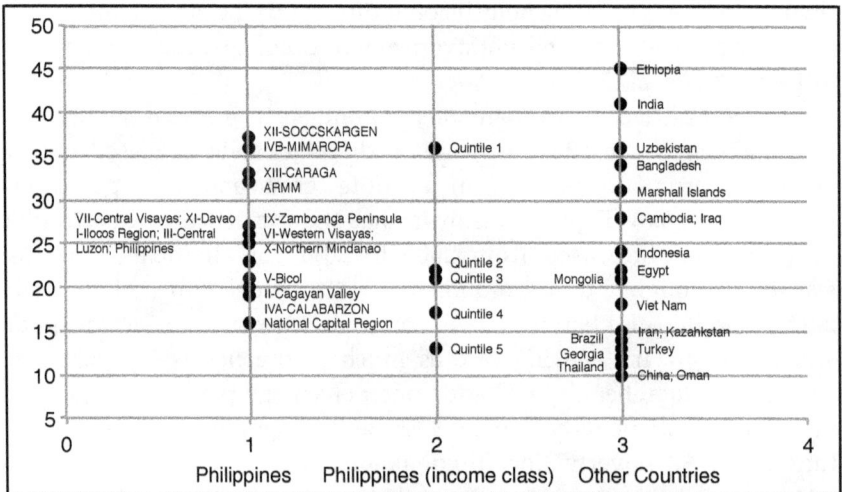

Source: World Bank's World Development Indicators and National Demographic Health Survey 2013.

FIGURE 5.5
Health Expenditure by Source of Funds, 1991–2013 (%)

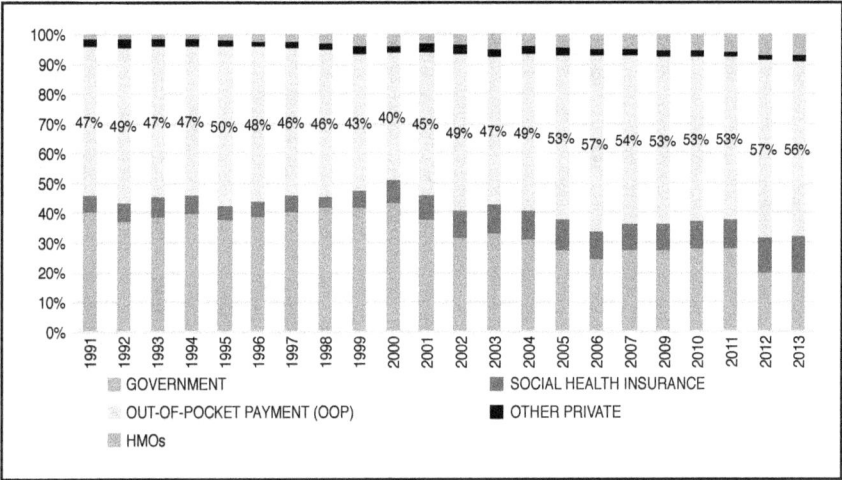

Source: National Health Accounts, Philippine Statistics Authority.

FIGURE 5.6
Budget of the Department of Health, 2007–14 (pesos)

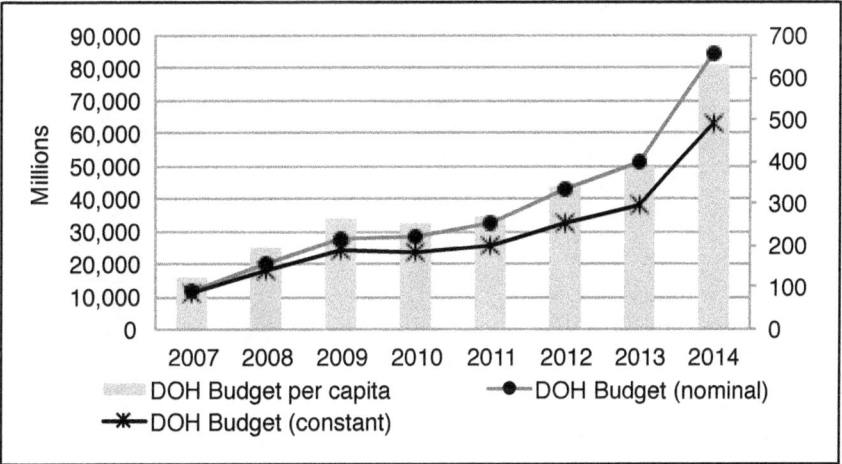

Source: Department of Health.

FIGURE 5.7
Proportion of Households by Income Quintile Incurring Catastrophic Payments,
Selected Years (%)

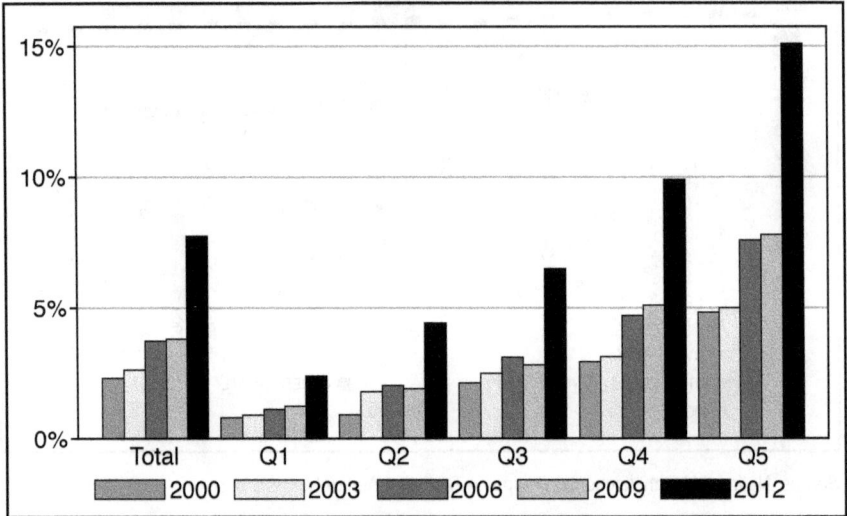

Source: Bredenkamp and Buisman 2015.

FIGURE 5.8
Proportion of Population by Socioeconomic Status Experiencing Illnesses and
Visiting a Health Facility, 2013 (%)

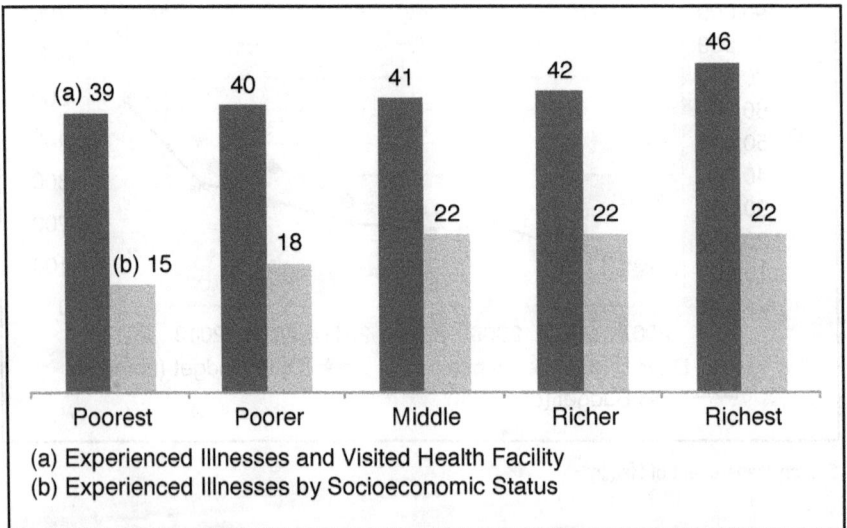

(a) Experienced Illnesses and Visited Health Facility
(b) Experienced Illnesses by Socioeconomic Status

Source: PSA (Philippine Statistics Authority) and ICF International 2014.

TABLE 5.2
Key Health Expenditure Indicators in Selected Countries, 2013

Area/Country	GDP per Capita (current $)	GDP per Capita (constant 2005 $)	Health Expenditure per Capita (current $)	Health Expenditure per Capita (PPP $)	Share of Health Expenditure in Total Government Expenditure (%)	Share of Out-of-Pocket Expenditure in Total Health Expenditure (%)
OECD	32,108.19	37,994.60	4,579.00	4,652.38	17.54	13.98
Brunei	41,344.04	25,490.29	973.56	1,811.61	7.42	7.94
Cambodia	1,090.12	748.78	75.76	228.71	7.73	59.74
Indonesia	3,491.93	1,853.81	106.63	293.30	6.63	45.81
Laos	1,759.78	818.25	32.41	95.20	3.46	39.99
Malaysia	10,933.49	7,373.99	423.43	938.29	5.88	36.11
Myanmar	1,203.84	...	14.40	36.66	1.50	68.20
Philippines	2,870.54	1,665.29	121.60	287.33	8.55	56.67
Singapore	56,286.80	38,087.89	2,507.43	3,578.05	12.46	56.79
Thailand	5,519.36	3,425.70	264.35	658.24	17.01	11.27
Vietnam	2,052.29	1,077.91	111.17	308.30	9.33	49.41

Notes: PPP = purchasing power parity; OECD = Organization for Economic Co-operation and Development.
Source: World Bank's World Development Indicators 2015.

Responsiveness is achieved when individuals' legitimate expectations regarding the non-health-enhancing aspects of the health
system are met (Silva n.d.). It encompasses dignity, confidentiality,
autonomy, prompt attention, quality of basic amenities, access to
social support networks during care, and choice of care provider.
Hence, responsiveness, which is measured against legitimate
expectations, is not to be confused with patient satisfaction, which
represents a complex mix of individually determined perceived
needs based on personal or societal experience. The last available
responsiveness data comes from a multi-country study which shows
that the Philippines has an above-average score of 6.51, ranking 8th
out of 35 selected countries (mean of 5.75, range 4.31–7.44) (de Silva
and Valentine n.d.).

IV. What Has Been Accomplished So Far and What Gaps Remain?

Over the years the Philippines undertook reforms to address rising
challenges in the health sector. However, what seems to be lacking
is a clearly articulated, aspirational and unified vision for the system,
without which overlaps and contradictions remain unresolved. As
referred to earlier, the establishment of the NHIP in 1995 signalled
the country's shift from a purely budget-financed and publicly
delivered system (supply/input driven) to one where government
funds and private prepayments flowed through patients, and private
providers complemented public providers (demand driven). Yet,
the shift was never completed, leaving the country straddling both
supply- and demand-driven systems and unable to fully reap the
benefits of either. This is manifested in the policies of the last
five years. The national government massively scaled up enrolment
of the bottom 40 per cent of the population en masse into PhilHealth
and made enrolment compulsory. Government healthcare facilities
were enhanced through the Health Facilities Enhancement Program
for the primary purpose of getting them accredited by PhilHealth.
Meanwhile, the DOH continued to support inputs for government
health facilities through significant budget support, expanded

programmes for access to medicine and the deployment of health workers and internally developed information and communications technology (ICT) solutions. There also remains a bias towards easily quantifiable inputs (medicines, human resource, facility upgrading, enrolment into insurance) rather than outputs (e.g., utilization) or outcomes (e.g., intermediate outcomes such as efficiency, quality, safety, and final outcomes such as health outcomes, financial protection and responsiveness) when monitoring and reporting supposed gains. These have, in turn, compromised the purchasing power of PhilHealth to extract efficiency and quality from healthcare providers, and have weakened accountability of government providers, particularly LGUs.

A. Governance

Nearly twenty-five years after the devolution of health services to LGUs, the DOH has yet to fully embrace its role of being an enabler rather than a direct provider of health services — that is to develop long-term strategies and detailed policy agenda, set standards and enforce regulations, capacitate LGUs to be the frontline providers, harness and align the private sector, work with the legislative body for key policies, raise the profile of health in other sectors to address social determinants, and promote inclusive policy discourse. A few examples illustrate these.

The DOH publishes the National Objectives for Health (NOH) during the start of every administration, but the NOH merely articulates targets and remains silent on priorities and strategies. A health financing strategy and human resource for health (HRH) master plan were prepared in 2011 and 2013, but the lack of formalized policies supporting these strategies and plans failed to ensure implementation or adherence. Similarly, programme-specific strategies and frameworks for disease control programmes do not include sections on engaging the private sector, despite it constituting almost 50 per cent of service delivery.

In terms of HRH, the more than two decades Doctors-to-the-Barrio programme and the similar subsequent programmes for nurses and midwives continue to be stop-gap measures for municipalities without doctors and inadequate numbers of nurses and midwives; all these without addressing the underlying causes, which include limitations on the share of the LGU budget for personnel services and the lack of sanctions and incentives for LGUs to recruit and maintain the appropriate HRH staffing.

In terms of drugs, the programmes for access to medicine have markedly reduced drug prices by as much as 80 per cent and have demonstrated a reliable supply chain and logistics. But no nationwide policy or infrastructure has been set up to systematically reduce drug prices in the market, despite medicines being significant drivers of OOPs and legal mandates permitting the government to set maximum drug retail prices and control retail and distribution monopolies that may lessen access to lower-priced medicines.

Various experiences of corporatized DOH hospitals and LGU-owned health economic enterprises have illustrated the benefits of fiscal and management autonomy, as can be seen in improvements in service delivery and appropriateness of referrals, although less in affording financial protection. However, minimal guidance has been put forward regarding the governance of government hospitals. DOH-managed hospitals continue to receive budgetary allocation without clarity on its role and difference from LGU-managed hospitals.

As to having a fair and transparent process for determining which publicly purchased health services and commodities the population is entitled to, only the Formulary Executive Committee is institutionalized to perform such a function for drugs, with no coordinative mechanism in place for the different government health funders — the DOH, PhilHealth, Philippine Charity and Sweepstakes Office (PCSO), Philippine Amusement and Gaming Corporation (PAGCOR) and LGUs — to agree on what to purchase. Efforts to incorporate health interventions and technology assessments are being initiated but are slowed by capacity constraints. The lack thereof has made the system vulnerable to strong lobby groups and stalled decisions on service coverage.

From 2010 to 2016, seven health-related laws had been enacted, but many other dated laws still need to be updated. Foremost of these dated laws are the Medical Act of 1959, Pharmacy Act of 1969 and the Hospital Licensing Act of 1965, which continue to govern the practices of medicine, pharmacy and licensing of hospitals despite the massive changes that have been taking place.

The DOH's initial large-scale public–private partnership (PPP) project (i.e., Modernization of the Philippine Orthopedic Center) focused on increasing service capacity instead of designing an alternative business model where the revenue stream is mainly PhilHealth reimbursements rather than OOPs. No framework is likewise in place to regulate the operations and harness the potential of private health insurance and health maintenance organizations, which account for 9 per cent of total health spending. No guidelines currently exist on coordination of benefits and harmonization of systems, standards and processes.

A major gap is apparent in the ability of the DOH to hold different stakeholders accountable. This is underpinned by the failure to institute a platform and interoperability standards in a timely manner for information systems, thus delaying the digitization of health-related transactions. The DOH relies on nationwide surveys, that seldom give provincial and municipal-level estimates, or aggregated administrative data, which makes quality control challenging. The policy environment for ICT is weak, with healthcare providers able to invoke privacy concerns to justify withholding certain needed data. Hence, even though the DOH mandated the submission of key data as a prerequisite for hospital licensing in 2015, the compliance rate has not been optimal. There is a lack of coordination with the Philippine Statistics Authority (PSA) to strengthen civil registration and vital statistics. Efforts to engage the citizens and civil society organizations have been minimal, with the DOH's hospital advisor website the only mechanism in place that systematically collects feedback on health service delivery. These factors have contributed to inadequate evidence which could have guided the DOH and the national government in their allocations of national transfers and other support mechanisms to reduce health inequity, particularly in the poorest areas that are burdened with high incidences of disease.

B. Financing

Financing involves three basic functions: generating funds for health, pooling these into single or multiple funds, and using pooled funds to purchase health services on behalf of a population group. Purchasing is considered effective when it is able to link equitable distribution and efficient, transparent and accountable use of resources with people who are ensured access to quality health services that will not leave them impoverished (Resilient and Responsive Health Systems 2014).

With epidemiologic and demographic transitions, increasing health threats, empowered and demanding citizenry, and rapid development of new medicines and technology, it is anticipated that the sector will require ever-increasing financial resources. Raising more revenues can mean tapping new sources or addressing various sources of inefficiencies and plugging leakages. The DOH budget quadrupled over the last five years, mostly coming from the earmarked taxes from sales of tobacco and alcohol. A significant portion of this was allocated for health insurance subsidies (see Table 5.3) and for upgrading DOH and LGU hospitals and clinics. The PhilHealth premium has also been increased marginally, but considering its mandate, both the premium and collection efficiency remain low. LGU budget allocation is still highly dependent on preferences of local chief executives (see Figure 5.9).

The national and local governments *passively* purchase health services from individual government health facilities through budget support. Since this amount is fixed — regardless of output or outcomes — government health facilities compensate by building private rooms/wards and by having patients pay out-of-pocket for medicines, supplies and diagnostic services. Despite a population coverage of 92 per cent, PhilHealth has yet to fully recognize and leverage its purchasing power.

Traditionally, PhilHealth has been viewed as "the means to help people pay for healthcare services", or providing financial assistance rather than affording financial protection. In late 2011, this began to change when PhilHealth shifted from the fee-for-service provider

TABLE 5.3
Department of Health Budget and PhilHealth Premium Subsidy Allocation,
2010–16 (billion pesos)

Year	Department of Health Total Health Budget	PhilHealth Premium Subsidy Allocation	Share in Total Health Budget (%)
2010	24.6	2.00	8.0
2011	31.8	3.50	11.0
2012	42.2	12.03	29.0
2013	50.4	12.61	25.0
2014	83.7	35.29	42.0
2015	87.6	37.06	42.0
2016	122.63	43.90	35.7

Source: Department of Health.

FIGURE 5.9
Local Government Units Health Expenditure per Capita and Share to
Total Expenditure by Region, 2011

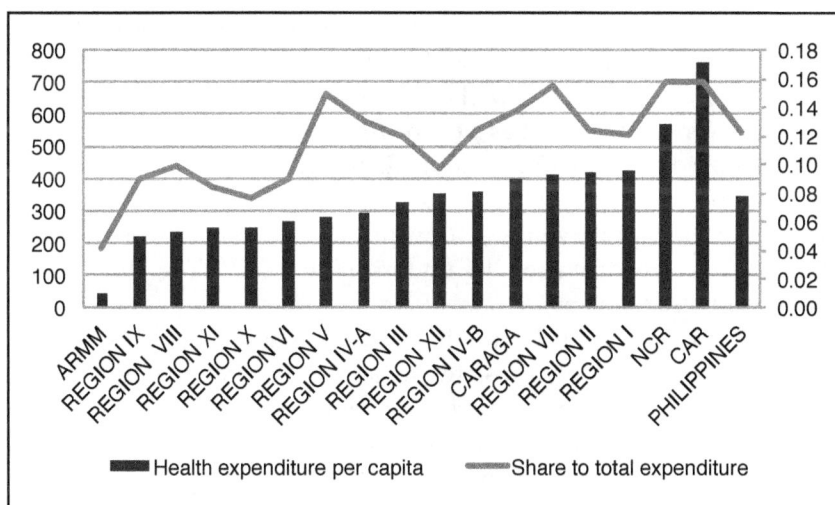

Source of basic data: Statement of Income and Expenditures, Bureau of Local Government Finance, Department of Finance.

payment scheme to case rates with a no balance billing (NBB) option for government-subsidized poor members seeking care in government hospitals. Although problems arise from the rates not having been supported by adequate costing studies, and the compliance rate to NBB among select government hospitals is only around 60 per cent, the shift to case rates has increased transparency and simplified the understanding of PhilHealth.

In 2012, PhilHealth began to further assert its purchasing role by designing a new benefit scheme guided by clinical pathways, backed by costing, with zero or fixed co-payment options, and which selectively contracts qualified healthcare providers. More than the actual benefits of the package, the value is largely its potential template or proof of concept of how PhilHealth can be an active purchaser and eventually redesign all its benefits.

However, despite the massive increase in enrolment, per capita benefit payments at a compounded annual growth rate of 8 per cent from 2007 to 2015, and total benefit payout tripling from P30 billion in 2010 to nearly P100 billion in 2015, its share of the total health expenditure has only increased from an average of 9–10 per cent to 14 per cent, and has yet to significantly reduce OOP. Its share in the revenues of many government and private hospitals remains small (e.g., 20 per cent for DOH hospitals), and this will persist if it continues to allow healthcare providers to charge unlimited co-payment or OOP.

Moreover, PhilHealth has yet to fully use its role as a purchaser to minimize fragmentation among different service levels, promote the use of primary care services, drive improvements in service quality and responsiveness, or provide additional incentives to facilitate service provision in underserved areas. The inability to fully assert itself can be accounted for in part by the passive agenda setting of its governing board, the institutional legacy of being part of a pension fund that translates to apprehensions among manage-ment and staff to support increasing benefit coverage, and a weak information system that does not give PhilHealth business intelligence to manage the healthcare providers it is currently empanelling.

Medicines account for as much as 62 per cent of OOP, resulting in numerous initiatives to improve both financial and physical access to drugs, medicines and devices (PSA 2014). In 1988, the Generics Act mandated physicians to prescribe drugs in their generic name in order to provide cheaper alternatives. The *Botika ng Bayan* (Community Pharmacy) initiative was launched to expand the retail distribution of medicines, as well as to ensure that the cheaper alternatives are geographically accessible. These steps contributed to more generic drugs being dispensed than branded drugs in 2013, despite a recent study by Wong et al. (2013) showing that the majority of patients were not offered generic alternatives in drug outlets (see Figure 5.10).

FIGURE 5.10
Proportion of Patients Offered Generic Alternatives by Region (% of drugstores)

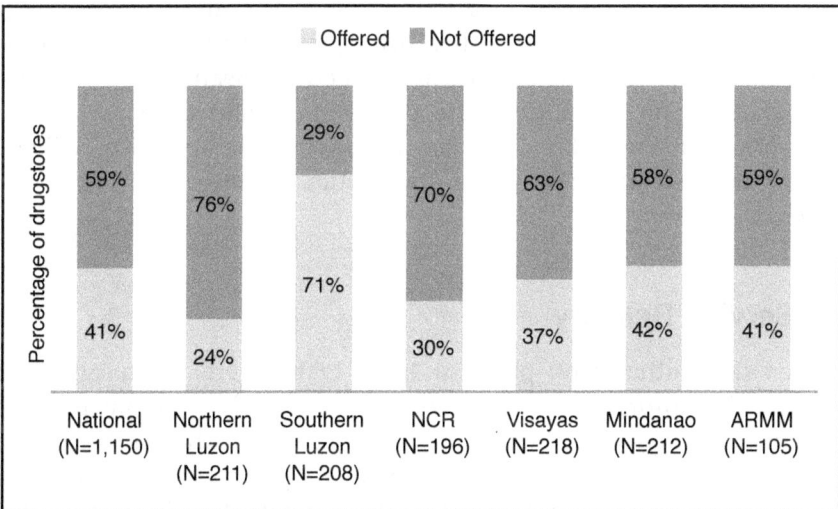

Notes: NCR = National Capital Region; ARMM = Autonomous Region in Muslim Mindanao.
Source: Wong et al. 2014.

The Universally Accessible Cheaper and Quality Medicine Act in 2008 further aimed to lower the cost of relevant drugs in the market by enabling the DOH to promote competition and mandate price limits if market competition proved ineffectual in lowering prices. In 2009, for the first and only time, the DOH applied this mandate of setting maximum retail prices, for twenty-two drug molecules. The DOH's Pharmaceutical Division also started several medicine access programmes in 2009 to further help bring down prices of medicines through bulk procurement. Unfortunately, information gaps from patients and providers alike contributed to poor uptake and utilization, while the lack of coordination with PhilHealth has resulted in inefficient overlaps between DOH access programmes and PhilHealth benefits (META 2013). For example, DOH-retained hospitals contracted in PhilHealth's Z benefit package for breast cancer are reimbursed the full amount, even if the hospital already receives the cancer drugs for free through the access programme. More importantly, it has become an excuse for PhilHealth to delay the financing of an explicit pharmaceutical benefit package, which would be a more appropriate and sustainable mechanism to assure geographic and financial access to needed medicines. Nonetheless, the Pharmaceutical Division has started to publish a drug price reference index, which aims to guide government procuring bodies, healthcare providers and patients on the appropriate procurement and purchase prices. The prices in the index could be used as mandatory price ceilings. Plans are also under way for diagnostics to have a similar price reference index.

C. Service Delivery

When devolution took place in 1991, LGUs were technically and financially unprepared to respond to their new responsibilities. Despite twenty-five years of devolution, only a handful of LGU health systems have succeeded in delivering quality health services without risk of impoverishing their constituents. Key ingredients for these successful LGUs included strong leadership by a local chief executive, fiscal and management autonomy for the health providers, and strategic use of PhilHealth reimbursements. The latter contributed to increased investments in infrastructure and equipment, better compensation and motivated health staff.

Another key aspect of service delivery is integration between the different delivery platforms — primary, secondary, tertiary. Because health facilities are licensed and paid (either as budget or health insurance reimbursement) as discrete individual facilities rather than as a system, there is no incentive to refer to the appropriate level or do early intervention at the primary level. This is evident in

PhilHealth's benefit payout profile, where acute gastroenteritis (diarrhoea) and pneumonia continue to be among the top reimbursed conditions.

Nationally, the lack of and inequitable distribution of supply inputs is apparent: the bed-to-population ratio has decreased over the years with no substantial increase in hospital or hospital beds, even with the continued increase in population (see Figure 5.11). At least 60 per cent of all medical practitioners work in urban areas, with the top three regions having the most and least healthcare workers corresponding to the richest and poorest regions, respectively (HHRDB 2013). The average availability of innovator and generic medicines among government healthcare providers are 8 per cent and 27 per cent, respectively. Underfunded, understocked and understaffed government health facilities leave patients with no choice but to seek care in private health facilities, which are often perceived to provide better quality of care, even if the OOP is high (META 2013).

FIGURE 5.11
Total Hospital Beds and Bed Capacity per 10,000 Population, 1976–2012

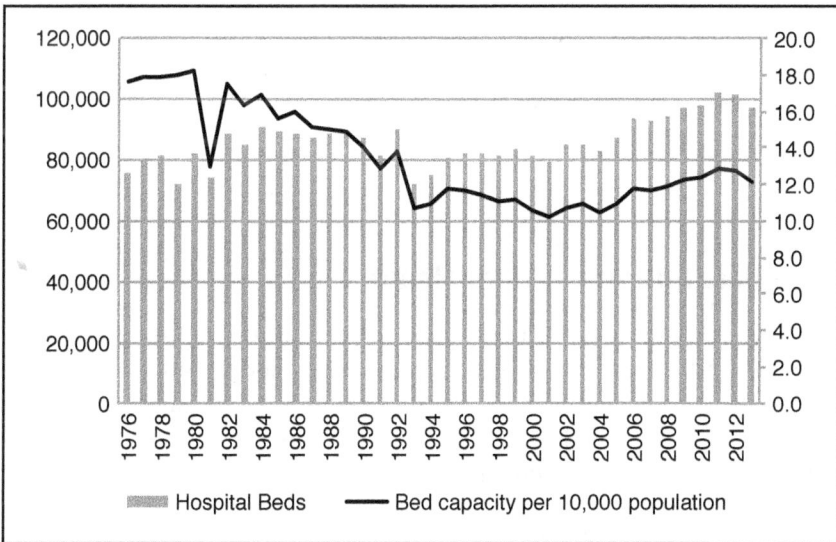

Source of basic data: Philippine Statistical Yearbook 2014, Philippine Statistics Authority.

While private health facilities provide the government with a faster option to scale rather than build up health facilities from scratch, the average hospitalization cost in the old fee-for-service payment scheme is three times more in private facilities than in government facilities, as shown in Table 5.4 (NDHS 2013). This difference was expected to be resolved by the shift to case rates, wherein PhilHealth pays the same rate to either public or private hospitals. But this was not realized, as private hospitals continue to charge the "balance bill" to OOP. Nonetheless, if the private sector is to be harnessed and aligned towards universal health coverage, their current business model has to change from one that is primarily reliant on OOP to a model that relies mostly on health insurance payments; a model that is seen with the increasing number of private hospitals that have begun working within the PhilHealth case rates and offering the zero OOP option.

TABLE 5.4
Average Costs of Hospital Care
(pesos)

Type of Cost	Government Hospital	Private Hospital
Average Total Hospital Bill	8,640	25,471
Average paid by PhilHealth (under Fee-for-Service Scheme)	3,221	7,278

Source: PSA and ICF International 2014. *Philippines: National Demographic and Health Survey 2013.*

D. Other Determinants of Health

There is collaboration with other sectors in addressing the social determinants and advancing universal health coverage, health security and health system resilience, but this collaboration is still limited and can be expanded further. The Department of Social Welfare and Development's Pantawid Pamilya Pilipino Program (4Ps) ties cash grants to several health-related conditions — from children getting immunized and taking deworming pills, to mothers availing of maternal health services from skilled health professionals in health facilities. The 4Ps have illustrated that health gains are possible through synergistic actions among different sectors. Another key area of collaboration is on the reduction of road traffic accidents. This needs stronger implementation of laws prohibiting driving under the effects of alcohol and requiring the use of seatbelts, and the construction of well-designed and high quality roads. Another ongoing collaboration is with the education sector, with the DOH beginning to utilize schools as strategic service delivery partners. Even with these collaborations, the DOH still needs to be more proactive in championing interventions that would improve living, working and schooling conditions.

V. Scenarios for Health in 2040

Over the last thirty years, the Philippines has been pursuing a piecemeal and incremental approach to health reform. The succeeding section discusses the implications of two different scenarios: Scenario 1 maintains and incrementally improves the status quo, while Scenario 2 pursues a bolder, more holistic approach that requires a complete shift to demand side. Table 5.5 provides a summary of the key characteristics of the two scenarios.

TABLE 5.5
Roles of Key Actors in Health System 2040

Key Actors	Scenario 1: Status Quo	Scenario 2: Alternative
Department of Health (DOH)	Determine entitlements; Raise revenues (through tax and other earmarks); Design, finance, deliver, regulate and monitor; Sets standards; Regulate and enforce.	Determine entitlements; Raise revenues (through tax and other earmarks, direct other national government financing towards single pool); Set service delivery standards (i.e., facilities, commodities, practice of profession); Regulate and enforce standards, including for private health insurance and health maintenance organizations (HMOs); Undertake surveillance; Monitoring and evaluation; Provide services in times of disaster; Coordinate and convene all other sectors; Design innovative public–private partnerships.

TABLE 5.5   (*continued*)

Key Actors	Scenario 1: Status Quo	Scenario 2: Alternative
DOH-retained Hospitals	End-referral centre by default, but functions like any Level 3 hospital; With implicit management and fiscal autonomy.	Formally included in service delivery networks providing highly specialized services (national reference laboratories, centres of excellence) and residency and fellowship training; Explicit management and fiscal autonomy.
PhilHealth	Determine entitlements; Raise revenues, through premium collection and investments; Set accreditation standards; Accredit healthcare providers.	Adopt entitlements and standards set by DOH; Raise revenues, through premium collection and investments; Negotiate prices of goods and services; Enter into contracts with healthcare providers and enforce provisions.
Local Government Units	Determine entitlements; Raise revenues, finance and deliver all health services; Grant hospitals management and fiscal autonomy (optional).	Raise revenues, finance and deliver population-based health services; Deliver all other services through health networks that have management and fiscal autonomy.
Private Healthcare Providers	Deliver without coordination, not integrated in service delivery networks.	Deliver in coordination with public providers, fully integrated in service delivery networks.
Private Health Insurance	Design benefit packages without coordination with PhilHealth.	Design benefit packages that supplement mandated entitlements.

A. Governance

The most crucial step is clarification of roles — identifying who is primarily in charge of determining entitlements, setting standards, financing, purchasing, delivering service, regulation and quality assurance, surveillance and monitoring and evaluation (M&E). Until this is resolved, the question as to "Who pays for what?" will persist, even when the appropriate questions should have been "Who pays?", "Who delivers?" and "What criteria have to be fulfilled for a particular health service/commodity to be publicly financed?"

Under Scenario 2, the DOH's role is more focused on policymaking and regulation, while PhilHealth becomes the main purchaser. The DOH is proposed to be the sole institution that sets out the services every Filipino is entitled to, while PhilHealth becomes responsible for purchasing these. Consequently, the DOH must adopt a transparent priority-setting process that will be the basis for expanding the list of entitlements. The scenario implies that the DOH will refrain from supplying specific inputs through its national programmes — commodities, human resources, health facility enhancement grants or ICT solutions — as these may only serve to diminish PhilHealth's purchasing power and undermine provider autonomy. All entitlements, regardless of whether these health services, pharmaceutical benefits and curative, rehabilitative and palliative interventions are public or not, are to be paid by the purchaser as long as these are at the individual level (e.g., vaccines, tuberculosis drugs). The only exceptions will be population-based services, which will be the responsibility of LGUs. As much as possible, those determined as public health commodities will be taken out of the private market, especially if their unregulated use poses risks to public health. Otherwise, the market prices of these public health commodities will be tightly regulated.

With the purchaser–provider split (i.e., government and private healthcare providers deliver services), Scenario 2 proposes that government healthcare providers need to be afforded management and fiscal autonomy, as this will be necessary to ensure that the perceived benefits of improving responsiveness and accountability and reducing the cost of service provision (Ryan, Parker and Brown 2000) take place.

Scenarios for service coverage by 2040 are summarized in Table 5.6.

TABLE 5.6
Scenarios for Service Coverage by 2040

Indicator	Scenario 1: Status Quo	Scenario 2: Alternative
Service Coverage	Dependent on health facility and PhilHealth membership classification.	Uniform for all Filipinos.
Expansion Process	Ad-hoc.	Systematic, participatory and transparent priority-setting process in place.
Public health commodities	Mostly excluded in PhilHealth benefit package, but with some overlaps. Available at no cost in public facilities only and available in the private market at variable prices.	Included in PhilHealth benefit package; freely available in both public and private facilities; not available in the private market, or, if available, consider price cap/ceiling.
Inclusions	Inpatient, day surgery, outpatient.	Inpatient, day surgery, outpatient, rehabilitative, palliative, transfers, pharmaceutical benefit.

The ability to harness credible information in a timely manner for strategic, operational and day-to-day concerns supports strategic management of the health sector, ensures strength and staying power of reform programmes, and enables the government to be responsive to emerging threats. New and valid information can be generated through basic or applied research, household surveys and administrative data, which, under Scenario 2, the DOH would be heavily investing in, given its focus as steward of the health system. A strong, dedicated M&E unit will be needed within the DOH.

Under the current scenario, health programmes are implemented as stand-alone amidst overwhelming recognition of the role social determinants play in improving health. This was the logic behind the

4Ps, for which education and health conditions were enveloped into a primarily social welfare programme. For many high-burden diseases like tuberculosis, the impact of medical management runs second only to social interventions. Thus, Scenario 2 will strive to integrate health programmes into other social programmes using a whole-of-government approach.

B. Health Financing

Table 5.7 presents the two scenarios in terms of health financing by 2040. The goal of reducing the share of OOP to 30 per cent or less of total health expenditure from the current 56 per cent requires the system to shift from OOP to a predominantly publicly prepaid system (i.e., from government revenues allocated for health and from mandatory and voluntary health insurance contributions) complemented by caps on allowable OOP or co-payments.

A predominantly publicly financed system is considered the global best practice. In the European Union (EU) alone, 73 per cent of healthcare was publicly financed in 2010. Turkey, for example, increased public spending to the EU average, which has led to the reduction of nearly 10 percentage points in the share of direct payments by households. Thailand, after launching its universal coverage scheme, scaled up its public financing and halved the share of direct payments. More prepayments can be mobilized as the formal labour sector base expands and as the country becomes more affluent. Specifically, the mandatory health insurance contributions can be raised from the current 2.5 per cent to at least 5 per cent of monthly payroll, coupled by the removal of the income ceiling of P35,000. An alternative premium schedule using a prorated per capita (rather than per family) scheme based on the number of dependents can also be considered.

From having multiple purchasers in the DOH, LGUs, PAGCOR, PCSO, PhilHealth and individual households, Scenario 2 envisions a single and active national purchaser that will consolidate the prepaid funds and extract efficiency, effectiveness and quality from healthcare providers. The smaller pools of health assistance funds from agencies such as the PCSO and PAGCOR will be aligned and redirected into

TABLE 5.7
Scenarios for Health Financing by 2040

Indicator	Scenario 1: Status Quo	Scenario 2: Alternative
Flow of resources	Money follows facilities (in public setting) and patient (in private setting); Incomplete shift to demand-side financing.	Money follows the patient (regardless); Complete shift to demand-side financing.
Revenue generation for health	National and local taxes; High out-of-pocket payments; Low insurance prepayments.	National and local taxes; High insurance prepayments; Low out-of-pocket payments.
Pooling of funds	Limited, with many smaller pools.	Extensive, single national pooled fund.
Purchasers	Department of Health, local government units, PhilHealth, Philippine Charity Sweepstakes Office, Philippine Amusement and Gaming Corporation and Priority Development Assistance Fund are all passive purchasers; PhilHealth is a financial intermediary.	PhilHealth as the main active purchaser.
Purchasing power	Low.	High.
Contracted unit	Individual facilities (fragmented, no complementation.	Networks (integrated primary and specialty care, complementary).
Provider payment mechanism (PPM)	Line item budget; Case rates; Capitation.	Annual global budget (based on diagnosis-related groups/case-mix); Performance/results-based block grants.
Basis for reimbursement rates of selected PPM	Average.	Costing exercise.
Purchaser–Provider split	No.	Yes.

the bigger pool. These can be channelled as health insurance premiums for the remaining 8 per cent of the population that needs to be covered, or redirected to fund services that are still not included as part of the entitlements. Furthermore, budgetary allocations for inputs — drugs, commodities, deployment programmes and the like — shall be pooled as part of the purchaser's funds. All these efforts to increase the size of the pool are crucial, because it enables the fund to pay fair reimbursements. The pooling of PAGCOR and PCSO funds into this single fund will also minimize the discretionary manner that presently characterizes how these agencies provide health-related financial assistance.

As the benefits are expanded, financial protection improved and health insurance contribution levels of the formal labour sector increased, the current contributions for the poor, near-poor and other eligible individuals and families that the national government fully subsidizes will be increased to approximate the increased levels of the formal labour sector and ensure sustained funding of the expanded benefits. If the sin taxes cannot fully finance these subsidies, new earmarks from value added tax (VAT) collections, a special (health) levy on sugared beverages, financial transaction tax, lottery, tourism tax, and mobile phone tax can be considered.

Scenario 2 proposes that the contracting is done with service delivery networks and not with stand-alone health facilities. Network-based contracts give every network member — clinics and hospitals — incentives to efficiently use resources, as every member benefits from the savings. Specifically, networks are incentivized to keep the population healthy, provide the appropriate level of care, and minimize redundant investments. It incentivizes the establishment of strategically located specialty centres rather than many redundant one-stop shops, and facilitates cross-subsidization of operational costs and the setting up of referral transport services.

When healthcare providers are contracted separately, there are no incentives for appropriate use and judicious referral, pushing healthcare providers to look after their own survival instead of coordinating and making the best use of resources. Thus, in a setting without a nationwide health facility blueprint or investment plan and with poor guidelines to ensure equitable distribution of healthcare provider capacity, providers always gravitate towards areas with high market potential — defined as the capacity of people for OOP — rather than underserved areas. To recoup their investments faster, providers are biased towards capital-intensive services with higher income potential, even if these are not necessarily the most needed or cost-effective. As a result, Scenario 1 perpetuates inequality in investments, since urban areas with larger populations and better capacity to pay continue to gain better access.

Network-based contracting has been shown to work in many parts of the world, including in Thailand, which had several years of success by contracting a district hospital (hub) with a network of more than ten primary care clinics (spokes). Locally, LGU-owned healthcare providers can form or can be mandated to organize a province-based network, which can be legally established into a government-owned and controlled corporation or economic enterprise. This will render the required agility, self-sufficiency and political neutrality that will be conducive for accountability. It can either compete with the private networks or subcontract aspects of its operations to the private sector, since it is not bound to a political leadership operating within three-year election cycles.

In terms of provider payment, Scenario 2 proposes a fairly calculated and systematically costed global budget for the contracted networks. For commodities that are determined to be of public health significance and/or currently bulk-procured by the DOH, PhilHealth will be allowed to arrange the bulk purchase and distribution of these commodities. PhilHealth must also enact and strictly enforce policies on co-payment ceilings; otherwise the OPP will remain a problem.

With its enhanced role as government health purchaser, PhilHealth needs to reassess its capacity to deliver on this task. Its current human resource complement is still largely designed for LGU and informal sector marketing, enrolment and collections-related functions. With 92 per cent population coverage and the national government fully subsidizing the poor and the informal sector population, it now needs to focus and gain competencies related to purchasing, such as contract management, health market analysis, price negotiations and advanced-level fraud detection.

C. Health Service Delivery

Table 5.8 describes the required shift in the DOH's role to enable and support service delivery by providers and balancing this with protecting the interests of the patients. For medicines that will not be purchased in bulk, the DOH can implement an e-procurement system similar to the Department of Budget and Management's Procurement Service (PS-DBM). This will promote transparency and sustainably lower risk for persistent bid failures, especially among government healthcare providers.

TABLE 5.8
Scenarios for Health Service Delivery by 2040

Indicator	Scenario 1: Status Quo	Scenario 2: Alternative
Medicines and other technologies	Address service delivery gaps (medicine entitlement programmes); Drug Price Reference Index.	Develop infrastructure for drug e-procurement system that limits procurement price.
Human resources	Address service delivery gaps (deployment programmes).	Address overall supply and quality gaps (expansion of training programmes, policies on return service, licensing and accreditation).
Information and communications	Multiple systems, not interoperable; Department of Health (DOH) and PhilHealth create software/ programs.	Multiple systems with single standard, hence interoperable; DOH and PhilHealth set standards, licences, and regulates software/programs.
Gatekeeping	Non-existent.	Required (Primary Care Provider for All).
Health facilities and public–private partnerships	Business model is based predominantly on out-of-pocket payment.	Business model of health facilities is based predominantly on PhilHealth reimbursements and earmarked sin taxes.

To address the inequitable distribution of health human resources, the DOH needs to look at both pre-service curriculum and in-service career pathways and incentives. An ideal pre-service curriculum has to have a strong emphasis on the service component and a primary care orientation. Examples of successful models are the University of the Philippines' School of Health Sciences, which preferentially admits individuals who come from underserved areas and are willing to return and serve in their hometowns, and Ateneo de Zamboanga School of Medicine, which has a higher than 95 per cent retention rate. Deployment programmes have to be reimagined and branded as a viable alternative career path or as a career-enhancing stint, instead of its current personnel augmentation orientation.

The DOH can also push for new laws that would allow additional categories of the health workforce, task-shifting and team-based care. For example, to ensure access to primary care services in the context of the physician shortfall, training nurses to become nurse practitioners can be a viable option. Their role is similar to a general practitioner, only with less authority to prescribe medication and make referrals for other services (Seale, Anderson and Kinnersley 2005). They can work independently and take on the responsibility of their patient's health without the supervision of a physician.

The DOH also needs to strengthen training capacities of all DOH hospitals as regional teaching and training institutions and regional reference laboratories by creating thousands of new *plantilla* positions for residency and fellowship training, as well as faculty positions. This is expected to create a virtuous cycle of educators and trainees. A consortium between public and private healthcare providers will also ensure that trainees in private healthcare facilities are adequately exposed to the needs of the majority of the population.

State-of-the-art ICT systems form the backbone of evidence-based decision-making that would literally enable knowledge "at the fingertips", especially for decision-makers. However, both the DOH and PhilHealth have to transition their role from developers of ICT platforms to creating standards and regulating health-related ICT products and services. There should be a recognition that the government would never be able to render the 24/7 ICT support often required from those who develop application systems.

A shelved initiative of PhilHealth from a few years back captures this essence. The health information technology provider (HITP) policy for electronic claims (e-claims) sought to minimize the corporation's ICT burden by setting standards for the e-claims platform, then accrediting a number of ICT suppliers who in turn provide their services to thousands of healthcare providers. Another model is through outsourcing similar to the online civil registration system of the then National Statistics Office (now the Philippine Statistics Authority).

The DOH will also provide guidance and standards and build up the capacity of LGUs and private healthcare providers in health promotion and in disaster mitigation and resilience interventions. It will champion national legislation and policies that will restrict access to tobacco, alcohol and a diet high in sugar and salt while promoting a healthy lifestyle and diet, exercise and activities aimed at mitigating climate change, including transforming hospitals into low carbon hospitals and expanding green mass transportation.

While the Health Facilities Enhancement Program is intended to upgrade health facilities, it still does not address the lack of health facilities in many other areas. And while it has supported upgrading, the upgrading has not fully responded to the changing demographic and epidemiological picture that demands chronic care. To catch up with the infrastructure gaps and respond to the changing care needs, the expected fifteen-year equivalent of the 20 per cent of the 85 per cent of incremental sin taxes earmarked for health can be immediately used in full to help fund a rapid scale-up with private sector partners. Subsequent collections will be part of the availability payments to private sector partners as they come due. This can be used to design a more appealing PPP option for the private sector. Based on the 2016 estimates of P64.2 billion in incremental sin tax revenues, the expected amount available for supply-side investments would be 10.9 billion. Simply multiplying this amount by fifteen years would give a projected amount of P16.45 billion, which can be converted into health PPP projects of up to P30 billion with matching private sector mobilization that can be implemented immediately. More importantly, with the earmarked sin taxes funding the availability payments, the business model of health PPP projects would be consistent with the universal healthcare goals of ensuring financial protection. Indeed, health PPPs cannot be designed similar to other PPPs, where user fees are the primary cost recovery measure made available for the private partners. In a demand-driven health insurance based system, where access to healthcare services is not driven by capacity to pay but by health insurance membership, both earmarked sin taxes and health insurance benefit payments should be the complementary revenue sources for the private partners.

D. Patient-Centeredness

Scenario 2 describes a demand-driven system, where the patient is at the centre and his/her choices are valued. The poor will not be constrained to seek care only from a public provider. The choice of where to access care will also not penalize them, such that public health commodities previously available only in public facilities will also be accessible in other institutions. Initiatives to enable informed choice are also promoted. Patient navigators such as PhilHealth's Customer Assistance, Relations and Empowerment (CARES) will be scaled up and their reach will be expanded — from hospitals to clinics and the communities. Pending government-wide freedom of information legislation, a liberal data sharing or access policy can be enacted to improve accountability and system responsiveness.

VI. Realizing the Vision

Box 5.2. An Envisioned Case of a Filipino Family in 2040

Jose and Alicia are minimum wage earners. They live in Cavite but work in a factory in Mandaluyong City, Metro Manila. Efficient public transportation means they commute for only an hour every day. They live close to a fresh market, which enables Alicia to prepare healthy meals for them to take to work. In the factory, strict enforcement of occupational health standards ensures that workers are comfortable and do not face health risks. On a day when Jose is not feeling well, he goes to the nearest clinic, where he is treated with utmost respect and care. When Alicia needs to be admitted to a government hospital, she only has to give her name to the hospital clerk and all is taken care of. Upon discharge, Alicia gets her pack of take-home medicines and does not have to pay anything from her pocket. And because the hospital service is complete, Jose is able to continue working even as Alicia is confined. An episode of sickness does not destabilize Jose and Alicia's lives.

Thailand and Turkey embarked on their quests of universal health coverage in 2000 and 2003, respectively. In less than fifteen years Thailand was able to improve access to services and drop OOP share of total health expenditure to 12 per cent. Turkey was able to lower its infant mortality rate to one comparable to the OECD average. What the OECD did in thirty years, Turkey was able to do in nine. In these two countries, visions for universal health coverage were adopted, institutions were transformed and individuals were empowered with the necessary skills to implement the vision.

The steps described in Scenario 2 will enable the required competencies and organizational structures to be determined. Clearly, the government capacity to produce and use knowledge needs emphasis more than ever. Thailand and Turkey have demonstrated that when society is mobilized, is informed, and actively demands their universal health coverage entitlements, no health system reform is impossible to achieve. Universal health coverage can be done, and it can be done quickly.

Note

1.   Acknowledgements due to Ida Marie Pantig, Lorra Angelia Sayson, Nel Jason Haw and Mikaela Limcaoco.

References

Arcand, J. "Undernourishment and Economic Growth: The Efficiency Cost of Hunger". Presentation to the European Media Seminar on Global Food Security, Royal Swedish Academy of Agriculture and Forestry, Stockholm, 15 October 2001 <http://www.fao.org/News/2001/stockholm/arcandfull.pdf>.

Banzon, E., J.A. Lucero, B.L. Ho, M.E. Puyat, E.J. Quibod, and P.A. Factor. "Public-Private Partnerships Options toward Achieving Universal Health Coverage in the Philippine Setting". PIDS Discussion Paper Series 2014-48. 2014.

Barro, R., "Determinants of Economic Growth: A Cross-Country Empirical Study". NEBR Working Paper 5698. 1996.

Bausch, D.G., and L. Schwarz. "Outbreak of Ebolavirus Disease in Guinea: Where Ecology Meets Economy". PLOS Neglected Tropical Diseases 8, no. 7 (2014): e3056 <https://doi.org/10.1371/journal.pntd.0003056>.

Blaxter, M. *The Health of the Children: A Review of Research on the Place of Health in Cycles of Disadvantage*. London: Heinemann Educational Books, 1981.

Bloom, D., D. Canning, and D. Jamison. "Health, Wealth, and Welfare". In *Health and Development: A Compilation of Articles from Finance & Development*, edited by Jeremy Clift, pp. 10–15. Washington, DC: IMF, 2004 <https://www.imf.org/external/pubs/ft/health/eng/hdwi/hdwi.pdf>.

Bloom, D., D. Canning, and J. Sevilla. "The Effect of Health on Economic Growth: A Production Function Approach". *World Development* 32 (2004): 1–13 <http://doi.org/10.1016/j.worlddev.2003.07.002>.

Bredenkamp, C., and L. Buisman. "Universal Health Coverage in the Philippines: Progress on Financial Protection Goals". World Bank Policy Research Working Paper 7258. 2015 <http://www-wds.worldbank.org/external/default/WDSContentServer/WDSP/IB/2015/05/06/090224b082e49ae2/1_0/Rendered/PDF/Universal0heal0ial0protection0goals.pdf>.

Fu-Lai Yu, T., Y. Wai-Kee, and D. Kwan. *International Economic Development: Leading Issues and Challenges*. London: Routledge, 2014.

Gallup, J.L., and J.D. Sachs. "The Economic Burden of Malaria". *American Society of Tropical Medicine & Hygiene* 64, nos. S1–S2 (2001): 85–96 <http://www.ajtmh.org/content/64/1_suppl/85.full.pdf+html>.

Grundy, J., V. Healy, L. Gorgolon, and E. Sandig. "Overview of Devolution of Health Services in the Philippines". *Electronic Journal of Rural and Remote Health Research, Education, Practice and Policy* 3 (2003) <http://www.rrh.org.au/publishedarticles/article_print_220.pdf>.

Hai, W., Z. Zhao, J. Wang, and Z. Hou. "The Short-Term Impact of SARS on the Chinese Economy". *Asian Economic Papers* 3 (2004): 57–61.

Hartigan-Go, K., M. Valera, and M.K. Visperas. "A Framework to Promote Good Governance in Healthcare". AIM Working Paper Series 13-021. 2013.

Institute for Health Metrics and Evaluation. "GBD Profile: Philippines". 2010 <http://www.healthdata.org/sites/default/files/files/country_profiles/GBD/ihme_gbd_country_report_philippines.pdf>.

Jamison, D., J. Breman, A. Measham, G. Alleyne, M. Claeson, D. Evans, P. Jha, A. Mills, and P. Musgrove. *Disease Control Priorities in Developing Countries*, 2nd ed. Washington, DC: World Bank, 2006.

Kottasova, I. "World Bank: Cost of Ebola Could Top $32 billion". CNN, 9 October 2014 <http://edition.cnn.com/2014/09/24/business/ebola-cost-warning/> (accessed 5 November 2014).

Lavado, R., V.G. Ulep, and L. Lagrada. "Burden of Health Payments in the Philippines". Paper presented during the Workshop on Dissemination of Study Results: The Financial Burden of Health Payments, Manila, Philippines, 23–24 March 2011 <http://iris.wpro.who.int/bitstream/handle/10665.1/10590/RS_2011_GE_13_PHL_eng.pdf?sequence=1>.

Lewis, R., A. Alvarez-Rosete, and N. Mays. *How to Regulate Health Care in England? An International Perspective.* London: King's Fund, 2006.

Mayer, D. "The Long Term Impact of Health on Growth in Latin America". *World Development* 29, no. 6 (2001): 1025–33 <http://doi.org/10.1016/S0305-750X(01)00026-2>.

Mexican Commission on Macroeconomics and Health. "Investing in Health for Economic Development: Executive Summary". Cholula, Puebla: Universidad de las Americas, 2004.

Murray, C.J., J.A. Salomon, and C. Mathers. "A Critical Examination of Summary Measures of Population Health". *Bulletin of the World Health Organization* 78, no. 8 (2000): 981–94 <http://doi.org/ 10.1590/S0042-96862000000800008>.

National Research Council (US). *Accounting for Health and Health Care: Approaches to Measuring the Sources and Costs of Their Improvement.* Washington, DC: National Academies Press (US), 2010.

OECD (Organisation for Economic Co-operation Development). "OECD Health Data 2001: A Comparative Analysis of 30 Countries". 2001 <http:// www.oecd.org/els/health-systems/oecdhealthdata2001acomparative analysisof30countries.htm>.

———. *Health at a Glance 2011: OECD Indicators.* Washington, DC: OECD, 2011 <http://www.oecd.org/els/health-systems/49105858.pdf>.

OECD and WHO (World Health Organization). "Infant Mortality". In *Health at a Glance: Asia/Pacific 2014: Measuring Progress towards Universal Health Coverage,* pp. 16–17. Washington, DC: OECD, 2014 <http://www.oecd-ilibrary.org/docserver/download/8114231ec006.pdf?expires=1443937411&id=id&accname=guest&checksum=F48E4535E153B07AD2047F6492608E13>.

Preker, A., and A. Harding. *Innovations in Health Service Delivery: The Corporization of Public Hospitals.* Washington, DC: World Bank, 2003.

Price-Smith, A. *The Health of Nations: Infectious Disease, Environmental Change, and their Effects on National Security and Development.* Cambridge, MA: MIT Press, 2002.

PSA (Philippine Statistics Authority) and ICF International. *Philippines: National Demographic and Health Survey 2013.* Manila: PSA; Rockville, MD: ICF International, 2014.

———. "Family Income and Expenditure Survey 2012". Manila: PSA, 2014.

Resilient & Responsive Health Systems. "What is Strategic Purchasing for Health?" 2014 <http://resyst.lshtm.ac.uk/sites/resyst.lshtm.ac.uk/files/docs/reseources/Purchasing%20brief.pdf>.

Robine, J-M. "The Relevance of Population Health Indicators". *J Epidemiol Community Health* 57, no. 5 (2003).

Romualdez, Alberto G. Jr., Jennifer Frances E. dela Rosa, Jonathan David A. Flavier, Stella Luz A. Quimbo, Kenneth Y. Hartigan-Go, Liezel P. Lagrada, and Lilibeth C. David, edited by Soonman Kwon and Rebecca Dodd. "The Philippines Health System Review". *Health Systems in Transition* 1, no. 2 (2011) <http://www.wpro.who.int/philippines/areas/health_systems/financing/philippines_health_system_review.pdf>.

Ryan, N., R. Parker, and K. Brown. "Purchaser-Provider Split in a Traditional Public Service Environment: Three Case Studies of Managing Change". *Public Policy and Administration Journal* 9, no. 1 (2000): 206–21 <http://eprints.qut.edu.au/4824/1/4824.pdf>.

Seale, C., E. Anderson, and P. Kinnersley. "Comparison of GP and Nurse Practitioner Consultations: An Observational Study". *British Journal of General Practice* 55 (December 2005) <http://bjgp.org/content/55/521/938.long>.

Silva, A. "A Framework for Measuring Responsiveness". WHO GPE Discussion Paper Series 32. n.d. <http://www.who.int/healthinfo/paper32.pdf>.

Silva, A., and N. Valentine. "Measuring Responsiveness: Results of a Key Informant Survey in 35 Countries". WHO GPE Discussion Paper Series 21. n.d. <http://www.who.int/healthinfo/paper21.pdf>.

Statistics Canada. "2. Health Status Indicators Based on Vital Statistics". 2015 <http://www.statcan.gc.ca/pub/82-221-x/2013001/quality-qualite/qua2-eng.htm>.

UNICEF (United Nations Children's Fund). *The State of the World's Children 2009*. New York: UNICEF, 2008.

Wong, J., R. Baclay, R. Duque, P. Roque, G. Serrano, J. Tumlos, and A. Ronsing. "The Prevalence of Philippine Prescribing, Dispensing, and Use of Behavior in Relation to Generic Drugs and their Risk Factors". PIDS Discussion Paper Series 2014–17. 2014.

WHO (World Health Organization). *The World Health Report 2000 Health Systems: Improving Performance*. Geneva: WHO, 2000.

———. *Making Pregnancy Safer: The Critical Role of the Skilled Attendant: A Joint Statement by WHO, ICM and FIGO*. Geneva: WHO, 2004.

———. *Neonatal and Perinatal Mortality: Country, Regional and Global Estimates*. Geneva: WHO, 2006.

———. "Maternal Mortality". 2014 <http://www.who.int/mediacentre/factsheets/s348/en/>.

———. "Health Status Statistics: Mortality". 2015 <http://www.who.int/healthinfo/statistics/indhale/en/>.

WHO and Commission on Macroeconomics and Health. *Macroeconomics and Health: Investing in Health for Economic Development*. Geneva: WHO, 2001.

Xu, K., D. Evans, K. Kawabata, R. Zeramdini, J. Klavus, and C. Murray. "Household Catastrophic Health Expenditure: A Multicountry Analysis". *The Lancet* 362 (2003): 111–17 <http://doi.org/10.1016/S01406736(03)13861-5>.

6

Environmental Resources, Shocks and National Well-Being[1]

James Roumasset, Majah-Leah Ravago,
Karl Robert Jandoc and Clarisa Arellano

This chapter deals with promoting the common good through better energy, resource and environmental policies as well as improved management of natural disaster risks, including climate change. Increasing gross domestic product (GDP) will be insufficient to meet the aspirations of the Philippine people for higher levels of living, inasmuch as GDP does not measure welfare. Largely because of the omission of these elements, we begin with a discussion of green accounting — the method of extending national income accounting to include the degradation of the environment and the depletion of natural resources.

As we discuss in the second part, comprehensive national income accounting can be further extended to include natural disasters and other shocks to the ecological–economic system. Even policy distortions can be accounted for by including them as constraints to the system. Thus, environmental resource conservation, disaster preparedness and policy reform all become potential sources of welfare growth. The later section deals with the mission of sustainable development, particularly how the Sustainable Development Goals (SDGs) relate to the mission of improving the welfare of Filipinos.

I. Increasing Levels of Living in the Face of Environmental Degradation and Resource Depletion

Stewardship of natural resources and the environment should not be treated as a separate objective from management of the economy (World Commission on Environment and Development 1987). The fundamental premise of sustainable income and green accounting, which have a long history in the Philippines and other countries, is that nature and the economy are part of the same system (the *environomy*) as shown in Figure 6.1. And one system requires one unifying measure of performance.

FIGURE 6.1
The Environomy

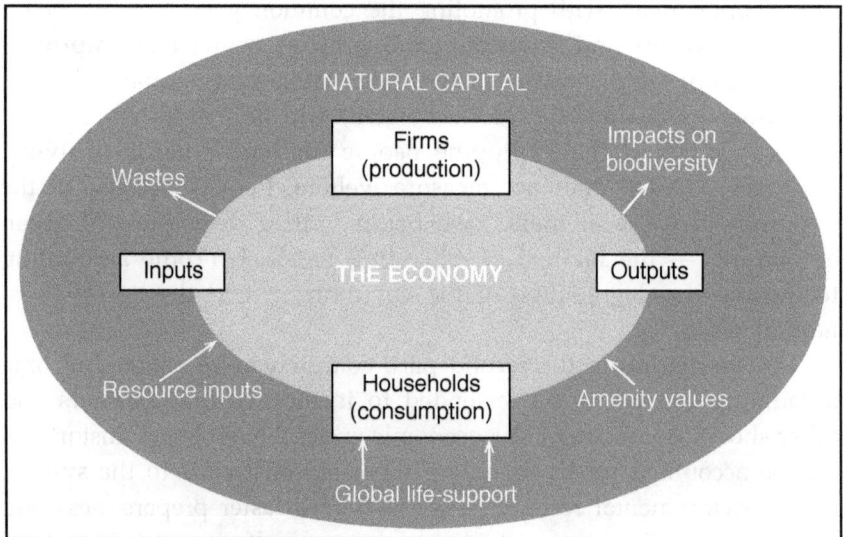

Source: Adapted from Burnett and Roumasset 2010.

To convert the most common indicator of the size of an economy, GDP, into a measure of national well-being, several adjustments must be made.[2] It is well known that GDP overestimates public welfare by failing to deduct depreciation — that portion of investment that simply replaces capital which has worn out or become obsolete. Deducting capital depreciation from GDP yields net domestic product (NDP). And since income is a better measure of welfare than production, we need to subtract the income earned in the Philippines by foreigners, add income earned by Philippine citizens abroad, and add remittances to the Philippines by non-citizens. The result is national income (NI). For the same reason that depreciation of plant and equipment has been subtracted, we also need to subtract depreciation of natural capital, i.e., the lost present-value from mining, forest depletion/degradation, and extraction of other natural resources. Using appropriate prices and accounting for all goods and services that affect human welfare results in an improved index of national well-being — green national income (GNI).

The ultimate vision of national accounting in the Philippines is to supplement the existing system of national accounts so that depletion of natural resources and the degradation of the environment can be treated in a consistent fashion with capital depreciation and better approximate economic welfare.

GNI is NI minus environmental degradation and natural capital depletion, the latter being the counterpart of depreciation of produced capital (plant and equipment). GNI also measures *sustainable income* in the sense that if total capital accumulation were added to consumption, then that level of hypothetical consumption could be sustained indefinitely (Lange et al. 2010). The same accounting framework is sometimes used to provide a criterion for sustainability: If net investment after deducting natural depletion and environmental degradation is positive, then the economy is said to be sustainable.

Green accounting initiatives in the Philippines have been going on for twenty years. The early accounts were reckoned in terms of NDP after deducting environmental and resource degradation (see Box 6.1). Due to data limitations, these accounts were partial in nature and underestimated the real cost of depletion and degradation. For example, deforestation and depletion of marine resources were not included. Here, we review more recent attempts at green accounting

Box 6.1. Box 1: History of Green Accounting in the Philippines

Environment and Natural Resources Accounting Project (ENRAP). Handled by the Department of Environment and Natural Resources (DENR) and funded by USAID in 1991, this was the first initiative measuring natural capital depreciation in the Philippines focusing on forest and mineral asset accounts, costs of preventing pollution, costs imposed by pollution, and valuation of non-market household uses of the environment (Hecht 2000). ENRAP explicitly recognized "nature" as a separate productive economic sector. Unfortunately, it was hampered by data constraints and unable to produce reliable policy implications (Hecht 2000).

Integrated Environmental Management for Sustainable Development–Environment and Natural Resources Accounting (IEMSD–ENRA). Headed by the National Statistical Coordination Board in 1995 with assistance from the UN (Hecht 2000), this implemented the UN's System of Integrated Environmental and Economic Accounting (SEEA) framework. It concentrated on developing accounts for environmental assets measured in physical and monetary terms and considered adjustments relating to depletion, defensive expenditures and degradation (Virola and Lopez-Dee 2005). Depletion and degradation costs of soil erosion and air/water pollution from the conventional net domestic product (NDP) were used to compute "environmentally adjusted NDP". But due to data limitations, resource depletion only covered water resources, and degradation costs were underestimated.

ENRA II Project. This second phase of ENRAP aimed to institutionalize the Philippine Economic–Environmental and Natural Resources Accounting (PEENRA) System. Executive Order 406 (1997) established PEENRA units in the National Economic Development Authority (NEDA), DENR and the National Statistical Coordination Board (now Philippine Statistics Authority) that updated, revised and expanded environmental indicators and accounts to include land, mineral, water, forest and fishery. However, these efforts were not integrated into the GDP accounts and instead produced separate accounts of natural capital depletion.

Box 6.1. (continued)

Philippine Wealth Accounting and Valuation of Ecosystem Services (Phil-WAVES). This ongoing project, which began in 2012, aims to provide national asset accounts for minerals and mangroves, as well as ecosystem services accounts based on studies from project sites in Southern Palawan and Laguna Lake by employing the SEEA framework.

and discuss the improvements in resource depletion and pollution. Data limitations dictate that this study will provide only a rough estimate of how much needs to be deducted from NI on the grounds of environmental resource issues and natural disasters in order to convert NI into a measure of welfare. For example, in 2013 the losses due to resource depletion, environmental degradation and damage from Typhoon Yolanda were equivalent to approximately 9 per cent of NI.

If prudent resource use and environmental policies are followed, the amount deducted from GNI shrinks as a percentage of NI such that environmental resource management becomes a source of growth. This indeed appeared to have been the case in the early 1990s, based on the ENRA project described in Box 6.1. However, subsequent statistics compiled by the World Bank and illustrated in Figure 6.2 suggest that this optimistic result has not continued and that environmental resource management in the 2000s has not been a source of welfare growth. However, the figures used in going from NI to GNI in Figure 6.2 were limited to minerals, forests and energy resources for the case of resource depletion, and carbon and particulate emissions in the case of environmental degradation.

Due to the aforementioned problems with previous attempts at green accounting, we now turn to the task of constructing resource depletion and environmental degradation accounts for 2000–13. Figures 6.3a to 6.3d show the available data on natural resource depletion and environmental degradation, expressed in nominal monetary values. The sum of these four factors, plus particulate emissions,[3] is the difference between NI and GNI.

FIGURE 6.2
Gross National, National, and Green National Income, 2008–13
(billion pesos at constant 2000 prices)

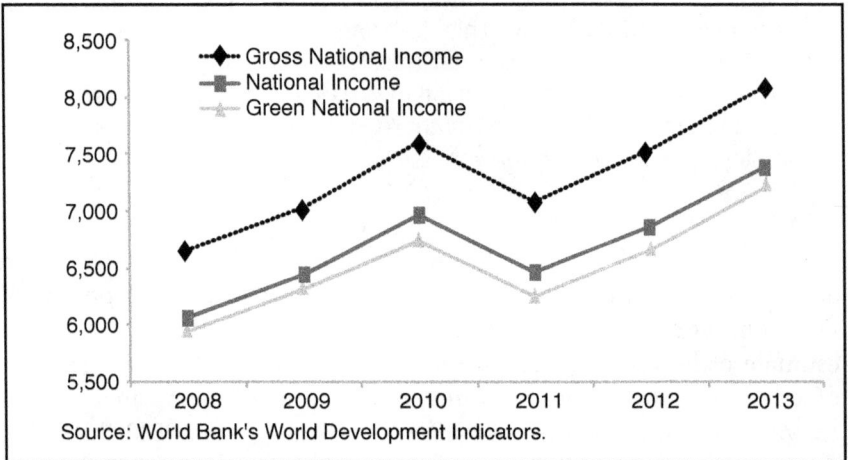

Source: World Bank's World Development Indicators.

FIGURE 6.3
Cost of Natural Resource Depletion and Environmental Degradation, 2000–2013
(million dollars at current prices)

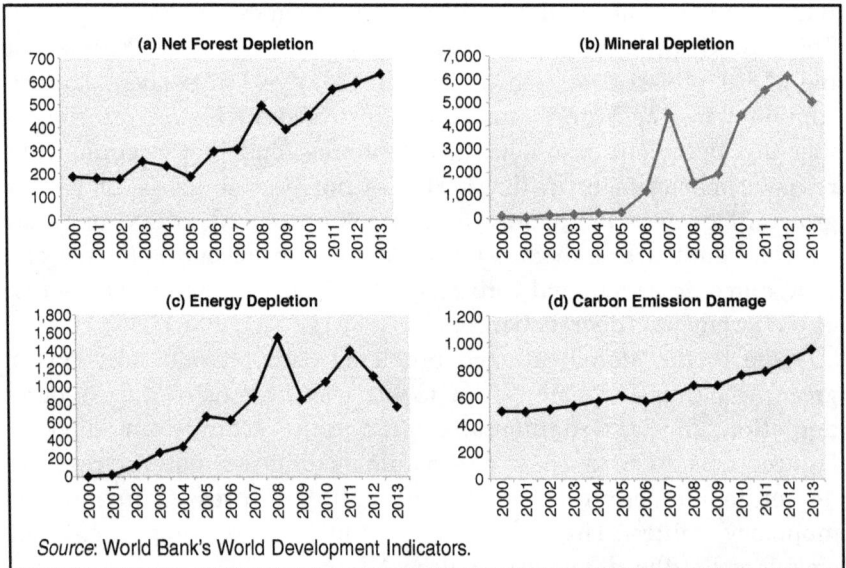

Source: World Bank's World Development Indicators.

Inasmuch as the World Development Indicators only allow the aggregation of a very few components of resource depletion and environmental degradation, other sources were used to provide additional information for other components (see Box 6.2). In terms of outdoor air quality, indicators show that the particulate matter 2.5 ($PM_{2.5}$) levels in Baguio City have become slightly worse, while Metro Manila, Cebu City and Cagayan de Oro City have maintained $PM_{2.5}$, sulfur dioxide (SO_2) and nitrogen dioxide (NO_2) levels within the Philippine National Air Ambient Quality Guideline Value. As to indoor air pollution, around half of the Philippine population is exposed to pollution caused by fuelwood or charcoal use (World Bank 2009). For water pollution, as of 2007, out of the 19 Priority Rivers identified by the Department of Environment and Natural Resources (DENR), 13 conformed with DENR's water quality criteria regarding dissolved oxygen but only 8 conformed with standards for biochemical oxygen demand.

Box 6.2. Other Measures of Environmental Degradation and Natural Resource Depletion

Indicators of environmental degradation and natural resource depletion can be classified according to physical measures (quantity and quality) and related economic cost due to illnesses (morbidity) and deaths (mortality). The table below provides supplementary figures for these indicators.

Quantity (Concentration) and Quality	Economic Cost[a]
Outdoor Air Pollution	
Particulate Matter 2.5 ($PM_{2.5}$). The standard is 35 µg/m³ annually or lower. The main drivers of high $PM_{2.5}$ concentration are rapid urbanization, transport and expansion of manufacturing and industrial production (Arcenas 2009).	Morbidity. Almost 55 per cent of illnesses are attributed to outdoor air pollution. Associated cost is P950 million (in 2007 prices) per year, with about half of it accounted for by productivity loss.

Box 6.2. (continued)

Quantity (Concentration) and Quality	Economic Cost[a]
Sulfur Dioxide (SO$_2$). The standard is 80 µg/m^3 annually or lower. High concentrations can be due to high numbers of diesel vehicles burning sulfur-containing diesel fuels and industrial facilities burning high sulfur (3 per cent) fuel oil (EMB 2004). Nitrogen Dioxide (NO$_2$). A major source of NO$_2$ is burning of coal, oil and gas.	Mortality. Over 15,000 people died in 2003 due to diseases linked to outdoor air pollution. Total annual cost of mortality ranges from P5.5 billion to P75 billion.
Indoor Air Pollution	
Solid Fuel Use. Around half of the Philippine population is exposed to pollution caused by fuelwood or charcoal use (World Bank 2009), and the use of solid fuel is skewed towards the poor, according to Household Energy Consumption Survey.	Morbidity. In 2003, most of the 450,000 cases of related diseases occured among children aged 0–4 years. Cost for all cases is estimated at P1.5 billion. Mortality. Deaths due to related diseases (i.e., TB, lung cancer, pneumonia, etc.) reached about 6,000 in 2003, with cost ranging from P4.6 billion to P28 billion.
Water Pollution	
Fresh Surface Water. For 19 priority rivers, only 13 conformed with the dissolved oxygen (DO) standard and 8 with the biochemical oxygen demand (BOD) standard. Marine Waters. Indicators include coliform counts and other physicochemical indicators. Over time, 8 out of 14 test sites in Manila Bay showed improved total coliform content. Manila Bay also passed the criteria on pH, oil and grease, and ammonia levels, but failed in nitrates and orthophosphates.	Morbidity. In 2003, more than 33 million Filipinos fell ill with water-quality diseases, the bulk of which were due to diarrhea. Cost for all cases is estimated at P21 billion. Mortality. Related diseases (i.e., diarrhoea, typhoid, cholera, etc.) killed 11,000 children under 5 years old in 2003, with 4,000 deaths for the rest of the population. Costs for these deaths range from P42 billion to P107 billion.

Box 6.2. (continued)

Quantity (Concentration) and Quality	Economic Cost[a]
Deforestation	
The deforestation rate from 1990 to 2005 was about 2.2 per cent annually (World Bank 2009), but there was forest appreciation starting from 1996 (Carandang 2008) as secondary forests were recovering due to decreased use of forestlands for fuelwood extraction and a shift from large-scale users of forest resources to small-scale community users (Carandang 2008).	

[a]*Source*: World Bank 2009.

Figure 6.4 augments the data shown in Figure 6.3 with other measures of environmental degradation and natural resource depletion. The grey line shows natural resource depletion from 2003 to 2013. The black line is the adjusted environmental degradation measure, which now accounts for mortality and morbidity costs from outdoor and indoor air pollution, as well as water, sanitation and hygiene. The result shows that resource depletion appears to have reached a turning point. This is presumably because forest depletion is self-limiting. Once depletion has sufficiently depleted forest stocks, remaining forested areas are less accessible, such that depletion slows, even with inadequate governance. There is no such self-limiting effect with environmental degradation, which is still increasing. Adding the two curves, we find that total depletion and degradation (TDD) increased slightly from 2003 to 2007 and then remained roughly constant until 2013.

FIGURE 6.4
Depletion and Degradation, 2003–13
(million pesos at constant 2000 prices)

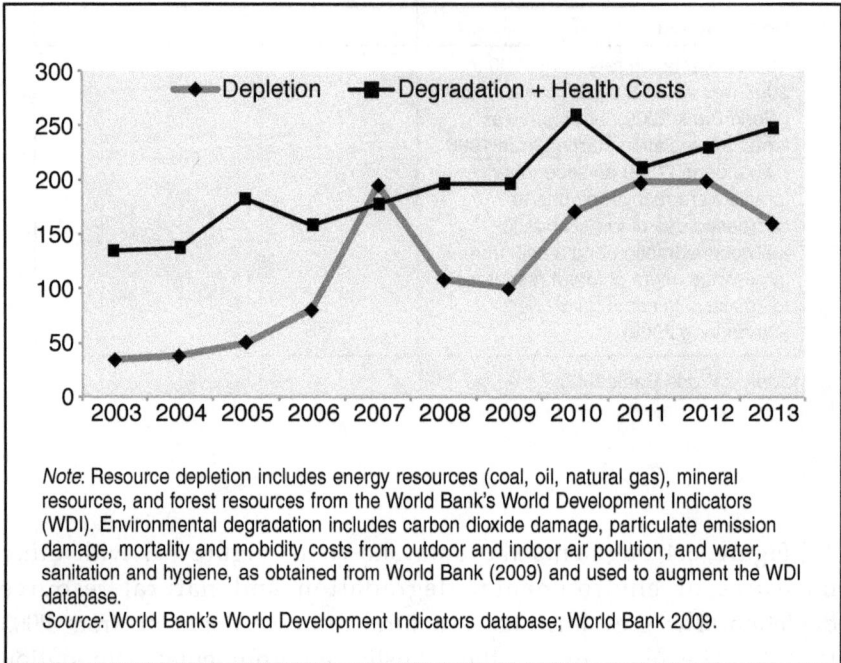

Note: Resource depletion includes energy resources (coal, oil, natural gas), mineral resources, and forest resources from the World Bank's World Development Indicators (WDI). Environmental degradation includes carbon dioxide damage, particulate emission damage, mortality and mobidity costs from outdoor and indoor air pollution, and water, sanitation and hygiene, as obtained from World Bank (2009) and used to augment the WDI database.
Source: World Bank's World Development Indicators database; World Bank 2009.

Table 6.1 compares partial values of TDD in selected ASEAN countries. In the Philippines, TDD as a percentage of NI decreased from 3.1 per cent in 2010 to 2.3 per cent in 2013. Since estimates for both depletion and degradation are only partial (i.e., they do not cover all categories such as marine resources and health costs; pollution estimates only cover productivity losses and do not include the value of statistical life), these regional comparisons may be misleading in the sense that what is left out varies across countries. For both 2010 and 2013, depletion includes net forest depletion, mineral depletion and energy depletion. Degradation includes carbon dioxide and particulate emission damage. However, values for particulate emission damage were only available for 2010.

TABLE 6.1
Total Depletion and Degradation (TDD) Values in Selected ASEAN Countries, 2010 and 2013
(billion dollars at current prices)

Country	2010				2013			
	Depletion	Degradation	TDD	% of National Income	Depletion	Degradation	Total	% of National Income
Philippines	5.99	2.20	8.19	3.08	6.51	0.96	7.47	2.29
Malaysia	19.17	2.49	21.66	9.05	20.91	2.55	23.47	7.76
Indonesia	35.60	8.08	43.68	5.95	32.52	6.46	38.97	4.41
Thailand	12.11	3.55	15.66	5.13	15.83	3.40	19.23	5.32

Note: Numbers may not sum precisely because of rounding.
Source: World Bank's World Development Indicators.

Figure 6.5(a) sets out two possible scenarios for both natural-resource depletion and environmental degradation (including health costs of degradation). These are the non-sustainable or weak growth scenario represented by the black lines (WG) and the sustainable or strong growth (SG) scenario represented by the grey lines. The WG scenario assumes that the share of natural resource depletion as a percentage of national income will stay constant at 2 per cent until 2040 (increasing solid black line). On the one hand, the quantity of resource depletion will slow down (even without improved governance) for the simple reason that there will be less forests and marine resources to deplete. On the other hand, the scarcity value would increase due to both the physical scarcity and higher incomes by 2040. Without clear evidence on which force would dominate, our WG scenario for resource depletion remains at current rates. Regarding environmental degradation, we assume in the SG scenario that it stays constant at 3 per cent of NI until 2040 (rising dotted black line), in association with the expected increase in the numbers of petrol and diesel vehicles, electricity consumption and the size of the industrial sector.

The SG scenario assumes improved natural resource management such that depletion falls to zero by 2040.[4] In the medium-run, depletion of marine and terrestrial stocks of renewable resources should be negative, since they have been depleted below their optimal levels. We assume that by 2040 the value of renewable stocks is held constant as sustainable fishing and forestry policies only harvest stock growth. Non-renewable reserves can also be held constant by offsetting extraction with exploration and discoveries of new deposits.

In accordance with the country's Intended Nationally Determined Contributions submitted to the United Nations Framework Convention on Climate Change (UNFCCC) in 2015, the SG scenario for environmental degradation holds the value of emissions constant at its current level (constant grey dashed line, approximately P275 billion). By 2040 this becomes 0.6 per cent of NI. That is, TDD as a percentage of NI optimistically falls by an order of magnitude by 2040.

Figure 6.5b compares GNI with SG and WG projections for TDD. NI is assumed to increase at the optimistic rate of 7 per cent for both cases. In the WG case, TDD remains at 5 per cent of NI, whereas

FIGURE 6.5
Possible Scenarios on Depletion, Degradation and Green National Income, 2015–40
(billion pesos at constant 2000 prices)

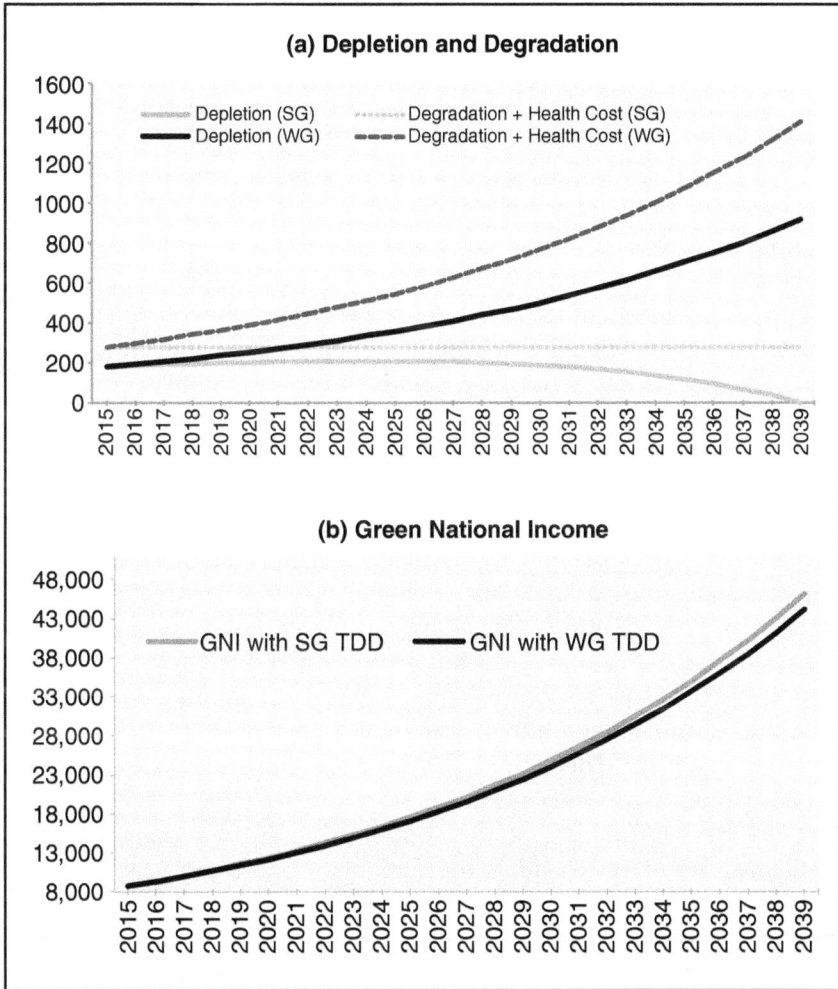

(a) Depletion and Degradation

Depletion (SG)
Depletion (WG)
Degradation + Health Cost (SG)
Degradation + Health Cost (WG)

(b) Green National Income

GNI with SG TDD   GNI with WG TDD

it falls to 0.6 per cent in the SG scenario. Improved environmental and resource management results in economic welfare, as represented by GNI, growing faster than NI at an average rate of 7.2 per cent up to 2040.

Since even a partial measurement of TDD is already 5 per cent of NI, amounting to P407 billion in 2013 (P161 billion for depletion, P246 billion for degradation, both at constant 2000 prices), well-being is substantially lower than it would have been without that subtraction. The country's NI for 2013 was P8.169 trillion (PSA 2014). If the full value of TDD is around 7 per cent of NI and that is reduced to around one-tenth of that percentage, this means that GNI can grow about 0.4 per cent faster than NI from 2016 to 2040.

There are several factors that are currently impeding efficient environmental and resource management. One of the clearest is the failure to impose emission taxes according to the marginal damage costs of pollution. Similarly, congestion charges can internalize much of the spillover effects of driving, which are currently causing enormous traffic delays in Manila and elsewhere. Another is the underpricing of forest and water resources, documented in the 1970s and 1980s (Repetto et al. 1989; Roumasset 1991) and continuing to the present.

While most of the literatures in both resource economics and sustainable development presume that natural resources are over-exploited, the opposite is also possible. Failing to pursue efficient exploration, development and extraction of mineral resources can be equally damaging to GNI. For example, consider a mineral resource (e.g., a copper or gold deposit in Mindanao) worth $6 billion in present value terms after deducting extraction and environmental costs. Banning extraction of the resource reduces the country's wealth by $6 billion. In green accounting this should be treated as a capital loss, commensurate with depletion. That is, the mining ban decreases GNI by $6 billion.

The basic principle of efficient mining is to extract minerals until the market price equals the foregone opportunity cost plus any environmental damage costs. This would allow much higher royalties than are currently being collected. On the other hand, the royalties must not extract the rents from mineral exploration and development to the point where it is unattractive. The challenge is to develop incentives for mineral exploration and development, while at the same time capturing a large share of mineral rents for the Filipino people (Garnaut 2010; Lange et al. 2010).

Similarly, deforestation policies can be improved, not so much by banning logging but by selection of logging concessionaires who obtain the highest present value from forest areas. On public forestlands, this can be done by auctioning logging concessions and charging logging royalties in accordance with the lost present value due to reductions in both ecosystem services and timber stocks.

II. Risk Management and Policy Reforms Can Increase the Growth of Well-Being

A. Accounting for the Likelihood of Natural Disasters

Due to the random occurrence of natural disasters such as typhoons, earthquakes, volcanic eruptions, tsunamis and other geological processes, as well as the impact of climate change on rainfall patterns, sea levels and temperatures, the importance of disaster preparedness and resiliency is becoming more crucial and could be a potential source of welfare growth.

The theoretical construct underlying green accounting typically abstracts from uncertainty. Accordingly, GNI cannot measure the performance of a country's risk management. Before generalizing comprehensive welfare accounting to include uncertainty, it is useful to recall that GNI measures sustainable income — that hypothetical level of consumption that could be sustained into the future (Smulders 2008). Accordingly, another name for GNI is *environmentally sustainable income*. By abstracting from the possibility of adverse shocks to the *environomy*, GNI overstates sustainable income. Just as GNI accounts for the extent to which falling stocks of natural capital reduce sustainable income (Weitzman and Lofgren 1997), we can account for the extent to which future adverse events reduce sustainable income as well. We call the resulting construct *comprehensive national income* (CNI). This is illustrated in Figure 6.6. CNI is sustainable income after accounting for the possibilities of natural disasters and damage from climate change.

The black (eventually dashed) line represents the projected growth of GNI, assuming that no disaster hits the country. The grey line illustrates what happens to GNI when a disaster hits at time t. Since sustainable income has been overstated before the disaster hits, it suddenly records losses in physical and human capital and

FIGURE 6.6
Comprehensive National Income (CNI)

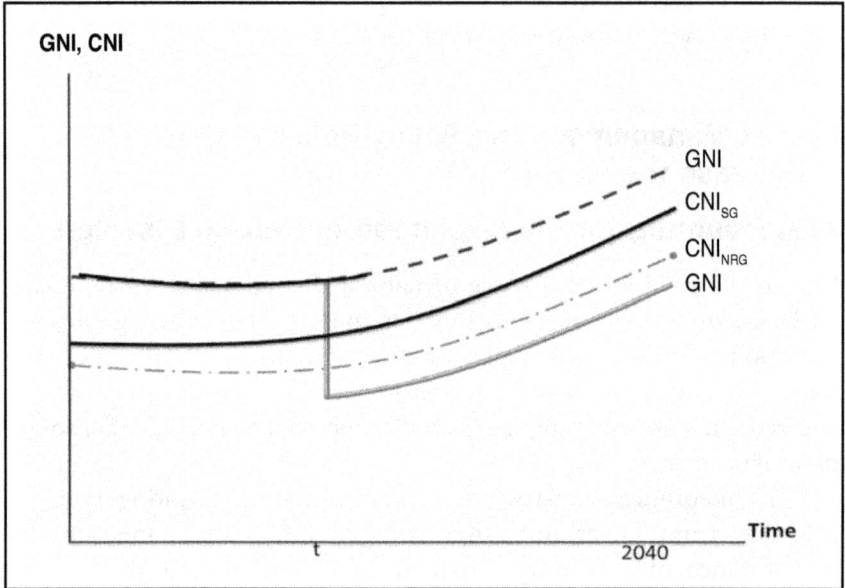

jumps downwards. In 2013, the impact of Yolanda alone amounted to P334 billion (at constant 2000 prices) in terms of damage and losses. This is almost 4.1 per cent of NI for that year (NEDA 2013).[5]

Once we allow for the likelihood of natural disasters, sustainable income is considerably reduced, as illustrated by the non-resilient growth CNI_{NRG} (grey dashed) line. There is no kink in CNI_{NRG} because sustainable income has already been reduced before the disaster hits (after accounting for the probability of asset loss).[6] The solid black line represents a more optimistic scenario (CNI_{SG}), wherein government takes cost effective precautionary and other risk managing measures that enable the economy to grow at a rate equal to, or even faster than, the growth rate of GNI. In the CNI_{NRG} scenario, the government only partially prepares for the disaster, leading to a slower growth rate as well as a reduced level of sustainable income.

B. Managing Disaster Risk: The Many Levels of Precaution and Response

This leaves the question of how public policy can be designed to balance the available ex-ante and ex-post controls to maximize expected well-being, given the event distribution, with particular attention to natural disasters. Investments in disaster preparedness have been shown to deliver very high rates of return. In a meta-analysis that compiles several case studies on disaster, Shreve and Kelman (2014) find that for every dollar of investment in preparedness, \$3–\$30 worth of benefits (avoided damage) are obtained, depending on the nature of avoidance actions and the type of disaster or hazard.

Given the projected increase in both the occurrence and intensity of extreme natural events (Cinco et al. 2013), improved institutional capability on disaster risk management is needed. The recent experience of natural disaster such as typhoons Frank (international name: Fengshen) in 2008, Ondoy (Ketsana) and Pepeng (Parma) in 2009, Pablo (Bopha) in 2012, and Yolanda (Haiyan) in 2013 have raised government and private sector awareness regarding the need for preparedness.

Disaster management in the Philippines dates back to the 1930s. The lead agency then was the Civilian Emergency Administration (CEA), which was mandated to formulate and execute policies and plans for the protection and welfare of the civilian population under extraordinary and emergency conditions. CEA is the earliest precursor of what we know today as the National Disaster Risk Reduction and Management Council (NDRRMC). Republic Act 10121 of 2010 reconstituted the National Disaster Coordinating Council (NDCC) into NDRRMC after more than three decades of its existence. The NDRRMC is empowered with a mandate on policymaking, coordination, integration, supervision, monitoring and evaluation functions related to disaster risk management. The secretary of the Department of National Defense is the chair, with the secretaries of the Department of Interior and Local Government, Department of Social Welfare and Development, Department of Science and Technology (DOST), and economic planning secretary/director-general of the National and Economic Development Authority (NEDA) as vice-chairpersons.

The NDRRMC was established after the Strategic National Action Plan (SNAP) on Disaster Risk Reduction (DRR) was formulated and Executive Order 888 was signed. SNAP provided a road map for sustaining disaster risk reduction initiatives in the country and promoting good practices of individuals, organizations, local government units (LGUs) and the private sector. Through Executive Order 888 and Administrative Order 1, LGUs are mandated to adopt and use the DRR guidelines. The experience from typhoons Ondoy and Pepeng provided the impetus to revisit and review the existing setup for disaster management in the country.

Prior to the formation of the NDRRMC, Republic Act 9729 of 2009 created the Climate Change Commission (CCC) with the mandate of coordinating, monitoring and evaluating government programmes and action plans relating to climate change. The CCC has the status of a national government agency and is attached to the Office of the President. In principle, the NDRRMC and the CCC have aligned their activities by harmonizing the Local Climate Change Action Plans and Local Disaster Risk Reduction Management Plans by the LGUs. As the coordinating agency, NEDA is tasked to build capacity among the local, regional and national level government offices to integrate DRR in their respective plans. The Midterm Update of the Philippine Development Plan 2011–16 (NEDA 2013) included spatial considerations in directing the focus of government interventions according to the following categories: (i) the number or magnitude of poor households in the province; (ii) the provincial poverty incidence, or the proportion of poor individuals to the provincial population; and (iii) the province's vulnerability to natural disasters (floods and landslides, in particular).

Despite these institutional achievements, the country's ability to efficiently respond to disaster can be improved and is continually being tested by each disaster event. The NDRRMC (2011) cited several constraints and issues that thwart efficient disaster management: (i) ineffective vertical and horizontal coordination among member agencies; (ii) limited coverage by governmental and partner organizations due to resource constraints; (iii) ineffective LGU capacities, such as the lack of managerial and technical competencies; (iv) limited funds, equipment and facilities for monitoring and early warning; (v) insufficient hazard and disaster risk data and information; (vi) inadequate mainstreaming of disaster risk management in development planning and implementation; (vii) poor enforcement of environmental management laws and other relevant regulations; and (viii) inadequate socio-economic and environmental management programmes to reduce the vulnerability of marginalized communities.

Clearly, managing the risk of natural disasters is a complex job due to the heterogeneous nature of disasters and the various stakeholders and potential actions involved. Improving national policies towards better disaster risk management requires a conceptual framework. We start with the illustration in Figure 6.7. The grey boxes show the nature of damage likelihoods before and after various actions have been taken, while the black ovals illustrate the five levels of disaster management:

(i)   Mitigation, e.g., of climate change (inasmuch as earthquakes, volcanoes, and even climate change are largely exogenous to the Philippines, it may be appropriate to skip this step, except as a member of the community of nations).

(ii) Ex-ante reduction of exposure (disaster prevention), which includes risk and hazard mapping, rezoning, relocation of residences, public infrastructure (e.g., drainage and dikes), building strengthening (e.g., engineering design), education and awareness among communities, building capacity of DRR professionals and practitioners.

(iii) Early warning and response.

(iv) Ex-post loss reduction, which includes relief, timely information and communication, dredging, healthcare, relocation.

(v)   Coping, which includes rebuilding, rehabilitation, recovery and ex-ante financial preparation for the same, e.g., through external or self-insurance.

Even though optimal risk management is a recursive process, investments in each of these levels of control are interdependent. The costs and benefits at each level depend on what investments are made at other levels. Attempts to apply simple rules of thumb (e.g., "an ounce of prevention is worth a pound of cure") are likely to be counterproductive.

FIGURE 6.7
Natural Disaster Risk Management Framework

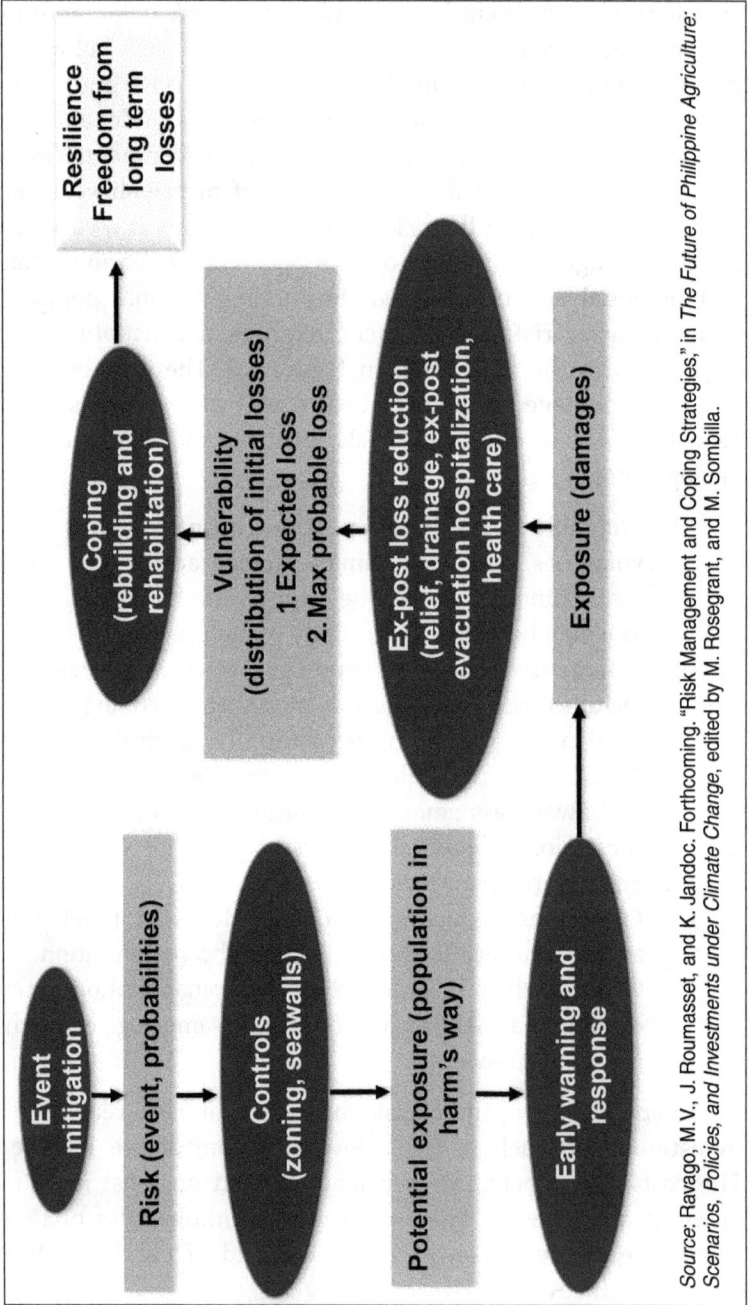

Source: Ravago, M.V., J. Roumasset, and K. Jandoc. Forthcoming. "Risk Management and Coping Strategies," in *The Future of Philippine Agriculture: Scenarios, Policies, and Investments under Climate Change*, edited by M. Rosegrant, and M. Sombilla.

In principle, if the likelihood distributions (grey boxes) can be estimated for each configuration of actions (black ovals), then least-cost methods of achieving a particular resilience level can be computed. Given the extreme complexity of this problem, one possible simplification is illustrated by the vulnerability box. Instead of estimating the entire likelihood distribution, one estimates a key characteristic of said distribution, such as *expected loss* or *maximum probable loss*. Even with this simplification, however, this task exceeds current administrative capabilities. In order to deliver improved disaster management that increases the growth rate of CNI, these modelling capabilities must be further developed. This is in line with the government's call for capacity building to strengthen statistical agencies.

Table 6.2 provides a matrix of the levels of disaster management as illustrated in Figure 6.7 against the thematic areas as provided for in the NDRRMC plan, including National Disaster Response Plan. The table also shows the government agencies in charge of the various thematic areas.

In the past three years, the country has made significant strides in terms of utilizing scientific knowledge in the delivery of early warning systems. The DOST's Project Nationwide Operational Assessment of Hazards (NOAH) has developed state-of-the-art geo-hazard vulnerability maps and raised the level of awareness among Filipinos. DOST's PAGASA has also upgraded its equipment in the last five years, enabling them to provide real time typhoon alerts and weather updates, thereby promoting improved disaster management.

Moving forward, the country and its multilateral partners are capitalizing on the experience and lessons learned from typhoon Yolanda (Haiyan) in 2013. The extensive damage challenged capabilities for rebuilding, rehabilitation, recovery and coordination. The government's commitment is key to sustaining relief and rebuilding capabilities inasmuch as it concomitantly builds the capacity of government to respond to future disasters.[7] The outpouring of aid, both technical and financial, from local and international donors was critical, but also underscored the importance of having a single government agency with overall authority to coordinate the various stakeholders.

TABLE 6.2
**Levels of Disaster Management and Corresponding Thematic
Areas and Agencies Responsible**

Level of Disaster Management	Thematic Area	Agencies Responsible
Event mitigation	Disaster prevention	...
Ex-ante reduction of exposure	Harm mitigation	Department of Science and Technology[a] Department of Public Works and Highways (DPWH) National Economic and Development Authority (NEDA) Office of Civil Defense (OCD) Department of Environment and Natural Resources (DENR) Department of Finance (DOF)
Early warning and response	Disaster preparedness	Department of the Interior and Local Government (DILG)[a] Philippine Atmospheric, Geophysical and Astronomical Services Administration (PAGASA) Project Nationwide Operational Assessment of Hazards (NOAH) Weather Philippines Philippine Institute of Volcanology and Seismology (PHIVOLCS) Philippine Information Agency (PIA) OCD
Ex-post loss reduction	Disaster response	Department of Social Welfare and Development (DSWD)[a] Department of Health (DOH) Department of Transportation and Communications Civil Aviation Authority of the Philippines National Grid Corporation of the Philippines
Coping (rebuilding, rehabilitation and recovery)	Disaster rehabilitation and recovery	NEDA[a] OCD National Housing Authority DPWH DOH DSWD

Note: Thematic Area is based on the National Disaster Risk Reduction & Management Council Plan.
Note: a. Lead Agency.

The Yolanda experience also clarified the need for financial preparation. The Department of Finance (DOF) has developed a Disaster Risk Financing and Insurance Strategy (DOF 2015) consisting of various financial instruments targeted at national, local, and household levels, with a view to reducing the impact of disasters on the poorest and most vulnerable sectors of society. At the national level, stand-by emergency credit for urgent recovery worth $400 million was put in place by the Japan International Cooperation Agency in 2015. Catastrophe bonds are also being considered. At the local government level, pilot projects for provincial government catastrophe insurance and city disaster-risk financing are being tested. At the household level, a potential residential disaster insurance pool is being studied. On the other hand, the tendency to assume that insurance subsidies and mandates are the best tools of risk management runs counter to the framework discussed above.

To sustain the gains achieved thus far, further enhancement of disaster management capabilities, including at the local government level, is needed. A more comprehensive assessment of capabilities along the lines of Figure 6.7 will promote better disaster risk reduction and management and contribute to the growth of national well-being.

C. Policy Reform as a Source of Growth

There are feasible possibilities for producing material goods and environmental amenities, as illustrated in the outer frontier in Figure 6.8. However, all economies suffer from inevitable inefficiencies due to policy distortions and operate at some point inside the frontier as shown. The good news is that "greedy growth", the strategy of advancing the slice of the economic pie for special interests at the expense of both the environment and the general public, is not necessary; nor is extreme environmental protectionism that puts resources off limits and accordingly precludes an important source of growth. Instead, by removing policy distortions, it is possible to move in a "win-win" direction and improve both material consumption and environmental amenities (Ravago et al. 2010).

Conventional economics emphasizes moving the frontier out by increases in produced and human capital (e.g., learning). The correct measure of total capital accumulation nets out resource depletion and environmental degradation as well as conventional depreciation. Economic theory tells us that the growth rate of per capita income in a closed economy converges to the growth rate of technological change. Inasmuch as 2 per cent is considered a rapid rate of technological change, convergence theory suggests that a per capita income growth rate of 5 per cent is unattainable in the long run. Fortunately, convergence theory leaves out two important sources of growth, in addition to the prospects for improved environmental and disaster management discussed in Part I. First, since the Philippine economy is an open one, domestic savings can be supplemented by foreign investment as a source of capital growth. Second (and the concern of this section), sustained efficiency improvements can be a source of growth as the economy moves from the interior point in Figure 6.8 to a point closer to the frontier.

FIGURE 6.8
Relationship between Material Consumption and Environmental Amenities

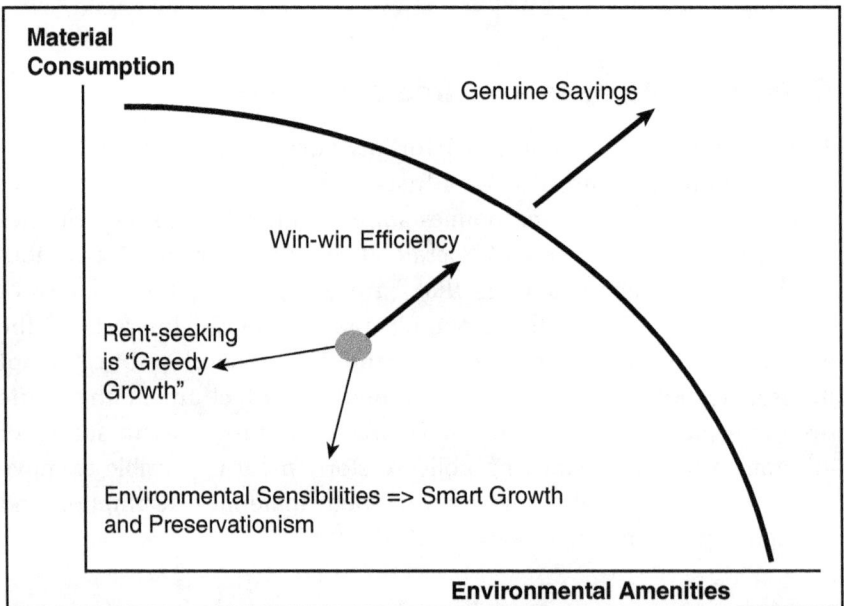

Source: Adapted from Endress and Roumasset 1996.

One source of efficiency gains is distortions and unnecessary friction inhibiting international trade, such as restrictions by the National Food Authority on grain trade (e.g., Clarete 2008). Similarly, removing policies that inhibit mutually beneficial exchanges in the domestic market, such as restrictions on land sales, can increase efficiency (Fabella 2014). An example of a distortion in energy policy that is currently inhibiting welfare growth is the policy of subsidizing renewable sources of power generation through a feed-in-tariff (FIT), discussed in the following section.

D. Stimulating Renewable Energy: High Cost vs. Efficient Methods

As a dramatic illustration of how well-intentioned policies can reduce efficiency and welfare, suppose that the Renewable Energy Act of 2008 was further strengthened to mandate that all power in the Philippines will be generated from renewable sources. Figure 6.9 provides an

FIGURE 6.9
The Economic Cost (Waste) of a Feed-in-Tariff

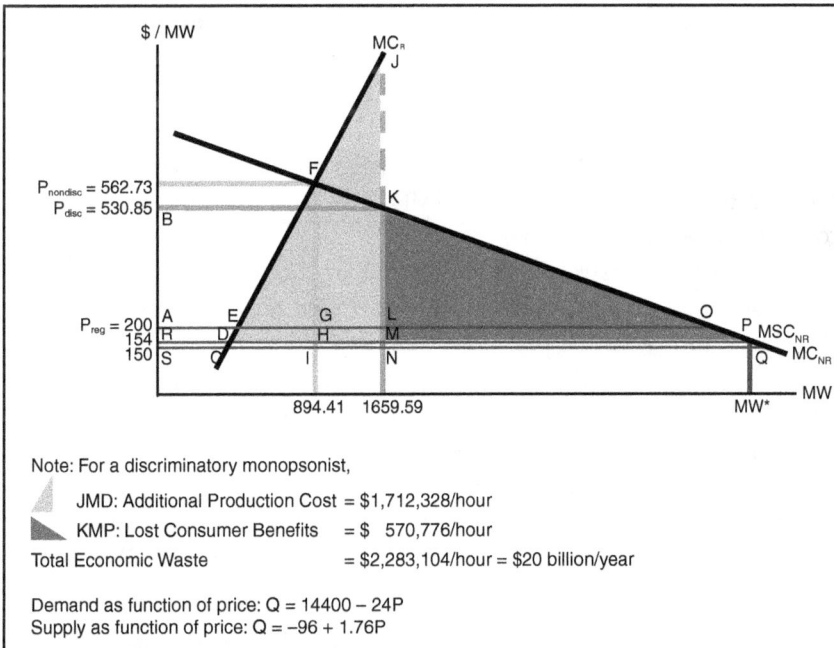

Note: For a discriminatory monopsonist,

    JMD: Additional Production Cost = $1,712,328/hour
    KMP: Lost Consumer Benefits   = $ 570,776/hour
    Total Economic Waste   = $2,283,104/hour = $20 billion/year

Demand as function of price: Q = 14400 − 24P
Supply as function of price: Q = −96 + 1.76P

illustration of how policy distortions shrink the economy in the context of subsidizing renewables. Electricity can be produced by a non-renewable fuel (coal) or by renewable sources such as wind and solar. The marginal cost of non-renewably sourced power (MC_{NR}) is based on the import price of coal. The higher marginal social cost of the non-renewable power (MSC_{NR}) is due to carbon and other emissions from burning coal. Meanwhile, the cost of renewably sourced power (MC_R) is rising, largely because of the differential suitability of different locations. The optimal solution in this case is at MW*, where the demand (D) intersects with MSC_{NR}. This can be simply achieved by setting an emission tax equal to the difference between MSC_{NR} and MC_{NR}. Suppose the policy is instead to displace all non-renewable power with renewable power. This can be done by setting a uniform FIT equal to the price that equates demand with renewable supply, minus MC_{NR}. This is the non-discriminating price ($P_{nondisc}$) in Figure 6.9.

Since setting a uniform FIT may have an unacceptable impact on prices, suppose that instead the regulatory authority acts as a perfectly discriminating monopsonist and pays every supplier the marginal cost. The regulator sets the price such that the revenue represented by the rectangle BKNS in Figure 6.9 just equals the subsidy outlays represented by the triangle JNC. The loss in consumer surplus will equal the area defined by the triangle KMP. Note that moving from a non-discriminating to a discriminating monopsony reduces the loss in consumer surplus from the triangle FHP to triangle KMP. However, doing so also increases the excess burden from the supply side from the area FHD to a larger triangle JMD. Thus, there is no ex-ante reason to prefer one over the other.

In order to illustrate the magnitude of these excess burdens from both consumer and producer sides, we undertake a numerical exercise that takes into account plausible numbers from the current electricity market. We assume that the elasticity of supply and demand at the currently observed points are 0.5 and 1.1, respectively. We assume that for a typical hour the demand for non-renewable energy at the regulated price of $200/MW is around 9,600 MW and that the marginal cost of non-renewables is $150/MW, considering that the marginal cost for generation from coal is around $0.07/kWh (Meller and Marquardt 2013) and 45 per cent of the retail price is due to generation cost. The marginal social cost of non-renewables is assumed to be \$4 more than the marginal cost, reflecting damage from both CO_2 and SO_2.[8] With these assumptions, the excess burden on the producer's side from a perfectly non-discriminating monopsonist (triangle FHD) is \$147,015 for a typical hour (around \$1.2 billion a year), while the excess burden on the consumer's side (triangle FHP) is \$2,004,750 for a typical hour (around \$17 billion a year). These two excess burdens sum up to more than \$18 billion in a year, which is around 6 per cent of GDP for the Philippines in 2014.

The shaded areas of Figure 6.9 represent the economic costs (waste) of a perfectly discriminating monopsony. The excess burden from the producer's side is around \$15 billion a year, while the excess burden on the consumer's side is around \$5 billion a year. The sum is roughly \$20 billion, or 7 per cent of GDP in 2014. Interestingly, the attempt to mitigate against the price increase, while decreasing the loss of demand-side excess burden, increases supply-side excess burden even more, due to the greater amount of power that must now be produced by renewables.

Since regulatory authorities are unable to act as discriminating monopsonists, however, the excess burden could well be more than 7 per cent. Not knowing the costs of different types of renewable energy in different locations, the authorities tend to assign a uniform price to each type of renewable. This means, for example, that the higher subsidies for solar power will displace some amount of more cost-effective wind power.

This exercise shows how moving towards a policy of energy self-sufficiency and 100 per cent renewability can have a major downward effect on welfare and its growth rate. But moving in the opposite direction (towards lower subsidies) will have the opposite effect.

By facilitating an efficient transition to a greater reliance on renewable energy without the use of high-cost subsidies, policy reform can improve levels of living as indexed by sustainable income. Since there are inevitable forces that will tend to make NI growth slower than GDP (e.g., a declining growth rate of remittances as Philippine incomes increasingly converge towards those in developed countries), policy reforms as well as improvements in environmental and disaster management can ensure that levels of living increase at the same or a greater rate than GDP.

E. Political Economy and Institutional Reform

It is one thing to articulate policies that can increase the growth of well-being and another thing to render those policies politically feasible. To the extent that reforms can be packaged in approximately win-win combinations, their political feasibility is enhanced (Buchanan 1985). For example, the opponents of a major mining deal will be less influential if the use of royalties paid to the government from that venture are transformed into expenditures that transparently promote the common good, such as investments in education. Part of the royalties can also be invested into a conservation trust fund, such that residual environmental costs (after appropriate safeguards) are offset by commensurate environmental benefits.

Institutional reform is also needed to render efficiency-enhancing policies effective. For example, management policies for public forestlands need to provide incentives for selecting concessionaires that will maximize the long-run value of the resource (including carbon sequestration and ecosystem services). This can be done with the combination of auctions for the selection of concessionaires, royalty assessments based on the lost present value from harvesting, payments for ecosystem services, and performance bonds for enforcement against excess depletion. While marine resource management has already been devolved to local government, technical and financial assistance from national government are needed for determination of optimal catch rates, enforcement, and assessment of governance mechanisms such as individual transferable quotas.

Further conclusions regarding these higher levels of analysis are unwarranted. Institutional design and political feasibility are components of the economics of the *second* and *third best* (Dixit 1999; Roumasset 2015). While there are some broad principles that can be further developed and applied — e.g., regarding the comparative advantage of national and local governments (Roumasset 1989, 1997) — these only become useful once the more fundamental first-best policies have been articulated as discussed above. For example, one cannot meaningfully propose to "transform" mineral royalties into human capital and conservation accounts without first determining what percentage of the in-situ resource price (net of extraction costs) should be paid in royalties. The proposition that government should specify how resource royalties should be transformed into productive investments derives from the now-defunct Hartwick rule, that resource depletion should be governed by the Hotelling principle and that resource royalties should be reinvested in capital formation in order to sustain consumption levels indefinitely. We know now that while optimal resource depletion should indeed be governed by an extended version of the Hotelling rule, capital accumulation should be governed by an entirely separate principle, known in economics as the Ramsey equation (Endress et al. 2005).

III. Sustainable Development and the UN Sustainable Development Goals

In 2015 the Philippines acceded in principle to the UN's 2030 Agenda for Sustainable Development. Part of the aim of the agenda is to "protect the planet from degradation, including through sustainable consumption and production, sustainably managing its natural resources and taking urgent action on climate change, so that it can support the needs of the present and future generations" (UN 2015). As a testament to this focus, nine of the seventeen goals comprising the agenda are specific to climate change, natural resources, the environment, and disaster risk management:

   (i)   Goal 6: Ensure availability and sustainable management of water and sanitation for all;

   (ii)   Goal 7: Ensure access to affordable, reliable, sustainable and modern energy for all;

   (iii) Goal 8: Promote sustained, inclusive and sustainable economic growth, full and productive employment and decent work for all;

   (iv) Goal 9: Build resilient infrastructure, promote inclusive and sustainable industrialization and foster innovation;

(v)   Goal 12: Ensure sustainable consumption and production patterns;

(vi)   Goal 13: Take urgent action to combat climate change and its impacts;

(vii) Goal 14: Conserve and sustainably use the oceans, seas and marine resources for sustainable development;

(viii) Goal 15: Protect, restore and promote sustainable use of terrestrial ecosystems, sustainably manage forests, combat desertification, and halt and reverse land degradation and halt biodiversity loss; and

(ix)   Goal 17: Strengthen the means of implementation and revitalize the global partnership for sustainable development.

By themselves, these goals do not provide a guide for formulating public policy. As illustrated in the previous section, some goals may be in conflict with others. In other cases, prioritization among goals remains ambiguous. The main challenge for the government is to interpret and operationalize these goals for environmental protection, disaster risk mitigation and climate change policies in ways that do not contradict the primary government responsibility of promoting the common good as provided for in the 1987 Constitution. The government previously signified its intention to achieve some of these goals; for instance, by its Intended Nationally Determined Contributions to the UNFCCC. The commitment to reduce greenhouse gas (GHG) emissions by 70 per cent by 2030 may seem excessive, even relative to the non-resilient growth scenario, even though the NRG scenario was based on rather exaggerated assumptions. The government has also prioritized adaptation over mitigation of climate change, noting that mitigation can be a function of adaptation. For example, adaptation investments that improve the robustness of forest and marine ecosystems will also sequester carbon from the atmosphere, thereby aiding global mitigation.

In the same document, the Philippine government has recognized that the country should not drastically sacrifice the common good and instead contribute "its fair share in global climate action". This means that climate mitigation efforts not resulting from adaptation initiatives must emanate from global agreements, and, for Philippine efforts not to undermine the country's own development goals, the reduction of GHG emissions in the Philippines should be aided by financial and technical assistance from developed countries.

The problem in public policy formulation in many countries, as well as in the Philippines, emanates from the plethora of ill-defined and often contradictory objectives. For example, policies regarding farmer and food security, land reform, electricity, and disaster management, include the objectives of sustainability, self-sufficiency, renewability, affordability, reliability, inclusivity, security, and resiliency. Since each of these objectives may subtract from others, the pursuit of too many objectives is likely to lead to a *mission impossible*. Goal 7, for example, calls for ensuring "access to affordable, reliable, sustainable and modern energy for all", while Goal 13 requires taking "urgent action to combat climate change and its impacts". Advocates of renewable energy may interpret these goals as requiring subsidies of renewable energy to reduce carbon emissions from fossil fuels. As discussed previously, these subsidies make electricity more expensive, thereby creating a contradiction between the goals of affordability and sustainability.

Moving forward, the key is to find ways to reconcile these goals without sacrificing the common good. In the context of the affordability versus sustainability paradox, there are ways to reduce pollution and stimulate innovation in renewable energy without direct price subsidies of renewable electricity generation (Fischer et al. 2014). In particular, emission taxes commensurate with domestic pollution damages can be implemented.

Absent a strong and binding global agreement and assuming that carbon-induced damages in the Philippines are 5 per cent of worldwide damages,[9] the Philippine carbon tax should be $1.25 per tonne of carbon dioxide, given a global social cost of carbon of $25/MtCO_2.[10] Since a megawatt hour of electricity from coal generates about 0.98 tonnes of carbon dioxide,[11] the tax on coal-generated power should be around $1.23/MWh. Adding another $7.88/MWh to take local pollutants (SO_2, NO_X and TSPs) into account would increase the tax to $9.11/MWh — 4.6 per cent of the current electricity price of approximately $200/MWh.[12] By directly internalizing the costs of pollution and thereby inducing the correct adjustment of both fuel mix and quantity of power produced, the high economic costs of FIT subsidies can be avoided entirely and with only a modest effect on the price of electricity.

IV. Conclusions

Inasmuch as GDP does not serve as an index of well-being, what needs to be done so that CNI also grows at 7 per cent? First, note that a robust economy will reduce the extent of net out-migration and retard the growth of remittances. This force will tend to make NI, and therefore GNI, grow more slowly than GDP. To offset this negative force, total environmental degradation and the depletion of natural capital must decline as a percentage of NI. Even a partial accounting of depletion and degradation shows that GNI is almost 6 per cent less than NI. Gradually reducing this rate towards zero in the strong/ sustainable scenario thus becomes a source of growth. For example, if the true depletion and degradation is 8 per cent of NI, reducing TDD to 0.6 per cent by 2040 would add an average of almost a third of a per cent to the growth rate of well-being. This would be enough to offset the declining growth rate of remittances inasmuch as remittances are also about 8 per cent of GNI. On the other hand, if TDD were to worsen, it may make attaining a 7 per cent growth of well-being unattainable.

The prospect of natural disasters and economic policy distortions can be accounted for in the same spirit. Less-than-optimal risk management and economic policies are reducing the GNI welfare index below its potential. Improving risk management and resiliency policies can similarly increase the growth rate of national well-being (as measured by CNI), as the economy moves closer to its potential.

Likewise, the removal of policy distortions is a potential source of economic growth. For example, the replacement of distortionary subsidies of renewable energy with emission taxes can move the economy closer to the economic frontier and thereby increase the growth rate of well-being.

In the case of resource management, the challenge is to maximize the present value of existing resource stocks by policies that incentivize resource extraction and harvesting at efficient levels. Since existing forest stocks are below efficient levels, this requires improved governance to reverse deforestation not only by reforesting prospective forestlands but by incentivizing the sustainable use of existing forest stocks. Similarly, existing laws that grant local governments control over municipal-level fisheries can be complemented by national assistance in enforcing fishing regulations, such as the establishment of catch quotas and allocations. Mining policies should incentivize exploration through tax incentives while simultaneously preventing excessive extraction through increased royalty assessments. In the case of pollution, the key is to face firms with the full costs of their production; e.g., by means of emission taxes and/or cap and trade systems.

Continued rapid socio-economic development in the Philippines is unlikely to be achieved unless environmental resource management, resiliency and other economic policies are reformed. In particular, since a falling growth rate of remittances will reduce the growth rate of comprehensive income, the size of TDD will need to fall so that a 7 per cent increase in GDP will not be inconsistent with a 7 per cent increase in welfare. To the extent that risk-management is improved and policy constraints are relaxed, it is even possible for welfare to increase at 7 per cent while GDP grows at a slightly slower rate. Without these reforms, worsening pollution, congestion and resource degradation are likely to make the goal of 7 per cent welfare growth infeasible.

Since "what gets measured gets managed" (Heal 2012), there is a pronounced need to improve the capability to measure GNI and CNI. Fortunately, the Philippine government has previously committed to strengthening statistical agencies and improving the institutional capability for official statistics to be more disaggregated, frequent, timely and accessible (Balisacan 2015) and for climate change modelling and damage assessment.

Notes

1. See Endress et al. (2005) for theoretical details.
2. The difference between the marginal cost of electricity and its marginal social cost is the marginal damage cost. The marginal cost to the Philippines of an additional unit of global carbon was taken as double the share of

the Philippines in world population times the world social cost of carbon (see Gayer and Viscusi 2016 on the necessity of using the domestic as opposed to the global cost of carbon). The cost of particulate matter and SO_2 from producing electricity from coal was taken to be twice the social cost of carbon.

3. Nordhaus (2015) argues that an efficient and politically feasible carbon tax for each country should be even lower than that indicated by its share of world GDP, which is less than 1 per cent for the Philippines (see also Gayer and Viscusi 2016). Our use of a 5 per cent share reflects the Philippines' greater vulnerability to climate change. If the Philippines participates in a stronger and more binding treaty than the Paris Agreement, the Philippine carbon tax should be much higher in the future.

4. The global social cost of carbon (SCC) in this chapter (\$25/MT of carbon dioxide) is obtained as a midpoint of the SCC reported in Nordhaus (2011) and the United States Environmental Protection Agency (2013, revised August 2016). Nordhaus reports an SCC of \$12 per MT of carbon dioxide, while the EPA reports an SCC of \$37 per MT carbon dioxide.

5. US Energy Information Administration (EIA) <https://www.eia.gov/tools/faqs/faq.cfm?id=74&t=11>.

6. Jaramillo and Muller (2016) estimate the marginal cost for SO_2, NO_x and TSPs from power generation in the United States to be around \$0.05/kWh (\$50/MWh). To adjust for willingness-to-pay in the Philippines, we multiply this number by the ratio of U.S. per capita national income to Philippine per capita national income (15.75 per cent). A caveat to this number is that it does not take into account the greater concentration of the Philippine population and hence its greater exposure (Roumasset and Smith 1990). The assumptions behind these numbers can be improved by specific research on the marginal damage cost of SO_2, NO_x, and TSPs in the Philippines.

References

Arcenas, Agustin B. *Environmental Health: Economic Costs of Environmental Damage and Suggested Priority Interventions: A Contribution to the Philippines Country Environmental Analysis.* Manila: World Bank, 2009.

Balisacan, A.M. "Philippine Statement Delivered to UN Summit for the Adoption of the 2030 Agenda for Sustainable Development". 70th Session of the United Nations General Assembly, New York, 27 September 2015.

Buchanan, J.M. *Liberty, Market and State: Political Economy in the 1980s.* New York: New York University Press, 1985.

Burnett, K. and J. Roumasset. "Sustainable Science: Overview for Further Research". In *Sustainable Science for Watershed Landscapes*, edited by J.A Roumasset, K.M. Burnett, and A.M. Balisacan. Singapore: Institute of Southeast Asian Studies; and Los Baños, Philippines: SEARCA, 2010.

Carandang, Antonio P. *The Forestry Sector: Costs of Environmental Damage and Net Benefits of Priority Interventions: A Contribution to the Philippines Country Environmental Analysis*. Manila: World Bank, 2008.

Cinco, T., F. Hilario, R. de Guzman, and E. Ares. "Climate Trends and Projection in the Philippines". PAGASA (Philippine Atmospheric, Geophysical and Astronomical Services Administration), 2013.

Clarete, R. "Options for National Food Authority Reforms in the Philippines". In *From Parastatals to Private Trade: Lessons from Asian Agriculture*, edited by S. Rashid, A. Gulati, and R. Cummings Jr. Baltimore: John Hopkins University Press, 2008.

DENR–EMB (Department of Environment and Natural Resources–Environmental Management Bureau). "National Air Quality Status Report (2003–2004)". 2004.

———. "National State of the Brown Environment Report (2005–2007)". 2009.

Dixit, A. *The Making of Economic Policy: A Transaction-Cost Politics Perspective*. Cambridge: MIT Press, 1999.

DOF (Department of Finance). "Philippines: New Initiatives to Boost Resilience against Natural Disasters". 2005 <http://www.dof.gov.ph/index.php/philippines-new-initiative-to-boost-resilience-against-natural-disasters/>

Endress, L. and J. Roumasset. "The Yin and Yang of Sustainable Development: A Case for Win-Win Environmentalism". *Journal of the Asia Pacific Economy* 1, no. 2 (1996): 185–94.

Endress, L., J. Roumasset, and T. Zhou. "Sustainable Growth with Environmental Spillovers". *Journal of Economic Behavior and Organization* 58, no. 4 (2005): 527–47.

Fabella, R.V. *Comprehensive Agrarian Reform Program (CARP): Time to Let Go*. UP School of Economics Discussion Paper 2014-02. 2014.

Fischer, C., R. Newell, and L. Preonas. *Environmental and Technology Policy Options in the Electricity Sector: Interactions and Outcomes*. CESifo WP 4757. 2014.

Garnaut, R. "The New Australian Resource Tax Rent". University of Melbourne, 2010 <https://www.melbourneinstitute.com/downloads/news_and_events/The%20New%20Australian%20Resource%20Rent%20Tax%20200510%20v5.pdf>.

Gayer, T., and W.K. Viscusi. "Determining the Proper Scope of Climate Change Policy Benefits in U.S. Regulatory Analyses: Domestic versus Global Approaches". *Review of Environmental Economics and Policy* 10, no. 2 (2016): 245–63.

Hartwick, J. "Intergenerational Equity and the Investment of Rents from Exhaustible Resources". *American Economic Review* 67 (December 1977): 972–74.

Heal, Geoffrey. "Reflections — Defining and Measuring Sustainability". *Review of Environmental Economics and Policy* 6, no. 1 (2012): 147–63.

Hecht, Joy E. *Lessons Learned from Environmental Accounting: Findings from Nine Case Studies*. Washington, DC: IUCN–The World Conservation Union, 2000.

Jaramillo, P., and N. Muller. "Air Pollution Emissions and Damages from Energy Production in the US: 2002–2011". *Energy Policy* 90, issue C (2016): 202–11.

Lange, G., K. Hamilton, R. Giovanni, L. Chakraborti, D. Desai, B. Edens, S. Ferreira, B. Fraumeni, M. Jarvis, W. Kingsmill, and H. Li. *The Changing Wealth of Nations: Measuring Sustainable Development in the New Millennium*. Washington, DC: World Bank, 2010.

Meller, H., and J. Marquardt. *Renewable Energy in the Philippines: Costly or Competitive?* Germany: Deutsche Gesellschaft für Internationale Zusammenarbeit (GIZ) GmbH., 2013.

NDRRMC (National Disaster Risk Reduction and Management Council). *National Disaster Risk Reduction and Management Framework*. NDRRMC, 2011 <http://www.ndrrmc.gov.ph/>.

NEDA (National Economic Development Authority). *Reconstruction Assistance on Yolanda: Build Back Better*. Pasig City, Philippines: NEDA, 2013 <http://www.neda.gov.ph/wp-content/uploads/2013/12/RAY-DOC-FINAL.pdf>.

———. *Reconstruction Assistance on Yolanda: Implementation for Results*. Pasig City, Philippines: NEDA, 2015 <http://yolanda.neda.gov.ph/wp-content/uploads/2015/11/RAY-2.pdf>.

Nordhaus, William. "Estimates of the Social Cost of Carbon: Background and Results from the RICE-2011 Model". Cowles Foundation Discussion Paper No. 1826. Yale University, 2011.

———. "Climate Clubs: Overcoming Free-Riding in International Climate Policy". *American Economic Review* 105, no. 4 (2015): 1339–70.

PSA (Philippine Statistics Authority). PSA, 2014 <http://psa.gov.ph/>.

Ravago, M.V., J. Roumasset, and A. Balisacan. "Economic Policy for Sustainable Development vs. Greedy Growth and Preservationism". In *Sustainability Science for Watershed Landscapes*, edited by J.A. Roumasset, K.M. Burnett, and A.M. Balisacan. Singapore: Institute of Southeast Asian Studies; and Los Baños, Philippines: SEARCA, 2010.

Ravago, M.V., J. Roumasset, and K. Jandoc. "Risk Management and Coping Strategies". In *The Future of Philippine Agriculture: Scenarios, Policies, and Investments under Climate Change*, edited by M. Rosegrant, A. Balisacan, and M. Sombilla. Forthcoming. Related UP School of Economics Discussion

Paper 2015-15: <http://www.econ.upd.edu.ph/dp/index.php/dp/article/view/1485/967>.

Repetto, R., W. Magrath, M. Wells, C. Rossini. *Wasting Assets: Natural Resources in the National Income Accounts*. Washington, DC: World Resources Institute, 1989.

Republic of the Philippines. "Intended Nationally Determined Contributions". Document communicated to the UNFCCC, October 2015.

Roumasset, J. "Decentralization and Local Public Goods: Getting the Incentives Right". *Philippine Review of Business and Economics* 26, no. 1 (1989).

———. "Natural Resource Management for Sustainable Development in the Philippines". *Journal of Agricultural Economics and Development* (January 1991).

———. "Designing Institutions for Water Management". In *Decentralization and Coordination of Water Resource Management*, edited by D. Parker and Y. Tsur. Netherlands: Kluwer Academic, 1997.

———. "Reflections on the Foundations of Development Policy Analysis". In *Sustainable Economic Development: Resources, Environment, and Institutions*, edited by A. Balisacan, U. Chakravorty, and M. Ravago. Netherlands: Elsevier, 2015.

Roumasset, J., K. Burnett, and H. Wang. "Environmental Resources and Economic Growth". In *China's Great Transformation*, edited by L. Brandt and T. Rawski. Cambridge: Cambridge University Press, 2008.

Roumasset, J.A., and K.R. Smith. "Exposure Trading: An Approach to More Efficient Air Pollution Control". *Journal of Environmental Economics and Management* 18, no. 3 (1990): 276–91.

Shreve, C.M., and I. Kelman. "Does Mitigation Save? Reviewing Cost-Benefit Analyses of Disaster Risk Reduction. *International Journal of Disaster Risk Reduction* 10 (2014): 213–35.

Smulders, Sjak. "Green National Accounting". In *The New Palgrave Dictionary of Economics*, 2nd ed., edited by S. Durlauf and L. Blume. UK: Palgrave-Macmillan, 2008.

Stiglitz, J., A. Sen, and J.P. Fitoussi. "Mis-measuring Our Lives: Why GDP Doesn't Add Up". Commission on the Measurement of Economic Performance and Social Progress (France), New Press, 2010.

UN (United Nations). *System of Environmental-Economic Accounting 2012: Central Framework*. New York: UN, 2014.

———. *Transforming Our World: The 2030 Agenda for Sustainable Development*. New York: UN, 2015.

United States Environmental Protection Agency (US EPA). "The Social Cost of Carbon: Estimating the Benefits of Reducing Greenhouse Gas Emissions".

2013 <https://www.epa.gov/climatechange/social-cost-carbon> (accessed 10 January 2017).

Virola, R.A., and E.P. Lopez-Dee. "Green GDP towards Sustainable Development: The Philippine Experience". National Statistical Coordination Board (NSCB) Technical Paper. Philippines: NSCB, 2005.

Weitzman, M.L., and K. Lofgren. "On the Welfare Significance of Green Accounting as Taught by Parable". *Journal of Environmental Economics and Management* 32, no. 2 (1997): 139–53.

World Bank. "The Philippines: Country Environmental Analysis". Report by the Sustainable Development Department, East Asia and Pacific Region. Washington, DC: World Bank, 2009.

———. "World Development Indicators". Various years <http://data.worldbank.org/data-catalog/world-development-indicators>.

World Commission on Environment and Development. *Our Common Future.* Oxford: Oxford University Press, 1987.

7

Energy: Power Security and Competitiveness[1]

Majah-Leah Ravago, Raul Fabella, Ruperto Alonzo, Rolando Danao and Dennis Mapa[2]

According to one set of official projections, if the Philippine economy were to grow at 7 per cent per annum, close to the rate achieved in recent years, then by 2040 the country's per capita income would be P316,173 ($6,873) at constant 2000 prices[3] — a sharp increase from the 2015 level of P74,453 ($1,618). This is an optimistic forecast, given that annual per capita income growth over the past twenty-five years averaged only about 2 per cent. The impressive growth attained during the period 2011–16 was mainly driven by private and government consumption, which was, in turn, partly fuelled by overseas Filipinos' remittances (BSP 2015).

The sustainability of the recent growth remains tenuous. One constraint is the perennially high cost of power, as well as an inadequate power supply that cannot support the country's potential growth. The challenge lies in both the sourcing and timing of additional power supply to meet the growing demand and avert a recurrence of the power crisis that took place in the early 1990s, while also reducing the cost of power. Energy supply and cost are central to an improved investment climate that in turn generates a higher productivity growth.

Philippine power costs are high by regional standards; within the Association of Southeast Asian Nations (ASEAN), it ranks second to Singapore. Thus, the country struggles to attract mobile capital, a reason why manufacturing growth has lagged in recent decades. We have elsewhere labelled the slower manufacturing growth compared to services as "development progeria" (Daway and Fabella 2015), where services forge ahead to developed-country levels in low-income countries. This translates into slow growth and slow poverty reduction.

Republic Act (RA) 9136, otherwise known as the Electric Power Industry Reform Act (EPIRA) of 2001, has the well-intentioned objective of opening up access to, and fostering competition in, the retailing of electricity so as to lower the price for consumers. However, electricity prices in the Philippines remain among the highest in Southeast Asia. Figure 7.1 shows the trends in electricity tariffs for residential and industrial customers in selected Asian economies. In 2013, for example, the Philippines' residential rate was $0.14/kWh, much higher than the rate in Singapore ($0.12/kWh), Thailand ($0.08/kWh), Indonesia ($0.04/kWh), and Malaysia ($0.06/kWh). While the Philippines' industrial rate ($0.10/kWh) was a close second to the highest rate in Singapore ($0.11/kWh).

Several factors explain the Philippines' high power cost despite the fact that 25–29 per cent of its fuel source is from relatively lower-cost hydro and geothermal. As will be explained below, these include fuel mix, taxes and subsidies, low reserves and low generation capacity per capita, average size of generation plants, overall efficiency, volatility, and the absence of competition in Power Supply Agreement (PSA) contracting (Fabella 2016).

The EPIRA mandates all industry participants to unbundle their own operations according to their functions and, consequently, unbundle their rates, charges and costs. Figure 7.2 shows the breakdown of Meralco's (Manila Electric Company) tariff for its residential, commercial and industrial customers. With regard to the retail price of electricity for residential consumers, a household that consumes about

FIGURE 7.1
Electricity Tariffs in Selected Asian Economies (constant 2005 US$)
(a) Residential and (b) Industrial

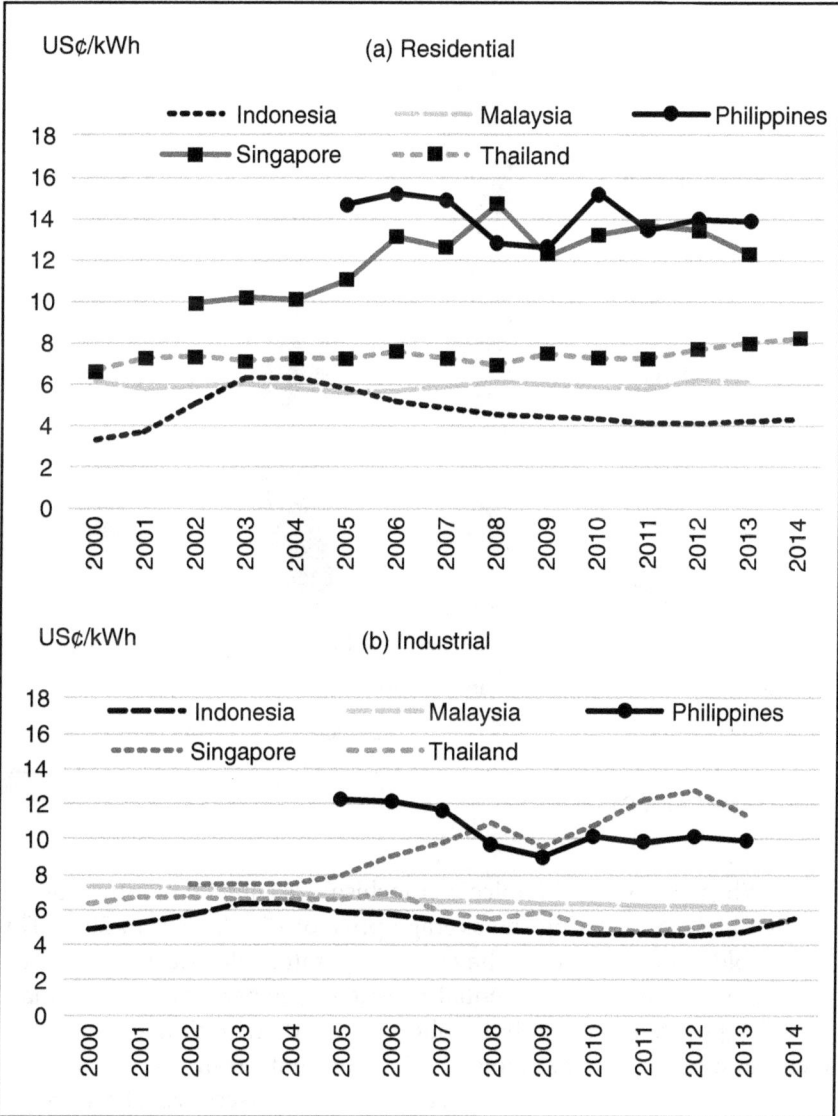

Source: Enerdata n.d., "Energy Data".

FIGURE 7.2
Manila Electric Company's (Meralco) Breakdown of Tariff

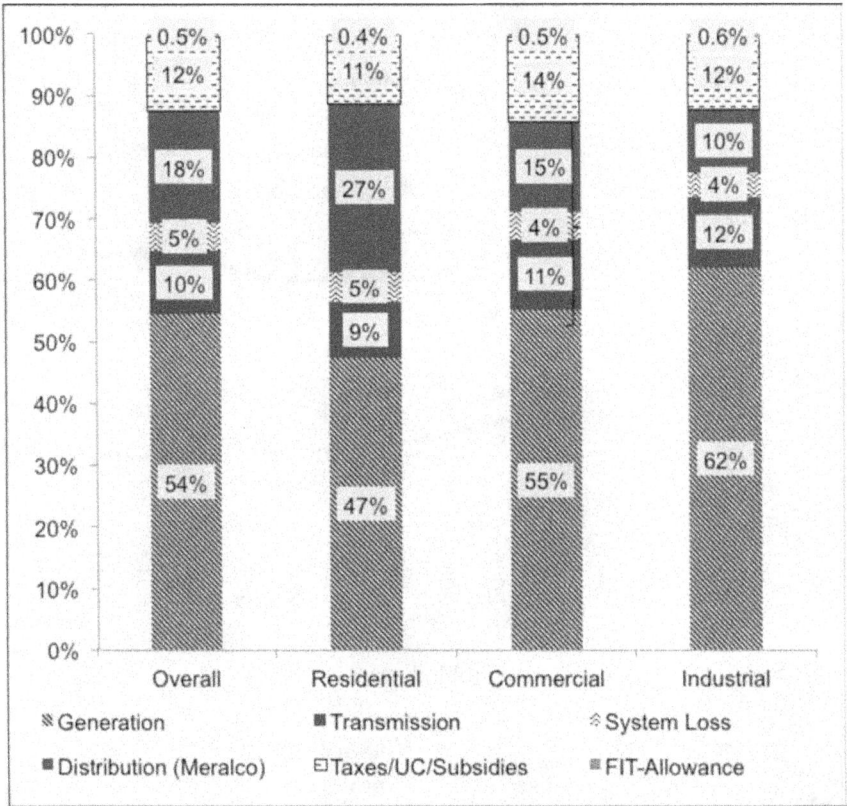

Source: Manila Electric Company 2015.

200 kWh a month in Meralco's franchise area has a monthly bill of about P1,888 ($41), using the average price of P9.68/kWh in 2015. This household would typically have a refrigerator, electric fan, flat iron, TV set, and radio. For residential consumers, generation charges make up 47.4 per cent of the bill, followed by distribution charges that include supply and metering at 27.2 per cent. Transmission charges make up about 9 per cent. Transmission losses are about 5 per cent. Taxes and subsidies are 11 per cent and the feed-in tariff (FIT) allowance is 0.4 per cent.

In this chapter, we focus on the generation sector. We present two possible forward-looking scenarios running up to 2040 to illustrate how policy reforms with regard to fuel mix can potentially lower power rates. A significant reduction in the blended generation charges that make up 47.4 per cent of the total bill will clearly improve the economic well-being of Filipino consumers. The numerical computation illustrates that to bring the price of power down, the optimal fuel mix is not constant over time but should exploit the opportunities opened up by less costly resources while taking environmental (including health) costs into account. We also provide an assessment of the power sector's performance and suggest broad key reforms and alternative pathways needed for the sector to contribute to the overall vision of a strong-growth economy.

I. Baseline Assessment of Power Sector Performance

The sustainability of the economic growth during the last four years remains tenuous. The Philippine investment rate has remained at well below 25 per cent of gross domestic product (GDP), while the saving rate is now at 25 per cent of GDP — making the Philippines a net lender to the world. Government investment as a percentage of GDP remains at less than its target level of 5 per cent. To achieve the Filipino 2040 vision, growth must quickly become investment-driven, with the investment rate at 25–27 per cent of GDP. This would mean a government capital outlay of 6–7 per cent and a private investment rate of 21–22 per cent. This is an immense departure from the historical level of approximately 1.5 per cent of GDP for government infrastructure spending and 17 per cent for the private investment rate.

These investment targets have not been attained in the last quarter of a century. On the one hand, the government will be hard-pressed to try to reach this level of government capital outlay unless it addresses the causes of the spending gridlock and miserable absorptive capacity. An increase in government contracting activity (GCA) is a way to address this. On the other hand, the private investment rate will not rise to desired levels unless the known traditional hurdles to investment are cleared: the almost unbearably lengthy, costly licensing procedures; the highly uncertain and sometimes inconsistent nature of regulation; the high cost of doing business; and the closing of many areas (agriculture and mining) to large-scale investment projects. One sizeable source of investment is foreign direct investment (FDI), which the Philippines has repeatedly rebuffed. The country's share in total FDI in ASEAN is only about 1 per cent. Investment friendliness is far from being the Philippines' competitive strength.

After the passage of EPIRA in 2001, the power industry has undergone a major shift in structure, from a predominantly government-led monopoly in generation and transmission to a private sector–led and more competitive environment. This has brought expectations that electricity prices will eventually go down due to forthcoming new investments in power generation. Fourteen years after EPIRA was passed, significant milestones have been achieved, including the establishment of the Wholesale Electricity Spot Market (WESM), removal of some cross subsidies, unbundling of functions to reflect their true costs, and the establishment of the Energy Regulatory Commission (ERC) and the Joint Congressional Power Commission (JCPC) to enhance oversight. However, implementation delays in completing the privatization of assets and transfer of management of the contracted generation companies under independent power producers (IPPs) to IPP administrators have pushed back the end-goal of establishing retail competition and open access (RCOA) in the power sector.

A. Resource Availability and Power Consumption Mix

After EPIRA, new investments in natural gas and additional coal came online and expansion of geothermal and hydro replaced some of the more expensive diesel. Figure 7.3 shows the trend in installed capacity mix by fuel source from 1991 to 2015. In the early 1990s, the capacity mix was composed mostly of renewable energy and others (mostly diesel). As new sources came online, the mix became diverse and included natural gas after 2001. By 2015, coal constituted 32 per cent of the mix, renewable energy 33 per cent, natural gas 15 per cent, and the remaining 20 per cent consisted of diesel, bunker fuel, and other oil-based products. The passage of the Renewable Energy Law (RA 9513)

FIGURE 7.3
Installed Capacity Mix by Share, 1991–2015

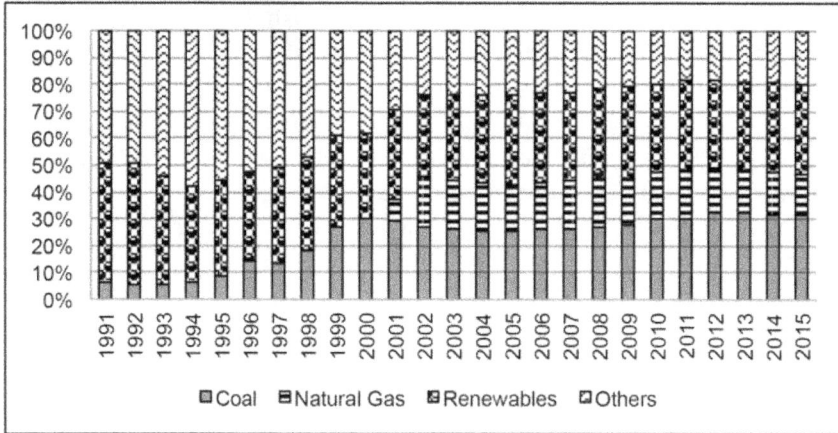

Coal   Natural Gas   Renewables   Others

Source: Department of Energy (DOE).
Note: "Renewables" consist of hydropower, geothermal, wind, solar, and biomass. "Others" consist of oil-based products, petroleum, and diesel. Off-grid generator not included in installed capacity.

in 2008 encouraged investments in renewable energy production in solar, wind, biomass, and run-off-river hydro, expanding the green energy share in generation capacity.

By grid, the capacity mix varies as may be dictated by location and basic resource availability. The national electricity grid is divided into Luzon, the Visayas, and Mindanao, following the major island groupings of the country. Natural gas production is only found in Luzon and constitutes 41 per cent of the grid capacity. Coal production is largest in the Luzon grid at 36 per cent. In the Visayas grid, renewable energy, mainly geothermal, has the largest share at 36 per cent of grid capacity. Coal also occupies a substantial share at 30 per cent, followed by oil-based sources, including diesel and petroleum, at 25 per cent. In Mindanao, renewables have the biggest share at 54 per cent, with hydro dominating at 47 per cent of the total grid capacity. Coal is small at 10 per cent. The projected capacity mix in 2019, including the committed and indicative projects, in the three grids will be varied, especially in Mindanao, where more coal will figure in the mix.

B. Load (Consumption) Profile

In terms of power consumption, Figure 7.4 shows the monthly load (consumption) curve. For Luzon, demand usually peaks during the summer season, mainly driven by residential use of air-conditioning units and electricity consumption of industries. On a daily basis, power consumption on weekdays starts to rise at 7 a.m., as people prepare for their daily routine, then peaks at around 11 a.m. to 12 noon. From the midday peak, consumption goes down and reaches a trough between 4 and 5 p.m., when people are traveling home, then peaks again at around 7 p.m. Daily off-peak is from 1 to 6 a.m.

In the Visayas, the typical trend is stable from January to December. Geothermal covers most of the baseload in the Visayas. Interestingly, unlike Luzon, where geothermal generation is constant, the Visayas uses some of its geothermal power to meet its peak. Although the region occasionally imports power from Luzon, the direction of trade is usually from the Visayas to Luzon. In Mindanao, consumption peaks during the summer and holiday seasons, when

FIGURE 7.4
Luzon, Visayas and Mindanao Monthly Load Curve, 2013

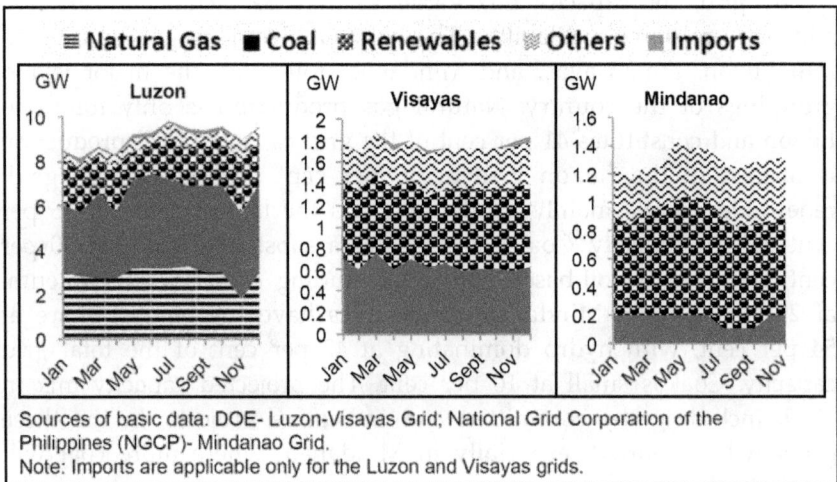

Sources of basic data: DOE- Luzon-Visayas Grid; National Grid Corporation of the Philippines (NGCP)- Mindanao Grid.
Note: Imports are applicable only for the Luzon and Visayas grids.

people from Mindanao working in either Luzon or the Visayas make their way back home. Hydro generation comprises the baseload of Mindanao.

C. Power Supply and Demand Indicators

Benchmarking power supply and demand indicators of the Philippines relative to other countries indicates that there is limited supply of power in the Philippines vis-à-vis consumption (Table 7.1). In 2014 the Philippines had 17.95 GW capacity serving 100 million Filipinos. In comparison, its neighbours Thailand and Malaysia had 44.83 GW and 32.46 GW of power capacity serving their populations of 68 million and 30 million, respectively. Electricity consumption per capita in the Philippines is the lowest compared to other ASEAN countries. In contrast, the price per kWh is among the highest. It should be noted that Thailand, Malaysia and Singapore trade in electricity, and this potentially helps keep power costs low.

TABLE 7.1
Power Supply and Demand Indicators in Selected Asian Countries, 2014

	Electricity generation per capita[a] (kWh/cap)	Per capita electricity use[b] (kWh/cap)	Installed electricity capacity[c] (GW)	Share of renewables in electricity capacities[d] (%)	Pop'n (million)[e]
Philippines	772	633	17.95	32.86	100
Indonesia	901	789	53.87	12.25	253
Malaysia	4,773	4,388	32.46	20.06	30
Singapore	8,949	8,586	13.18	1.95	6
Thailand	2,523	2,508	44.83	18.05	67
China	4,153	3,590	1,405.03	30.94	1,364
Japan	8,066	7,444	311.53	26.88	127
South Korea	10,797	9,928	93.71	11.68	50

TABLE 7.1   (*continued*)

	Residential prices[f] (USc05/kWh) (for 2013)	Industrial prices[g] (USc05/kWh) (for 2013)	GDP US$ at constant price and exchange rate (2005) per capita[h]	Electricity transport/ distribution losses[i] (kWh/cap)
Philippines	13.84	9.91	1,650	73
Indonesia	4.19	4.82	1,878	85
Malaysia	6.07	6.17	7,295	193
Singapore	12.32	11.44	37,203	44
Thailand	8.03	5.33	3,457	157
China	4.55	6.38	3,826	239
Japan	22.60	16.26	37,607	367
South Korea	8.82	7.87	24,550	364

a. Net Generation is the amount of gross generation less the electrical energy consumed at the generating station(s) for station service or auxiliaries. Note: Electricity required for pumping at pumped-storage plants is regarded as electricity for station service and is deducted from gross generation (EIA 2015).
b. Net Consumption is the consumption of electricity computed as generation plus imports, minus exports, minus transmission and distribution losses (EIA 2015).
c. Installed capacity.
d. Renewables share in electricity production or generation (Enerdata).
e. World Development Indicators.
f. In real prices constant at 2005 US$ cents (Enerdata).
g. Constant 2005 US$ prices and exchange rate (Enerdata).
h. Constant 2005 US$ prices and exchange rate (Enerdata).
i. Transmission and distribution loss is electric energy lost due to the transmission and distribution of electricity. Much of the loss is thermal in nature (EIA 2015).

The trend in net electricity generation[4] and consumption among selected Asian countries is shown in Figure 7.5. Relative to its neighbours, both generation and consumption per capita have been low in the Philippines since 1990. While generation has seen tepid growth, population growth has increased faster in the Philippines than its neighbours.

FIGURE 7.5
Electricity Net Generation and Consumption Per Capita

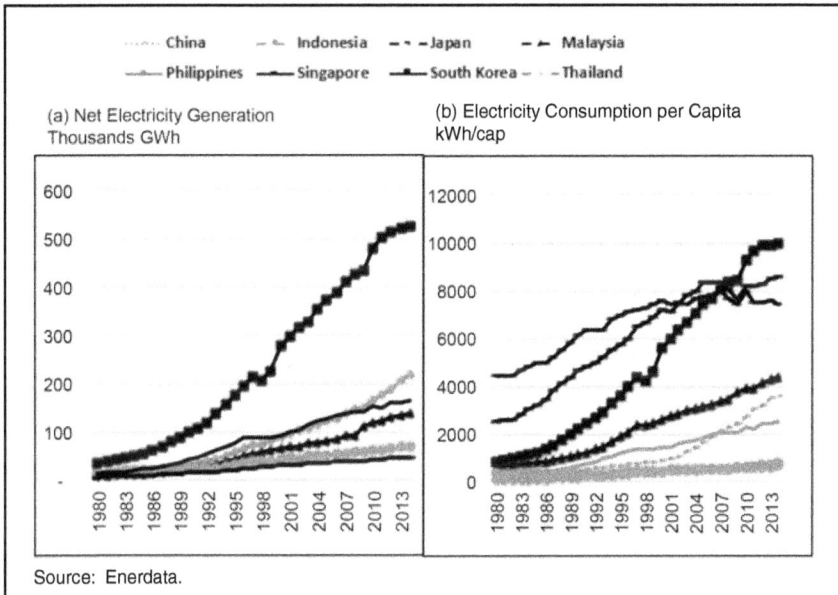

Source: Enerdata.

D. Energy and Climate Change

In 2008, RA 9513, or the Renewable Energy Act, was passed, mainly to (i) reduce dependence on fossil fuels, thus insulating the country's exposure to price fluctuations in the international markets, and (ii) increase utilization and development of renewable energy resources as tools in preventing harmful emissions. To implement this law, the Department of Energy (DOE) released Circular 2015-07-0014, prescribing the policy for maintaining a fuel mix of 30-30-30-10; i.e., 30 per cent coal, 30 per cent renewables, 30 per cent natural gas, and 10 per cent others. The 30 per cent share of renewable energy resources in the country's total power-generating capacity is facilitated through the implementation of the feed-in tariff (FIT) system.

Given this policy, what is the current status and where is the country heading, in terms of investments in generating capacity? Figure 7.6 shows the various renewable energy (RE) sources in the Philippines from 1991 to 2014. The graph shows that the biggest source is hydropower, followed by geothermal. Other renewable sources include wind, solar and biomass. The share of renewable energy to total energy historically has been high for the Philippines. The share was about 38 per cent in the 1990s and averaged at about 33 per cent in 2011–14.

FIGURE 7.6
Renewable Resources and Renewable Share to Total Energy

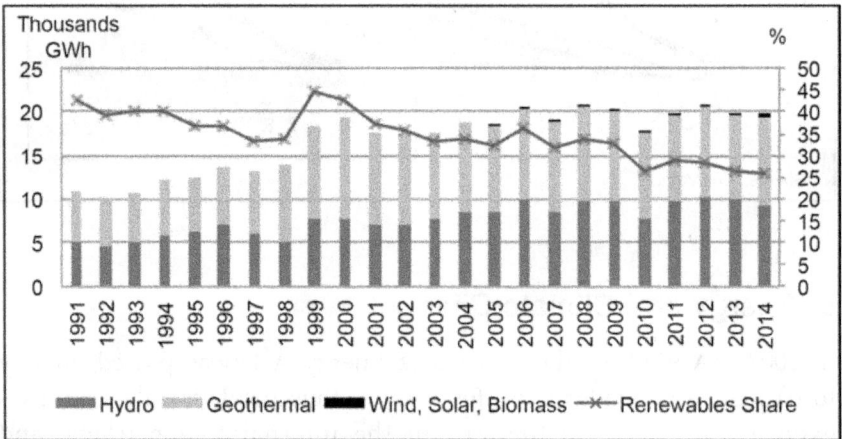

Sources of basic data: DOE and Enerdata 2015.

If, by 2040, technological innovation shall have driven down the cost of RE relative to conventional sources, then the target 30 per cent share of RE may be redundant and FIT no longer necessary to encourage RE technologies for power generation.

With regard to the second objective of the Renewable Energy Act, even in the absence of an agreement on complete participation in climate change, the Philippines' share of renewables in total energy source has been the highest relative to its Asian neighbours since 1991, as seen in Figure 7.7a. In 2014 the Philippines' share stood at 33 per cent, China at 23 per cent, Japan at 15 per cent, and Indonesia at 12 per cent. How does this translate in terms of carbon emissions? Figure 7.7b shows the carbon footprints of these countries relative to the highest two emitters. For the Philippines, the share of the renewables is very high and total carbon emissions are very small.

Furthermore, power generation is not the only source of carbon gas emissions in the Philippines. Transport is another major source of carbon gas emissions. Table 7.2 shows, that, in fact, in the last three decades of the twentieth century, transportation was a heavier emitter of greenhouse gases than electricity. By 2012, however, power generation was releasing 60 per cent more carbon dioxide than transport. The search for clean technologies, therefore, holds for these two sectors.

FIGURE 7.7
Renewable Resources and CO_2 Emissions

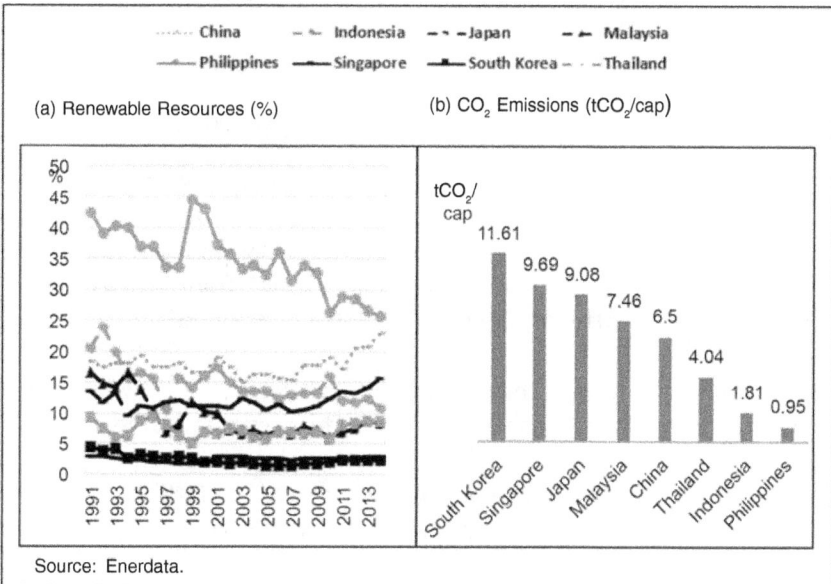

Source: Enerdata.

TABLE 7.2
Carbon Dioxide Emissions
(million tonnes)

Period	Electricity and heat production	Transportation
1971–80	90.13	98.4
1981–90	108.83	105.43
1991–2000	181.49	216.31
2001–10	284.72	243.14

Source: World Resources Institute (2014).

While the share of renewables may already be high, the prescribed target of 30 per cent share for coal is already lower than the 32 per cent share in installed capacity[5] in 2015 and the 42 per cent gross generation capacity[6] in 2014. These benchmarks will be higher, since the new capacity said to be coming on-stream is largely coal (e.g., Redondo Power Plant in Subic, Zambales). The Asian Development Bank (ADB) outlook for the Philippines (2013) sees coal constituting about 70 per cent of the fuel mix in the Philippines in 2035.

II. The Philippines in 2040: Strong vs. Weak Growth

Two scenarios for the Philippine economy up to 2040 are identified in Figure 7.8. The first scenario, the strong-growth scenario, assumes an average GDP growth rate of about 7 per cent annually from 2016 to 2040. With low population growth that ranges from 1.5 per cent to 0.6 per cent for 2016–40,[7] per capita GDP growth would therefore average about 6 per cent.

Accompanying this high economic growth is the well-known demographic dividend. That is, productivity rises due to the increased number of people in the workforce relative to dependents (Lee and Mason 2006). Strong reforms are needed to reduce fertility, including investment in human capital and expanded work opportunities. Reducing the fertility rate is the critical element for the demographic transition. Strong political will is also needed to increase the contraceptive prevalence rate from the current figure of 55 per cent to 70 per cent.

FIGURE 7.8
Strong and Weak Growth Scenarios of GDP per Capita, 2016–40

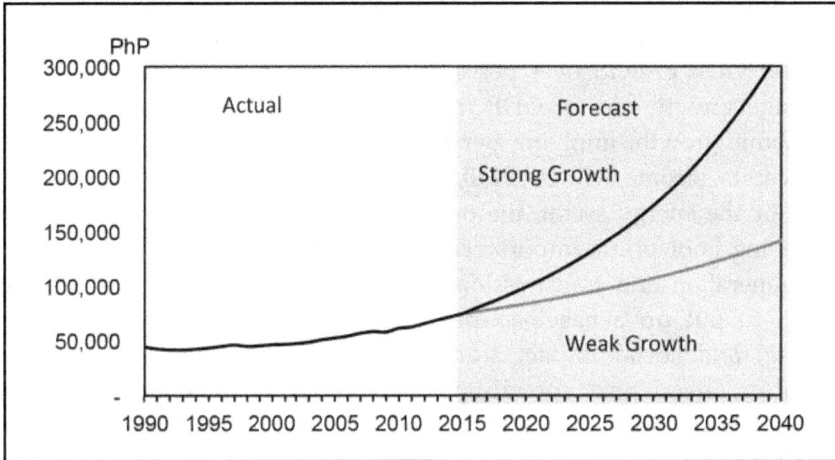

Authors' calculations.
Note: GDP per capita (constant 2000 prices) from 1990 to 2015 (actual) and 2016 to 2050 (projected).

Continuous investment in human capital is important, including the additional two years of schooling with the implementation of the K to 12 programme. The latter is particularly relevant for women, as increased education of women is a strong determinant of lower fertility. In turn, an increase in years of schooling may be expected to boost real wages, particularly for young workers.

The changing age structure due to a reduction in the country's total fertility rate (TFR) is a necessary but not a sufficient condition for harvesting the demographic dividend. Reforms must be made in the labour market to provide young workers with higher employment opportunities. The strong-growth scenario simulates an increased employment rate coupled with a lower fertility rate and increased years of schooling (that is, the additional two years). Under the strong-growth scenario, the "support ratio" will be higher than 0.50 starting from 2025 and will be highest at 0.55 from 2055 to 2065. This scenario creates a relatively wider demographic window of opportunity. This means that, in 2025, 50 effective workers are supporting themselves and 50 effective consumers. By 2040, 54 effective workers are supporting themselves and 46 other effective consumers, thus providing the economy with additional savings.

The alternative "weak-growth scenario" assumes an average annual GDP growth of 4 per cent from 2016 to 2040, similar to the average growth rate of GDP from 1990 to 2012. With this projected economic growth, implying per capita income growth of 2.6 per cent, per capita income will be P140,791 ($3,061) by 2040.

For the energy sector, the power subsector in particular, long-term visioning is of prime importance as investments in most new facilities for generation and transmission are lumpy in nature. It takes several years to put up a baseload power plant, especially when environmental and social impact studies are required. Thus, it is critical to plan ahead and coordinate the power requirement and the corresponding generation and transmission that will support the vision of strong growth.

Forecasts of electricity consumption for 2040 under the two scenarios were obtained using a single-equation error correction model, a dynamic model that integrates short-run dynamics with a long-run relationship (see Danao and Ducanes 2016 for details of the model). In the present case, the short-run dynamics is modelled by relating annual growth rates of electricity consumption to growth rates of the predictor variables: GDP, electricity price, and temperature. The long-run relationship between electricity consumption and real GDP appears as an extra term in the model. Because there may be disequilibrium (referred to as "disequilibrium error") in the short run, this extra term is regarded as the error correction mechanism (ECM), which corrects for the disequilibrium. ECM was estimated using annual data from 1992 to 2015. The forecast values were computed by assuming that electricity price and temperature follow their historical trends.

Figure 7.9 shows the trend in actual total electricity consumption[8] for 1990–2015 together with the forecasts for 2016–40, both including transmission losses and utilities' own-consumption. The forecasted trend is the electricity consumption that supports the assumed GDP per capita growth under each scenario. Electricity consumption is expected to grow at an annual average rate of 4.3 per cent under

FIGURE 7.9
Strong and Weak Growth Scenarios of Electricity Consumption, 2015–40

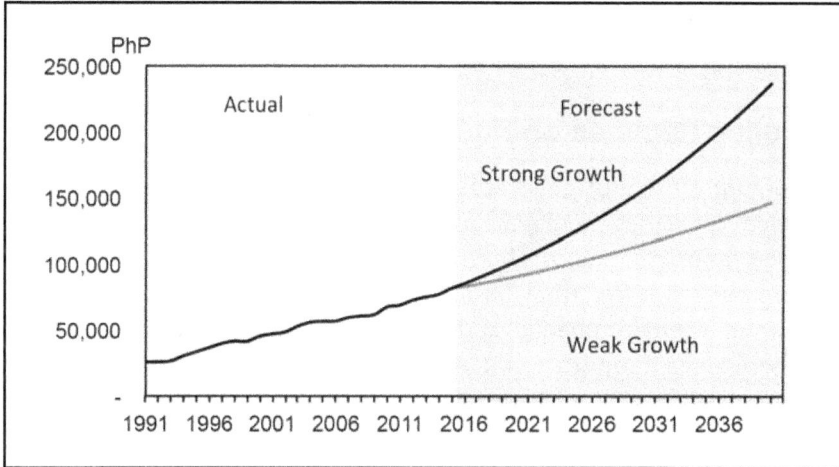

Authors' calculations.

the strong-growth scenario but only 2.4 per cent under weak-growth. We consider the forecasts as lower bounds if we allow for the possibility of lower electricity prices and higher temperatures. However, electricity consumption will also be influenced by demand-side management through the use of more efficient appliances, lighting fixtures, and smart metering (see, for example, Strbac 2008; Moura and de Almeida 2010; EIA 2014). Thus, the net effect on electricity consumption is unclear. Since electricity consumption in the model is primarily driven by aggregate real GDP, it cannot reflect the effects of changes in the components of GDP. Future modelling efforts should account for the structural changes within the economy, i.e., the gross value added share of agriculture, industry and services.

What is the needed generating capacity that corresponds to the vision of strong-growth and the possibility of weak-growth, and at what electricity prices? The policies that the government takes are critical in influencing the outcome.

We did a numerical exercise to compute the required generating capacity at each projected electricity consumption level for the two scenarios. Formal modelling requires that supply and demand be determined simultaneously at each point in time. For illustration purposes, electricity consumption is modelled separately when computing the generation requirement.

A. Policy Regimes on Fuel Mix

To calculate the net generating capacity, estimates are needed for installed capacities from various fuel sources by grid in Luzon, the Visayas, and Mindanao. This requires determining the optimal mix of fuel sources over time based on the least-cost rule while taking into account environmental and health concerns. Inasmuch as a fully theoretical and operational model of investment planning and coordination is yet to be developed for the Philippines, we do not compute the optimal fuel mix. We focus instead on the conceptual issues and illustrate how policies with regard to fuel mix might affect the growth trajectory of the country and the well-being of Filipinos — in particular, how fuel mix affects the blended generation charges that constitute 47.4 per cent of the consumers' electricity bill.

For the two scenarios, strong- and weak-growth projections, we consider the policy of the government as stated in the DOE Department Circular 2015-07-0014, "Guidelines for the Policy of Maintaining the Share of Renewable Energy (RE) in the Country". The policy statement in Section 2 of the circular is "to maintain the share of RE in power generation ... by adopting at least 30 percent share of RE in the country's total power generation capacity". For the numerical exercise, the fuel mix is pegged at 30 per cent share of RE, 30 per cent natural gas, 30 per cent coal, and 10 per cent others. The 30-30-30-10 fuel mix in the installed capacity is hereinafter referred to as Policy 1.

Under the strong-growth scenario, we present three other policy regimes on fuel mix. Policy 2 favours increased utilization of the lower-cost resources but accounts for environmental costs. The ADB (2013) forecasts coal, currently the cheapest fuel, as being the main fuel source in Asia and the Pacific through 2035. For the Philippines, the ADB (2013) forecasts coal to be about 70 per cent of the fuel source in

2035 under their business-as-usual scenario. Policies 3 and 4, with an eye towards the objectives of RA 9513 or the Renewable Energy Act of 2008, consider a fuel mix that favours the increased use of renewables, both conventional and variable.

Moreover, our computation under the strong-growth scenario considers four policy regimes that target the following installed capacity fuel mix by 2040: (i) 30-30-30-10; (ii) utilization of lesser-cost resources; (iii) increased use of conventional renewables (hydro and geothermal); and (iv) increased use of variable renewables (solar and wind) and biomass. Inasmuch as we do not model for the optimal fuel mix, the policy regimes above are just four of the many possible configurations of fuel mix. A caveat is in order for Policy 3: the fuel share of conventional renewables in our assumption is for illustration purposes, as the share may hit a hard constraint depending on the availability of natural reserves, e.g., water for hydropower.

Table 7.3 presents our assumptions about the fuel mix for the Philippines and the corresponding power consumption mix under the four policy regimes. We consider the type of load and geographical location (grid) in our assumption of fuel mix. For Luzon, fuels for baseload include coal, natural gas, geothermal, base hydro and other renewables. These other renewables include the variable solar, wind, and run-off river hydro, which are considered "must-dispatch" together with biomass. Mid-merit and peak loads include peaking hydro, peaking natural gas, and oil. For the Visayas and Mindanao, baseload fuels include coal, geothermal, base hydro and the must-dispatch variable renewables, while mid-merit and peak loads include peaking hydro and oil.

To obtain the aggregate fuel mix for the country, we first compute the level of gross installed capacity and power consumption for each type of fuel for each grid. Summing up the required gross installed capacity across all grids for each fuel and dividing it by the aggregate gross installed capacity, we obtain the aggregate fuel mix for the country. The same method is applied for the aggregate consumption mix. This is done for each of the policy regimes. The aggregate installed capacity mix and consumption mix is presented in Table 7.3.

We still apply the fuel mix assumption provided in Table 7.3 for all cases, even if policy regime 2 follows the increased utilization of a lower-cost resource.[9]

TABLE 7.3
Assumptions on Fuel Mix Share for Policy Regimes 1, 2, 3 and 4

	Installed Capacity Mix				
	Coal	Natural Gas	Conventional RE	Variable RE	Others
Policy 1: 30-30-30-10					
2016	35	15	29	4	16
2022	30	24	27	4	15
2028	29	28	27	4	12
2034	30	29	26	4	11
2040	30	30	26	4	10
Policy 2: Utilization of the lesser-cost resource					
2016	35	15	29	4	16
2022	38	14	29	3	16
2028	40	15	29	3	13
2034	44	15	28	2	10
2040	49	14	27	2	8
Policy 3: Increased utilization of conventional renewables (hydro and geothermal)					
2016	35	15	29	4	16
2022	31	15	34	5	15
2028	29	15	34	10	12
2034	27	15	35	14	9
2040	24	15	36	16	8
Policy 4: Increased utilization of variable renewables (solar, wind, biomass, run-off river hydro)					
2016	35	15	29	4	16
2022	31	15	33	7	15
2028	29	15	33	11	12
2034	27	15	34	15	9
2040	24	15	35	18	8

	Coal	Natural Gas	Conventional RE	Variable RE	Others
			Power Consumption Mix		
Policy 1: 30-30-30-10					
2016	44	20	32	1	3
2022	37	30	29	1	2
2028	36	34	25	3	2
2034	37	35	22	4	2
2040	38	35	20	5	2
Policy 2: Utilization of the lesser-cost resource					
2016	44	20	32	1	3
2022	47	21	28	1	3
2028	50	20	27	1	2
2034	55	17	25	1	2
2040	63	11	24	1	1
Policy 3: Increased utilization of conventional renewables (hydro and geothermal)					
2016	44	20	32	1	3
2022	38	21	37	2	2
2028	36	17	40	4	2
2034	33	15	43	7	1
2040	31	15	43	10	1
Policy 4: Increased utilization of variable renewables (solar, wind, biomass, run-off river hydro)					
2016	44	20	32	1	3
2022	38	20	37	3	2
2028	36	17	38	7	2
2034	33	15	38	12	1
2040	31	13	38	16	1

Source: Authors' calculations.
Notes: 2016 data are a carry over of the fuel mix as of June 2015. Conventional renewables include hydro (19 per cent) and geothermal (10 per cent). Variable renewables include wind (2 per cent) and solar (1 per cent); biomass (1 per cent) is also added here.
*Sum not equal to 100 due to rounding.
See Ravago et al. (2016) for the fuel mix by grid and share allocation of installed capacity by load, baseload and mid-merit to peaking plus ancillary.

B. Assumptions on Fuel Price

The evolution of power generation price for each type of fuel largely depends on how technology develops over time (see Viswanathan et al. 2006; ADB 2013; van Kooten 2013; Knittel et al. 2015). One can think of many price trajectory possibilities. We use the following five cases with regard to generation price to illustrate the effects of these price trajectories on the blended generation charge:

Case 1: Baseline
        Policy 1 – 2015 prices constant for the next 24 years.
        Policies 2, 3, 4 – 2015 prices plus emissions charges constant for the next 24 years.
Case 2: Prices of RE incorporate FIT degression rates in policies 1 to 4.
Case 3: Annual decrease in average RE prices by 3 per cent in policies 1 to 4.
Case 4: Annual decrease by 8 per cent and 3 per cent in the price of solar and RE, respectively, in policies 1 to 4.
Case 5: All prices change simultaneously, applying Energy Information Administration (EIA) projections on fuel prices in 2015 in policies 1 to 4.

Case 1 is the baseline where the current 2015 average generation charges are assumed to remain constant in 2016–40. The purpose is to determine the projected installed capacities and blended generation charges under the assumption that future fuel prices will remain the same. This is applied to policy regime 1 of 30-30-30-10. For policy regimes 2, 3 and 4, carbon emissions charges are added. The incorporation of emissions charges is an attempt to reflect the true social cost, albeit incomplete. The full social cost would have to incorporate local pollution, including cost of particulates and sulphur dioxide. This may be larger than the emissions charges (see chap. 6 by Roumasset et al. in this volume and Roumasset and Smith 1990), but an estimate for the Philippines is wanting. Cases 2, 3 and 4 relax the constant price assumption of must-dispatch renewables only while all other fuel prices remain constant, as in case 1. Case 5 is where all fuel prices change simultaneously following the growth projections of the U.S. EIA. In all cases, policy regimes 2, 3 and 4 incorporate emissions and local pollution charges. The performance of each of cases 2 to 5 is measured against the baseline case.

Table 7.4 presents the fuel prices for case 1. Panel (a) shows the average generation charge in 2015 for each type of fuel source by grid in Luzon, the Visayas, and Mindanao. This is the generation price applied in policy regime 1. These are adjusted to incorporate the negative externality from carbon emissions (column b) to obtain generation charges for policy regimes 2, 3 and 4 (panel a+b). The generation charges are adjusted by imposing the appropriate emission charges per kWh of the corresponding CO_2 emissions.

Following Roumasset et al. (chap. 6, this volume), we use a global social cost of carbon (SCC) (\$25/MT of CO_2) obtained as the average of the SCC reported in Nordhaus (2011) and the United States Environmental Protection Agency (2013, revised August 2016). We assume that carbon-induced damages in the Philippines are 5 per cent of worldwide damages, and, without a strong and binding global agreement, the Philippine carbon tax should be \$1.25 per MT of CO_2 (see Box 7.1 for the conversion and computation of emission charges).

TABLE 7.4
Fuel Prices for Case 1, 2015 Prices Constant for the Next 24 Years
(P/kWh)

Fuel Type	Policy 1 (a)			Emissions Charge* (b)	Policies 2, 3 and 4 (a+b)		
	Luzon	Visayas	Mindanao		Luzon	Visayas	Mindanao
Social Cost of Carbon							
Coal	3.89	4.65	4.65	0.0566	3.95	4.71	4.71
Geothermal	4.52	5.01	5.01	...	4.52	5.01	5.01
Hydro	4.56	3.86	2.93	...	4.56	3.86	2.93
Must-Dispatch RE	7.16	7.16	7.16	...	7.16	7.16	7.16
Natural Gas	4.41	...	...	0.0317	4.44	...	...
Oil	10.18	6.79	8.24	0.0426	10.22	6.83	8.28

Sources of basic data: Meralco 2015, "Average Generation Charge by Fuel Type" for Luzon; kuryente. org 2015, "Power Supply Agreements"; Visayan Electric Company (VECO) 2016, "Generation Rates" for Visayas and Mindanao. See Box 7.1 on the computation of emissions charges.

Box 7.1. Notes on carbon emissions

Since carbon emissions are a global public bad, the social cost of carbon (SCC) is the appropriate measure to use to incorporate its cost. SCC is the value of the long-term damage caused by a one-ton increase in global carbon emissions in a given year. A range of estimates is given by several studies; for example, $25 per tCO_2 (Tol 2013), $12 per tCO_2 in 2005 dollars (Nordaus 2011), $36 per tCO_2 (Shelanki and Obstfeld 2015).

Is the value of SCC the appropriate charge to reflect the true cost in the Philippines? Gayer and Viscusi (2016) argue that the proper scope of domestic regulation for a public bad should consider the net "benefits of a policy across the political jurisdiction whose citizens will bear the cost of the policy" (p. 2). They further note that without any binding world agreement regarding climate change mitigation, "there is no clear justification for one nation to include the benefits to other nations from policies for which the one nation incurs all of the costs" (p. 13). Gayer and Viscusi (2016) suggest downscaling the SCC by the nation's share of world GDP as an appropriate scope of policy regulation regarding carbon emissions. Nordhaus (2015) argues that an efficient and politically feasible carbon tax for each country should be even less than that indicated by its share of world GDP. The Philippines share in world GDP is 0.44 per cent. However, we use a 5 per cent downscaling factor to reflect the Philippines' greater vulnerability to climate change (Roumasset et al. 2016). The Philippine carbon tax should be much higher in the future, according to the GDP share of countries participating in the new treaty (Nordhaus 2015), if a stronger and more binding treaty than the Paris Agreement emerges.

Following Roumasset et al. (chap. 6, this volume), we use a global SCC ($25/MT of CO_2), which is obtained as a midpoint of the SCC reported in Nordhaus (2011) and the United States Environmental Protection Agency (2013, revised August 2016). Nordhaus reports an SCC of $12 per MT of CO_2, while the EPA reports an SCC of $37 per MT of CO_2. Absent a strong and binding global agreement, and assuming that carbon-induced damages in the Philippines are 5 per cent of worldwide damages, the Philippine carbon tax should be $1.25 per MT of CO_2, given a global social cost of carbon of $25 per MT of CO_2.

Box 7.1. (continued)

Using the conversion factor from the US Energy Information Administration (EIA) (https://www.eia.gov/tools/faqs/faq.cfm?id=74&t=11), a megawatt hour of electricity from coal generates about 0.98 MT of CO_2: $\left(\dfrac{2.17\ lbs\ CO_2}{kWh} \times \dfrac{1{,}000\ kWh}{1\ MWh} \times \dfrac{1\ MT}{2204.62\ lbs}\right) = 0.98$ MT. The same formula is used for natural gas and oil but applying the corresponding pounds of CO_2 per kWh conversion factor.

The emissions charge on coal-generated power should be around \$1.23/MWh $(=^{\$1.25}/_{MT\ CO_2} \times ^{0.98\ MT\ CO_2}/_{MWh})$. In terms of pesos per kWh, the emissions charge is P0.0566/kWh $(=^{\$1.23}/_{1{,}000\ kWh} \times ^{P46}/_{\$1})$.

The NTRC (2016) has proposed emissions charges in the range of P100–P1000 (\$2.2–\$21.7 at P1=\$46) per $MtCO_2$ following the range of carbon taxes being implemented in other countries. NTRC recognizes SCC but uses their suggested range in illustrating the revenue generated from the imposition of a carbon tax. A midpoint value of the suggested range of NTRC is \$11.96 per $MtCO_2$. Following the same process of downscaling by 5 per cent, the emission charge for the Philippines is \$0.598 per MT of CO_2.

The other four cases are the "what-if" analyses relative to the baseline case. Case 2 takes into account the degression rates in the FIT, which is already in place as per ERC Case No. 2011-006 and ERC Resolution 10, Series of 2012. Incorporation of FIT will alter the price of must-dispatch renewables in policy regimes 1 to 4. The FIT and degression rate is based on the adjusted 2016 rates as per ERC Case No. 2015-216 RC, where biomass, hydro, solar, and wind have FIT of P7.0508, P6.4601, P8.69, and P7.40, respectively. The same circular notes that degression rates for solar and wind no longer apply. The degression rate for biomass and hydro is 0.5 per cent two years after the effectivity of FIT.

Case 3 is a scenario where prices of renewables decrease. This is a bottom-up exercise because we ask the question: by how much, *at the minimum*, will prices of renewables have to go down for policies 1 and 4 to perform better. This exercise results in a 3 per cent annual decrease in the overall average price of the solar, wind, biomass, and run-off river hydro. This annual decrease in the average price of these renewables is reflected in policy regimes 1 to 4 under case 3.

Case 4 considers the trend in the decrease in the price of solar. Feldman et al. (2014) reported that the prices of photovoltaic (PV) systems for the United States have fallen by 6–8 per cent per year on average since 1998. We use an 8 per cent reduction in solar prices and a 3 per cent reduction in other renewables, as in case 3, to further illustrate when policy regime 4 becomes superior to other policy regimes.

Table 7.5 presents the prices of must-dispatch RE under Cases 2, 3 and 4.

TABLE 7.5
Price Assumption of Must-dispatch RE under Cases 2, 3 and 4
(P/kWh)

	Case 1 (Baseline)	Case 2 Price of RE incorporating FIT degression rates	Case 3 Annual decrease in average RE prices by 3%	Case 4 Annual decrease by 8% and 3% in the price of solar and RE
2016	7.16	7.16	7.16	6.98
2022	7.16	7.06	5.96	5.36
2028	7.16	6.97	4.96	4.19
2034	7.16	6.88	4.14	3.33
2040	7.16	6.8	3.44	2.67

Case 5 illustrates what happens when all fuel prices change simultaneously. The evolution of generation charges for each type of fuel source largely depends on how technology develops over time. The heightened concerns over the environment and the energy crisis in the 1970s have since prompted research and development programmes in finding ways towards increased efficiency of coal power plants (Viswanathan et al. 2006). Denmark, Germany and Japan have been actively pursuing the development of an ultra-supercritical coal power plant that utilizes stronger high-temperature materials (World Coal Association 2015), enabling the power plant to utilize coal efficiently, thereby reducing carbon emissions. The shale gas boom and "fracking" technology would also affect the relative prices of fuel sources (Stephenson 2015). The glut of shale gas in the United States that brought down the price of natural gas by almost 70 per cent in 2008–12 has provided incentives for generators to switch from coal to gas (Knittel et al. 2015). Technology on renewable sources is likewise evolving, including the development of batteries that address the intermittent nature of these sources (van Kooten 2013; International Renewable Energy Agency [IRENA] 2015).

To capture the changes in technology, we apply the growth projections of EIA (2016 and 2017) on fuel prices in 2015 (from Table 7.4) to come up with a projection of fuel prices until 2040 for the Philippines. Table 7.6 presents the projection on fuel prices used under case 5.

TABLE 7.6
Price Assumption under Case 5
(P/kWh)

| Grid | Fuel | No Emission Charge | | | | |
| | | Policy 1 | | | | |
		2016	2022	2028	2034	2040
Luzon	Coal	3.89	4.19	4.29	4.43	4.56
	Geothermal	4.52	4.52	4.89	5.29	5.72
	Hydro	4.56	4.56	4.50	4.44	4.38
	Must-Dispatch RE	7.16	7.46	7.14	6.84	6.55
	Natural Gas	4.41	7.42	8.54	8.46	8.29
	Oil	10.18	23.39	27.45	32.44	37.64
Visayas	Coal	4.65	5.00	5.12	5.29	5.45
	Geothermal	5.01	5.01	5.42	5.86	6.34
	Hydro	3.86	3.86	3.80	3.75	3.70
	Must-Dispatch RE	7.16	7.46	7.14	6.84	6.55
	Natural Gas	...	...	...	...	...
	Oil	6.79	15.60	18.30	21.63	25.10
Mindanao	Coal	4.65	5.00	5.12	5.29	5.45
	Geothermal	5.01	5.01	5.42	5.86	6.34
	Hydro	2.93	2.93	2.89	2.85	2.81
	Must-Dispatch RE	7.16	7.46	7.14	6.84	6.55
	Natural Gas	...	...	...	...	...
	Oil	8.24	18.93	22.21	26.25	30.46

TABLE 7.6   (*continued*)

Grid	Fuel	No Emission Charge				
		Policies 2 to 4				
		2016	2022	2028	2034	2040
Luzon	Coal	3.95	4.24	4.35	4.49	4.62
	Geothermal	4.52	4.52	4.89	5.29	5.72
	Hydro	4.56	4.56	4.50	4.44	4.38
	Must-Dispatch RE	7.16	7.46	7.14	6.84	6.55
	Natural Gas	4.44	7.46	8.57	8.49	8.32
	Oil	10.22	23.44	27.49	32.48	37.68
Visayas	Coal	4.70	5.06	5.18	5.35	5.50
	Geothermal	5.01	5.01	5.42	5.86	6.34
	Hydro	3.86	3.86	3.80	3.75	3.70
	Must-Dispatch RE	7.16	7.46	7.14	6.84	6.55
	Natural Gas	...	...	...	...	...
	Oil	6.83	15.64	18.35	21.67	25.14
Mindanao	Coal	4.70	5.06	5.18	5.35	5.50
	Geothermal	5.01	5.01	5.42	5.86	6.34
	Hydro	2.93	2.93	2.89	2.85	2.81
	Must-Dispatch RE	7.16	7.46	7.14	6.84	6.55
	Natural Gas	...	...	...	...	...
	Oil	8.28	18.97	22.25	26.29	30.50

Source of basic data: U.S. EIA (2016) and U.S. EIA (2017).

For illustration purposes, we still apply the fuel mix assumption provided in Table 7.3 for all cases, even if policy regime 2 follows the increased utilization of a lower-cost resource. Given the generation price and the fuel mix assumptions under the four illustrative policy regimes and five cases of evolution of fuel price, the required installed capacities for strong- and weak-growth scenarios are calculated using our computation.

Appendix Table 7.A provides the computation, parameters, formulas and assumptions used to estimate the projected installed capacity and gross generation for each grid — Luzon, the Visayas, and Mindanao.[10]

The result of computation for the Philippines is presented in Table 7.7. Gross installed capacities and gross generation are summed

TABLE 7.7
Generation Capacity in Strong and Weak Growth Scenarios, 2015–40

Indicator	2015	2016	2022
Strong Growth Scenario			
Population Growth Rate (%)	...	1.46	1.21
GDP per Capita (P)	74,453	79,299	110,216
GDP per Capita Growth Rate (%)	...	6.51	5.72
Electricity Consumption = Gross Generation (MWh)	81,896,000	85,434,660	111,382,600
Installed Capacity (MW)	18,279	18,983	24,143
Blended Generation Charge (P/kWh)			
Policy 1: 30-30-30-10 fuel mix	...	4.35	4.38
Policy 2: Least-cost resource	...	4.38	4.37
Policy 3: Increased conventional RE	...	4.38	4.43
Policy 4: Increased variable RE	...	4.38	4.47
Weak Growth Scenario with Policy 1			
Population Growth Rate (%)	...	1.68	1.57
GDP per Capita (P)	74,453	76,155	87,550
GDP per Capita Growth Rate (%)	...	2.29	2.39
Electricity Consumption = Gross Generation (MWh)	81,896,000	83,204,540	95,137,580
Installed Capacity (MW)	18,279	18,539	20,912
Blended Generation Charge (P/kWh)	...	4.35	4.38

Indicator	2028	2034	2040
Strong Growth Scenario			
Population Growth Rate (%)	1.05	0.84	0.61
GDP per Capita (P)	154,741	219,707	316,173
GDP per Capita Growth Rate (%)	5.89	6.11	6.35
Electricity Consumption = Gross Generation (MWh)	143,576,000	184,496,300	236,865,100
Installed Capacity (MW)	30,545	38,682	49,096
Blended Generation Charge (P/kWh)			
Policy 1: 30-30-30-10 fuel mix	4.42	4.46	4.47
Policy 2: Least-cost resource	4.34	4.32	4.29
Policy 3: Increased conventional RE	4.50	4.58	4.65
Policy 4: Increased variable RE	4.57	4.70	4.82

TABLE 7.7 (*continued*)

Indicator	2028	2034	2040
Weak Growth Scenario with Policy 1			
Population Growth Rate (%)	1.40	1.21	1.04
GDP per Capita (P)	101,441	118,873	140,791
GDP per Capita Growth Rate (%)	2.56	2.76	2.93
Electricity Consumption = Gross Generation (MWh)	109,676,600	126,681,700	146,383,200
Installed Capacity (MW)	23,803	27,185	31,103
Blended Generation Charge (P/kWh)	4.42	4.46	4.47

Authors' Calculations (Constant Fuel Prices, Downscaled NTRC Average Carbon Tax).
Notes: 1. Strong growth scenario has an annual 7 per cent GDP growth rate and low variant
population growth rate.
2. Weak growth scenario has an annual 4 per cent GDP growth rate and medium variant
population growth rate.
3. Policy 1: 30-30-30-10 mix. Policy 2: Increased utilization of the lower-cost resource.
Policy 3: Increased use of conventional renewables. Policy 4: Increased use of variable
renewables. Policies 2, 3 and 4 take account of emissions charges.
4. The result for each grid is given in Ravago et al. (2016).

across grids to obtain the values for the country corresponding to
the four policy regimes under the strong-growth scenario and policy
regime 1 under the weak-growth scenario. Under the strong-growth
scenario, regardless of policy regime, the results show that the country
needs to increase its installed capacity from 18.2 GW in 2015 to about
49 GW in 2040; a 169 per cent increase to support the 7 per cent annual
growth from 2016 to 2040. This required installed capacity in 2040 is
close to the 2012 installed capacity of Thailand and Indonesia, which
are at about 53 GW and 48 GW, respectively. Gross generation would
increase from 81,896 GWh in 2015 to 236,865 GWh in 2040; a 189 per
cent increase. Under the weak-growth scenario, the results show that
the country needs to increase its installed capacity from 18.2 GW in
2015 to about 31 GW in 2040; a 70 per cent increase. Gross generation
would increase from 81,896 GWh in 2015 to 146,383 GWh in 2040; a
78 per cent increase.

Meeting the required installed capacity is a necessary but not a sufficient condition for the improvement of the well-being of Filipinos. Recall that the objective of this study is to improve the well-being of Filipinos. The price consumers pay to access and consume electricity matters. This is reflected by the blended generation charge, which constitutes 47 per cent of total bill to residential consumers (Meralco 2015). Therefore, a significant reduction in the blended generation charges will improve the economic well-being of Filipino consumers.

Focusing on the strong-growth scenario, Figures 7.10 to 7.14 show the results on the projected trends of the blended generation charge for the five cases of possible evolution of fuel prices. For each of these cases, we compare the performance of the four policy regimes on fuel mix: Policy 1: 30-30-30-10 mix (the current policy stance of the government); Policy 2: increased utilization of the lower-cost resource; Policy 3: increased use of conventional renewables; and Policy 4:

FIGURE 7.10
Case 1 (Baseline constant fuel price) – Generation Price Projections

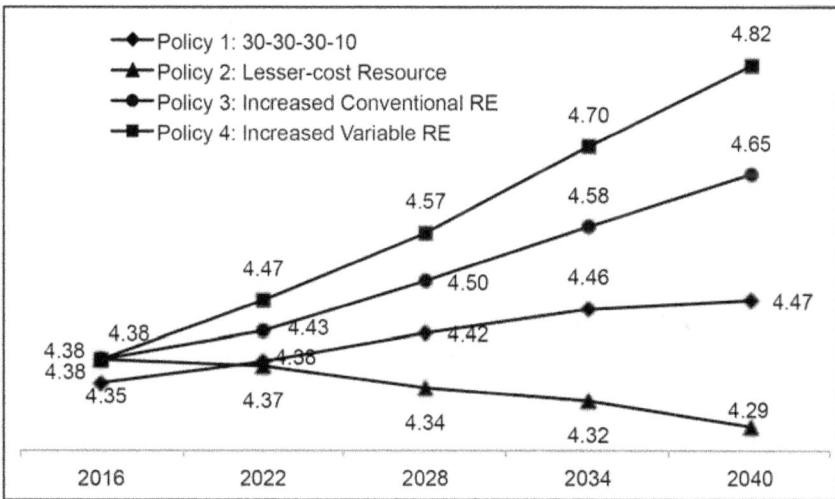

Source: Authors' calculations.
Note: Policy regimes on fuel mix: 1) 30-30-30-10 mix, 2) increased utilization of the lower-cost resource, 3) increased use of conventional renewables, and 4) increased use of variable renewables. Policy regimes 2, 3 and 4 take account of the emissions charge.

FIGURE 7.11
Case 2 – Generation Price Projection When Prices of RE Incorporate FIT Degression Rates (P/kWh)

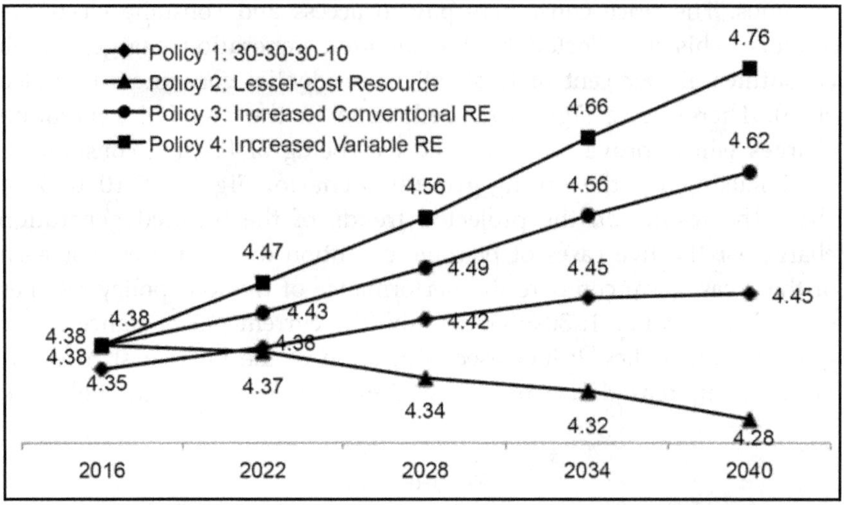

Authors' calculations.

FIGURE 7.12
Case 3 – Generation Price Projection with Annual Decrease in Average RE Prices by 3% (P/kWh)

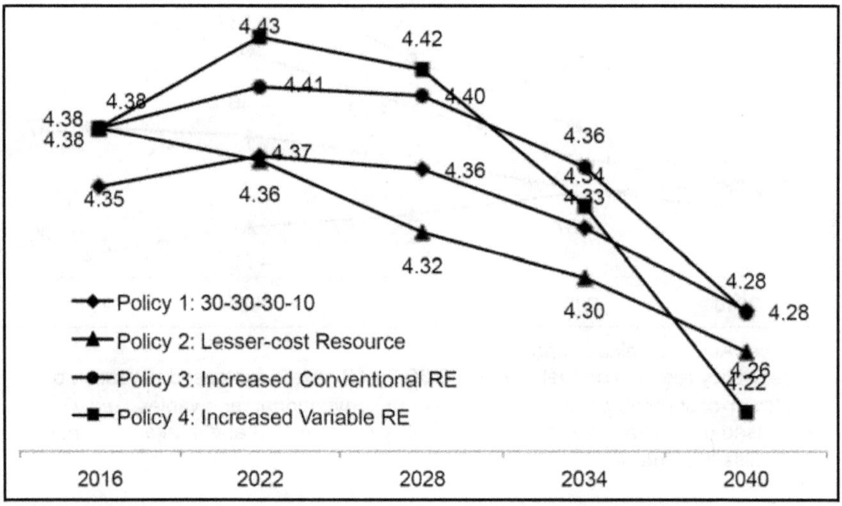

Authors' calculations.

FIGURE 7.13
Case 4 – Generation Price Projection with Annual Decrease by 8%
in the Price of Solar and 3% in RE (P/kWh)

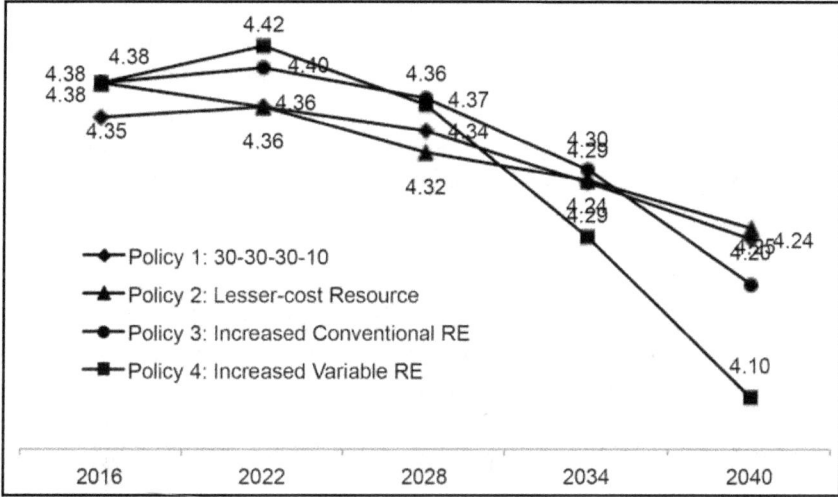

Authors' calculations.

FIGURE 7.14
Case 5 – Generation Price Projection when All Fuel Prices Change
Simultaneously (P/kWh)

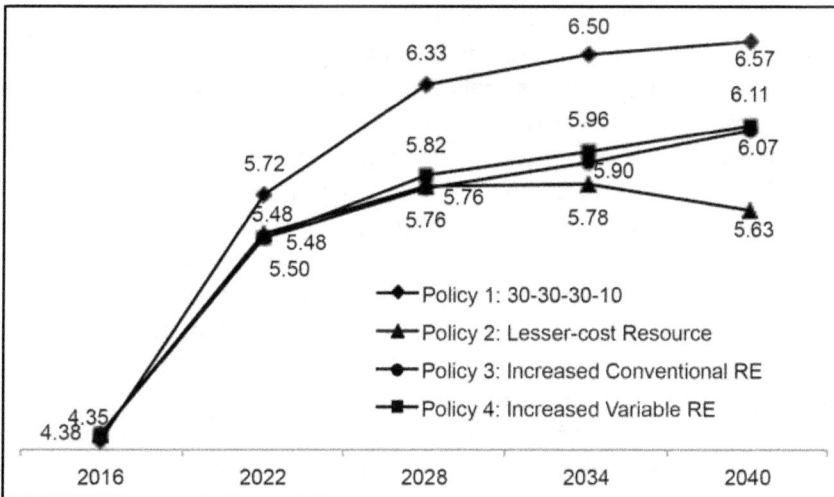

Authors' calculations.

increased use of must-dispatch renewables. Policy regimes 2, 3 and 4 take account of the emissions charge. It should be noted that in all five cases of possible evolution of fuel prices, the fuel mix assumptions under the four policy regimes remain the same as given in Table 7.3.

Holding fuel technology and prices constant at 2015 values (case 1), Figure 7.10 shows that policy regime 2 performs best, where the blended generation charge will decrease by 2.21 per cent, from P4.38/kWh in 2016 to P4.29/kWh in 2040. On the other hand, maintaining the 30-30-30-10 "balanced aspiration" would be costly. Following policy regime 1, the blended generation charge is projected to increase from P4.35/kWh in 2016 to P4.47/kWh in 2040; an increase of 2.77 per cent. Policy regime 3 of increasing the fuel share of conventional renewables such as hydro and geothermal performs better than policy regime 4, but this may not be a realistic assumption given the hard constraints of natural reserves. Increasing the share of must-dispatch renewables, policy regime 4, at current generation prices, can lead to an increase of 9.87 per cent in the blended generation charge by 2040.

Holding fuel prices constant from 2015 to 2040, this exercise shows that there is a better alternative to the balanced aspiration on fuel mix, which mandates the maintenance of 30 per cent share of renewables. Policy regime 2 could potentially help in bringing the cost of power down by lowering the cost of the blended generation charge. While fixed fuel prices are assumed under case 1, the problem is dynamic in nature. Policy regime 2 is the utilization of the lower-cost resource, where coal is favoured since it is presently the cheapest. Depending on how technology evolves, policy regime 2 favours whichever has the lower cost, not necessarily coal.

Figure 7.11 shows the projected generation price trends under case 2 when FIT degression rates are incorporated in the prices of must-dispatch renewables. Case 2 lowers the prices of must-dispatch renewables, while prices of other fuel sources remain the same as in case 1. The analysis shows that the performance rank of the four policy regimes is the same as in case 1. As expected, the generation charges under policy regimes 3 and 4 go down in 2040 relative to our benchmark provided in case 1 in Figure 7.10.

Figure 7.12 presents the results for case 3 when we allow for a 3 per cent annual decrease in the average prices of must-dispatch renewables. It must be noted that case 3 is a bottom-up exercise because we ask the question to what extent the price of renewables must go down for policy regime 4 to perform better. Figure 7.12 expectedly shows that policy regime 4 gives the lowest blended generation charge by 2040. If technology of solar, wind, run-off river hydro, and biomass evolves accordingly, then policy regime 2 transforms into policy regime 4; i.e., increased utilization of the lower-cost resource — in this case, must-dispatch renewables.

Figure 7.13 shows the results for case 4, which is a variant of case 3. Solar price is projected to decrease by 8 per cent annually and average prices of must-dispatch renewables to decrease by 3 per cent. As expected, the results show that policy regime 4 gives the lowest blended generation charge by 2040, at P4.10/kWh. Similarly, if technology of solar changes rapidly, then policy regime 2 transforms into policy regime 4, increased utilization of the lower-cost solar resource.

Figure 7.14 shows the results for case 5, where all fuel prices are assumed to change simultaneously. EIA (2016) projections were applied to the 2015 fuel prices for the Philippines in the conduct of this exercise. The EIA annual average growth projection for coal up to 2040 is at 0.50 per cent, which is relatively lower than other fuel sources at 2.50 per cent for natural gas, 4 per cent for oil, and −0.64 per cent for must-dispatch renewables. Policy regime 2, the utilization of the lower-cost resource, performs best, posting a blended generation charge of P5.68/kWh.

To reiterate, our overriding objective is to improve the well-being of Filipinos by lowering the price of electricity in an economically efficient manner. Our computation illustrates that the optimal fuel mix is not constant over time, but it should exploit the opportunities opened up by less costly resources while taking environmental and health costs into account.

An important caveat is that the fuel mix in the four policy regimes is based on current and projected prices and the current situation. This does not account for the intermittency cost of renewable generation capacity and the cost of integrating renewables into the grid, which may require additional investment. For example, a 16 MW wind turbine in Scotland requires a grid investment of £4 billion (House of Lords 2008, vol. 2, p. 252). In Britain, a 34 per cent share of renewables in their generation and transmission imposes a likely cost of £6.8 billion a year, or an extra 38 per cent increase (House of Lords 2008, vol. 1, p. 252). The intermittent nature of renewable generation, such as in wind and solar, requires additional investment in new capacity from reliable conventional sources (or even in nuclear energy) to serve as back-up sources (Van Kooten 2010). In the United Kingdom, the pursuit of a 15 per cent renewables target requires roughly doubling the requirement for new capacity.

III. Proposed Targets from 2016 to 2040

We have translated the government's "2040 vision" in terms of per capita income growing to P316,173 ($6,873) in 2040, at constant 2000 prices from the 2015 level of P74,453 ($1,618). This means that per capita income has to grow at 6 per cent per year. In section I, we built a strong- and weak-growth scenario. The vision in 2040 is realized in the strong-growth scenario, whereas a business-as-usual case is illustrated in the weak-growth scenario. We then asked what was required from the energy sector to attain the vision by focusing on the fuel mix policy and how it can influence the electricity price.

We then outlined measurable indicators and proposed indicative targets constituting energy security through to 2040 (Table 7.8). We take energy security to have three dimensions: accessibility, affordability, and reliability. Accessibility is defined as the percentage of the population that have access to electricity. In 2012, 87.5 per cent of Filipinos had access to electricity. The target for the current administration (2016–22) can be 90 per cent. The indicator for affordability is the price that consumers pay. Our analysis in Section I focused on the generation costs that make up 47 per cent of the electricity bill. Since EPIRA, the generation sector has already been privatized. The government can facilitate a more competitive environment by not mandating a fuel mix, but rather by letting the market work. Following market signals, the generation sector will rationally adhere to the utilization of the least-cost resource. The targets under affordability correspond to the results presented in Figure 7.10.

TABLE 7.8
Measurable Indicators and Proposed Targets

	Benchmark year units	2012–15	2016–22	2022–28	2028–34	2034–40	Remarks
1. Accessibility	2012 (% of pop)	87.5	90	92	94	95	2012 is based on WB.
2. Affordability: Price (full cost including health & environmental cost) – Gen Charge	2015 (P/KW)	4.38	4.37	4.34	4.32	4.29	2015 BGC based on MERALCO prices. Projection based on authors' preliminary calculations.
3. Reliability: Loss of Load Expectation (LOLE)	2015 (days/year)	1.2	1.1	1	1	0.9	2015 is based on WB estimates. 1 day optimal LOLE is based on del Mundo 1991.

Sources of basic data: WDI (2014); Meralco (2015); del Mundo (2015).

The third dimension for energy security is reliability, which can be measured using the engineering concept called "Loss of Load Expectation" (LOLE). It is defined as the expected number of times in a year that the available generation capacity, considering scheduled- and forced-outages of power plants, will not meet system daily peak demand; i.e., the number of days in a year that there will be "brownouts" (blackouts) caused by unscheduled power plant outages. In the United States and Europe, a standard LOLE is approximately 0.3 to 0.1 days per year. In the Philippines, LOLE has been previously estimated to be 1.2 days per year (Del Mundo 2014). The target for the current administration is to shorten the LOLE to 1.1 days per year.

IV. Key Reforms and Alternative Pathways

A. Investment Coordination in Generation, Transmission and Distribution

Given the long gestation period to build a power plant, the benefits from planning ahead far exceed the costs. Concomitant with investment in generation are the coordinated investments in transmission and distribution infrastructure. A well-conceived master plan that accounts for the current assessment of the industry and provides incentive-compatible arrangements will attract investors to bet on the country for the long term. Coordination has never been the Philippines' strong suit, and we have to do much better in this regard in the next twenty-five years. A master plan coordinating investment in generation, transmission and distribution infrastructure must be drawn up at the start of the new administration. This is critical if the Philippines wants to sustain economic growth. An equally decisive factor is the coordination between investment in power generation and investment in upgrading the grid.

The stability and consistency of government policies are important to foster and encourage private investment in power generation. Timeliness of implementation is also crucial. The ERC, for example, has to decide on numerous petitions for tariff adjustments. Delays due to a cumbersome and contentious accounting review process cost the distribution utilities (DUs) money, which is eventually passed on to captive consumers. The ERC's recent move to outsource the review process to the market through the Competitive Selection Process (CSP) will free the ERC of a considerable burden: it is now the DUs' responsibility to convince the ERC of the transparency and competitiveness of their power supply agreements (PSA). If the CSP is found wanting, the ERC simply subjects the PSA to a Swiss challenge. As to who determines the acceptability of the CSP, the ERC can coordinate with the Philippine Electricity Market Corporation (PEMC) or the Public-Private Partnership (PPP) Center, which has developed some capability on market testing. As to the issue of the PSA contract template, we recommend that a portfolio approach be developed in lieu of a per-plant approach to auctioning. This means that the bidders may not necessarily be power generation plants but may indeed be power supply aggregators (e.g., various power types such as baseload and peaking) who can handle the numerous financial minutiae (e.g., risk sharing among the parties).

Uncertainty in the policy environment discourages the inflow of private investment in the power sector; the same results draw from gaps and weaknesses in the physical network, such as the grid connection. It is foolhardy to invest in assets that will become stranded. The few investors who may come in are those likely to demand higher returns for higher risks, or those whose comparative advantage is in extracting compensation from the national government and navigating the bureaucratic maze rather than in efficient operations.

B. Government Investment in the Transmission Highway

Section 8 of EPIRA created the National Transmission Company (TRANSCO), which assumed the electrical transmission function of the National Power Corporation (NPC). TRANSCO is owned by the Power Sector Assets and Liabilities Management Corporation (PSALM), which is mandated to privatize its assets either through an outright sale or a concession contract. To privatize the electrical transmission function, the Congress, through RA 9511 enacted in December 2008, awarded the franchise to the NGCP, a consortium consisting of Monte Oro Grid, Calaca High Power Corp, and State Grid Corporation of China.

The franchise granted NGCP the authority to engage in the business of conveying or transmitting electricity through a high voltage backbone system of interconnected transmission lines, substations and related facilities, and for other purposes. The nature and scope of the franchise also granted NGCP the authority to construct, install, finance, manage, improve, expand, operate, maintain, rehabilitate, repair and refurbish the present nationwide transmission system.

Prior to the congressional franchise, one of TRANSCO's responsibilities, as provided in Section 9 of the EPIRA, was to improve and expand its transmission facilities, consistent with the Grid Code and the Transmission Development Plan (TDP). TRANSCO was also required to submit any plan for expansion or improvement of its facilities for the approval of the ERC. One of TRANSCO's modes of financing the expansion of its transmission facilities was through loans (e.g., from the ADB and JICA).[11] With the award of the franchise, these responsibilities now rest solely with the NGCP, along with financing and seeking the approval of the ERC for any investment in expanding the transmission facilities. Approval by the ERC of any investment would need to consider the cost implication to consumers, as the investment recovery is ultimately passed on to consumers. Our suggestion is that financing and investment should be separate from the regulatory structure of the transmission tariff. Since government owns the transmissions assets, TRANSCO should play the lead role in planning, investment and expansion of transmission facilities. Financing, for example, could be in the form of PPP or through the government treasury, depending on the efficacy of the investment. Depending on the mode of financing, consumers can partly finance the expansion, similar to Norway and Chile (Oren et al. 2002).

It is critical to make investment in transmission expansion incentive-compatible with key stakeholders, consumers, the private sector and government. In the Philippines, the long wait by the NGCP for ERC's approval in consideration of the increase in retail cost is likely to inhibit investment in transmission, which could lead to congestion and, ultimately, higher costs for consumers. Investment in transmission expansion offers great potential benefits for efficiency by increasing access to low-cost generation, improving reliability and mitigating market power. Better transmission could potentially reduce the marginal cost of transmission (Joskow 1976), which will eventually lower average wholesale prices.

C. Regulatory Oversight Coordination in Support of a Competitive Market

The recent passage of the Philippine Competition Act, which provides for a National Competition Policy and the creation of the Philippine Competition Commission (PCC), bodes well for a regulatory regime that has more resources and is more transparent. It should be stressed that the PCC and the ERC must work in harmony to ensure that "forum shopping" is avoided and no industry participant exercises significant market power.[12]

Agencies should recognize the limitations of their own capacity as well as the strengths of other agencies. In particular, ERC has now issued a circular mandating CSP. In the interim, DUs are to prove that their PSA contracts went through transparent and open competitive bidding.

As part of EPIRA's unbundling of the sector, the NGCP, a private for-profit entity, enjoys a monopoly franchise over grid operations. While NGCP won its franchise through competitive bidding, PCC and ERC should ensure that NGCP as system operator does not engage in monopoly pricing. They should also ensure, together with the DOE, that new investments in transmission facilities are on time to meet future demand and that proper maintenance is in place at all times to avoid system failure.

D. Reconciling Two Seemingly Contradictory Instruments: EPIRA and RE Law

The power industry has two major legal instruments: the EPIRA (RA 9136) and the RE Law (RA 9513). An examination of these two laws suggests that they may be working at cross purposes, with the EPIRA apparently being undermined by the RE Law. Reconciling the disparate objectives is necessary preparatory to reforming these laws.

The long-term national goals are articulated in the EPIRA. Foremost among them are to ensure the quality, reliability, security and affordability of the supply of electric power; to make sure that transparent and reasonable prices of electricity prevail in a regime of free and fair competition, and full public accountability; to promote the utilization of indigenous and new RE resources in power generation to reduce dependence on imported energy; and to accelerate the total electrification of the country.

In 2008, the RE Law was passed with the objective of (i) reducing dependence on fossil fuels, thus insulating the country's exposure to price fluctuations in international markets, and (ii) increasing utilization and development of RE resources as tools in preventing harmful emissions.

The main conflict between the two laws lies in how certain provisions of the RE Law seem to run counter to EPIRA's goals of "affordability of the supply of electric power" and "reasonable prices of electricity". In particular, the FIT system under the RE Law raises the price of electricity paid by the consumer.

One way of reconciling "the goals of economic growth and development with the promotion of health and safety, and the protection of the environment" is to address the negative environmental and health effects of carbon emissions from power generation based on fossil fuel through carbon taxes; i.e., directing policy right at the source of the harmful spillovers. The carbon taxes will internalize the negative externality, and the revenues generated can be used to finance investments in environmental and health protection.

E. Reform of the Electric Cooperatives

One black hole in the power landscape of the Philippines is the operation of some electric cooperatives (ECs), where financial viability is constantly in question. One reason is the role of local politics in the capture of management. Cooperatives are run on the one-member, one-vote modality — a political and inefficient modality. This results in political capture. Cooperatives must move towards the corporatist lines of one-share, one-vote. This incentivizes greater efficiency and attention to the bottom line. Management should then be passed to the hands of those with most to lose if the company fails. Wresting cooperatives from the claws of politics is tricky and needs political courage. Denial of power to a population as the ultimate weapon is politically costly for the national government. The efforts of the National Electrification Administration (NEA) at providing subsidies for corporatization has resulted in a meagre harvest. The target is the eventual consolidation of small DUs into only a handful of more financially robust DUs run on corporatist lines and open to private investors. This will also greatly unburden the ERC.

To make ECs more efficient, the EPIRA gives them the option of conversion to either a stock cooperative or stock corporation. DOE Circular 2004-06-007 urges ECs to "undertake structural and operational reforms ... through collaboration with the private investor-operators to gain access to private sector capital and management expertise". This initiative needs to be monitored more closely, highlighting "best practices" where private sector participation leads to cheaper, more reliable electricity services.

F. Investment in Research and Development

Attention also needs to be directed towards energy research and development (R&D). In fact, the Philippine Development Plan (PDP) 2011–16 cites the need for stronger energy R&D, particularly on RE. Current initiatives are focused on non-food feedstock development for biodiesel and bioethanol in support of the country's biofuels programme. In this regard, partnership among government, academe and the private sector should be harnessed.

Two government agencies are at the forefront of energy R&D: the DOE and the Department of Science and Technology (DOST). The DOE performs its energy research testing and laboratory services through two divisions: the Geo-scientific Research and Testing Laboratory, and the Lighting and Appliance Testing Laboratory. As such, they do not really engage in basic research.

The DOST's Philippine Council for Industry, Energy, and Emerging Technology Research and Development (PCIEERD) is the agency that is more closely associated with basic research. Its governing council is composed of seven members from the government (DOST, Department of Public Works and Highways, Department of Transportation and Communication, DOE, Commission on Higher Education, Board of Investments–Department of Trade and Industry, Department of Budget and Management) and three from the private sector. Despite the interagency nature of PCIEERD, government resources allocated to energy R&D remain limited, and coordination among government agencies involved in energy R&D is generally lacking. A glaring example of this lack of coordination is in the development of jatropha for biodiesel production in the mid to late 2000s. While the scientific community was still studying the technical feasibility of using oil from this plant as biodiesel, two competing government-owned and -controlled corporations (i.e., Philippine Forest Corporation and the Alternative Fuels Corporation) had already embarked on a massive jatropha planting programme, which simply went to waste. As academician and former DOST secretary Emil Javier remarked, the jatropha endeavour was a case where the policy preceded the technology.

Meanwhile, nuclear energy, a competitive source of power, remains untapped. The 600 MW Bataan Nuclear Power Plant (BNPP), construction of which started in 1976, was ready to be commissioned by the mid-1980s, but the Cory Aquino administration decided to mothball it for safety and political reasons. Critics cited the Three Mile Island incident in the United States in March 1979, where a nuclear reactor suffered a partial meltdown. Even more immediate was the Chernobyl disaster in Ukraine in April 1986, which happened two months into the Cory Aquino administration. This was considered a level 7 event — the maximum category in the International Nuclear Event Scale. There have been attempts to revive interest in operating the BNPP, but anti-nuclear sentiments have prevailed.

V. Concluding Remarks

To attain the goal of strong economic growth, we estimated electricity consumption to grow at an annual average rate of 4.3 per cent. Focusing on the generation sector, we illustrated how policy reforms on fuel mix could potentially reduce blended generation charges that make up 47 per cent of the total electric bill of households. The results of our simulations showed that a policy that supported the increased utilization of less costly resources could potentially decrease the blended generation charge. On the one hand, with the base-case assumption that technology and, hence, fuel prices would remain constant at 2016 prices from 2016 to 2040, the emergent policy would imply increased utilization of coal as fuel, since this is by far the cheapest. With this assumption, blended generation charge could potentially decrease in 2040. On the other hand, if technology for variable RE could evolve rapidly to bring fuel prices down by at least 3 per cent from today's current average prices, then this would point to the increased utilization of variable RE resources.

The paramount objective in our numerical exercises was to improve the well-being of Filipinos by lowering the price of electricity in an economically efficient manner. The results of the five simulations with regard to generation price illustrated that the optimal fuel mix should not be constant over time but should exploit the opportunities opened up by less costly resources.

We also assessed the power sector's performance and suggested broad key reforms and alternative pathways. The current *Philippine Energy Plan (PEP) 2012–2030* identifies major policy thrusts as follows: ensure energy security, expand energy access to promote a low-carbon future, climate-proof the energy sector, promote investment in the energy sector, and develop regional energy plans. By 2040, it is hoped that a fully functioning wholesale electricity market will be in place — one that covers not just spot sales and purchases by generation companies and distribution utilities, but longer-term sales and purchases of different durations as well. The EPIRA itself points out the policy reforms needed to achieve its objectives. For an efficient, competitive electricity market, retail competition and open access (RCOA) should be fully rolled out under a stable policy regime that completes the full implementation of the EPIRA.

Filipino 2040 encompasses a set of long-term goals based on the standard of living that Filipinos want to have in twenty-five years. Certainly, a comprehensive plan is essential to realizing this vision. With this as our guidepost, we outlined measurable indicators and proposed indicative targets constituting energy security for the next four administrations prior to year 2040.

Looking forward, we take energy security to have three dimensions: accessibility, affordability, and reliability. The indicator for affordability is the price that consumers pay. Our analysis focused on the generation costs that make up 47 per cent of electricity bills. Since the enactment of the EPIRA, the generation sector has mostly been privatized. The government can facilitate a more competitive environment not by mandating a fuel mix but rather by letting the market work. Following market signals, the generation sector will rationally adhere to the utilization of the least-cost resource.

Notes

1. This chapter is made possible by the generous support of the American People through the United States Agency for International Development (USAID) to the Energy Policy and Development Program (EPDP). The EPDP is a four-year programme implemented by the UPecon Foundation, Inc. The contents or opinions expressed in this chapter are the authors' sole responsibility and do not necessarily reflect the views of USAID or the United States Government or the UPecon Foundation, Inc. Any errors of commission or omission are the authors' and should not be attributed to any of the above.

2. The authors gratefully acknowledge the valuable review and comments of Dr Francisco Viray that became the basis of the calculation of required generation capacity and blended generation charge. The authors acknowledge the input of Dr Geoffrey Ducanes in the modelling of electricity consumption. They also thank the excellent research assistance of EPDP's Shirra de Guia, J. Kat Magadia, Miah Pormon, Tim Guanzon, and Mico del Mundo. Mari-An Santos, Jean Lau Wang, Donna Bajaro, Renzi Frias and Rainer dela Cruz assisted in the finalization of this chapter.

3. For this chapter, the currency exchange rate used is P46 = US$1.

4. Net electricity generation or production is the amount of gross generation less the electrical energy consumed at the generating station(s) for station service or auxiliaries (EIA 2015).

5. Installed capacity is the maximum output — commonly expressed in megawatts (MW) — that generating equipment can supply to system load, adjusted for ambient conditions (EIA 2015).

6. Gross generation capacity is the total amount of electric energy produced by generating units and measured at the generating terminal in kilowatt hours (kWh) or megawatt hours (MWh) (EIA 2015).

7. See Ravago et al. (2016) for more details about the two scenarios and our assumptions on the population projections.

8. Total electricity consumption includes transmission losses and utilities' own consumption.

9. Ideally, as prices adjust in various cases, the share of fuel mix also adjusts.

10. See Ravago et al. (2016) for full details of the computation.
11. See ADB Project Number: 36018, Loan Number: 1984, dated January 2012 and JICA Report in <http://www.jica.go.jp/english/our_work/evaluation/oda_loan/post/2007/pdf/project13_full.pdf>.
12. As of September 2016, the PCC and ERC are in the final stage of drawing a memorandum of understanding in coordinating their work.

References

ADB (Asian Development Bank). *Energy Outlook for Asia and the Pacific.* Mandaluyong City, Philippines: ADB, 2013*a* <http://adb.org/sites/default/files/pub/2013/energy-outlook.pdf>.

————. *Asian Development Outlook 2013: Asia's Energy Challenge.* Mandaluyong City, Philippines: ADB, 2013*b* <http://adb.org/sites/default/files/pub/2013/ado2013.pdf>.

BSP (Bangko Sentral ng Pilipinas). "Economic and Financial Statistics: Overseas Filipinos' Remittances". 2015 <http://www.bsp.gov.ph/statistics/efs_ext3.asp>.

Danao, R., and G. Ducanes. "An Error Correction Model for Forecasting Philippine Aggregate Electricity Consumption". EPDP WP 2016-05. 2016 <http://www.upecon.org.ph/epdp/working-paper-forecasting-05/>.

Daway, S., and R. Fabella. "Development Progeria: The Role of Institutions and the Exchange Rate". *Philippine Review of Economics* 52, no. 2 (2015).

Del Mundo, R. "Competition and Security of Supply in Philippine Electricity Market". Presentation at the EPDP Conference 2016: Toward Inclusive and Sustainable Energy Development, Makati, 12–13 January 2014.

DOE (Department of Energy). Department Circular 2004-06-007. 2004 <https://www.doe.gov.ph/department-circular-no-2004-06-007>.

————. "Power Statistics". 2012, 2013, 2014 <https://www.doe.gov.ph/philippine-power-statistics>.

————. "Philippine Energy Plan". 2014 <https://www.doe.gov.ph/pep>.

————. Department Circular 2015-07-0014. 2015 <https://www.doe.gov.ph/department-circular-no-dc2015-07-0014>.

————. "Power Development Plan 2009–2030". 2015 <https://www.doe.gov.ph/2009-2030-PDP>.

————. "Electric Power Supply Demand Outlook for 2012–2030". n.d. <http://www2.doe.gov.ph/Presentations/Visayas%20Power%20Summit%20-%20April%2026.pdf>.

————. "Mindanao Outlook". n.d. <http://minbizcon.com/wp-content/uploads/2013/08/Department-of-Energy.pdf>.

EIA (US Energy Information Administration). "Annual Energy Outlook 2014 with projections to 2040". 2014 <http://www.eia.gov/forecasts/aeo/pdf/0383(2014).pdf>.

————. *Annual Energy Review*. 2015 <http://www.eia.gov>.

————. *Annual Energy Outlook*. 2016 <https://www.eia.gov/outlooks/aeo/data/browser/#/?id=1-AEO2016&cases=ref2016~ref_no_cpp&sourcekey=0>.

————. "How Much Carbon Dioxide is Produced per Kilowatthour When Generating Electricity with Fossil Fuels?" 2016 <https://www.eia.gov/tools/faqs/faq.cfm?id=74&t=11>.

Electric Power Industry Reform Act (EPIRA) of 2001 <https://www.doe.gov.ph/epira-ra-9136>.

Enerdata. n.d. "Carbon Emissions" <https://yearbook.enerdata.net/#CO2-emissions-data-from-fuel-combustion.html>.

————. n.d. "Energy Data". <https://yearbook.enerdata.asia/southeast-asia-electricity-production-and-data.html#renewable-in-electricity-production-share-asean-countries.html>.

ERC (Energy Regulatory Commission). ERC Case No. 2015-2016 RC. Manila: ERC, 2016.

Fabella, R. "The Market Testing of Power Supply Agreements: Rationale and Design Evolution in the Philippines". EPDP WP 2016-03R. 2016 <http://www.upecon.org.ph/epdp/working-paper-psa-03/>.

Feldman, D., G. Barbose, R. Margolis, T. James, S. Weaver, N. Darghouth, R. Fu, C. Davidson, S. Boot, R. Wiser. "Photovoltaic System Pricing Trends". US Department of Energy, 2014 <http://www.nrel.gov/docs/fy14osti/62558.pdf>.

Gayer, T., and K. Viscusi. "Determining the Proper Scope of Climate Change Benefits in US Regulatory Analysis: Domestic versus Global Approaches". *Review of Environmental and Economics Policy* 10, no. 2 (2016): 245–63 <https://www.brookings.edu/wp-content/uploads/2016/08/rev-environ-econ-policy-2016-gayer-reep-rew002.pdf>.

House of Lords. *The Economics of Renewable Energy: Volume I Report*. 2008 <http://www.publications.parliament.uk/pa/ld200708/ldselect/ldeconaf/195/195i.pdf>.

————. *The Economics of Renewable Energy: Volume II Evidence*. 2008 <http://www.publications.parliament.uk/pa/ld200708/ldselect/ldeconaf/195/195ii.pdf>.

IRENA (International Renewable Energy Agency). "Renewable Power Generation Costs in 2014". 2015 <http://www.irena.org/documentdownloads/publications/irena_re_power_costs_2014_report.pdf>.

Joskow, P.L. "Contributions to the Theory of Marginal Cost Pricing". *Bell Journal of Economics* 7, no. 1 (1976): 197–206.

Knittel, C., K. Metaxoglou, and A. Trindade. "Natural Gas Prices and Coal Displacement: Evidence from Electricity Markets". NBER Working Papers, 2015 <http://www.nber.org/papers/w21627>.

Kuryente.org. "Power Supply Agreements". 2015 <http://www.kuryente.org.ph/>.

Lee, R., and A. Mason. "What is the Demographic Dividend?" *Finance and Development: A Quarterly Magazine of the International Monetary Fund* 43, no. 3 (2006) <http://www.imf.org/external/pubs/ft/fandd/2006/09/basics.htm>.

Meralco (Manila Electric Company). "Metro Manila Electricity Prices". 2015 <http://www.meralco.com.ph/consumer-information/rates-archive>.

―――. "Typical Consumer Rates". 2015 <http://www.meralco.com.ph/consumer-information/rates-archive>.

―――. "Generation". 2015 <http://www.meralco.com.ph/consumer-information/rates-archive>.

Moura, P., and A. de Almeida. "The Role of Demand-side Management in the Grid Integration of Wind Power". *Applied Energy* 87, no. 8 (2010): 2581–88.

NGCP (National Grid Corporation of the Philippines). "Typical Load Curve by Fuel Source for Each Grid during Peak Demand (Wet and Dry Season)". 2014.

―――. "Typical Daily Visayas to Luzon Hourly HVDC Loading during Peak Demand (actual data)". 2014.

Nordhaus, William. "Estimates of the Social Cost of Carbon: Background and Results from the RICE-2011 Model". Cowles Foundation Discussion Paper No. 1826. Yale University, 2011.

Oren, S., G. Gross, and F. Alvarado. "Alternative Business Models for Transmission Investment and Operation: National Transmission Grid Study, Appendix C". 2002 <http://eetd.lbl.gov/publications/alternative-business-models-for-trans> (accessed March 2016).

Ravago, M.V., R. Fabella, R. Alonzo, R. Danao. D. Mapa. "Energy: Power Security and Competitiveness". EPDP Working Paper 2016-01R. 2016 <http://www.upecon.org.ph/epdp/working-paper-fil-2040-energy-01/>.

Renewable Energy Law (RA 9513). 2008 <https://www.doe.gov.ph/laws-and-issuances/republic-act-no-9513>.

Republic Act (RA) 9511. <http://lia.erc.gov.ph/documents/359>.

Shelanki and Obstfeld. "Estimating the Benefits from the Carbon Dioxide Emissions Reductions". 2015 <https://obamawhitehouse.archives.gov/blog/2015/07/02/estimating-benefits-carbon-dioxide-emissions-reductions>.

Stephenson, M. *Shale Gas and Fracking: The Science behind the Controversy*. UK: Elsevier, 2015.

Strbac, G. "Demand Side Management: Benefits and Challenges". *Energy Policy* 36, no. 12 (2008): 4419–26.

Tol, R. "Targets for Global Climate Policy: An Overview". *Journal of Economic Dynamics and Control* 37, no. 5 (2013): 911–28.

Van Kooten, G. "Wind Power: The Economic Impact of Intermittency". *Letters in Spatial and Resources Sciences* 3, no. 1 (2010): 1–17.

———. "Economic Analysis of Feed-in Tariffs for Generating Electricity from Renewable Energy Sources". In *Handbook on Energy and Climate Change.* Cheltenham, UK: Elgar, 2013 <http://www.elgaronline.com/view/9780857933683.00017.xml> (accessed 20 November 2015).

Visayan Electric Company (VECO). "Generation Rates for Visayas and Mindanao". 2016 <http://www.veco.com.ph/>.

Viswanathan, R., K. Coleman, and U. Rao. 2006. "Materials for Ultra-supercritical Coal-fired Power Plant Boilers". *International Journal of Pressure Vessels and Piping* 83, nos. 11–12 (2006): 778–83.

WDI (World Development Indicators]). "Development Indicators". 2014 <http://databank.worldbank.org/data/reports.aspx?source=world-development-indicators>.

World Coal Association. "Reducing CO_2 Emissions". 2015 <https://www.worldcoal.org/reducing-co2-emissions/high-efficiency-low-emission-coal>.

WRI (World Resources Institute). "Data Sets". 2014 <http://www.wri.org/resources/data_sets>.

Appendix

TABLE 7.A
Parameters and Formulas Used in the Computations

	Parameter	Variable	Unit	Formula	Description
1	Electricity Consumption	EC	GWh	...	Projected using error correction model (Figure 7.9). Equal to Gross Generation.
2	Share of Electricity Consumption by Grid	a	%		Historical average from 1991 to 2014: 74% for Luzon, 13% for Visayas, 13% for Mindanao.
3	Electricity Consumption by Grid	EC_G	MWh	$EC \times \frac{a_G}{100} \times 1000$	G refers to Grid: Luzon, Visayas, and Mindanao 1 GW = 1000 MW
4	Load Factor	LF_G	%		This is the average load divided by the peak load in a specified time period. Based on the DOE's Philippine Energy Plan assumptions per grid; 73% for Luzon, 69% for Visayas, 72% for Mindanao. Assumed constant for all years.
5	Peak Demand by Grid (Non-Coincident)	PD_G	MW	$\frac{EC_G}{LF_G \times 8,760hrs}$	Based on the DOE's Power Development Plan computation of peak demand.
6	Peak Demand (Non-Coincident)	PD		$\sum_G PD_G$	Summing the peak demand across grid to obtain the peak demand for the Philippines is based on DOE Power Statistics (2014).

TABLE 7.A (continued)

	Parameter	Variable	Unit	Formula	Description
7	Regulating Reserve	RR_G	MW	$PD_G \times .04$	Assists in frequency control by providing automatic primary and/or secondary frequency response, equivalent to 4% of peak demand.
8	Contingency Reserve	CR_G	MW	—	Intended to take care of the loss of the largest synchronized generating unit or the power import from a single grid interconnection, whichever is larger. The Sual Power Plant Unit 1 with 0.647 GW capacity is assumed to serve as CR_G; Kepco-Salcon Unit 1 with 0.100 GW capacity for Visayas; a coal-fired power plant with 0.105 GW capacity for Mindanao.
9	Dispatchable Reserve	DR_G	MW	—	Second-largest unit capacity online. The Sual Power Plant Unit 2 with 0.647 GW capacity is assumed to serve as DR_G; Kepco-Salcon Unit 2 with 0.100 GW capacity for Visayas; a coal-fired power plant with 0.105 GW capacity for Mindanao.
10	Capacity Share by Load (Load L: Base, Mid-merit, Peaking)	CF_{LG}	%	—	Based on the DOE's Power Development Plan capacity share assumptions by grid for base, mid-merit, and peaking loads respectively for all grids: 67%, 23%, 10%.

#	Name	Symbol	Unit	Formula	Description
11	Net Installed Capacity by Load	NIC_{LG}	MW	$PD_G \times CF_{LG}$	Required installed capacity by base, mid-merit, and peaking load net of maintenance and station service.
12	Net Installed Capacity for Ancillary	NIC_{AG}	MW	$RR_G + CR_G + DR_G$	Required installed capacity to satisfy ancillary services net of maintenance and station service.
13	Maintenance Capacity Factor	b	%		Assumed to be 90% of gross installed capacity.
14	Station Service Capacity Factor	c	%		Assumed to be 90% for base and 95% for mid-merit, peaking, and ancillary services of gross installed capacity + maintenance service.
15	Gross Installed Capacity by Grid by Load	GIC_{LG}	MW	$\dfrac{NIC_{LG}/b}{c}$	Required installed capacity by base, mid-merit, and peaking load plus maintenance and station service.
16	Gross Installed Capacity for Ancillary by Grid	GIC_{AG}	MW	$\dfrac{NIC_{AG}/b}{c}$	Required installed capacity to satisfy ancillary services plus maintenance and station service.
17	Gross Installed Capacity by Grid	GIC_G	MW	$GIC_{LG} + GIC_{AG}$	Required installed capacity by Luzon, Visayas, and Mindanao.
18	Gross Installed Capacity	GIC		$\sum_G GIC_G$	Required installed capacity for the Philippines.
19	Share of Installed Capacity by Load by Grid	θ_{LG}	%	$\dfrac{GIC_{LG}}{GIC_G}$	Note: $\sum_L \theta_{LG} = 100\%$ (see Ravago et al. 2016 for details).

TABLE 7.A *(continued)*

	Parameter	Variable	Unit	Formula	Description
20	Fuel Source (Technology)	F	—		Fuel sources include coal, natural gas, conventional renewables, variable renewables, and oil. Conventional renewables include geothermal and hydro. Variable renewables include the must-dispatch solar, wind, biomass, and run-off river hydro.
21	Fuel Share by Load by Grid as Percentage of Installed Capacity	β_{FLG}	%		Share in the fuel mix by grid is percentage of installed capacity. (see Ravago et al. 2016 for details). Note that not all fuel sources or technologies are suitable for all types of load. Geographical location also matters. The following list the technologies by load and by grid: 1. Luzon — Baseload: coal, natural gas, geothermal, base hydro and the must-dispatch variable renewables. Note: $\theta_{LG} = \Sigma_F \beta_{FLG}$ Mid-peak-ancillary: peaking hydro, peaking natural gas, and oil. 2. Visayas and Mindanao — Baseload: coal, geothermal, base hydro and the must-dispatch variable renewables. — Mid-peak-ancillary: peaking hydro, and oil.

#	Description	Symbol	Unit	Formula	Notes
22	Per-unit Energy by Load by Grid	ρ_{LG}	%		Per-unit energy of baseload is assumed 67% for all grids. Per-unit energy of midmerit-peak-ancillary is assumed 5% for Luzon and Mindanao, and 2% for Visayas.
23	Share of Energy Consumption by Load by Grid	δ_{LG}	%	$\frac{\rho_{LG}}{LF_B}$	Per-unit Energy by Load/Load Factor.
24	Sum Total of Load Share in Peak Demand	d	%		The parameter (d) is based on the load duration curve in 2014 actual utilization of the different fuel sources. Based on DOE data, the shares in peak demand of base, midmerit, and peaking are 67%, 23%, and 10%, respectively. Mark-up for ancillary services is 15% of peak demand computed as $\frac{NIC_{A0}}{PD_G}$. Thus, sum total of load in peak demand, d = 115%.
25	Fuel Share by Load by Grid as Percentage of Electricity Consumption	μ_{FLG}		$\frac{\beta_{FLG} \times d}{\delta_{LG}}$	Share in the fuel mix by grid is the percentage of Power Consumption Mix (see Ravago et al. 2016 for details). Computed as fuel share (installed capacity) by load multiplied by the sum total of load share in peak demand (d) taken as a share of energy consumption by load divided by the share of energy consumption by load.
26	Generation by Fuel Source by Grid	G_{FG}	kWh	$EC_G \times \mu_{FLG} \times 1000$	
27	Fuel Price by Grid	GP_{FG}	P/kWh		Given in Tables 7.4–7.6.
28	Generation Cost by Fuel Source by Grid	GC_{FG}	P	$G_{FG} \times GP_{FG}$	
29	Blended Generation Charge by Grid	BGC_G	P/kWh	$\frac{\Sigma_F GC_{FG}}{\Sigma_F G_{FG}}$	
30	Blended Generation Charge	BGC	P/kWh	$\frac{\Sigma_{FG} GC_{FG}}{\Sigma_{FG} G_{FG}}$	

8

Development Finance[1]

Gilberto M. Llanto

Substantial resources for financing critical development expenditures will be needed to sustain the current economic momentum and meet future socio-economic aspirations. Where should the country get its financial resources to implement priority measures? This chapter looks at three main sources of funds — households and firms, donors, and foreign investors — and examines long-term implications with reference to taxation, the overall financial system, public–private partnerships (PPP), official development assistance (ODA), and remittances. It is imperative for the government to substantially raise tax revenues and rely more on domestic borrowing. ODA and PPP should be used to strategically finance infrastructure needs and emerging regional public goods, respectively. Financial reforms should be geared towards providing access to poor households and micro, small and medium enterprises, as well as financial education for overseas Filipinos and their families, to widen their investment horizons. Related financial inclusion policies and interventions are an important component for achieving the country's long-term vision.

Figure 8.1 provides a convenient framework highlighting the task of raising and channelling funds from the three main sources identified above to be used in policy-determined development

FIGURE 8.1
Framework of Development Finance in the Philippines

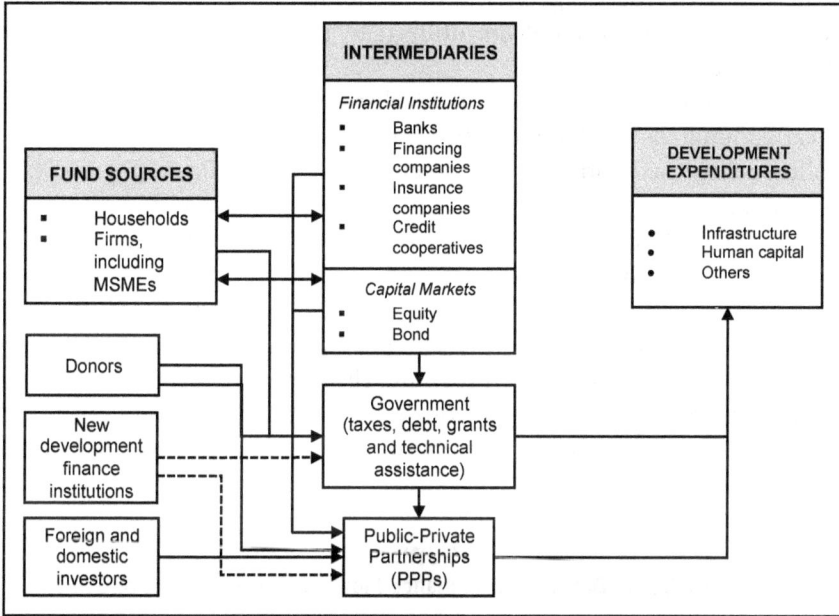

expenditures. The new development finance institutions such as the Asian Infrastructure Investment Bank (AIIB) are specifically included in the figure to indicate their potential as another major source of infrastructure finance for the Philippines. In the case of the AIIB, the People's Republic of China (PRC) is positioning itself as the largest international source of loans for infrastructure. The bilateral Philippine–PRC relationship will have a major bearing on how the country can access this source of long-term loans.

Households and firms pay taxes to the government, while the process of financial intermediation transforms the savings of households and firms into an adequate supply of finance for the use of the private and public sectors. Donors provide the government with loans, grants and technical assistance (TA), while foreign and domestic investors participate in PPP by taking an equity position, providing debt finance and engaging in the operation and maintenance (O&M) of infrastructure facilities such as rail, ports, toll roads and airports.

Private domestic and foreign investors also tap the financial and capital markets for resources to invest in PPPs for infrastructure. Public sector loans, grants, PPP schemes, and TA provided by donors to the government are utilized to finance critical development expenditures.

In 2014 the main source of development finance was lending by local commercial banks and other financial institutions (P3.56 trillion), followed by tax and non-tax revenues (P1.91 trillion) (Figure 8.2). Other sources of development finance are project and programme loans through ODA, national government domestic and foreign borrowings, remittances, and foreign direct investments (FDI). Since 2000, FDI flows to the Philippines have averaged about 1.3 per cent of gross domestic product (GDP) (Llanto and Navarro 2014). This is very low compared to most neighbouring economies, and it highlights the importance of addressing key policy, regulatory and institutional issues that weaken the interest of foreign investors in the Philippines.

FIGURE 8.2
Major Philippine Development Finance Flows, 2000–2013 (as % of GDP)

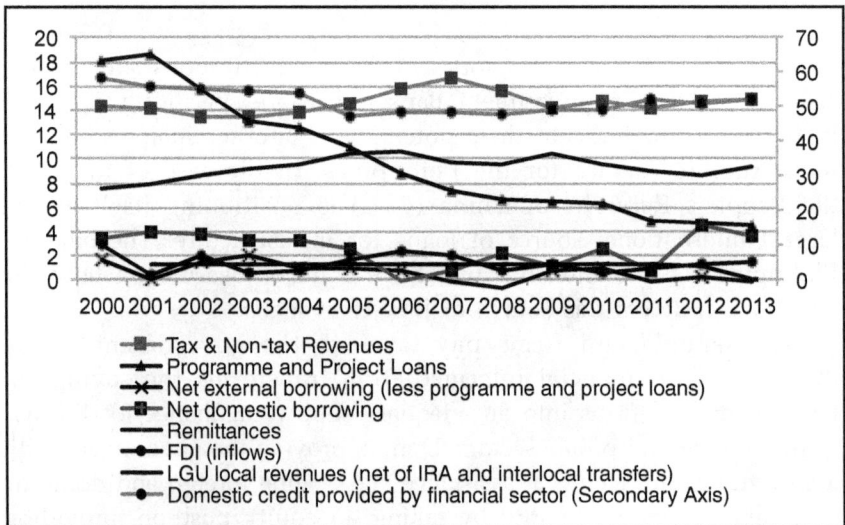

FDI = foreign direct investments; LGU = local government units.
Source: Llanto and Navarro (2014*a*).

I. Taxation

A. Tax Effort

The Philippine tax effort (that is, tax revenue-to-GDP ratio) is low relative to other ASEAN countries, especially the high-middle-income countries of Thailand and Malaysia (Figure 8.3). The tax-to-GDP ratio was 16.5 per cent in Thailand and 15.2 per cent in Malaysia in 2010–13, compared to the Philippines' 12.4 per cent, although the Philippine figure has increased somewhat in recent years.

FIGURE 8.3
Tax Revenue to GDP Ratio in Selected Asian Countries, 1990–2013
(%)

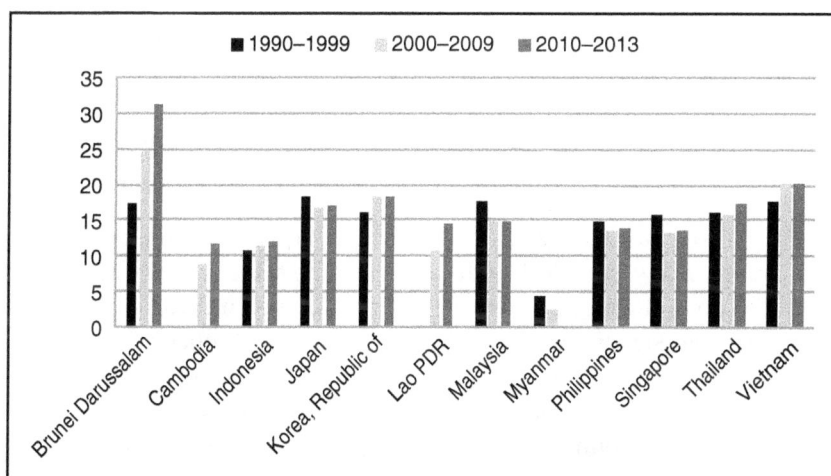

Note: Median averages, computed by author.
Source of raw data: International Monetary Fund's World Revenue Longitudinal Data.

The Philippines is not behind other countries when it comes to the instruments for taxation and the corresponding statutory tax rates (Table 8.1). Its statutory tax rates are higher than those of neighbouring countries. But having higher tax rates does not necessarily lead to higher tax collections. In fact, other ASEAN countries with lower tax rates have a better tax collection performance.

TABLE 8.1
Tax Rates in ASEAN Member States, Japan and Korea (%)

Country	Corporate Income Tax	Personal Income Tax (top schedule)	Indirect Tax		
			VAT/GST	Sales	Service
Brunei Darussalam	18.5	n/a	n/a	...	...
Cambodia	20	20	10	...	...
Indonesia	25	30	10	...	...
Japan	23.9	45	5	...	...
Korea, Republic of	22	38	10	...	...
Lao PDR	24	24	10	...	...
Malaysia	24	28	6	...	...
Myanmar	25	25	...	5–120	5
Philippines	30	32	12	...	...
Singapore	17	20	7	...	...
Thailand	20	35	7	...	...
Vietnam	20	35	10	...	...

Sources: Ernst & Young 2014, 2016*a*, 2016*b*, 2016*c*; KPMG Asia Pacific Tax Centre 2013.

A narrow tax base and inefficient tax administration are behind the country's low tax effort. Individual income taxes are only effectively imposed on and collected from formally employed individuals and tax-abiding professionals. Individual income taxes are collected through a withholding system imposed on private and public sector employees; and in the case of self-employed individuals, such as professionals (e.g., lawyers, accountants, engineers, consultants, etc.), through self-declaration of taxable incomes. High-net-worth individuals (e.g., those receiving incomes in the form of interest, dividends and stock options) are taxed at a final withholding rate of 10 per cent in the case of dividend income from a domestic corporation and at 20 per cent in the case of interest on peso bank deposits, deposit substitutes and trust funds.

Business persons and professionals generally avail themselves of various tax deductions to reduce taxable incomes. There is a need for a comprehensive review of individual income taxation that will consider tax rates, coverage, method of taxation (e.g., final tax on dividend income versus graduated rates on employment income), and administrative procedures for filing. There is also a need to review the taxation of individuals to make it a more effective instrument of tax collection.

Corporate income taxes are collected mostly from a relatively small number of SMEs and large enterprises. A large number of establishments are microenterprises, which contribute little to tax collection. These are generally single proprietorships and operate in the fringes of the shadow economy. The Department of Trade and Industry (DTI 2011) reported that as of 2011 there are 820,255 establishments in the country, of which 90.6 per cent are micro-enterprises, 9 per cent are SMEs, and 0.4 per cent are large enterprises. There is a need to review corporate income taxation to make it more effective in collecting taxes from corporate establishments. It is important to expand the taxable base. In general, tax policy should eschew unnecessary tax exemptions and incentives to corporates and individuals (e.g., exemption of senior citizens from payment of value-added tax [VAT]). A decomposition of tax collection growth indicated that the tax base component explains about 80 per cent of total tax collection increases from corporate and individual income taxes and VAT in 2011–12 (International Monetary Fund [IMF] 2013).

More developed economies such as Japan, the Republic of Korea and Singapore rely more on taxes on income and wealth, while developing economies saddled with weaker tax administration generally depend more on indirect taxes (Figures 8.4a and 8.4b).

Indirect taxes are a more significant source of revenue for the Philippines than direct taxes. Indirect taxes are composed of the VAT on consumables and services, excise tax on petroleum products, alcohol, tobacco and others. Recent tax reforms centred on increasing the VAT and excise tax on liquor and tobacco have yielded very significant revenues for development spending (e.g., health, conditional cash transfers), based on the canons of simplicity and ease of administration.

Clearly, the Philippines must undertake more vigorous tax collection efforts to deliver its development commitments. Its low tax effort is explained by several factors: low tax compliance by taxpayers, narrow tax base brought about by non-inclusion of many individuals and micro and small enterprises in the tax net, weak tax administration,

FIGURE 8.4a
Share of Direct and Indirect Taxes to GDP in Selected Asian Countries, 2002–13 (%)

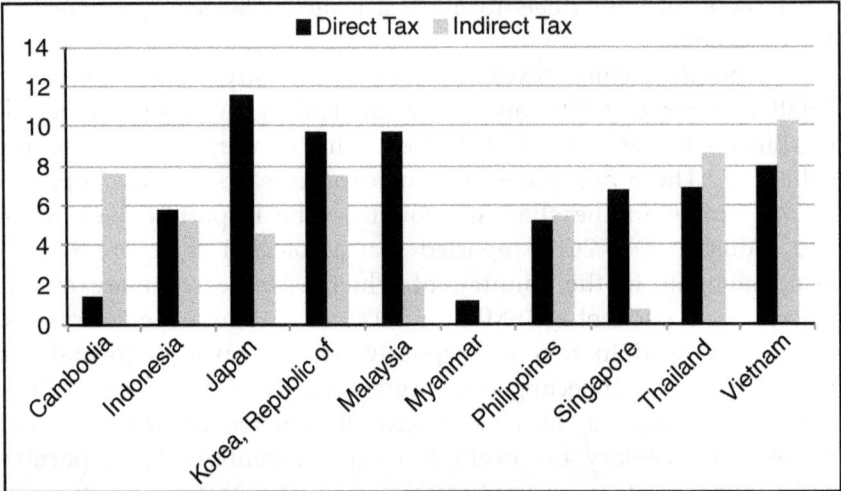

Note: Percentages are median averages. Direct taxes include individual income tax revenue, corporate income tax revenues, taxes on payroll and workforce revenue, and property tax revenue. Indirect taxes include value added tax (VAT) revenue, excise taxes, and trade revenues.
Source of raw data: International Monetary Fund's World Revenue Longitudinal Data.

FIGURE 8.4b
Share of Direct and Indirect Taxes to GDP in Selected Asian Countries, 2014 (%)

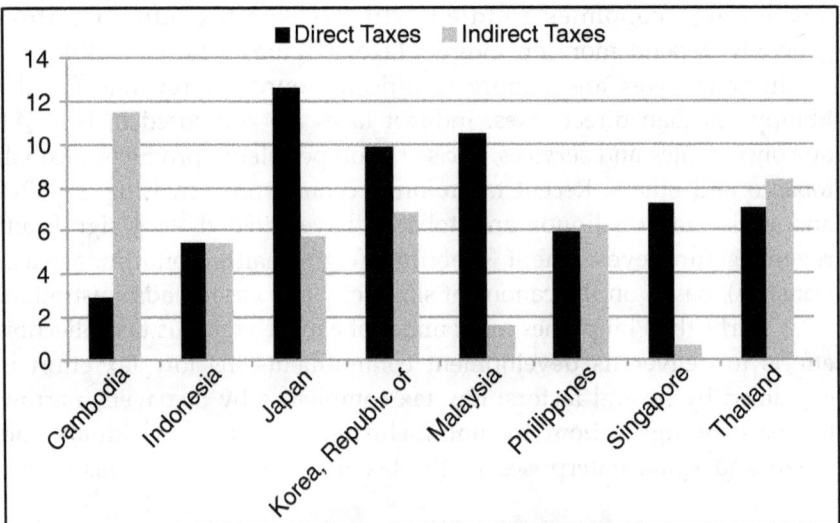

Source: IMF's World Revenue Longitudinal Data.

and tax exemptions arising from fiscal incentives given to meet the country's investment objectives. As the economy grows, the shadow economy or the informal sector will shrink, and this presents a timely opportunity to expand the tax base. However, if the past is a prologue to the future, it looks like the low tax effort will persist unless the government exercises the political will to reform the tax policy and tax administration.

One approach would be to increase consumption taxes, because these are easier to administer and collect. However, this is lopsided. What is needed is a comprehensive review of direct and indirect taxation, with a view to craft a system that would yield substantial revenues but at the same time be equitable, progressive and competitive with the tax systems of other ASEAN countries. It should also be noted that tax harmonization is an important objective of the ASEAN Economic Community (AEC).

Admittedly, in light of the country's experience with the Comprehensive Tax Reform Program in the late 1990s, it will be difficult to undertake a comprehensive tax reform programme. The government had exerted a great effort to prepare a well-designed tax system only to find that the tax reform programme passed by Congress was an inferior package. However, this experience should not deter efforts to undertake a comprehensive tax review.

Local government units (LGU) currently have a minor role in improving the overall tax effort. This is due to generally weak local tax revenue collections. Various studies have documented the dependence of LGUs on fiscal transfers, chiefly on internal revenue allotments (IRA), grants and other funds from the national government, which has led many LGUs to give less priority to local revenue mobilization (Manasan 2005, 2007; Llanto 2011, 2012). The inability of LGUs to raise substantial local revenues also stems from the inadequacy of their taxing powers (Llanto 2011) and poor local tax administration. The national government has retained control over major sources of tax revenues. The principal sources of local incomes are the IRA, property tax, business tax, and service and business income from various local economic enterprises. Only cities and provinces are authorized to collect real property taxes, and municipalities only receive their share collected by provinces. Revenue-productive taxes controlled by the national government include corporate and individual income taxes, VAT, and excise tax on tobacco, liquor and petroleum products (Llanto 2011). Notwithstanding the limitations to their taxing authority, LGUs have not maximized their revenue potential, and there is scope for increasing local taxes, such as local business taxes and real property taxes, especially in growing urban centres. Local constituents will not be averse to paying additional taxes once they see and experience the benefits of better local governance.

B. Key Issues and Recommendations

In the immediate term, policymakers should conduct a comprehensive review of tax policy and improve tax administration. The objective is not only to raise tax collections but also to ensure that the Philippine tax system is equitable and competitive with other ASEAN countries.

The tax reform effort should include finding broad-based taxes. Expanding the taxation of consumer products may be one way of increasing tax revenues. The government may want to look into the taxation of products and services coursed through online transactions, especially those transacted with companies abroad (UP 2004). While the Bureau of Internal Revenue (BIR) has already implemented (in 2013) the guidelines on the taxation of e-commerce transactions through Revenue Memorandum Circular Number 55-2013, effective monitoring will be necessary to ensure compliance of concerned agents, such as online shoppers, banks, credit card companies, freight forwarders and others (Vicente 2006).

LGUs have to improve collection of real property taxes and local business taxes. Tax on idle private lands and a special levy on lands that have benefited from infrastructure financed by the government have not been used by LGUs to improve local revenue generation. In 2013, total real property tax collection reached around P41.2 billion, which is equivalent to 0.36 per cent of GDP. Real property tax collection had about a 31 per cent share to total local revenues in 2009–13.

Outstanding issues in real property tax that must be resolved are as follows: (i) outdated schedule of market values; (ii) multiple taxes on property ownership and transfers; (iii) relatively high transfer taxes, which discourage formal transactions; (iv) weak enforcement of property-related taxes; (v) lack of uniform property valuation systems and methodologies; (vi) political intervention in property valuation; (vii) limited use of information technologies in the appraisal process; and (viii) non-provision for formal education and training of assessors/appraisers (Department of Finance [DOF] 2013).

LGUs should contribute their share in increasing the overall tax effort by improving local revenue collection through reforms in local tax policy and tax administration. The 1991 code has set certain limits on the taxing powers of LGUs and has somewhat diminished the taxing power of provinces in favour of cities. There is a need to review the tax assignment of cities, municipalities and provinces to improve overall efficiency of tax collections.

Congress should enact the Fiscal Responsibility Bill, where a proposed new spending will not be approved without a pre-identified effective source of financing. In this regard, a moratorium on revenue-eroding measures should be agreed upon in the Legislative Executive Development Advisory Council (LEDAC). Any proposed measure that will result in the erosion of the tax base should not be taken lightly.

Necessary reforms in tariff and customs administration should be implemented immediately, such as installing a national single window in the Bureau of Customs and providing the right incentives, including strictly applying appropriate negative sanctions on erring customs personnel. Trade revenue is still an important source of revenue, although trade liberalization and various free trade agreements have reduced its relative revenue contribution. In 2012, trade revenue amounted to around 2.7 per cent of GDP, compared to 6.1 per cent for corporate and individual income taxes and 4.1 per cent for VAT and excise taxes (IMF's World Revenue Longitudinal Data).

Policymakers should work with counterparts to implement key agreements among the ASEAN countries for tax harmonization. Two provisions related to taxation provided in the AEC Blueprint signed in 2007 require the following: (i) enhancement of the withholding tax structure, where possible, to promote the broadening of the investor base in ASEAN debt issuance; and (ii) avoidance of double taxation among all member countries by 2010. The objective is to have competitive tax rates and improve tax administrations among member countries.

II. Financial System

Taxes will remain a significant source of Philippine development finance. However, tax revenues cannot fully cover the enormous development spending needs of the next twenty-five years. The government must continue to tap financial and capital markets to finance development expenditures. Net domestic borrowing by the government was on average 2.5 per cent of GDP in 2000–2013 and 2.9 per cent in 2011–13. The percentage share of domestic borrowing to total borrowing has been increasing since 2009. A highly liquid domestic financial market has fully supported the government's financing requirements. The government has reduced its dependence on foreign borrowing over the past few years. This was reduced from an average of 0.5 per cent of GDP for the period 2000–2013 to 0.4 for 2011–13 (Llanto and Navarro 2014). Foreign loans are mostly dollar-denominated, with only a relatively small amount in yen (Samurai bonds). The government still maintains an exposure, albeit minor, to foreign borrowings for strategic and prudent reasons and has effectively managed currency risks and the possible negative impact of rising U.S. interest rates on dollar-denominated loans. In the near future it may have no immediate need to alter the present borrowing mix that favours domestic over foreign loans, and this could be the trend as the domestic financial system matures and develops.[2]

The Philippines needs robust and resilient financial and capital markets to mobilize and channel the savings of households and firms into productive investments, especially long-term investments. There is a need to develop long-term finance for long-term investments of private companies, especially those that are expanding and investing in long-term assets. Financial intermediation is largely through the banking system, as the Philippines, like many other Asian countries, has remained reliant on commercial banks. In the longer term the equity and bond markets need to become more important instruments for mobilizing long-term financing.

A. Banking System

The past two decades have demonstrated the strength and resiliency of the country's banking system in the face of regional and global financial crises and the recent volatility in global financial markets. The reforms instituted by the regulatory authorities in the form of the Bangko Sentral ng Pilipinas (BSP), the Securities and Exchange Commission (SEC), the Insurance Commission, and the DOF were instrumental in strengthening the financial system. Adherence to global financial and banking standards imposed by the Basel Committee on Banking Supervision was one of the crucial reforms pursued by BSP.

As of 2015, there are a total of 28,471 financial institutions in the country, of which 62.2 per cent are non-bank financial institutions and 37.8 per cent are banks. In recent years, the percentage share of banking units has increased from 35.9 per cent in 2010. Figure 8.5 shows that the bulk of Philippine financial resources are with universal and commercial banks, with a share of 73 per cent of the total resources of P15,381.70 billion in 2015 (BSP 2015e).

FIGURE 8.5
Share of Philippine Financial Resources by Type of Institution, 2014 and 2015
(%)

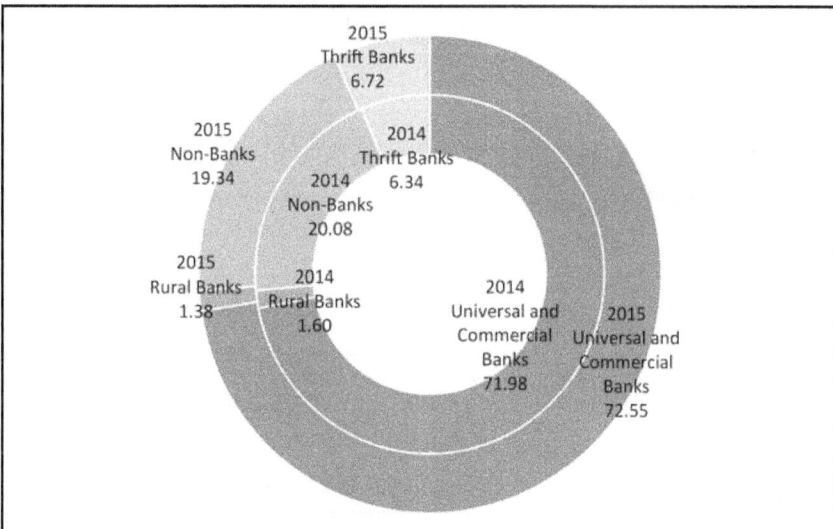

Source of basic data: BSP 2015, *Banking Statistics*.

The majority of banking institutions are universal banks (51 per cent of the total banking system), followed by rural and cooperative banks (25 per cent), thrift banks (19 per cent) and commercial banks (5 per cent). Currently, there are 5,398 universal banks, 503 commercial banks, 2,628 rural banks and cooperative banks, and 1,927 thrift banks. Key baseline indicators of the banking system show, first, an increase in total assets and deposits at an average annual growth rate of 12.7 per cent and 13.8 per cent, respectively, and second, the status of non-performing loans and acquired real and other properties that banks are trying to unwind (Table 8.2).

Key performance indicators point to the robustness and resiliency of the banking system (Table 8.3). A comparison with ASEAN peers

TABLE 8.2
Key Baseline Indicators of the Banking System, 2010–15
(billion pesos)

Indicators	2010	2011	2012	2013	2014	2015
Total Assets[a]	6,918.30	7,335.60	8,049.70	9,970.80	11,169.00	11,202.20
Total Deposits	5,125.10	5,360.70	5,753.60	7,608.90	8,524.60	8,615.20
Total Loan Portfolio (Gross)	3,276.90	3,726.50	4,191.30	4,897.00	5,832.40	5,887.80
Gross Non-Performing Loans (Gross NPL)[b]	118.3	120.4	105.7	135.5	134.8	140.8
Net Non-Performing Loans[c]	...	...	...	28.6	34.7	37.9
Real and Other Properties Acquired (ROPA)	137.1	120.4	113.6	118.4	111	108.1

Note: Preliminary data used for 2015.
[a] Figures adjusted to net off the account "Due from Head Office" with "Due to Head Office" of branches of foreign banks.
[b] Loans Classified as Past Due and Already Non-Performing plus Items in Litigation.
[c] Gross Non-Performing Loans minus Specific Allowance for Credit Losses (per Circular No. 772, Series of 2012; effective 1 January 2013).

TABLE 8.3

Key Indicators of the Philippine Banking System, 2010–June 2015 (%)

Indicator	2010	2011	2012	2013	2014	Jun-15
Profitability						
Earning Asset Yield[a]	5.9	5.6	5.2	4.5	4.3	4.3
Funding Cost[b]	2.1	2	1.8	1.2	1	1.1
Interest Spread[c]	3.8	3.6	3.4	3.2	3.2	3.2
Net Interest Margin[d]	3.9	3.8	3.6	3.3	3.3	3.4
Non-Interest Income to Total Operating Income[e]	37.2	35.8	38.3	38.9	31.2	31.4
Cost-to-Income[f]	63.6	65	63.5	60.3	62.4	62.3
Return on Assets (ROA)[g]	1.4	1.5	1.6	1.6	1.3	1.3
Return in Equity (ROE)[g]	12.2	12.1	12.4	13.3	10.9	10.7
Liquidity						
Cash and Due from Banks to Deposits (TLP)	25.9	25.3	25.4	33.6	29.1	27.3
Liquid Assets to Deposits[h]	59.7	56.5	57.5	59.5	55.7	55
Loans, Gross to Deposits	64.5	70	73.5	64.4	68.4	68.4
Asset Quality						
Restructured Loans to Total Loan Portfolio	1.5	1.2	1	0.7	0.6	0.6
Loan Loss Reserves (LLR) to TLP	4.3	3.9	3.7	3.3	2.8	2.8
Gross Non-Performing Loans (NPL) to TLP	4.4	3.8	3.4	2.8	2.3	2.4
Net NPL to TLP	1.1	1	0.7	0.6	0.6	0.6
NPL Ratio net of IBL	4.7	3.9	3.5	2.9	2.4	2.4
NPL Coverage (LLR to Gross NPL)	98.1	102.7	109.6	118.7	119.8	117.9
Non-Performing Assets (NPA) to Gross Assets	4.3	3.8	3.3	2.6	2.3	2.3
NPA Coverage (NPA Reserves to NPA)	56.9	62.4	68.1	73	77.1	76.5
ROPA to Gross Assets Ratio	2.3	1.9	1.6	1.3	1.1	1
ROPA to Coverage Ratio	19.7	22.1	23	25.1	29.5	27.5
Distressed Assets	9.5	7.9	6.8	5.6	4.6	4.6

TABLE 8.3 *(continued)*

Indicator	2010	2011	2012	2013	2014	Jun-15
Capital Adequacy						
Total Capital Accounts to Total Assets[j]	11.7	12.6	13.1	11.3	12.2	12.8
Capital Adequacy Ratio (Solo)[k]	16	16.7	17.3	16.5	15.4	15.1
Capital Adequacy Ratio (Consolidated)[k]	16.9	17.6	18.4	17.7	16.2	16.1

[a] Ratio of interest to average earning assets.
[b] Ratio of interest expenses to average interest-bearing liabilities.
[c] Difference between earning asset yield and funding cost.
[d] Ratio of net interest income to average earning assets.
[e] Non-interest income includes dividends income.
[f] Ratio of non-interest expenses to total operating income.
[g] ROA and ROE refer to the ratios of net profit to average assets and capital, respectively.
[h] Cash and Due from Banks plus Financial Assets, net of amortization (net of financial assets in equity securities).
[i] Ratios are computed in accordance with the NPL definition under BSP Circular No. 772 (s. 16 October 2012).
[j] Total capital accounts include redeemable preferred shares.
[k] Ratio of qualifying capital total risk-weighted assets. In implementing the reforms under the Basel III standards, while the three major risks (credit, market and operational risks) are still covered by the calculation of risk-based capital, the qualifying capital was strengthened through the eligibility criteria for recognition as capital, including the required loss absorbency features of capital instruments. Data as of end-December 2012 onwards are for Universal and Commercial Banks and Subsidiary Thrift Banks; excludes Stand-Alone Thrift, Rural and Cooperative Banks.
Source: BSP 2015.

shows that Philippine banks are relatively well performing (Table 8.4). The Philippine banking industry is highly liquid and is always on the lookout for highly remunerative investments. Meanwhile, banks have parked their excess liquidity with special deposit accounts (SDAs) in the BSP, although recently the regulator has been sending strong signals of unwinding these SDAs.

TABLE 8.4
Key Monetary and Financial Indicators in Selected ASEAN Countries, 2014 (%)

Country	Year-on-Year Growth of Broad Money (M2)	Nonperforming Loans over Commercial Bank Loans	Rate per Annum of Return on Commercial Bank Assets	Rate per Annum of Return on Commercial Bank Equity	Risk-Weighted Capital Adequacy Ratios	Year-on-Year Headline Inflation Rate
Indonesia	11.87	2.07	2.74	21.35	18.72	6.39
Malaysia	6.99	1.65	2.97	15.78	14.58	3.14
Philippines	11.25	2.02	1.57	15.91	18.29	4.17
Singapore	3.41	0.76	1.12	13.35	15.92	1.02

Source: ADB Asia Regional Integration Center 2015.

Banks continue to provide loans to their traditional clientele — the non-financial corporate sector. Domestic credit provided to the private sector has been slightly increasing since 2010 (Figure 8.6). Domestic banks continue to finance short-term assets, consistent with the short-term orientation of their liabilities. Over time they have learned to lengthen loan maturities, but there remains a mismatch between short-term liabilities of banks and the long-term requirements of such investments as infrastructure. In 2013, Standard Chartered Bank placed the Philippines in the low-risk category in terms of leverage. This indicates the financial system's capacity to provide more loans. The banking system is very liquid, and there is scope for more lending.

FIGURE 8.6
Share of Philippine Financial Resources by Type of Institution, 2014 and 2015
(%)

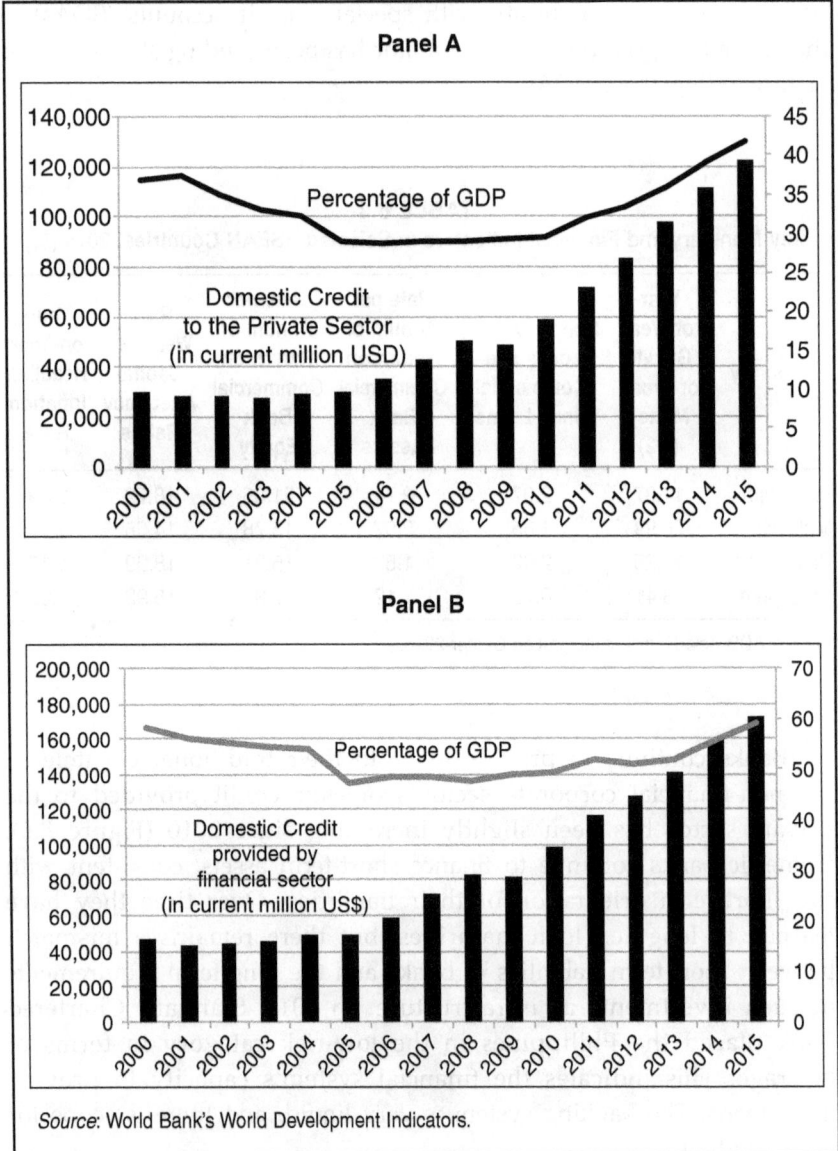

Source: World Bank's World Development Indicators.

Syndicated loans can be packaged to finance huge, long-gestating projects in the private and public sectors. However, in the absence of long-term products as alternative sources of financing, such syndicated loans may not be competitively priced. Alternatively, a corporation can choose to borrow directly from the public through the issuance of corporate notes. Listed corporate bonds are available in the website of the Philippine Dealing & Exchange Corp. If the corporation does not want to issue a bond, a commercial bank can arrange for the issuance of an initial public offering (IPO) for the company. However, only a few companies have chosen this approach to raising funds. They have, thus, depended on internal funds and bank loans for financing investments. The real challenge is to tease out competitive long-term financing from the financial system for long-term projects.

The short-term orientation of bank loans and the practical absence of long-term credit markets could be due to the lack of competition in the banking sector. It is a highly segmented sector, with universal and commercial banks catering to medium and large companies while thrift banks (smaller in capitalization) lend to small and medium companies. Micro and small enterprises borrow from microfinance and rural banks, the smallest in terms of capitalization and range of financial services provided. The BSP has adopted a permissive attitude towards bank consolidation, for example, by providing incentives to rural banks that would consolidate. However, the vast majority of banks, especially the smaller banks, have chosen to operate at their current level of capitalization and expertise. Many of those banks started as family-owned banks, which may be reluctant to give up family ownership and control. The regulator has to find a more nuanced approach to nudge banks to consolidate for financial strength and stability.

Congress has recently liberalized the entry of foreign banks with the view to having a more competitive banking system capable of providing better financial services in the future AEC. The presence of foreign players will definitely provide much-needed competition in the financial services industry.

B. Bond Market

The Philippine bond market consists of short- and long-term bonds, which are mostly issued by the national government. Government bonds may be issued in the form of treasury bills, fixed-rate treasury notes, retail treasury notes, and multicurrency notes, whereas commercial paper and corporate bonds comprise mostly floating rate debt instruments issued by large corporations. Most government bonds actively traded or issued are the fixed-rate treasury bonds and retail treasury bonds. Asian Bonds Online reports that, whilst the Philippine corporate bonds market is small, it has continued to grow rapidly in recent years, although it is still a rather thin market. Comparative figures across Asia corroborate this observation (Tables 8.5a and 8.5b).

TABLE 8.5a
Key Corporate Bond Market Indicators in Selected Asian Countries (I)
(%)

Country	Corporate Bonds Outstanding, 2013[a]			Corporate Bonds Issued, 2009–13	
	Size Over GDP	Foreign Exchange (FX) Share	3-Year Maturity over Total[b]	FX Share	Floating Share
People's Republic of China	16.4	9	24.4	9.1	1.5
Hong Kong, China	78.1	60.1	34.3	84.5	5.2
India	11.8	...	...	25.7	0.4
Indonesia	5.9	59.4	36.9	84	0.1
Korea, Republic of	90.1	11.9	45	15.6	5.5
Malaysia	48.4	17	15.7	36.5	0.2
Philippines	9.3	47.5	20.4	34.1	3.5
Singapore	46.6	31.3	26.8	18.6	3.8
Taiwan	49.6	...	...	8.3	1.5
Thailand	19.8	18.1	35.3	12.7	0.8

Note: Based on results from sampled Asian countries.
[a] Latest available, generally September 2013, except for India (2012). Data based on Asian Bonds Online include bonds by companies and financial institutions.
[b] Includes local currency corporate bond market only.
Sources: Deutsche Bank Research, Asian Bonds Online, CEIC, BIS, IMF, Dealogic as cited in Levinger and Chen 2014.

TABLE 8.5b
Key Corporate Bond Market Indicators in Selected Asian Countries (II)
(%)

Country	Market Concentration	Corporate Credit to GDP		Corporate Leverage, 2012
	Top 10 Share	Size over GDP	5-Year Corporate Annual Growth Rate	
People's Republic of China	23.7	139.4	22.6	104.6
Hong Kong, China	63.2	174.1	10.5	...
India	76.5	49.6	18.4	77.3
Indonesia	85.3	18.1	18.8	63.6
Korea, Republic of	70.5	111.4	8.5	80.6
Malaysia	60.9	...	...	77.3
Philippines	90.8	...	...	96.3
Singapore	58.4	69.9	7.3	...
Taiwan	86.5	...	...	...
Thailand	63.1	51.8	7.1	85.6

Note: Based on results from sampled Asian countries.
Sources: Deutsche Bank Research, Asian Bonds Online, CEIC, BIS, IMF, Dealogic as cited in Levinger and Chen 2014.

For a number of reasons, domestic and international players have not really entered the bond market. Some of the major issues that need to be addressed by the government and regulators are as follows: (i) lack of transparency; (ii) lack of organized trading, as the corporate bond market in the Philippines is bilateral and conducted over the counter, which means it lacks pricing and distribution information, and has no accurate picture of secondary market liquidity; (iii) high issuance costs; (iv) problems besetting institutional investors; (v) outmoded bankruptcy laws; and (vi) the need for increased regulatory supervision of corporate bond issuance (Espenilla 2004). In addition, the government needs to review the tax rate imposed on foreign investors investing in the Philippine capital market — currently at 30 per cent — and to review the restrictive rules on foreign investments.[3]

C. Equity Market

In mature economies, the equity market presents an important venue for raising capital and providing alternative investment opportunities. The Philippine equity market is underdeveloped, although there have been encouraging signs of growth. The equity market has been expanding in recent years in terms of total value turnover and volume of stocks traded (trade frequency). This indicates an increase in market liquidity. In 2014 the total value of market transactions was recorded at P2,130 billion, while the stocks volume reached about 815.2 billion shares (Figure 8.7). However, some indicators (market capitalization in Table 8.6; capital-raised-to-GDP ratio in Figure 8.8) show the middling status of the Philippine equity market.

FIGURE 8.7
Stock Market Transactions, 2006–14
(volume in million shares, value in million pesos)

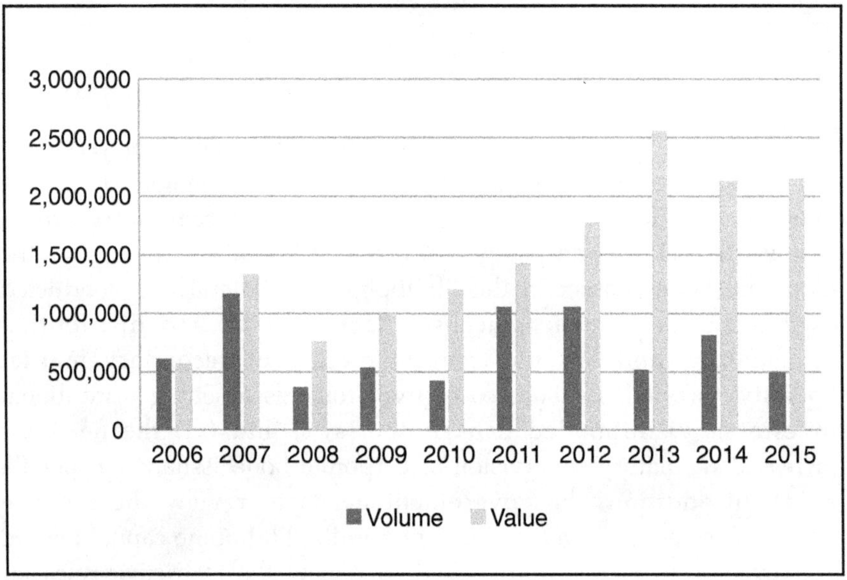

Source: BSP 2015d.

TABLE 8.6
Market Capitalization of Listed Companies in Selected ASEAN Countries, 2008–12
(% of GDP)

Country	2008	2009	2010	2011	2012
Indonesia	19.4	33	47.7	43.7	43.2
Malaysia	81	126.5	165.8	136.6	156.2
Philippines	29.9	47.6	78.8	73.8	105.6
Singapore	93.6	161.5	156.5	112	142.8
Thailand	37.6	52.4	87.1	77.7	104.7

Note: Market capitalization (also known as market value) is the share price times the number of shares outstanding. Listed domestic companies are the domestically incorporated companies listed on the country's stock exchanges at the end of the year. Listed companies does not include investment companies, mutual funds, or other collective investment vehicles.
Source: World Bank's World Development Indicators.

FIGURE 8.8
Capital Raised to GDP Ratio, 2012
(%)

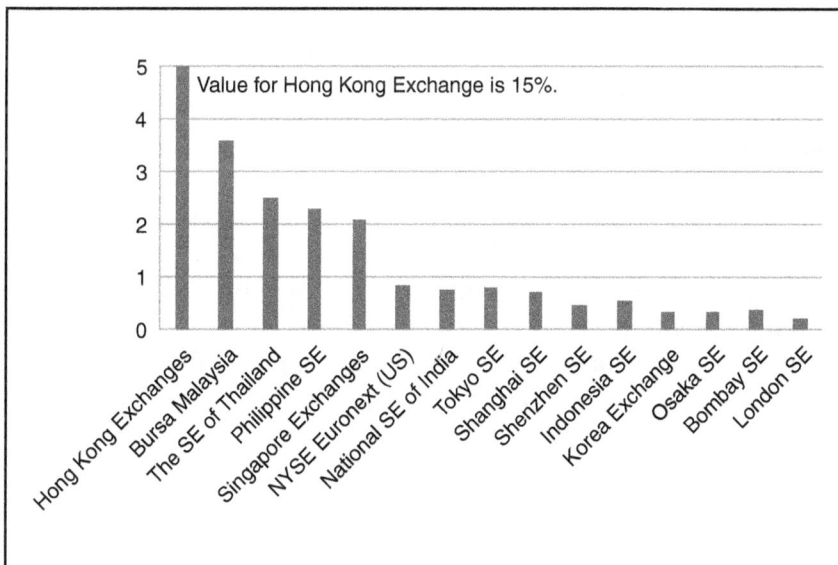

Sources: World Bank; World Federation Exchange as cited in Crisostomo, Padilla and Visda 2013.

The investor base is growing; but at 525,850 investor accounts, stock market investment continues to be limited to the few who have a high level of disposable income and are familiar with the intricacies of stock investments. The investor base is too small, but the potential number of investors is very large, which includes the millions of overseas Filipino workers (OFW) and their families who could have invested part of their remittances in the equity market instead of in real estate and consumption. There could be around 11.7 million households with bank accounts who are potential stock market investors, but these have not gone to non-bank deposit forms of investment, such as the stock market (Crisostomo, Padilla and Visda 2013). Other Asian economies have higher investor bases (e.g., Hong Kong, China with 35.7 per cent of its population; Malaysia, 12.5 per cent; and Singapore, 12.0 per cent).

The majority of investors are also based in Metro Manila. A 2009 survey of the Social Weather Stations reported that only around 1 per cent of Filipinos said they own any stocks. On the other hand, only 253 out of 800,000 companies registered and licensed by the SEC have their shares publicly listed in the Philippine Stock Exchange (PSE) (Crisostomo, Padilla and Visda 2013). The lack of understanding of the stock market, lack of trust and a negative perception of stock market investment have discouraged greater participation by potential investors. In this regard, the government, especially the SEC and PSE, has a large task in educating potential investors, in particular on the role and functions of the equity market and how it can be a good alternative to traditional bank deposits. More importantly, tough enforcement of auditing and disclosure requirements by the regulator and the PSE alike will be important steps to build investors' confidence. There is also a need to continue to reduce transaction costs faced by investors and review the relevance of certain issuances. For example, the requirements under BIR Revenue Regulation 1-2014 and BIR Revenue Memorandum Circular No. 5-2014 on withholding agents to submit an alphabetical list of payees of income payments subject to withholding taxes have triggered such an uproar in the business community that the Supreme Court issued a temporary restraining order against these issuances (Dumlao 2014; Tupas 2014).

D. Financing and Taxation of Micro, Small and Medium-sized Enterprises

There is a great potential for microenterprises and SMEs (or MSMEs) to be significant drivers of inclusive growth. In terms of employment, the DTI reports that of the 4.9 million jobs in 2012, 47 per cent were generated by microenterprises, 41.8 per cent by small enterprises, and 11.2 per cent by medium-sized enterprises. These enterprises contributed 35.7 per cent of the total value-added in 2012 (DTI n.d.).

However, lack of access to finance constrains growth and expansion. The compound annual growth rate of SME loans in the Philippines for 2011–14 was 6 per cent, compared to 12 per cent in Thailand and Indonesia. The SME loans-to-GDP ratio is lowest in the Philippines, at 9 per cent, compared to 105 per cent in Thailand, 55 per cent in Malaysia, and 36 per cent in Singapore (Deloitte 2015). Fewer Philippine SMEs are able to access loans than their counterparts in Malaysia, Thailand and Singapore (Figure 8.9).

The government has introduced several measures to provide SMEs with access to finance: mandatory lending (8 per cent of banks' loan portfolio for micro and small, and 2 per cent for medium-sized enterprises), a partial guarantee under the Small Business Corporation, and the Credit Surety Fund for cooperatives lending to a variety of small businesses. Government financial institutions have also been asked to develop SME lending programmes. Compliance with mandatory lending is shown in Table 8.7. Nevertheless, SMEs continue to face the problem of lack of access to finance. It could be that the failure to understand why the credit markets tend to exclude SMEs has led to inappropriate solutions. For example, the mandatory lending by private banks and the creation of SME lending programmes in government financial institutions are overly simplistic solutions.

There are several factors, other than the unwillingness of banks to lend to SMEs, that constrain their access to finance. Deloitte (2015) provided a summary of problems faced by SMEs: (i) a tendency of banks to overemphasize collateral while placing little emphasis on project feasibility; (ii) underdeveloped equity financing through the Philippine stock market; (iii) insufficient capitalization of financial institutions resulting in high-cost loans to SMEs; (iv) lack of credit

FIGURE 8.9
Sources of Small and Medium-sized Enterprise Financing in Selected Countries
(%)

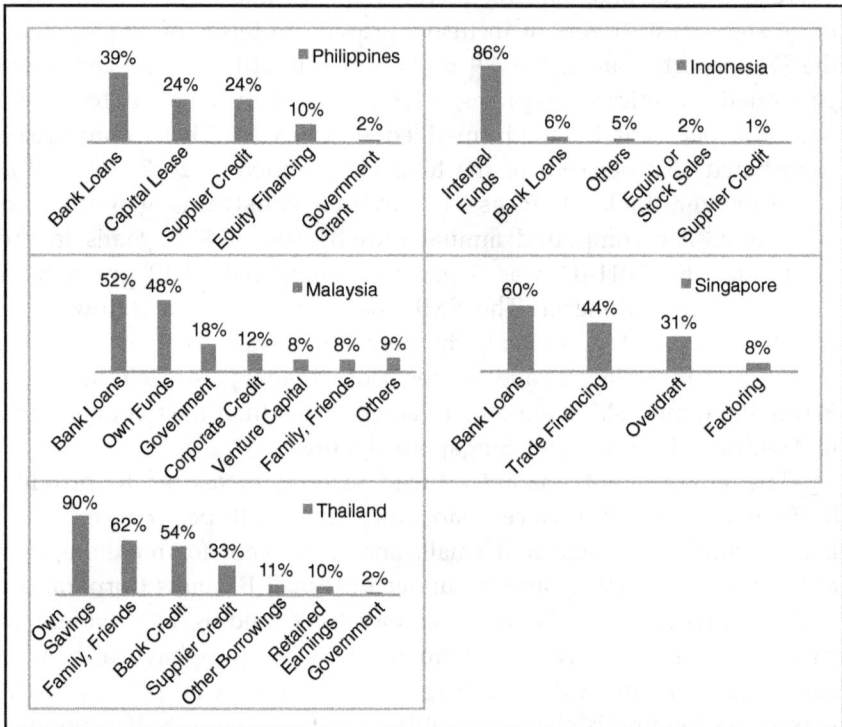

Source: Deloitte 2015.

information, and a highly centralized examination system; and (v) lack of guidance for preparing compliance documentation. In fact, for years, local researchers, especially those at the Philippine Institute for Development Studies, have highlighted all these factors, but the problems persist.

A review of the constraints to SME lending points to the inability of banks to overcome problems of information, underwrite SME loans, and manage credit risks and other risks arising from SME lending. In addition, many SMEs do not have the capacity to comply with various documentary requirements imposed by a strict regulatory

TABLE 8.7

Compliance with Magna Carta for Micro, Small and Medium-sized Enterprises, 2014 (billion pesos)

Compliance Indicators	Universal and Commercial Banks	Thrift Banks	Rural and Cooperative Banks	All Banks
Total Loan Net Portfolio, Net of Exclusions		491.01	101.86	4,003.53
Required Loan Portfolio for Micro, Small and Medium-sized Enterprises (MSMEs)				
10% for MSMEs	341.07	49.1	10.19	400.35
8% for Micro and Small Enterprises (MSEs) only	272.85	39.28	8.15	320.28
2% for Medium Enterprises (MEs) only	68.21	9.82	2.04	80.07
Actual Loan Portfolio for MSMEs				
Total for MSMEs	332.33	73.28	34.57	440.17
	(9.7%)	(14.9%)	(33.9%)	(11.0%)
MSEs only	134.70	36.12	25.27	196.09
	(3.9%)	(7.4%)	(24.8%)	(4.9%)
MEs only	197.63	37.16	9.30	244.08
	(5.8%)	(7.6%)	(9.1%)	(6.1%)

Note: Percentages in parentheses are Compliance Rates, defined as Actual Loans divided by Total Loan Net Portfolio, Net of Exclusions.
Source: BSP 2015a.

environment. The government's credit guarantee schemes and planned implementation of a credit scoring system for SMEs under the Central Credit Information Corporation can address the information and risk management constraints faced by SMEs.[4] Financial and business education should be extended to SMEs to enable them to undertake proper documentation and preparation of required feasibility studies. The lack of adequate collateral by SMEs can be addressed by establishing a secured transaction system, which provides the legal and regulatory framework for using movable property as collateral for SME loans. SMEs own a range of tangible and intangible assets, such as vehicles, inventory, sales contracts, *quedan* (a negotiable instrument showing ownership of a specified amount of product in a warehouse), account receivables, crops, livestock, fishponds, office and household appliances, and small industrial or agricultural machinery. These assets could be used to fill the collateral gap.

E. Financial Inclusion

Financial inclusion of poor households and MSMEs has become a rising global concern, and the Philippines is no exception. The BSP (2013, p. 1) defines financial inclusion as a state wherein there is effective access to a wide range of financial services for all Filipinos. Effective access means that financial services are appropriately designed, of good quality, relevant for actual use, and beneficial to the target market. The government has identified financial inclusion as an important strategy for inclusive growth.

A recent BSP (2015) survey reported the following: (i) 25 per cent of Filipino adults have never saved, 32 per cent used to save, and only 43 per cent presently have savings; (ii) of those with savings, only 32 per cent save in banks, while 68 per cent keep their savings at home; (iii) 65 per cent of unbanked adults cited lack of money as the main reason for not having a bank account; (iv) about 47 per cent of adults have outstanding loans; the main source of borrowing is informal — 62 per cent borrow from family, relatives or friends, while 10 per cent borrow from informal lenders; (v) in the past six months about 44 per cent of adults sent or received money, while 42 per cent made payments; (vi) only 3.2 per cent of adults have micro-insurance coverage; and (vii) clients rated themselves as only "somewhat satisfied" with how issues were resolved in most financial service access points.

Thus, in terms of usage of financial services, a relatively small segment of the population have deposit and loan accounts and insurance cover. This makes poor households dependent on informal lenders for liquidity, consumption and social protection requirements. Only 5 out of 10 Filipino adults have had transactions with banks, while there is low awareness of other access points for financial services, such as automated teller machines, e-money agents, non-stock savings and loans associations, and microfinance nongovernment organizations. The country also has a very low insurance penetration rate (ratio of insurance premiums to GDP) — at only 1.15 per cent in 2011. In 2010, Malaysia had an insurance penetration rate of 4.8 per cent, Singapore 6.1 per cent and Thailand 4.3 per cent. The country had estimated life insurance coverage of the population at only 18.3 per cent in 2011, indicating large room for growth of the insurance sector (Geron 2013). The more common forms of insurance are informal insurance schemes provided by cooperatives and similar organizations to their members. Llanto, Geron and Almario (2009) estimated that about 1.2 million adults are covered by informal insurance provided by around 11,000 cooperatives through mutual fund schemes that are not licensed by the Insurance Commission.

At present, government agencies (National Economic and Development Authority [NEDA] and DOF), financial regulators (BSP, SEC and the Insurance Commission) and the private sector (rural banks, cooperatives, and micro-insurance providers) are collaborating to expand financial inclusion.[5] Policy and institutional reforms have resulted in greater participation of private lending institutions (basically microfinance institutions) in providing small-scale clientele with access to deposit, credit and micro-insurance. The most recent report on the status of microfinance in the country shows that there are 6.9 million depositors with almost P42.4 billion in deposits and 5.3 million borrowers with P61.1 billion in outstanding loans (Mix Market n.d.). Client outreach is being expanded through mobile banking and use of information technology. Roman (2009) reported that there are 8 million users of e-money and 47 rural banks currently using mobile banking for microfinance operations; there were none in 2005. Some banks have lowered interest rates by 50 basis points on monthly rates on microfinance loans for clients who use the text-a-payment platform. The cost of domestic remittances has fallen from 6–7 per cent of the amount of remittance to 1 per cent. Some banks have also started to use mobile phone technology to provide access to financial services in areas without bank branches (Llanto and Navarro 2014). With respect to insurance, the latest data from the Insurance Commission show that micro-insurance coverage among Filipinos rose to 19.95 million (20.4 per cent of the population) in 2013, from 3.1 million (3.4 per cent of the population) in 2008, while data from the Rural Bankers Association of the Philippines show that the total number of clients of rural banks provided with micro-insurance rose by 153 per cent to 1.4 million in 2013, from around 543,500 in 2012 (Llanto 2015).

There are other types of financial services that will benefit the financially excluded, which should also be given serious attention by policymakers. These are disaster-risk financing, crop insurance and housing finance.

The Philippines is one of the most disaster-prone countries in the world, and when disasters such as typhoons, flooding and drought strike, it is the poor households, small farmers and fishers, and small-scale businesses that are most severely affected. There is a need to develop the financial resilience of households and small businesses and reduce their vulnerability to risks.

In this regard, the government has been assisted by the ADB and the Japan International Cooperation Agency with a contingency loan of $400 million, known as Stand-by Emergency Credit for Urgent Recovery, and a further loan of $500 million. A catastrophe-bond covering earthquakes and typhoons, designed with assistance from the ADB, is under consideration by the government. Catastrophe-risk insurance for provinces and cities is also at a pilot stage, with plans for a future roll out. These efforts are worth supporting and intensifying at both the national and local levels of government. They could be linked to micro-insurance providers to give risk protection to poor households and small-scale businesses.

Another financial service important for financial inclusion is crop insurance for small farmers, who face significant losses brought about by weather disturbances, pest infestation and plant diseases.

The government created the Philippine Crop Insurance Corporation (PCIC) in 1978 to provide crop insurance to rice and corn farmers. From a simple insurance scheme, crop insurance has evolved to cover multiple perils for crops, livestock and fisheries. However, coverage has remained low, and, worse, has been declining in recent years. From 1981 to 2000, PCIC was only able to provide insurance for a cumulative total of 2.8 million farmers. At its peak, in 1991, the programme serviced only around 336,000 farmers (PCIC n.d.).

Several problems beset implementation of the programme, resulting in its modest impact. Logistical and operational challenges, including high overhead costs and insufficiency of investment funds, weaken the impact of the crop insurance programme. Small farmers also view insurance premiums as additional production costs, thereby making enrolment to crop insurance prohibitive (Southeast Asian Regional Center for Graduate Study and Research in Agriculture). Several studies found the same challenges affecting the sustainability of the programme, including collected premiums being higher than marketing, operational and administrative costs; insufficient funding provided by the government; and heavy subsidies provided by the government to run the programme (Corpuz 2013; Estacio and Mordeno 2001; Congressional Policy and Budget Research Department 2012; Reyes and Domingo 2009). The government needs to address these operational issues, raise the awareness of farmers, and review the sufficiency of funding for the programme. It must also rethink the design of the current crop insurance programmes in view of recent innovations, such as index-based insurance products, that have been developed to overcome the weaknesses of traditional crop insurance (Roberts 2005).[6]

Providing the bottom 30 per cent of the income distribution with access to decent shelter is another major objective of the government. Rapid urbanization has swelled the ranks of the urban poor and created a tremendous demand for housing, social services and secure land tenure. Philippine housing and land markets have not kept pace with rapid urban growth (Llanto 2007). There seems to be significant market failures for the bottom 30 per cent of the income distribution, which has led the government to intervene in housing finance, production and regulation.[7] There are around 548,425 informal settler families (ISFs) in Metro Manila alone, of which around 104,219 are living along "danger areas" (see Chapter 3 for more details). The previous government allocated a five-year (2010–15) fund of P50 billion to provide housing to those ISFs in danger areas in Metro Manila. As of April 2015, the National Housing Authority (NHA) and the SHFC have provided housing for 78,601 out of the targeted 104,129 ISFs. In addition, in 2010–15 some 42,358 housing units were delivered in NHA resettlement sites for families affected by government infrastructure projects in Metro Manila and those in danger areas in Bulacan, Pampanga, Laguna and Rizal.[8] The CMP has been considered most responsive to the housing needs of low-income families, but it has limited outreach. The programme has not scaled up, and currently faces problems of land acquisition (Ballesteros, Ramos and Magtibay 2015). There is a need to improve programme implementation, the undercapitalization of SHFC (and, by extension, its two major programmes), and, more importantly, to make housing markets function more efficiently (Llanto 2007).

F. Key Issues and Recommendations

There is a need for a bank consolidation policy that aims for a stronger and more efficient banking industry. There are no regulatory constraints to consolidation. Providing incentives for consolidation, improving the quality of banks' boards of directors, and increasing capitalization requirements are steps towards this objective. There has been a proliferation of many small banks with very limited scope for providing efficient financial services. Almost every month the BSP issues notices of receivership of rural banks, indicating an underlying weakness of the banking sector. There are too many small, undercapitalized and inefficient banks, which incidentally also lack professional management capacity. Philippine banks are too small and do not have the financial muscle and expertise to compete with their counterparts in the future AEC.

Financial education is needed to strengthen the demand side of the SME loans markets. Establishing a secure transactions system for movable collateral and implementing credit scoring of SMEs will address collateral gaps and information problems, respectively. There is a need to improve the legal and regulatory environment for SMEs by simplifying registry, business licensing and documentation requirements.

There is a need to develop the financial system's capacity to provide long-term finance for long-term investments. Infrastructure financing is one area that would benefit from a more efficient financial intermediation system. A bank-dominated financial system will always find it quite a challenge to raise long-term finance, which mature equity and bond markets could easily provide. Recent reforms have contributed to develop a long-term finance market. The 2015 Securities Regulation Code Implementing Rules and Regulations were amended to make the regulatory environment more conducive for the issuance of short-term and long-term commercial papers. Shelf registration is now allowed, firm underwriting is not mandated, and financial statements are valid for 225 days. However, much more needs to be done. In this regard, the following are recommended: (i) improve competition within the financial system, but at the same time allow a financially diverse system to operate (e.g., specialized lending institutions operating in niche markets, banks using innovative lending technologies or business models); (ii) strengthen financial and lending infrastructure, including commercial law, bankruptcy law, contract enforcement, and institutions such as the CIC that address information problems in small and medium-scale borrower markets; and (iii) create conditions for capital market development to improve access to longer-term finance (World Bank 2014).

Policy recommendations to foster financial inclusion cover several areas. Financial education is a critical need for MSMEs and poor and illiterate households. It could be incorporated into school curricula, training courses (in the case of MSMEs) and administered as early as primary school. More effective enforcement of consumer protection is another tool to build public confidence in financial and capital markets. There is a need to make the CIC fully operational as soon as possible. It needs good staff and substantial resources to accomplish its mandated tasks. There is merit in developing appropriate regulation and supervision of mobile banking, IT-enabled financial services, and various types of financial innovations to foster financial inclusion.

There is a need to balance the expansion of financial inclusion through emerging technologies on the one hand and stability of the financial sector on the other. The government and regulators should support the development of back-end infrastructure, such as payment switches, credit bureaus, and collateral registry (Llanto 2015).

The government is on the right track in developing catastrophe-risk insurance, and this could be linked to micro-insurance providers to develop an effective delivery mechanism to poor households and small-scale businesses. Agricultural insurance such as crop insurance is an important aspect of financial inclusion of small farmers and small-scale agribusiness. There is a need to review the programmes for low cost and socialized housing, including the need to strengthen the SHFC, the government's main implementation arm.

III. Public–Private Partnerships

Greater creativity is required in tapping non-traditional sources of finance, such as PPP and the newly created international financial institutions for development financing, such as AIIB, New Development Bank (established by Brazil, India, the PRC, Russia and South Africa), and the ASEAN Infrastructure Fund.

The focus here is on PPPs that use private expertise in financing, construction and O&M of infrastructure facilities to help address the lack of infrastructure. They can relieve the government of the burden of provision and free up resources that could be used for other societal expenditures (Llanto, Navarro and Ortiz 2015). PPPs started to be used in the country for infrastructure provision in the 1990s, more particularly to solve the power crisis. The successful utilization of this infrastructure procurement method emboldened policymakers to include it in the range of strategies for infrastructure provision. In the early 1990s, Republic Act 7718 (the Build-Operate-Transfer [BOT] Law) was enacted and authorized the financing, construction and O&M of infrastructure projects by the private sector and for other purposes. It was later amended in 1994. The BOT law established the policy and institutional framework for various PPP schemes, e.g., BOT, Build–Lease–Transfer, etc. (Llanto 2010; Llanto and Navarro 2012; Llanto and Zen 2013).

In the 1990s there was a considerable number of PPPs, which peaked in 1994 with 94 projects, amounting to $18.64 billion, mostly in the telecommunications and power sectors. In the following years the number of PPP projects drastically dropped from this peak level, never to recover. The lowest point for PPPs was in 1998–99, following the Asian financial crisis, when private capital retreated to safe havens (Figure 8.10). There was recovery in the number of PPPs around the first half of the Arroyo administration, but political, legal and regulatory issues weakened investor appetite and constrained their development and implementation.

FIGURE 8.10
Number of PPP Projects and Amount of Investments, 1990–2014

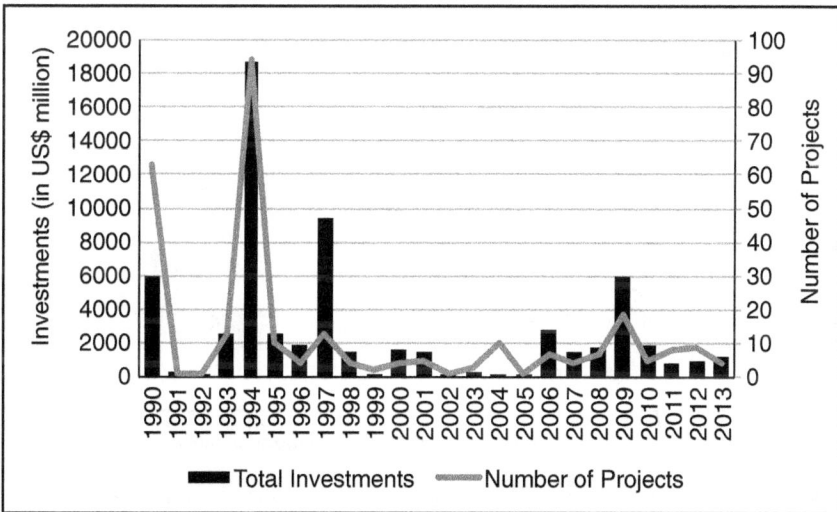

Source of basic data: World Bank's Private Participation in Infrastructure Database.
Note: The year in the horizontal axis refers to the financial closure year.

Despite the Philippines' relatively long experience with PPPs for infrastructure provision, only a few projects have been successfully brought to the implementation stage. Only 126 projects reached financial closure over the 1990–2013 period, of which the biggest were the North Luzon Expressway Project in 2001, with a total investment cost of $378 million, and the Manila Water concession in 1997, with $222 million (Figure 8.11). The electricity sector has the largest number (87) of successful projects, followed by the transport sector (22), comprising airports, railroads, roads, and seaports. The electricity sector also had the largest amount of investments, with $28.09 billion, followed by the telecommunications sector, with $21.74 billion.

FIGURE 8.11
Number of PPP Projects Reaching Financial Closure by Sector and Amount of Investments, 1990–2014

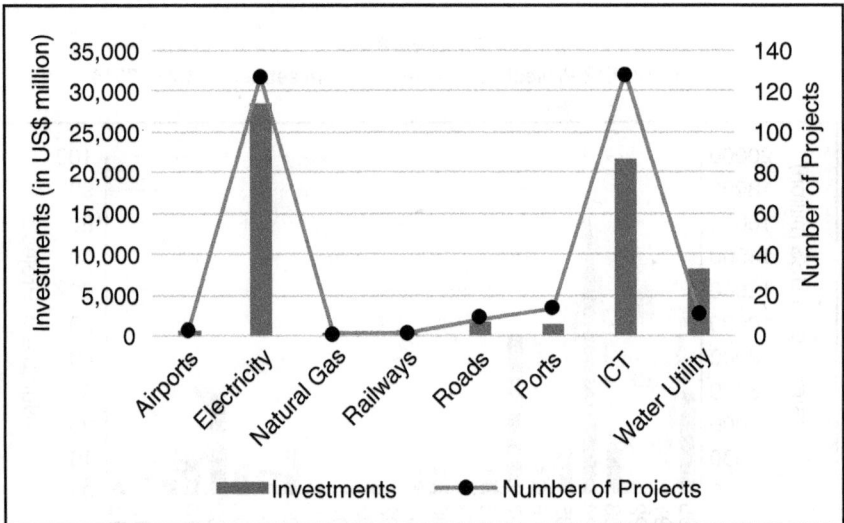

Source of basic data: World Bank's Private Participation in Infrastructure Database.

Data from the World Bank's Private Participation in Infrastructure Database listed a total of twelve PPPs that were either cancelled or distressed in 1991–2005. According to the World Bank, cancelled projects are those projects wherein the private sector has already exited by (i) selling or transferring its economic interest back to the government before fulfilling the contract terms; (ii) removing all management and personnel from the project; and (iii) ceasing operation, service provision, or construction for 15 per cent or more of the licence or concession period, following the revocation of the licence or repudiation of the contract. Meanwhile, distressed projects are those wherein the government or the operator has either requested contract termination or are in international arbitration. Five of those projects were from the electricity sector, with a total investment of $637 million. Two were from the water and sewerage sector, at $4.54 billion. And three were from the transport sector, at $1.18 billion.

The Aquino administration announced PPP as a major strategy for infrastructure provision and lost no time in addressing unresolved issues in PPP implementation inherited from prior years. Reform efforts centred on the following critical factors for successful PPP: (i) adequate legal and regulatory framework; (ii) building capacity in government agencies and the PPP Center; and (iii) financial support measures, such as the Project Development and Monitoring Facility (PDMF) and viability gap fund. Thus, the institutional framework for project preparation and approval was improved and strengthened through better coordination between NEDA and a revitalized PPP Center, now an attached agency under it.[9] The PDMF was established with funding from donors and government, to help government agencies during the preparatory stages of planned PPP projects. Consultants and transaction advisors are made available for better project preparation and formulation (Table 8.8). These reform efforts have now started to pay off, with several projects awarded, under procurement or in other stages of the PPP process (Table 8.9).

The government should continue to use PPPs to provide infrastructure. However, there is great merit in maintaining vigilance over factors that have constrained or slowed down PPP implementation in the past. Those factors cover issues affecting project identification, procurement, financing, and O&M. It is well known that infrastructure projects are often subject to rent-seeking activities and political patronage. The antidotes to such are greater transparency, empowerment of civil society as monitors of the entire range of procurement processes, competitive bidding, and strict enforcement of rules and regulations on procurement. The Philippines has a mixed experience, but during its incumbency the Aquino administration demonstrated how good governance could improve the procurement of infrastructure.

TABLE 8.8
Major Reform Milestones in PPP in 2014

Key Area	Major Reform Milestones
Policy Enhancements and Streamlined Processes	Amendment of the Build-Operate-and-Transfer (BOT) Law into the Public-Private Partnership (PPP) Act, including pertinent provisions on right-of-way acquisition (ROWA)
	Amended guidelines for the appraisal of PPP projects, including PPP Center as ICC-CabCom Secretariat for PPP projects
Improving capacities of PPP Players	Implementing Rules and Regulations (IRR) of the Executive Order on Alternative Dispute Resolution (ADR), with PPP Center to conduct massive information campaign once the IRR has been enacted
	Policy guidelines on sector-specific PPPs (education, health, and agriculture)
	Contract standardization initiative
	Upgrading of the Project Development and Monitoring Facility (PDMF) Panel of Consulting Firms
	Launch of the PPP Knowledge Portal — a comprehensive database of all knowledge and information about the PPP Program and projects
	Printing and dissemination of the PPP Manual for National Government Agencies (NGAs)
	Enhanced LGU PPP strategy, including the PPP Internship Program for select LGUs; and partnerships with other capacity development institutions

Source: Llanto and Navarro 2014a.

TABLE 8.9
Public–Private Partnership Projects under the Aquino Administration

Implementation	Metro Manila Skyway (MMS) Stage 3 MRT Line 7
Awarded	Daang Hari-SLEX Link Road (Muntinlupa-Cavite Expressway) Project PPP for School Infrastructure Project (PSIP) – Phase I NAIA Expressway Project (Phase II) PPP for School Infrastructure Project (PSIP) – Phase II Modernization of Philippine Orthopedic Center Automatic Fare Collection System Mactan–Cebu International Airport Passenger Terminal Building LRT Line 1 Cavite Extension and Operation & Maintenance Southwest Integrated Transport System (ITS) Project Cavite–Laguna Expressway
For Awarding	Integrated Transport System (ITS)–South Terminal Project
Under Procurement	Bulacan Bulk Water Supply Project Regional Prison Facilities through PPP Civil Registry System – Information Technology Project (Phase II) Operation and Maintenance of LRT Line 2 Laguna Lakeshore Expressway-Dike Project Development, Operations and Maintenance of the New Bohol (Panglao) Airport Development, Operations and Maintenance of the Laguindingan Airport Development, Operations and Maintenance of Davao Airport

TABLE 8.9 (*continued*)

Under Procurement (*continued*)	Development, Operations and Maintenance of Bacolod Airport Development, Operations and Maintenance of Iloilo Airport Davao Sasa Port Modernization Project
	New Centennial Water Source – Kaliwa Dam Project
	North–South Railway Project (South Line)
	Road Transport Information Technology (IT) Infrastructure Project (Phase II)
For Roll-out	LRT Line 6 Project LRT Line 4 Project

Source: Public-Private Partnership Center.

IV. Official Development Assistance

One of the major sources of development financing in the Philippines is ODA, which includes loans at concessional rates and grants from various donors. The Philippines has recently used it to finance poverty-related expenditures; e.g., conditional cash transfers; critical infrastructure such as roads, ports and airports; and budgetary support. ODA as source of development finance has an advantage over other types of finance, because the government can easily mobilize a relatively large ODA loan at concessional rates. An example is the ODA stream that came in the aftermath of Typhoon Yolanda (international name: Haiyan) to assist the government in reconstruction and rehabilitation of devastated areas. ODA loans to the Philippines have remained concessional and meet the 25 per cent grant element required by Philippine law (Llanto and Navarro 2014).

Although ODA has been on a decline globally because of the continuing sluggishness of rich economies, it would continue to play a strategic role in development finance. New priorities under the Sustainable Development Goals and regional public goods, such as climate change and public health, are populating the country assistance strategies of multilateral and bilateral donors, as well as the development agendas of developing countries.

In 2014 the total amount of ODA loans to the Philippines amounted to $11.2 billion, comprised of 76 loans and 449 grants (Table 8.10). The World Bank contributed the highest share in the ODA loans portfolio, with $4.45 billion (40 per cent share), which covers 20 out of 76 loans. It is followed by Japan, with $3.16 billion (28 per cent), covering 20 loans, and the ADB, with $2.23 billion (20 per cent) for 12 loans.

Infrastructure development received the largest share of the loans, at 39 per cent ($4.32 billion; 34 loans), followed by social reform and community development with 24 per cent, and governance and institutions development with 22 per cent. Moreover, NEDA (2015) reported that 70 programmes and projects equivalent to P187.8 billion have components relating to climate change strategies/interventions and disaster risk reduction, which have recently been recognized as crucial areas of concern. Meanwhile, ODA loans and grants supported the government's implementation of the Millennium Development Goals, with a total cost amounting to P262.6 billion covering 98 programmes and projects.

ODA will remain as a strategic source of development finance over the next twenty-five years, although it should be expected that the scale of ODA would decline as the country graduates into upper-middle-income status. The government should respond decisively to several ODA-related challenges: inefficiency in procurement, delays in fund releases, incomplete submission of liquidation reports, limited project management office staff, problems in obtaining government approvals and required clearances or permits, lack of LGU support for national infrastructure projects, adverse weather conditions, and problems on right-of-way and resettlement. These are not new issues, and there is certainly a need for stronger action on the part of the government to resolve them.

According to NEDA (2015), the financial performance of projects and programmes funded through the ODA in 2014 had significantly improved as a result of better absorptive capacity, as measured by disbursement level, disbursement rate and availment rate. From a level of $856 million in 2013, disbursement has doubled to around $1.7 billion, primarily owing to the large disbursements of programme loans amounting to $1.28 billion. The availment rate has also increased from 76 per cent in 2013 to 83 per cent in 2014 (Table 8.11).

TABLE 8.10

Annual Net Commitment of Active ODA Loans by Loan Type, 2005–14 ($ million)

Loan Type	2005	2006	2007	2008	2009	2010	2011	2012	2013	2014
Project	9,508	8,130	7,539	8,102	7,899	8,216	6,858	6,888	6,711	6,962
Programme	410	1,370	2,231	2,131	1,941	1,718	1,742	1,932	2,378	4,219
Total	9,918	9,500	9,770	10,233	9,840	9,934	8,600	8,820	9,089	11,181
Share to GDP (%)	9.6	7.8	6.5	5.9	5.8	5	3.8	3.5	3.3	3.9
Annual growth rate (%)	…	–4.2	2.8	4.7	–3.8	1	–13.4	2.6	3	23

Source: NEDA 2015.

TABLE 8.11
Disbursement and Availment Performance of ODA Loans, 2013–14

Indicators	Newly Signed Indicators		Continuing		Total	
	2013–14	2013–14	2013–14	2013–14	2013	2014
Disbursement Level ($ billion)	0.303	1.281	0.553	1.281	0.856	1.767
Programme	0.3	1.144	0.182	1.144	0.483	1.284
Project	0.003	0.137	0.371	0.137	0.374	0.483
Disbursement Rate (%)	88.73	105.33	50.96	105.33	60.01	76.13
Programme	88.43	98.7	80.71	98.7	85.34	99.42
Project	138.67	240.01	43.13	240.01	43.36	46.92
Availment Rate (%)	95.71	103.41	74.62	103.41	76.34	83.02
Programme	96.44	98.7	102.82	98.7	102.46	97.89
Project	52.82	171.96	68.05	171.96	70.6	68.84
Disbursement Ratio (%)	20.76	36.76	12.89	36.76	15.29	23.12
Programme	75.06	52.32	45.19	52.32	60.38	51.29
Project	2.82	10.55	9.54	10.55	7.78	9.4

Source: NEDA 2015.

There also needs to be better consistency and coordination of donor assistance with the Philippine Development Plan. An emerging area for fruitful collaboration with donors is the provision of key public goods, such as (i) disaster prevention, post-disaster rehabilitation and post-conflict transition, such as the Bangsamoro transition; (ii) social safety nets similar to conditional cash transfer programmes; and (iii) productivity-enhancing research and development and TA for capacity building, such as financing SME innovations (Llanto and Navarro 2014). In addition, ODA can be used for a more strategic and catalytic role in attracting private capital.

V. Remittances

In 2013, OFWs remitted $25 billion, compared to $17 billion in 2009. Remittances from overseas Filipinos averaged 9.2 per cent of GDP in 2000–2013 and 8.9 per cent of GDP in 2011–13, and have emerged as a new important source of funds for household consumption and investments in housing, education and health. To a great extent, overseas remittances have performed the dual function of (i) addressing the survival needs and sustenance of poor families and of (ii) providing a constant stream of liquidity that has partly financed the housing construction boom the country has experienced over the past several years and start-ups of microenterprises and microbusinesses in the informal sector (Llanto and Navarro 2014). They have also been instrumental in boosting the country's international reserves.

OFWs already use banks and remittance companies to send monies to their respective families. Those remittances form part of the banks' financial intermediation activities. Recipient households have also used remittances for productive investments in housing, education and health. However, there has been some concern that too much of the remittances find their way into real estate instead of being used to finance "more productive" investments such as infrastructure or to invest in better-earning financial instruments. The channelling of remittances to real estate may partly be explained by the limited financial options available to OFWs and their families. For example, they rarely make stock investments or invest in financial instruments other than traditional deposit accounts. There is therefore a case for comprehensive financial education for OFWs on the different financial instruments and other investment options available in the market. This will widen their investment horizons. Other options include securitization of remittance flows that enable banks to leverage remittance receipts for more lending, diaspora bonds for the government's long term-finance needs, and diaspora mutual funds (Terrazas 2010).

The Commission on Filipino Overseas (CFO) established the Diaspora Investment Program, which seeks "to work with financial institutions and intermediaries to develop new and innovative instruments and mechanisms such as diaspora bonds, remittance bonds and other mechanisms that tap into remittances and savings for development" (CFO website, as cited in Llanto and Navarro 2014). The experience of other countries (e.g., Israel, India, Ethiopia) on diaspora bonds has, however, been rather mixed.

VI. Conclusion

The funding requirements to maintain the country's development momentum are formidable, but they could be managed with proper policies and institutional arrangements, including the following.

First, the government must drastically increase its revenue mobilization efforts to raise substantial resources for an economy aspiring to be a high-middle-income one. It will have to raise tax revenues to a much more significant level than currently observed. The best option would be to conduct a comprehensive tax review that will consider tax yield, equity, widening of the tax base and competitiveness of the country's tax regime with those of other countries in the region. If the political climate does not support an omnibus or comprehensive tax reform programme, a second-best option would be to increase the yield of broad-based taxes, such as VAT and excise tax, by increasing the tax rate and ensuring the wide application of these taxes. LGUs should be asked to increase local tax efforts and contribute to the improvement of overall tax efforts.

Second, the government, through the DOF and BSP, must continue with astute debt management to ensure the least borrowing cost to the economy without sacrificing critical development spending. When domestic financial and capital markets mature and develop, domestic borrowing rather than foreign borrowing will be a more reliable and prudent source of financing. This will enable the economy to mitigate currency risks and help develop domestic debt markets.

Third, financial intermediation should be made more efficient through continuing policy and institutional reforms. Financial and regulatory reforms are necessary to make finance inclusive for MSMEs and poor households, and to create the environment for the development of long-term finance. Continuing policy support is needed for financial innovations and financial education. Inclusive finance should include other types of financial services, such as agricultural insurance for risk protection of small farmers and small-scale agribusiness, disaster risk financing for local communities and households, and housing finance for low-income households, especially those in informal settlements and danger areas.

Fourth, there is a distinct advantage in using PPP's to address the infrastructure deficit, which has been identified by past studies as a critical development constraint.

Fifth, while ODA is likely to decline, consistent with the country's graduation to upper-middle-income status, these funds should be used more strategically to finance emerging regional public goods, such as disaster risk financing and public health, which could not be funded from commercial sources.

Finally, there is a need for financial education of OFWs and their families to widen their investment horizons. Awareness and demand for alternative investment options will create incentives for the financial services industry to develop responsive financial instruments (e.g., securitization of remittance flows, diaspora bonds for the government's long-term finance needs, and diaspora mutual funds). Diaspora bonds could be one of those alternative financial options for OFWs and their families, but there is a need for a careful study in view of the mixed experiences of other countries with such bonds.

Notes

1. The author thanks the following for their research assistance: Ma. Kristina Ortiz, Cherry Madriaga and Pinky Padronia.
2. The Cabinet-level Development Budget Coordination Committee (DBCC) maintains that "in line with its liability management goals, the national government will continue to source [the] majority of its funding requirements from domestic lenders to help advance local capital market development as well as to reduce vulnerabilities to foreign exchange fluctuations" (de Vera 2015).
3. For details, see BSP Circular 818 at <http://www.bsp.gov.ph/downloads/ regulations/attachments/2013/c818.pdf> (accessed 27 December 2015)
4. Congress created the Central Credit Information Corporation (CIC) under Republic Act 9510 in 2008 to develop a credit scoring system that will help lenders in screening borrowers. Banks, quasi-banks, and their subsidiaries and affiliates, life insurance companies, credit card companies, and other entities are required to regularly submit basic credit data and updates. The CIC may include other credit providers to be subjected to compulsory participation. However, for a variety of reasons, the CIC has barely managed to implement its mandate. In fact, it has only recently started deliberating on the kind of information technology system that will become the backbone of the credit information database (Gamboa 2012).
5. The National Strategy for Financial Inclusion, building on the successful experience of the National Strategy for Microfinance formulated by the National Credit Council–Department of Finance, seeks (i) an effective partnership between government and the private sector, (ii) appropriate regulation and supervision frameworks, and (iii) support for financial innovations to improve financial inclusion.
6. An index policy operates differently. With an index policy, a meteorological measurement is used as the trigger for indemnity payments. These damaging weather events might be a certain minimum temperature for a minimum period of time; a certain amount of rainfall in a certain time

period (this can be used for excess rain and also for lack of rain/drought cover); attainment of a certain wind speed for hurricane insurance (Roberts 2005).

7. This discussion does not include housing markets for the non-poor, i.e., the middle- and high-income classes.

8. Source: "Housing and Urban Development Sector: Moving Forward (July 2010–April 2015)", a report submitted to the Housing Summit Stocktaking Session, 22 October 2015, by Land and Governance Innovations Consultants, Inc. The report provides a summary of land and housing issues: inadequate housing delivery mechanisms; limited availability of affordable land and housing units; weak, uncoordinated and lack of serious planning; and uncontrolled rural to urban migration.

9. In the past, the PPP Center (known initially as BOT Center) was attached to NEDA, then to the DOF, and in the final years of the Arroyo administration to DTI.

References

Ballesteros, M., T. Ramos, and J. Magtibay. "An Assessment of the Community Mortgage Program of the Social Housing Finance Corporation". PIDS Discussion Paper Series 2015-41. September 2015.

BSP (Bangko Sentral ng Pilipinas). "70. Compliance with Magna Carta for Micro, Small and Medium Enterprises". 2015a <http://www.bsp.gov.ph/banking/pbs_archives/2014/70.htm> (accessed 17 April 2018).

———. "National Strategy for Financial Inclusion: Our Platform to Provide Better Lives". 2015b <http://www.bsp.gov.ph/publications/speeches.asp?id=501> (accessed 18 October 2015).

———. "National Baseline Survey on Financial Inclusion". 2015c <http://www.bsp.gov.ph/downloads/publications/2015/NBSFIFullReport.pdf> (accessed 20 October 2015).

———. "Philippine Stock Market Transactions". Economic and Financial Statistics – Monetary, External and Financial Statistics. 2015d <http://www.bsp.gov.ph/statistics/efs_prices.asp>.

———. "22. Total Resources of the Philippine Financial System". 2015e <http://www.bsp.gov.ph/statistics/spei_pub/Table%2022.pdf> (accessed 17 April 2018).

Calica, A. "Palace: No Plans to Tax Text". *Philippine Star*, 26 November 2012.

CBPRD (Congressional Policy and Budget Research Department). "Review of the Philippine Crop Insurance: Key Challenges and Prospects". CPBRD Policy Brief 2012-6. November 2012.

CFO (Commission on Filipino Overseas). "Accomplishment". n.d. <http://cfo-linkapil.org.ph/about-us/accomplishment> (accessed 10 November 2015).

Chaudhur, N., and Y. Okamura. "Conditional Cash Transfers and School Enrollment: Impact of the Conditional Cash Transfer Program in the Philippines". Taguig City: World Bank, 2012.

Corpuz, J. "Case Study: Loan Guarantee and Insurance in the Philippines". Paper presented at the 4th World Congress on Agricultural and Rural Finance, 2013.

Crisostomo, R., S. Padilla, and M. Visda. "Philippine Stock Market in Perspective". Paper presented at the 12th National Convention on Statistics, Mandaluyong City, Philippines, 1–2 October 2013.

de Vera, Ben O. "PH Eyes Foreign Bond Sale before Yearend". *Philippine Daily Inquirer*, B1, 2 November 2015 <https://business.inquirer.net/201821/ph-eyes-foreign-bond-sale-before-yearend> (accessed 7 November 2015).

Deloitte Southeast Asia. "Digital Banking for Small and Medium-sized Enterprises: Improving Access to Finance the Underserved". 2015 <http://www2.deloitte.com/content/dam/Deloitte/sg/Documents/financial-services/sea-fsi-digital-banking-small-medium-enterprises-noexp.pdf> (accessed 10 October 2015).

DOF (Department of Finance). "Property Tax Reforms in the Philippines". Presented during the Fourth IMF–Japan High-Level Tax Conference, Tokyo, Japan, 2–4 April 2013.

DTI (Department of Trade and Industry). "SME Statistics". n.d. <http://www.dti.gov.ph/dti/index.php/resources/sme-resources/sme-statistics> (accessed 14 October 2015).

Ernst & Young. "Worldwide Personal Tax Guide: Income Tax, Social Security and Immigration 2014–15". 2014 <http://www.ey.com/Publication/vwLUAssets/Worldwide_Personal_Tax_Guide_2014-15/$FILE/Worldwide%20Personal%20Tax%20Guide%202014-15.pdf>.

———. "Worldwide Corporate Tax Guide". 2016*a* <http://www.ey.com/Publication/vwLUAssets/Worldwide_Corporate_Tax_Guide_2016/$FILE/2016%20Worldwide%20Corporate%20Tax%20Guide.pdf>.

———. "Worldwide Personal Tax and Immigration Guide 2016–17". 2016*b* <http://www.ey.com/Publication/vwLUAssets/Worldwide_Personal_Tax_

and_Immigration_Guide_2016-17/$FILE/Worldwide%20Personal%20Tax%20 and%20Immigration%20Guide%202016-17.pdf>.

———. "Worldwide VAT, GST and Sales Tax Guide". 2016c <http://www. ey.com/GL/en/Services/Tax/Worldwide-VAT--GST-and-Sales-Tax-Guide---Rates>.

Espenilla, N. "The Corporate Bond Market in the Philippines". 2004 <http:// www.bis.org/publ/bppdf/bispap26r.pdf> (accessed 12 October 2015).

Estacio, B., and N. Mordeno. "Agricultural Insurance: The Philippine Experience. Paper presented at the Corporate Planning Conference, Philippine Crop Insurance Corporation, 2001.

Gamboa, R. "Crawling Towards Centralized Credit". *Philippine Star*, 21 December 2012 <http://www.philstar.com/business/2012-12-21/888383/crawling-towards-centralized-credit>.

Geron, M.P. *Assessment of Microinsurance as Emerging Microfinance Service for the Poor: Case of the Philippines*. Mandaluyong City, Philippines: Asian Development Bank, 2013.

IMF (International Monetary Fund). *Tax Collections in the Philippines: An Empirical Analysis*. Washington, DC: IMF, 2013.

———. "Slower Growth in Emerging Markets, a Gradual Pickup in Advanced Economies". *IMF World Economic Outlook Update*. 2015a <http://www.imf. org/external/pubs/ft/weo/2015/update/02/pdf/0715.pdf>.

———. *Fiscal Monitor—Now is the Time: Fiscal Policies for Sustainable Growth*. Washington, DC: IMF, 2015b <http://www.imf.org/external/pubs/ft/ fm/2015/01/pdf/fmc1.pdf>.

KPMG Asia Pacific Tax Centre. *ASEAN Tax Guide*. 2013 <http://www.kpmg. com/Global/en/IssuesAndInsights/ArticlesPublications/Documents/asea n-tax-guide-v2.pdf>.

Levinger, H., and L. Chen. "What's behind Recent Trends in Asian Corporate Bond Markets?" In *Deutsche Bank Research, Current Issues, Emerging markets*. Frankfurt: Deutsche Bank, 2014.

Llanto, G.M. "Shelter Finance Strategies for the Poor: Philippines". *Environment & Urbanization* 19, no. 2 (2007): 409–23.

———. *Fiscal Decentralization in the Philippines*. Global Urban Economic Dialogue Series. Nairobi: UN Habitat, 2011.

———. "The Assignment of Functions and Intergovernmental Fiscal Relations in the Philippines 20 Years after Decentralization". *Philippine Review of Economics* 49, no. 1 (2012): 37–80.

———. "Financial Inclusion, Regulation and Education in the Philippines". ADBI Working Paper Series 541. August 2015.

Llanto, G.M., P. Geron, and J. Almario. "Philippines: Impact of Regulation on Microinsurance Development". CGAP Working Group on Microinsurance, 2009.

Llanto, G.M., and A. Navarro. *Development Finance and Aid in the Philippines: Policy, Institutional Arrangements and Flows Country Report*. Pasig City: NEDA and UNDP, 2014*a*.

———. "Financing Infrastructure in the Philippines: Fiscal Landscape and Resources Mobilization". PIDS Discussion Paper Series 2014-01. 2014*b*.

Llanto, G.M., A. Navarro, and M. Ortiz. "Infrastructure Financing, Public-Private Partnerships, and Development in the Asia-Pacific Region". MPDD Working Paper WP/15/01, UNESCAP. 2015.

Llanto, G.M., and F. Zen. "Governmental Fiscal Support for Financing Long-term Infrastructure Projects in ASEAN Countries". PIDS Discussion Paper Series 2013-08. 2013.

Manasan, R.G. "Local Public Finance in the Philippines: Lessons in Autonomy and Accountability". *Philippine Journal of Development* 32, no. 2 (2005): 32–102.

———. "Decentralization and Financing of Regional Development". In *The Dynamics of Regional Development: The Philippines in East Asia*, edited by Arsenio Balisacan and Hal Hill. Quezon City: Ateneo de Manila University Press, 2007.

Mix Market. "Philippines Market Overview". n.d. <http://mixmarket.org/mfi/country/Philippines> (accessed 17 April 2018).

NEDA (National Economic and Development Authority). *2014 ODA Loan Portfolio Review*. Pasig City: NEDA, 2015 <from http://www.neda.gov.ph/wp-content/uploads/2015/10/CY2014-ODA-Review-Overall-ao-30-June-2015-for-printing-FINAL.pdf>.

PA-LAMP (Philippines-Australia Land Administration and Management Project). "Land Administration Reform: Winning the War against Poverty". A Policy Studies Integration Report with revisions. 2002.

Philippine Crop Insurance Corporation (PCIC). "Crop Insurance in the Philippines: Security for Farmers and Agricultural Stakeholders". n.d. <https://www.preventionweb.net/files/3289_PCIC.pdf>.

Reyes, C., and S. Domingo. "Crop Insurance, Security for Farmers and Agricultural Stakeholders in the Face of Seasonal Climate Variability". PIDS Discussion Paper Series 2009-12. 2009.

Roberts, R. "Insurance of Crops in Developing Countries". *FAO Agricultural Services Bulletin* 159 (2005).

Terrazas, A. *Diaspora Investment in Developing and Emerging Country Capital Markets: Patterns and Prospects*. Washington, DC: Migration Policy Institute, 2010.

UP (University of the Philippines). "Towards a National Tax Policy for E-Commerce". PIDS Discussion Paper Series 2004-01. 2004.

Vicente, F. "Philippine Tax Leakages: An Assessment". Technical report for Economic Modernization through Efficient Reforms and Governance Enhancement (EMERGE). Makati City: EMERGE, 2006 <http://pdf.usaid.gov/pdf_docs/Pnadh572.pdf>.

9

Governance and Institutions[1]

Ronald U. Mendoza and Rosechin Olfindo

Poor governance and weak public institutions can undermine even the most well-crafted policies to promote inclusive development. Corruption, poor public service delivery, misallocation of resources, political instability, uncoordinated government agencies and deeply embedded patron–client relationships are among the challenges of governance and institutions that slow down or defeat any socio-economic reform agenda. In particular, corruption is a sizable problem in the Philippines, affecting all sectors and levels of government.

In this chapter we refer to *governance* as the manner in which public officials and institutions acquire and exercise the authority to facilitate collective action, craft public policy and provide public goods and services. On the other hand, *institutions* refers to the formal and informal rules that shape human interaction and their related enforcement mechanisms. Institutions therefore determine the possibilities for effective governance and collective action (see Figure 9.1). Both the government and market need institutions to function well. Otherwise, government and market failures are likely to litter the landscape instead of properly provided public goods and services. When government and markets work, then collective action outcomes — public goods and services — are more likely to succeed.

FIGURE 9.1
Framework on Governance, Institutions and Development

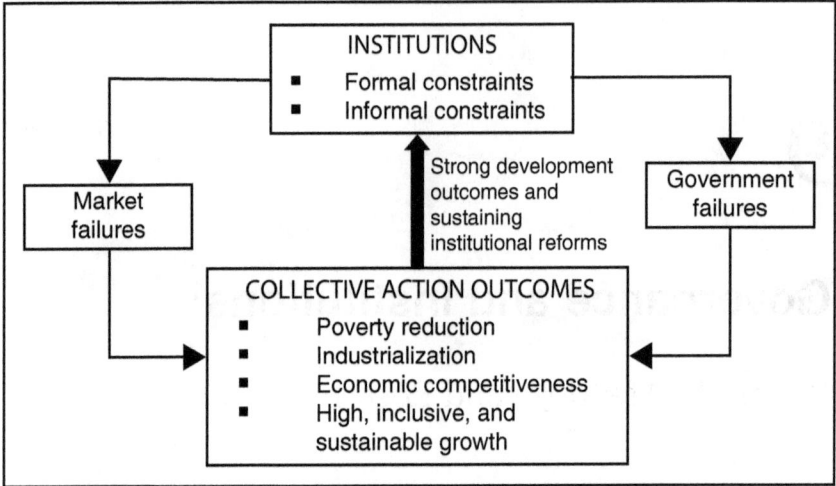

Note: This is an elaboration based on North (1993) and Fukuyama (2013).

It is widely acknowledged in the literature that poor governance and weak institutions are among the critical (Rodrik 2000, 2004, 2007; Nye 2011) constraints to investment and growth in the Philippines (see, for instance, ADB 2007; World Bank 2013; Aldaba 2014). Problems with governance, particularly corruption and political instability, weaken investor confidence and discourage the creation of much-needed jobs that can, in turn, potentially lift many Filipinos out of poverty. Weak institutions constrain the delivery of public goods and services that aim to enhance the supply and demand of labour, both of which are necessary to make economic growth more inclusive. As such, maintaining an environment stocked with adequate and well-functioning institutions is critical.

Poverty amidst weak public goods and services could also debilitate efforts to continue building stronger institutions. As well elaborated in the political science and economic development literature, reformists often struggle against traditional economic and political relationships that are deeply engrained due to a long history of poverty, dependence and patron–client relationships. Thus, the struggle to dramatically upgrade institutions to build a modern state and a competitive economy could also be described as a difficult transition that breaks away from a low-level equilibrium.

This chapter assesses the current state of play of governance structures and public institutions in the Philippines, as well as their key issues and challenges. It then presents policy options to reform public institutions and strengthen governance in the country. The proposals herein draw heavily on the literature as well as the consultations underpinning the strategic long-term visioning exercise for the Philippines.

I. State of Play

This section assesses the current state of governance structure and institutions in the Philippines compared to how they were a decade ago and with what neighbouring countries have achieved.

There are currently no cross-country objective data that measure the overall state of a country's governance and institutions. Due to the wide differences in rules and procedures among countries, defining what constitutes "good governance" and strong institutions is particularly challenging. For instance, the extent of corruption can be measured by the difference in procurement costs relative to materials purchased, but these are often limited, as procedures vary per country. Meanwhile, subjective data can better pick up crucial distinctions between the *de jure* and *de facto* institutional arrangements. Subjective data are typically based on the perceptions of businesses, individuals and experts, which are standardized across countries to allow for comparative analyses. Nevertheless, researchers acknowledge the limits of perceptions-based indicators, as they too can face measurement errors due to bias and imperfect information. Research studies on governance and institutions have relied on perception surveys when undertaking cross-country comparison, and supplement their analysis using individual country data.

In recent years the Philippines has made impressive strides in improving its governance and institutions, as shown by international benchmarking indicators. The improvements can be mainly attributed to the relatively more aggressive reforms undertaken by the government, aimed specifically at reducing the bureaucracy's vulnerability to corruption and creating a culture of transparency and accountability. These efforts have resulted in positive gains that are apparent in the increase in investor confidence and which will eventually lead to the expansion of the Philippine economy.

Among the widely used indicators of good governance are the World Governance Indicators of the World Bank. They measure good governance with respect to six key dimensions: voice and accountability, political stability, government effectiveness, regulatory quality, rule of law, and control of corruption. The Philippines has high scores in government effectiveness and voice and accountability but has low scores in political stability and control of corruption (see Figure 9.2). Since 2010, it has been apparent that the Philippines' scores in all six dimensions, including regulatory quality and rule of law, have been increasing at a much faster pace than those of other countries, as reflected in the improvement in the Philippines' relative rankings.

Compared with other members of the Association of Southeast Asian Nations (ASEAN), the Philippines is the only country that has improved its ranking in all six dimensions of governance between

FIGURE 9.2
Philippines' Scores in Governance Indicators, 2005–14

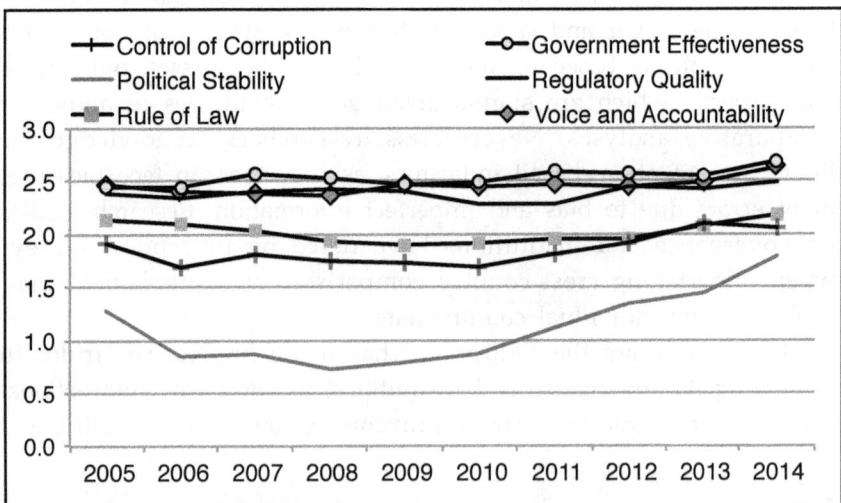

Source: Data from World Bank's Worldwide Governance Indicators.

2005 and 2014 (see Table 9.1). Among the ten countries, the Philippines and Indonesia have the highest scores in voice and accountability (both with a percentile rank of 53; 100 being the highest), but they also figure among the lowest scores in political stability (percentile ranks of 23 and 31, respectively). Despite improvements in relative rankings, the Philippines is still placed behind Singapore, Malaysia, Brunei Darussalam and Thailand in the dimensions of government effectiveness and control of corruption.

TABLE 9.1
Percentile Rank of Worldwide Governance Indicator Scores of ASEAN Countries, 2005 and 2014

Country	Government Effectiveness		Voice and Accountability		Control of Corruption	
	2005	2014	2005	2014	2005	2014
Singapore	99	100	51	45	98	97
Malaysia	84	84	43	37	63	68
Brunei Darussalam	70	82	24	29	62	72
Thailand	67	66	46	26	54	42
Philippines	56	62	49	53	35	40
Indonesia	39	55	45	53	20	34
Vietnam	49	52	9	10	25	38
Lao PDR	10	39	6	...	7	25
Cambodia	17	25	19	18	10	13
Myanmar	3	9	...	...	1	17

Country	Political Stability		Regulatory Quality		Rule of Law	
	2005	2014	2005	2014	2005	2014
Singapore	87	92	100	100	96	95
Malaysia	65	59	69	76	66	75
Brunei Darussalam	92	95	76	80	59	70
Thailand	22	17	65	62	55	51
Philippines	13	23	51	52	42	43
Indonesia	7	31	31	49	25	42
Vietnam	62	46	28	30	46	45
Lao PDR	30	61	9	21	13	27
Cambodia	35	45	35	37	11	17
Myanmar	20	12	1	6	2	9

Source: World Bank's Worldwide Governance Indicators.

Looking at other factors that affect a country's competitiveness, the World Economic Forum (WEF) reported that infrastructure and institutions are among the weaknesses of the Philippines, while macroeconomy, health and primary education are its strengths (see Figure 9.3). This is according to how these factors have fared in the basic requirements of a competitive country as reported in the WEF's Global Competitiveness Index. Over the last decade there has been no significant change in the order of these factors — infrastructure and institutions remain as bottlenecks, although they have shown slight improvements over the last decade, while health and primary education have deteriorated.

FIGURE 9.3
Philippines' Scores in Global Competitiveness Index Basic Requirements, 2006–7 and 2014–15

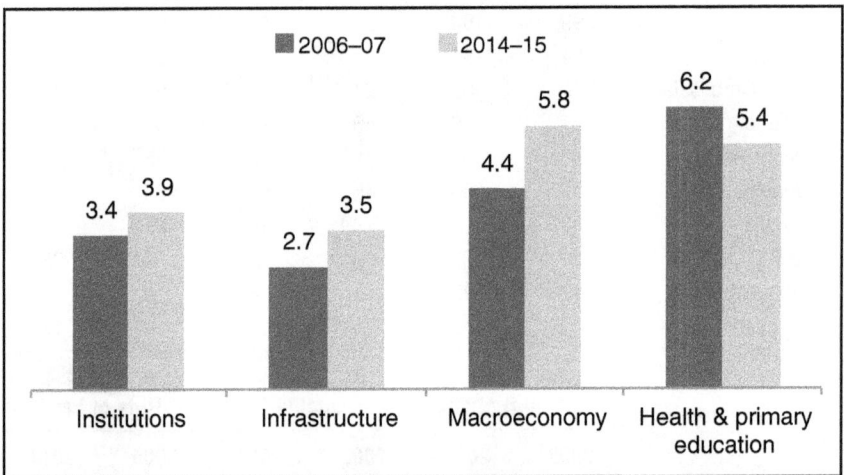

Source: World Economic Forum's Global Competitiveness Reports.

Among governance issues, corruption is the most problematic factor for doing business in the Philippines, and has remained so over the years (see Table 9.2). Businesses in neighbouring countries such as Thailand and Malaysia also faced corruption as the most problematic for doing business in 2014. However, compared with these

TABLE 9.2
Response Rates of Problematic Factors for Doing Business in the
Philippines, Thailand and Malaysia, 2006 and 2014

Problematic Factors	Philippines		Thailand		Malaysia	
	2006	2014	2006	2014	2006	2014
Corruption	21.5	17.6	14.7	21.4	8	17
Inadequate Supply of Infrastructure	15.2	15.9	6	6.3	5.8	4.4
Tax Regulations	4.4	13.3	8.2	2.4	8.3	4.4
Inefficient Government Bureaucracy	11.8	12.6	17.8	12.7	15.4	8.8
Tax Rates	3.7	9.7	2.5	2.6	7	6.6
Policy Instability	15.3	5.4	13.9	11.8	6.3	5.9
Restrictive Labour Regulations	2.5	5.3	2.6	0.5	8.3	3.4
Crime and Theft	3.8	4.1	0.2	1	5.4	9.5
Inflation	2.1	3.8	4.3	0.3	7.4	6.4
Inadequately Educated Workforce	0.8	2.3	10.2	6.2	6.7	3.9
Poor Work Ethic in National Labour Force	1	2.1	2.8	3.7	6	5.8
Insufficient Capacity to Innovate	...	2.1	...	6.3	...	5.1
Foreign Currency Regulations	0.3	1.9	2	0.1	8.1	3.4
Government Instability/Coups	13.6	1.9	7.7	21	1.1	5.2
Access to Financing	4.1	1.6	7.1	3.4	6	9.7
Poor Public Health	...	0.5	...	0.3	...	0.7

Source: World Economic Forum's Global Competitiveness Reports.

countries, the Philippines seems to have improved, as the proportion of responses citing corruption as the most problematic factor for doing business in 2014 was slightly lower than in 2005. During the same period, this proportion increased in the cases of Thailand and Malaysia.

While corruption remains the Philippines' top governance issue, data from Transparency International suggests that the country has made substantial improvements in this area in recent years (see Figure 9.4). The Philippines' score in the Corruption Perceptions Index

FIGURE 9.4
Philippines' Percentile Rank in Corruption Perception Index, 2005–14

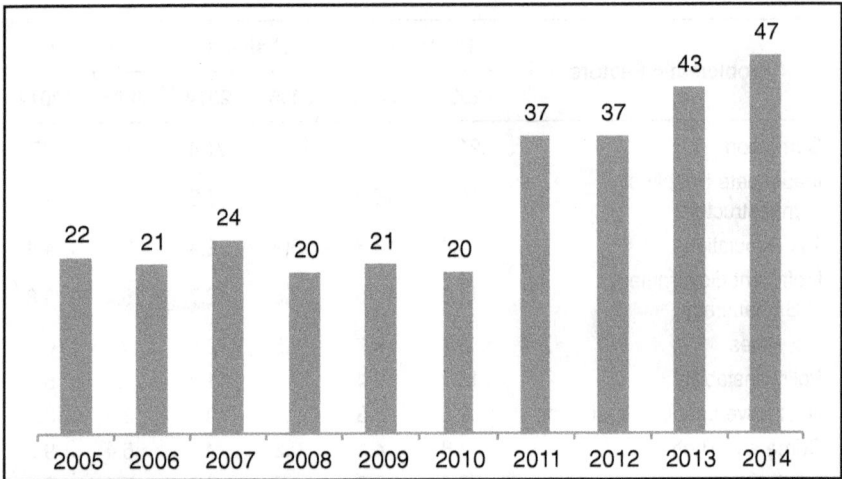

has improved since 2011, rising from being in the bottom 20 percentile to almost in the top 50 percentile by 2014. These improvements indicate that efforts by the government to reduce corruption have been recognized by businesses, although the relatively low standing of the country emphasizes the need to sustain these efforts.

A closer analysis of the reports explaining recent improvements in governance indicators suggests that they may be mainly attributed to President Benigno Aquino III's (2010–16) leadership and commitment to good governance. Reforms of public institutions, policies and programmes had been guided by three core principles: transparency, accountability and citizens' participation. Specifically, the Aquino administration pursued comprehensive initiatives that aimed to reduce corruption, improve public service delivery and enhance the business environment. Past administrations had also attempted to pursue strategic governance reforms, but they suffered from issues of low credibility and public trust, particularly in the case of the Estrada and Arroyo administrations, whose leadership suffered from allegations of corruption.

The reforms of the Aquino administration in key areas for participatory governance included providing access to government information by the general public. Specific examples include data on import transactions published by the Bureau of Customs (BOC), as well as the detailed budget information published by the Department of Budget and Management (DBM). These were complemented by efforts to build citizens' awareness of — and capability to engage in — the budget and policymaking process. Recent efforts to assess progress in budget transparency also suggest important gains, as the Philippines scored higher than many Southeast Asian countries in the Open Budget Index for 2015 (see Figure 9.5) of the International Budget Partnership and the Philippine Center for Investigative Journalism.

FIGURE 9.5
Open Budget Index Scores of Selected ASEAN Countries, 2012 and 2015

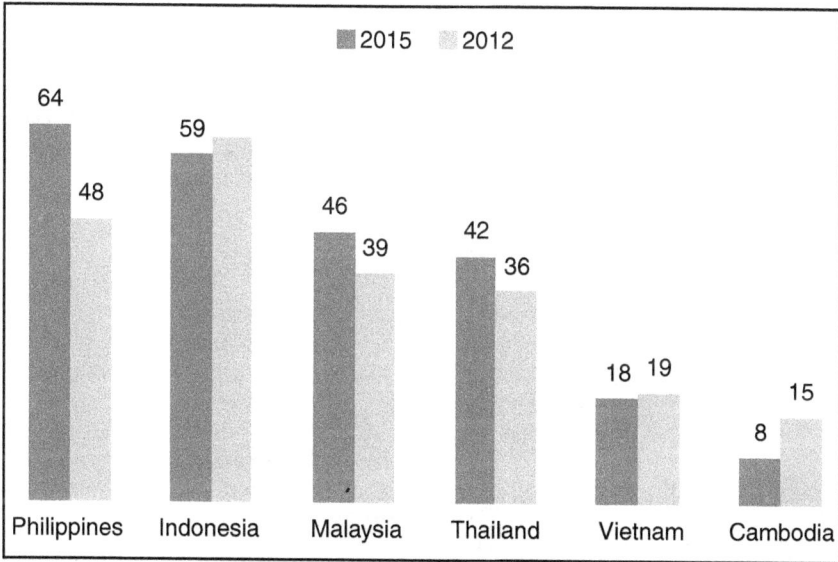

Source: International Budget Partnership's Open Budget Survey.

Moreover, government branches tasked with strengthening accountability have demonstrated important accomplishments in recent years. The Office of the Ombudsman, which serves as the government's key anti-corruption agency, is a case in point. Prior to recent reforms the ombudsman seemed far less efficient in exacting accountability from erring officials. In contrast, the incumbent ombudsman, who assumed office in 2011 and inherited a backlog of 11,000 criminal and administrative cases, has already resolved 6,200 cases within four years.[2]

These initiatives are clearly changing the perception of the international community with respect to transparency and accountability in Philippine political institutions.

These reforms contributed, in turn, to the country's credit rating being upgraded by agencies such as Fitch (from BB+ in 2011 to BBB– in 2013), Moody's (from Ba2 in June 2011 to Ba1 in October 2012) and Standard & Poor's (from BB in 2010 to BBB in 2014). According to Moody's, for example, the sustained upgrades over the past five years were driven by solid macroeconomic fundamentals and factors related to governance and institutions (see Table 9.3). Furthermore, the

TABLE 9.3
Reasons for Moody's Credit Rating Upgrade for the Philippines

Date	Upgrade	Main Factors	Governance and Institutions
15 June 2011	Ba3 to Ba2	Fiscal consolidation under the new administration; Sustained macroeconomic stability; Strengthened position in external payments; Significant pick-up in economic growth.	The government doubled its efforts to go after tax evaders and smugglers.
29 October 2012	Ba2 to Ba1	Promising economic performance despite deteriorating global demand; Enhanced prospects for growth in the medium-term; Stability in the financial system; Continued gains from enhanced revenue administration.	There were noted improvements in infrastructure spending. The peace agreement between the government and the Moro Islamic Liberation Front provides an environment for more investments.
3 October 2013	Ba1 to Baa3	Robust economic performance; Ongoing fiscal and debt consolidation; Political stability.	The popularity of the Aquino administration among the voters, as proven in the midterm-elections, translates to continued support to the reform agenda. Improvements in third-party assessments of institutional quality and international competitive-ness are pronounced.

TABLE 9.3   (*continued*)

Date	Upgrade	Main Factors	Governance and Institutions
11 December 2014	Baa3 to Baa2	Ongoing debt reduction and improvements in fiscal management; Stronger economic growth; Limited vulnerability to common risks currently affecting emerging markets.	Continued increase in cross-country rankings of competiveness, in line with the current administration's emphasis on good governance. Central bank's strong record in price and financial stability.

Source: Various Moody's reports.

Global Competitiveness Index (GCI) of the Philippines has increased since 2010, matched by improvements in the Ease of Doing Business Index (see Figure 9.6).

FIGURE 9.6
Philippines' Ease of Doing Business and Global Competitiveness Indices, 2010–15

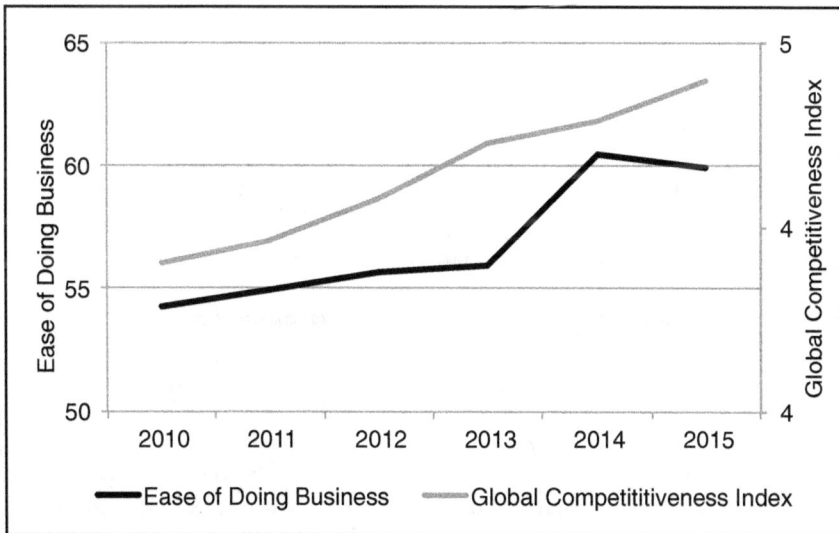

Note: Ease of Doing Business index shows the "distance to frontier" score, with 100 as the highest, while the Global Competitiveness Index ranges from 1 to 7.
Source: World Bank and World Economic Forum.

II. Issues and Challenges

While the previous section highlighted that governance indicators have improved in recent years, this section argues that there is more to be done in order to generate a substantial social impact. In particular, the Philippines still belongs to the bottom 50 per cent of countries facing corruption challenges. The reforms underlying improvements in governance indicators were focused on rebuilding the credibility of the government and restoring public trust, which were critical in paving the way for broader and deeper reforms. But because of the daunting task, these efforts have not yet had a significant impact on poverty, as the underlying factors that give rise to the deep-seated structural weaknesses in governance and institutions in the Philippines have yet to be addressed.

Figure 9.7 illustrates the framework for analysing the issues and challenges in promoting good governance and strengthening public

FIGURE 9.7
The Role of Institutions and Governance in Achieving the Filipinos' Vision by 2040

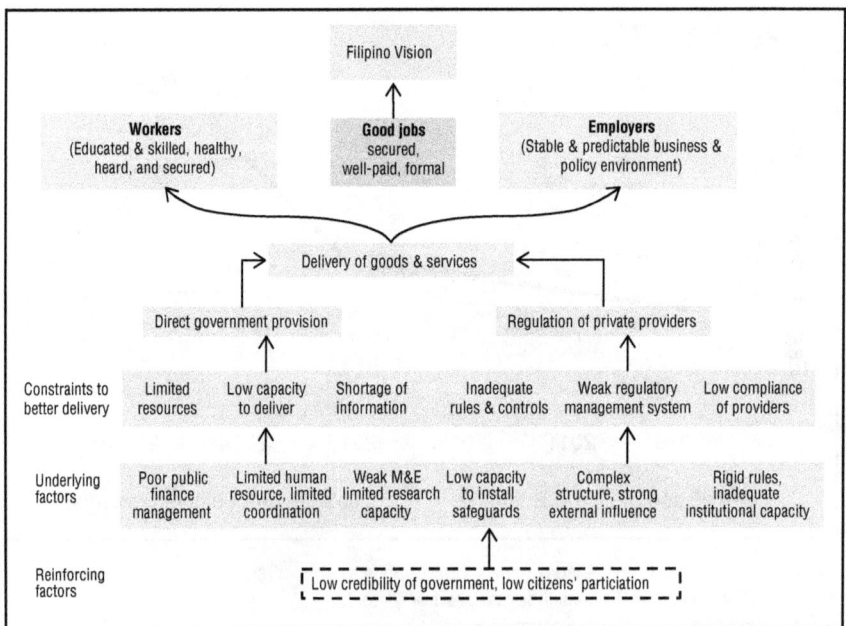

Note: Illustration is based on a review of literature.

institutions in the Philippines. The goal is to achieve the Filipinos' vision by 2040, and the role of the government is to provide an environment such that workers are able to take on "good jobs" and employers have the capacity to create such jobs. Ideally, this environment has the necessary goods and services, which are provided either directly by government or by private providers. However, there are constraints to effective delivery. The remainder of this section will attempt to identify the constraints, as well as the factors that give rise to them.

A. Limited Resources

The government needs resources to be able to deliver goods and services and to perform its administrative functions. It is only recently that the Philippines began to enjoy considerable fiscal space (see chapter 8 for more details). But for several decades the Philippines suffered from fiscal imbalances, which resulted in the low provision of public goods (e.g., infrastructure) and inadequate delivery of services (e.g., education, health, social protection). The tight budget has undermined the government's capacity to finance social expenditures as well as projects that could potentially improve its administrative efficiency, such as computerization. The limited resources can be attributed to the small revenue base and poor public finance management, spanning from tax collection to disbursement of public funds. Interestingly, this environment may have also fuelled a greater dependence on traditional relationships, particularly on how poor and low-income households turn to local political and economic patrons to be able to cope with a diminished and less credible state. Breaking from this low-level equilibrium requires mobilizing resources more effectively in order to resuscitate the fuller provision of public goods (de Dios 2007; Mendoza et al. 2015).

Yet, tax collection, in particular, has been low due to factors including low tax compliance (evasion and avoidance) and limited capacity for tax administration (Usui 2011). Local government units (LGUs) also have very low capacity to generate their own revenues and have mostly relied on internal revenue allotments (World Bank 2003). Moreover, there are issues in the allocation of expenditures that are compromised by various distortions, including allocation of resources to off-budget items that are not aligned with national government priorities, while weaknesses in the financial reporting system make comparing the budget with actual expenditures technically difficult (World Bank 2010).

In addition to creating leakages and the misuse of resources, poor management of public finances makes the system vulnerable to corrupt practices. For instance, the complex tax payment system opens up avenues for rent-seeking behaviour among government personnel. Wide discretion on the use of funds, particularly the ones allocated to lawmakers to provide the needs of their constituencies, have been subject to misappropriations, bribery and kickbacks, while the lack of transparency and consistency in reporting expenditures diminish the space to scrutinize how resources are used. Hence, while the old system triggered a hollowing out of the state, it also tended to feed more corrupt and traditional relationships and practices.

B. Low Capacity to Deliver

The delivery of public goods and services, particularly in areas and sectors where the private sector does not come in, is central to the government's role in ensuring equity. However, this role is constrained by the low implementation capacity to deliver such goods and services. An example is infrastructure — despite increases in the resources allotted to this sector, the low spending capacity of the government limits the number of projects that can be implemented. The quality of the human resources of the public sector could still be improved. The lack of qualified personnel limits the functions that agencies are required to perform, such as implementing programmes, collecting and consolidating information, and analysing critical information that can feed into policymaking. Many tasks entailing numerous steps to process permits and licences and facilitate coordination within the bureaucracy could be dramatically streamlined, as well as improved, through e-government investments. Ultimately, a leaner but technically more equipped public sector bureaucracy should be able to accomplish more and better services with far fewer but more productive bureaucrats.

Many studies have attributed low capacity of government personnel to low salaries relative to their counterparts in the private sector (for instance, World Bank 2000; NEDA 2011). Not only do low salaries prevent qualified people from joining the government, they also create a reason for employees to resort to graft and corruption. This behaviour among employees is also made possible by weak systems and procedures that can be easily manipulated. Corruption among government personnel is particularly rampant in agencies whose operations have direct contact with private individuals, such as in tax collection and procurement of goods and services. Minimizing this contact through streamlined procedures or stronger e-government platforms could dramatically reduce incentives and opportunities for rent seeking in many areas of government.

Another factor that contributes to the low quality of civil service is the existence of numerous key positions that are reserved for political appointees rather than for qualified personnel. An incumbent administration tends to put in these key positions new hires whose education and skills profile do not necessarily fit the position but who are hired because of political favours, especially during elections. This creates disincentives for qualified people to stay longer in the government. Professionalizing and stabilizing the civil service will be critical in this regard.

C. Shortage of Information

The government is required to make complex policy decisions that affect the whole economy. However, there is generally a shortage of information that can support these decisions. Policymakers often rely on their own intuition and experience when making decisions. As a result, decisions tend to be politically oriented. Underlying this constraint is the lack of reliable management information systems (MIS) within agencies that are capable of recording their operations and generating the relevant information that can support decision-making. In a study conducted by Ballesteros and Israel (2014), it was pointed out that the lack of a central monitoring and evaluation system within the agencies created difficulty in identifying and integrating information and data. Such record keeping is mostly undertaken at the local offices, and data are sent to the regional offices and then consolidated at the central office, resulting in a significant delay and in varying quality. Moreover, most administrative data are not open to the public, which also limits citizens' participation in data analysis.

There have been attempts by the government to improve its MIS, such as the computerization programmes dating back to the Ramos and Estrada administrations, but policy and institutional issues have created barriers. These issues include lack of coordination among agencies in setting up the network infrastructure, limited financial resources, continually changing government structures due to rationalization programmes, and limited absorptive capacity of government agencies (NITC 2000). While some government agencies have invested in MIS, they have largely been limited to supporting clerical functions.

D. Inadequate Rules and Controls

Rules and controls are necessary to ensure that public resources, both human and financial, are allocated and used efficiently and effectively. These include systems that track and monitor financial flows and the physical progress of projects, the systematic selection of potential beneficiaries of programmes, and periodic monitoring of programme outcomes, among others. When rules and controls are inadequate, they can potentially open up opportunities for discretion, manipulation and rent seeking, which lead to corrupt practices. In many government operations, notably in procurement of goods and services, tax collection and administration, and in programmes targeted at the poor, rules and controls are somewhat inadequate.

The procurement of goods and services by the government, for instance, has been subject to corrupt practices, which include collusion among bidders to attempt to increase the price, non-competitive bidding processes that ultimately favour one contractor, and delivery of substandard products and services that are eventually approved by government officials, among others (ADB 2012, 2013). These practices can be attributed to inadequate controls in procedures, to a lack of public awareness of such procedures, and to illicit accountability among concerned parties.

On programmes targeted at the poor, only a few of them use a systematic method to identify their beneficiaries, which often leads to benefits being diverted from those who need them the most. For example, livelihood assistance that provides cash grants to facilitate business start-ups among the poor often rely on the discretion of local community leaders to identify beneficiaries, who may opt to select allies, friends and relatives rather than those facing the greatest need. Once again, public service delivery is jeopardized, while traditional relationships are rewarded, leading to an erosion of trust in the provision of public goods. The conditional cash transfer (CCT), or the Pantawid Pamilyang Pilipino Program, is one of the few programmes to have embedded measures to limit discretion in its implementation.

E. Weak Regulatory Management System

When the private sector is involved in the provision of goods and services, regulation is critical to ensure that the goods and services provided serve the best interests of the public and, at the same time, create and facilitate conditions for effective and efficient markets. Several studies have indicated that the regulatory management system in the Philippines is generally weak (Cariño 2005; Llanto 2015). This can be attributed to a myriad of factors, such as the complex regulatory structure, contradictory laws, the low technical capacity of regulatory bodies, limited coordination among government agencies, but most notably to the strong influence of certain groups in the regulation process.

The strong external influence in regulation can be seen in many instances of government decisions that are more politically — rather than technically — driven. The regulators, many of them appointed by elected officials, are not immune from influence from forces outside the regulatory system, including powerful voices in society seeking protection of their economic position, or large domestic industry players seeking protection from foreign competition, who are also electoral constituents or campaign financiers, respectively. The vulnerability of the regulatory system to political manipulation is reinforced by the low transparency in making decisions, the weak evidence base on which these decisions are made, and the low integrity of higher officials tasked with sensitive regulatory oversight.

As the government veers away from direct provision to regulation, the weak regulatory management system in the Philippines has substantial implications for the quality of goods and services. General competition regulation will also have an affect on the country's competitiveness. While regulatory issues in the Philippines are much more apparent in the utility sectors, such as energy, water and telecommunications, the social sectors such as education and health, which also increasingly involve the private sector in service delivery (e.g., private schools and hospitals), are also not spared their negative effects. And as the country aspires to pursue innovative service delivery models — such as through public–private partnerships (PPPs) — combined with an ambitious international economic integration agenda (e.g., ASEAN), the load on a credible and professionalized regulatory system can only be expected to increase.

F. Low Compliance with Rules among Private Providers

The rules and regulations set forth by the government to extract from the private sector the goods and services that the public needs are only effective when they are complied with. There is a dearth of information on compliance, but available information on the quality of goods and services provided indicate that the compliance rate is low, particularly in areas that matter most for human capital development, such as education and health, and in addressing critical constraints to doing business, such as infrastructure. The low compliance among private providers can be attributed to the rigid rules in the provision of goods and services, which open up opportunities for rent seeking, combined with the generally inadequate regulatory capacity of agencies.

In the education sector, for instance, despite having better facilities and learning materials, some private schools lag behind public schools in terms of educational quality, as evidenced by the difference in the National Achievement Test (NAT) results. During the school year 2010–11, the mean percentage score (MPS) of public elementary school students was 70, while it was only 54 among private school students. The same pattern was recorded in secondary education, wherein the

MPS of public and private school students were 49 and 45, respectively (DepEd 2014). Despite having in place the right policies, standards and guidelines in the provision of private education, the lack of institutional capacity of the government to monitor the performance of the private sector gives rise to the poor delivery of these services.

Moreover, low compliance with regulations is also apparent in the provision of public goods, such as the transport infrastructure. An assessment of transport infrastructure in the Philippines indicated that the limited institutional capacity of agencies is the main challenge to the provision of infrastructure by the private sector (ADB 2013). Only a few transport projects went through a process of open and competitive bidding, which reflects the lack of capacity within sector agencies for project planning and preparation, as well as a lack of clear principles and rules for developing partnerships with the private sector.

Overall, most of the above factors that constrain the effective delivery of goods and services in the Philippines are common among developing countries, where resources are scarce and systems are less efficient. Developing countries in general are characterized by uncertain information, poverty, pervasive state influence in the economy, and centralization in decision-making (Grindle and Thomas 1991). But some developing countries, such as those in Southeast Asia, have been relatively more successful in addressing these challenges. It therefore takes an administration that has the credibility to initiate and undertake reforms, in order to build public trust, so that all actors can form collective action towards attaining the goal.

III. The Way Forward

This section presents policy options to address the above issues and challenges. While there is no single prescription to promote good governance and strengthen institutions in the Philippines, this section argues that there is a need for the "right" sequencing of reforms, starting from those that are easier to implement and face less political resistance, progressively building up towards more ambitious and deeper structural and political reforms. The *first round of reforms* should focus on simpler and more pragmatic reforms that aim to improve the delivery of goods and services that have immediate and significant impact on poverty reduction. These reforms are envisaged to trigger dramatic poverty reduction, in turn opening the window for the *second round of reforms*, which are more challenging to implement, as they address the deep-seated structural weaknesses in governance and institutions in the Philippines. Underlying this strategy is the "theory of change", whereby the long-term goals are first defined and then the necessary conditions to support these goals are mapped to the present institutional landscape.

The term "theory of change" is widely used in philanthropy, non-profit activities and government. It refers to an outcomes-based approach to promote a social change necessary to achieve a desired outcome. Specifically, the approach starts from defining the goal and then working backwards to identify the strategies necessary to achieve the goal. Essentially, theory of change is a way of thinking rather than a prescriptive set of policies to achieve the goal. It is a mapping out of the sequence of policies that can potentially lead to the goal. This approach is not new, but at its core are evaluation and informed social action (Vogel 2012).

In the Philippines, each administration has a defined goal, such as poverty reduction and inclusive growth. It also outlines the strategies to achieve these goals. However, what appears missing in the strategies is the sequencing of policies in a way that a particular policy change can affect the next policy change, leading to the achievement of the goal. The often noisy political environment could be part of the reason for this, as reforms appear to be much more opportunistic than strategic in nature. The theory of change elaborated in this chapter attempts to address the question of how to break free from the low level institutional and development equilibrium — moving from the traditional to a more modern institutional set for the country.

A. First Round of Reforms: Fixing Programmes that Create Jobs and Enhance Human Capital

The first round of reforms focuses on key areas where pragmatic governance reforms could yield immediate poverty reduction gains. It involves making the current programmes and services of the government work to enhance both the supply of and demand for labour. On the labour supply side it entails the following: (i) widening access to programmes and services such as education, health and social protection that effectively improve human capital; and (ii) increasing the capacity at the local level to deliver such services. On the labour demand side it entails the following: (i) providing the supporting policy environment that allows markets to expand; and (ii) lowering the costs of doing business, to encourage small businesses to grow.

1. Widening Access to Programmes and Services that Effectively Improve Human Capital

For many Filipinos, human capital investments combined with migration decisions (notably to fast-growing urban centres) offer a quick way for succeeding generations to escape poverty and rapidly increase their wage prospects (Paqueo et al. 2014). Essentially, this is the same job creation and labour migration pattern observed among other Asian economies that successfully industrialized and reduced poverty in the last few decades. To this end, the government has increased the budgetary allocations for education, health and social protection. However, there remain areas in the Philippines that are underserved, and the quality of services in these areas is low, as discussed in detail in chapters 4 and 5. While increasing the amount of resources seems to be the most obvious solution to low access and quality, improving governance in these sectors can also bring important gains while keeping the same budget envelope.

Improving the public financial management (PFM) system. The government has already come up with a PFM reform road map, which needs to be continued. Priority could be placed in strengthening PFM in education and health, so that increases in the budgetary allocations towards these sectors translate into improving both the access and quality of their services. It involves collective action, not only among oversight agencies such as in budget and management, audit, and finance, but also the financial units of the education and health departments. Making the PFM system more efficient and transparent can reduce leakages of funds allotted to these sectors, as well as promote accountability in the use of resources.

Using systematic targeting and strengthening monitoring and evaluation (M&E). Providing publicly financed services could mean focusing resources only on those who need such assistance and less on those who have the capacity to pay for privately provided services. Greater emphasis could therefore be placed on the formulation and adoption of targeting mechanisms to ensure that the individuals who receive government support are those who need them most. Moreover, M&E mechanisms can ensure that existing programmes are continually upgraded to yield a high impact and minimize leakages and waste. The government has made strides in embedding evidence-based M&E strategies in its key programmes, such as the CCT programme. The marked shift towards evidence-based targeting, monitoring, redress, and evaluation strategies could be seen as part of broader efforts to boost government transparency and accountability mechanisms.

Focusing public resources only on cost-effective programmes. Public resources are spent on many programmes whose impacts are hardly known. For instance, there are social protection programmes that are being implemented by many agencies that have existed for decades, but their impacts have never been evaluated. There is a need to evaluate the cost-effectiveness of existing programmes and services in order to determine whether or not they need to be expanded, redesigned or terminated. The same amount of resources can be used more efficiently if they are channelled to programmes and services that are proven to yield benefits to targeted beneficiaries and away from those that are ineffective.

Enhancing coordination among implementing agencies. Widening access to education, health and social protection programmes and services requires closer coordination among implementing agencies. Areas with an inadequate number of schools are likely to have inadequate numbers of hospitals and health clinics. There are also programmes that have similar objectives with similar target beneficiaries but which are being implemented by multiple agencies with limited coordination, spreading out resources and creating redundancy in the use of the government's human resource. In many areas there is a need for greater policy and programme coherence, so that fuller development outcomes may be more easily reached.

Making government data accessible to the public. The government can take advantage of research institutions to contribute to policymaking and programme management, particularly in honing government strategies and maximizing the impact of government-led initiatives. This is especially important when it comes to testing new programmes and scaling up current programmes. The successful institutionalization of these types of reforms could help ensure that public resources are spent responsibly and strategically, and contribute to the cultivation of a culture of evidence-based policymaking that supports and continues efficient and effective policies and discontinues inefficient and ineffective ones.

2. Increasing the Capacity at the Local Level to Deliver Services

Under the decentralized system, the assignment of service delivery, revenue mobilization and expenditure allocations is given to LGUs, although the national government still assumes the delivery of certain services. However, LGUs and local government agencies vary in their capacity to deliver services, and the areas in the Philippines where human capital investments are needed the most tend to have governance and implementation challenges. These areas are characterized by low economic activity, dispersed geography, persistence of conflict, and limited connectivity with markets, among others, that make policymaking particularly difficult.

Improving the quality of human resources, especially at the local level. There is a need to continue reforms to improve the quality of civil service, but priority can be given to local agencies, which are in charge of programme implementation and service delivery. Some local offices have inadequate human resources relative to the quantity of tasks they are required to deliver, while others have redundant positions and employees with overlapping functions. These often result in varying performance by the agencies in terms of meeting their targets, and consequently in the amount of budget they receive. In this regard there is also a need to fast-track the rationalization plans of line agencies to better evaluate human resource requirements in local offices, and to shift resources towards local offices that need these resources the most.

Using performance-based mechanisms to access national government funds by LGUs. LGUs differ in their abilities to generate adequate local revenues, such that national government agencies continue to deliver certain social services. The subsequent dependence on internal revenue allotments of many LGUs reinforces existing vertical fiscal imbalances and prevents local leaders from effectively carrying out their responsibilities. One possible approach to encourage low-revenue-generating LGUs to improve the delivery of their services is to utilize a performance-based mechanism that rewards good performance and incentivizes the efficient use of resources. This offers more funds as well as flexibility to LGUs that display concrete and measurable efforts to lessen their dependence on central government transfers. Put simply, well-performing LGUs could be rewarded with greater (and more flexible) access to resources, while LGUs with poor governance track records could be more adequately monitored, along with programmes that include stronger governance mechanisms (e.g., requirements for greater transparency).

Enhancing coordination between local and national governments. Strong local development outcomes will not necessarily take place automatically. Patron–client relationships and institutional backwardness in many parts of the country could frustrate the intended goals of participatory governance. There is still a role for centralized approaches, notably in terms of crafting a holistic strategy in allocating resources, designing programmes that are robust enough to stand implementation challenges at the local levels, and collecting and publishing data for broad groups of academia, civil society and think tanks to analyse and use in engaging both national and local authorities. Examples include allowing the public access to information on tax and other payments, and managing natural resource wealth by publicly disseminating mining revenues and receipts through the

Extractive Industries Transparency Initiative (EITI), whereby both national and local governments as well as mining companies are held accountable.

Encouraging political competition. In lieu of forthcoming deeper political reforms (e.g., anti-dynasty, pro-inclusive democracy and political party reform laws), it could be useful to create the incentives to compete politically for access to more (and more flexible) resources or support for public goods provision based on clear development outcomes and a framework of greater transparency and accountability. The existence of political dynasties can exert influence over local government spending patterns and subsequently local government outcomes. The disbursement of the so-called pork barrel was observed to favour local patrons. The resulting skew in the manner of distribution of public resources could run contrary to policy objectives such as poverty reduction (Mendoza et al. 2012).

Fostering cooperation among LGUs to realize scale economies. Local governments do not exist in isolation, nor can they function without cooperation from nearby localities. LGUs must be encouraged to form cooperation strategies to realize scale economies in public goods of which they would be contributing to the cost. This is important particularly in disaster-risk reduction and management that entail large costs, such as transport infrastructure, coastal management facilities and early-warning facilities, from which not only their constituents would benefit but also those of other LGUs.

3. Providing the Supporting Policy Environment that Allows Markets to Expand

Many studies have indicated that the slow economic growth of past decades could be attributed to a policy environment that is highly protectionist and restrictive, and which increases the cost of doing business in the Philippines (see, for instance, Medalla 1998; Fabella 2000; Clarete 2006; de Dios 2011; de Dios and Williamson 2013). Recently, the government has taken steps towards a new industrial policy, whereby incentives are properly designed to avoid rent seeking, such that clear, targeted and benchmarked outputs and activities must first be delivered before public support is granted to a firm, and to build transparency and accountability mechanisms on the firm and the government.

Evaluating existing investment incentive systems. Fiscal inducements such as income tax holidays, tax deductions and tax credits do not seem to exert a strong influence on investments (Aldaba 2007). One possible option is to incentivize and finance productivity-enhancing public goods such as infrastructure, health and education, which are likely to attract more investments (Clarete 1992; Reside 2007). Moreover, the adoption of performance-based incentive systems has the capacity to spur productivity in firms and entice investors to the Philippines. Recent policies taken by the Department of Trade and Industry (DTI) to concretely specify output targets and tie incentive measures to these targets are among the steps in this direction.

Reviewing regulatory barriers to investments. The government has also taken steps to review regulatory barriers to investments through the drafting of industry road maps in collaboration with the government, academe and industry associations. The road maps are useful in evaluating the rules and regulations affecting certain industries. For instance, some of the provisions of the laws affecting small industries have been found to be obsolete and need to be amended. These laws could inhibit the growth of businesses or discourage them from participating in formal markets. The road maps could serve as the basis for further review of existing regulations, particularly those that affect industries which are labour intensive.

Improving capacity to provide missing critical inputs. Infrastructure is the most critical missing input to better industry performance (chapter 3; see also Aldaba 2014). Transport infrastructure, in particular, can potentially connect markets and people and encourage more economic activities. However, the infrastructure sector is marred by severe governance challenges, such as low institutional capacity of the government to allocate, spend and manage resources for infrastructure or to integrate plans, including those at the local level. Efforts to improve governance in the area of infrastructure, however, also affect other sectors such as utilities (e.g., energy, water and communications) and social services (e.g., education, health and social protection). But in terms of prioritization of reforms, the government may need to first focus on those that affect all these key sectors.

Putting in place policies to encourage innovation and self-discovery. The government may devise incentives for first movers to encourage new investments. One readily implementable government intervention to promote self-discovery is through the provision of access to raw materials, intermediate inputs and shared service facilities (Aldaba 2014). The measure prompts firms, particularly micro, small and medium-sized enterprises (MSMEs), for instance, to use common service facilities and infrastructures, wherein machinery and equipment for a specific industry is provided to ensure that production gaps are addressed and value chains are strengthened. Given the exogenous boost in productivity in this setup, one successful firm or multiple firms benefitting from the inputs could consequently create more output or pursue more innovative activities with higher production value.

Enhancing coordination between public and private sectors. Finally, it would be difficult to envision the success of the aforementioned initiatives without first placing emphasis on formalized coordination mechanisms in fostering greater cooperation between the private and public sectors (Rodrik 2004; Aldaba 2014). The creation of industry development councils encourages deeper and more meaningful dialogues between the government and industry leaders. This in turn allows for a more nuanced and interactive policy evolution process, building in accountability through more transparent and evidence-based discussions and consultations. Increased cooperation could enable both parties to work more closely in identifying binding political constraints, developing appropriate interventions for industrial bottlenecks and formulating more strategic ways of investing public and private sector resources.

4. Lowering Costs of Doing Business to Encourage Small Businesses to Grow

Related to providing an enabling policy environment, this section emphasizes the need for policies targeted at small businesses. Markets are not necessarily inclusive (nor do they exist) in areas where poverty is rampant, due to a variety of factors, including both governance and market failures (Mendoza and Thelen 2008). The poor residing in remote areas are effectively excluded from formal markets because of their lack of connectivity, either physically (e.g., access to road networks) or through communications networks. Inadequate investments in human capital also prevent them from participating in formal markets. While informal markets offer some relief to a difficult environment where productivity-enhancing and poverty-reducing activities are capped, they are typically constrained, which prevents businesses from realizing scale economies.

Lowering the cost of doing business in the formal sector. Many of the small firms in the Philippines operate informally, which can mainly be attributed to the high transaction costs involved in participating in the formal sector. These include business registration, income tax payments and compliance with labour regulations. The systematic simplification of business processes could make it easier for smaller entrepreneurs to register their businesses, access government business-support programmes, tap into formal business networks and participate in private initiatives in aid of small and micro enterprises. A review of existing tax incentives for small businesses is necessary so as not to create disincentives to comply.

Supporting small entrepreneurs. Many of the poor resort to small-scale entrepreneurship because of limited access to wage employment, either due to their low skills or a lack of jobs in the areas where they live. Stamping out overregulation, developing and formalizing channels through which LGUs could assist social entrepreneurs and adopting enabling business environments encourage private enterprises. Two examples that tap the productive potentials of rural locales are the Farmer Entrepreneurship Program in Pangasinan — a joint initiative of the Jollibee Foods Corporation, Catholic Relief

Services and National Livelihood Development Corporation — and the Seaweed Federation in Parang, Maguindanao. In essence, this reform strategy focuses on the elimination of impediments to entrepreneurship in order to bolster local productivity. The recent creation of "Go Negosyo Centers" in various cities is also part of institutional reforms in this area. These centres essentially play a coordination role by helping to connect key stakeholders and provide a platform for more effective collective action to assist entrepreneurs and the innovation process.

Promoting local clusters. While the government is unlikely to play the lead role in forming value chains, it can nevertheless act as a catalyst by promoting the emergence of more extensive market connectivity involving small and medium scale enterprises by strategically channelling investments for entrepreneurial clusters through LGUs. In essence, the national government could correct information problems by investing in identifying and mapping potential value clusters and by leveraging social capital and greater familiarity of LGUs with existing local institutions and communities to jumpstart small and medium-scale business ventures. These local value clusters could then be closely integrated to regional or even interregional value chains in order to foster greater efficiency through greater specialization.

Building partnerships with local communities for projects that matter to them. The government may facilitate the development of relationships that underpin community-centric and community-specific business models. The success of Manila Water's "Tubig Para sa Barangay" Program and CocoTech's Livelihood Program hinge on the strength of partnerships between the local government and community-based organizations. Given that greater emphasis is placed on the role of the community in the initiative (the community as a business partner), community involvement is integral for the underlying business models to function (Ganchero and Manapol 2007). Behind this strategy are the promotion of local ownership and the cultivation of shared responsibility, including the formal and informal rules these entail. The role of LGUs could be viewed to be twofold: to lend legitimacy to the project through the leveraging of their social capital and to serve as a means to navigate local politics.

B. Second Round of Reforms: Address Deep-seated Structural Weaknesses

In addition to the above policy options, this section presents the key institutional reforms that should be pursued for continued economic development in the Philippines. They are categorized into the following four broad themes: (i) political and electoral reforms; (ii) social, development and asset reforms; (iii) economic competitiveness reforms; and (iv) public finance reforms and good governance innovations.

1. Political and Electoral Reforms

The objective of these reforms is to increase citizens' participation, whereby the majority of the population would be involved in democratic governance, political life and the electoral process. Major political and electoral reforms need to be undertaken to strengthen Philippine democracy through the enactment of crucial laws, such as those related to anti-political dynasty and pro-inclusive democracy, political party development and freedom of information (see Table 9.4). To allow for more active participation of LGUs in the development process, there is also a need to re-examine the Local Government Code and to make decentralization much more effective. In important ways, the country's decentralization could be part of a broader federalism initiative, but this requires many of the deep institutional reforms that complement decentralization, aligning better politics with governance and stronger development outcomes (Mendoza and Ocampo 2017).

For effective and responsive governance to be felt, political and electoral institutions need to be changed in such a way that the behaviour and belief systems of organizations are aligned with the welfare of the people. These reforms not only change the ways in which public hierarchies are formed but also promote the rule of law and adequate commitment and accountability of the government to its citizens. Other options to promote the rule of law and strengthen the anti-corruption drive include (i) the creation of an independent anti-corruption agency that would augment the powers of the Office of the Ombudsman and (ii) to draw on the experience of other developing countries, such as Thailand's National Anti-Corruption

TABLE 9.4
Status of Key Political and Electoral Reforms as of 2015

Reform	Key Feature	Selected References	Status as of 2015
Bangsamoro Basic Law Bill	Promoting inclusive governance in Mindanao	Schiavo-Campo and Judd (2005); Human Development Network (2005)	Pending
Anti-Political Dynasty Bill	Prohibiting family members and relatives from holding or running for elected local government positions	Mendoza et al. (2012); Solon, Fabella and Capuno (2009); de Dios (2007); Teehankee (2007)	Pending
Freedom of Information Bill	Requiring government agencies to allow public review and copying of all official information	Malaluan (2009); Habito (2010)	Pending
Political Party Development Act	Strengthening the political party system to develop genuine political development and democratization	Friedrich Edbert Stiftung (2009); Hutchcroft and Rocamora (2003)	Pending
Whistleblowers Protection Act	Extending security and benefits to individuals who volunteer information on graft and corruption in government		Pending
Reforms on the Sangguniang Kabataan Law	Prohibiting family members and relatives of national and appointed officials from sitting as Sangguniang Kabataan officials		Enacted into law in 2016
Revisiting the Local Government Code	Amending the Local Government Code to address the challenges in local service delivery	Capuno (2007)	Pending

Commission and Indonesia's Corruption Eradication Commission (KPK). Meanwhile, simple and transparent regulator and public administration systems and procedures in government operations, combined with serious investments in e-government, could also dramatically upgrade the governance landscape.

2. Social, Development and Asset Reforms

These cover the scope of constructive and well-designed programmes and policies that directly affect human development outcomes (see Table 9.5). As for asset reform, inequities arising from a skewed distribution of resources and assets open the door for government intervention that addresses these problems. The economic and social impact of the Comprehensive Agrarian Reform Program is still widely debated among various stakeholders and academics (Fabella 2014;

TABLE 9.5
Status of Key Social Development and Asset Reforms as of 2015

Reform	Key Feature	Selected References	Status as of 2015
Philippine Risk Reduction and Management Act	Strengthening disaster-risk reduction and management		Enacted into law in 2010
Reproductive Health Law	Guaranteeing universal access to methods on contraception, fertility control, sexual education and maternal care	Medalla (2002); Alonzo et al. (2004); Pernia et al. (2011); Pernia (2014); Pernia and Pernia (2015)	Enacted into law in 2012
Universal Health Care Act	Ensuring that all Filipinos, especially the poorest of the poor, will receive health insurance coverage from the Philippine Health Insurance Corporation		Enacted into law in 2013

TABLE 9.5 (*continued*)

Reform	Key Feature	Selected References	Status as of 2015
K-to-12 Basic Education Program	Expanding basic education an additional two years		Enacted into law in 2013
Amendments to the Philippines Fisheries Code	Prohibiting small-scale fishermen to fish in Manila Bay, among others	Habito (2010)	Amended in 2015
Social protection reforms	Converging social protection programmes: KALAHI-CIDSS, Pantawid Pamilya, Sustainable Livelihood Program		Implementation ongoing
Comprehensive Agrarian Reform Program	Redistributing public and private agricultural lands to farmers and farmworkers who are landless	Fabella (2003); Fabella (2014); Monsod and Piza (2014)	Pending
Mining Revenue Sharing Act	Providing a new revenue-sharing arrangement between the government and large-scale mining companies		Pending

Monsod and Piza 2014). In this regard, at the institutional level, effective asset reform is contingent on good governance and political will, and overcoming constraints at this level can lead to a greater impact and better performance (Habito 2010). Conversely, alternative solutions with the objective of addressing structural issues on land assets have also been proposed. In the midst of market failures such as imperfectly competitive markets and asymmetric information (e.g., when economies of scale prevail for a certain industry, thus leading to more market concentration), promoting competition in this setting can be an important driver of economic growth and innovation.

3. Economic Competitiveness Reforms

These reforms are aimed at encouraging competition to promote efficiency (see Table 9.6). The recent passing of the Fair Competition Law could be used to maintain a level playing field for the market economy, to protect and promote competition (from the perspective of both producers and consumers) and to stimulate the competitive process so that the market is able to function properly and bring about economic efficiency (Medalla 2002). Recently enacted laws, such as the Go Negosyo Act and Magna Carta for Micro, Small and Medium Enterprises, allow for these enterprises to access financing, technology, information and markets. These laws reflect the value of a government-wide thrust when it comes to developing and supporting MSMEs in the country (Habito 2010).

TABLE 9.6
Status of Key Economic Competitiveness Reforms as of 2015

Reforms	Key Feature	Selected References	Status as of 2015
Magna Carta for Micro, Small and Medium Enterprises (MSMEs)	Promoting, supporting, strengthening and encouraging the growth and development of MSMEs	Habito (2010)	Enacted into law in 2008
Go Negosyo Act	Establishing "Negosyo Center" in all provinces, cities and municipalities		Enacted into law in 2014
Fair Competition Law	Breaking the current monopolistic behaviour and unfair but very profitable trade practices of several corporations	Medalla (2002); Aldaba (2008); Habito (2010)	Enacted into law in 2015
Youth Entrepreneurship and Financial Literacy Program Act	Delivering highly relevant programmes to improve financial literacy among the youth		Enacted into law in 2015

TABLE 9.6 (*continued*)

Reforms	Key Feature	Selected References	Status as of 2015
Microfinance NGO Act	Strengthening NGOs engaged in microfinance operations for the poor		Enacted into law in 2015
Amendments to the Cabotage Law	Allowing foreign-flagged vessels to carry imported cargo directly to the final Philippine port of destination		Amended in 2015
Amendments to the BOT Law	Accelerating the procurement process for PPP projects and designating certain projects to be of national significance that will be shielded from adverse local government action	Llanto (2007*a*, 2007*b*)	Pending
Revisiting Ownership Restrictions in the Philippine Constitution	Relaxing foreign ownership restrictions of local firms	Sicat (2005); Foundation for Economic Freedom (2012); Mendoza and Melchor (2015)	Pending
Credit Surety Fund Cooperative Act	Enhancing accessibility of MSMEs, cooperatives and NGOs to credit facilities of banks		Pending

At the macro level, another way to accelerate the country's performance is by boosting foreign investments that will generate a myriad of benefits for the country, such as positive externalities and foreign capital (Sicat 2005). Augmenting this long-standing position is evidence that constitutional reform on the economic provisions with respect to foreign ownership or "Economic Charter Change",

particularly lifting restrictions, could positively affect foreign investment flows into the Philippines (Mendoza and Melchor 2015).
These new investments are associated with expansion of output,
increased productivity and reduction of unit costs of production in
the economy, which could also consequently enhance the level of
competition in the market (Sicat 2005). Nevertheless, such deep
reforms should be complemented with adequate safety nets that ease
the adjustments by different sectors facing the brunt of competition.
The importance of these complementary reforms should be strongly
emphasized if further international economic integration is to
be sustained through broad-based support from citizens and all
stakeholders.

4. Public Finance and Good Governance Innovations

These are related to the taxation and spending activities of the
government, taking into consideration the government's influence
on resource allocation and income distribution (see Table 9.7). The
more notable and definitive reforms that would attempt to update
the prevailing backward systems, such as the taxation of compensation income and the modernization of customs and tariffs, have
yet to be enacted into law. What is most problematic about this set
of reforms is the fact that taxation (via tariff and income taxation)
should translate to the provision of public goods and the proper
utilization of these public funds. However, since this may not
necessarily translate into reality in the context of a weak state, the
enactment of these laws may make the collection of funds more
efficient and equitable.

Although innovations in good governance are often combined
with public finance reforms (e.g., public expenditure tracking and
open procurement), these innovations can also come in other forms.
For instance, at the local level, these include innovations stressing
the importance of accessibility to information, an enabling policy
environment, aggressive civil society and the quality and leadership
of a local executive. There is evidence that transparency can lead to the
promotion of accountability and participation as well as the development
of trust in local leaders (Capuno and Garcia 2008, 2009).

TABLE 9.7

Status of Key Public Finance and Good Governance Innovations as of 2015

Reforms	Key Feature	Selected References	Status as of 2015
Sin Tax Reform Law	Restructuring the excise tax on alcohol and tobacco products		Enacted into law in 2012
Performance based grants (Seal of Good Governance, Performance Challenge Funds)	Creating an incentive mechanism for local government units to improve their performance	Brillantes (2001)	Implementation ongoing
Open and participatory budgeting process	Allowing the public to participate in decisions regarding the local budget	Brillantes and Fernandez (2010); Capuno and Garcia (2008, 2009)	Implementation ongoing
Reforms on Income Tax	Restructuring the income tax system	Diokno (2005); Quimbo and Javier (2015); Gloria et al. (2014)	Pending
Rationalization of Fiscal Incentives, Tax Incentives Management and Transparency Act	Reviewing the current incentive structure with a view to encourage more investments	Aldaba (2007); Reside (2006, 2007)	Pending
Customs Modernization and Tariff Act	Modernizing customs and tariff administration through full automation of operations	Llanto et al. (2014) Mendoza, Gloria and Pena-Reyes (2014)	Pending
Reforms on Local Public Finance	Improving the financing systems of local government units	Manasan (2005); Llanto (2009)	Pending

Notes

1. The authors acknowledge research assistance from the staff of the Asian Institute of Management Rizalino S. Navarro Policy Center, especially Louisa Camille Poco.
2. The statistics were sourced from presentations of the forum "Institutionalizing Anti-Corruption and Good Governance" organized by AIM in cooperation with Konrad Adenauer Stiftung (KAS).

References

ADB (Asian Development Bank). *Philippines: Critical Development Constraints*. Mandaluyong City: ADB, 2007.

———. *Philippines: Country Procurement Assessment Report 2012*. Mandaluyong City: ADB, 2012.

———. *Infrastructure for Supporting Inclusive Growth and Poverty Reduction in Asia*. Mandaluyong City: ADB, 2013.

Aldaba, R. "FDI Investment Incentive System and FDI Inflows: The Philippine Experience". PIDS Research Paper Series 2007-03. 2007.

———. "Assessing Competition in Philippine Markets". PIDS Research Paper Series 2008-23. 2008.

———. "The Philippine Manufacturing Industry Roadmap: Agenda for New Industrial Policy, High Productivity Jobs, and Inclusive Growth". PIDS Discussion Paper Series 2014-32. 2014.

Alonzo, R., A. Balisacan, D. Canlas, J. Capuno, R. Clarete, R. Danao, E. de Dios et al. "Population and Poverty: The Real Score". UP School of Economics Discussion Paper 2004-15. 2004.

Ballesteros, M., and D. Israel. "Study of Government Interventions for Employment Generation in the Private Sector". Paper for the Philippine Institute for Development Studies and Department of Budget and Management, 2014.

Brillantes, A. "Doing Things Differently: Innovations in Local Governance in the Philippines". *Philippine Journal of Public Administration* 45 (2001): 84–96.

Brillantes, A., and M. Fernandez. "Toward a Reform Framework for Good Governance: Focus on Anti-Corruption". *Philippine Journal of Public Administration* 54 (2010): 87–127.

Capuno, J. "The Quality of Local Governance and Development under Decentralization". In *The Dynamics of Regional Development: The Philippines in East Asia*, edited by A. Balisacan and H. Hill, pp. 204–44. Quezon City: Ateneo de Manila University Press, 2007.

Capuno, J., and M. Garcia. "Can Information about Local Government Performance Induce Civic Participation? Evidence from the Philippines". UP School of Economics Discussion Paper 2008-08. 2008.

———. "Earning Trust with Transparency: Performance Ratings and Trust in Local Officials in the Philippines". UP School of Economics Discussion Paper 2009-10. 2009.

Cariño, L. "Regulatory Governance in the Philippines: Lessons for Policy and Institutional Reform". Centre on Regulation and Competition Working Paper Series 113. June 2005.

Clarete, R. "General Equilibrium Effects of Investment Incentives in the Philippines". UP School of Economics Discussion Paper Series 1992-03. 1992.

———. "Ex-Post Effects of Trade Liberalization in the Philippines". In *Coping with Trade Reforms: A Developing-Country Perspective on the WTO Industrial Tariff Negotiations*, edited by S. Laird and S. Fernando de Cordoba. New York: Palgrave Macmillan, 2006.

de Dios, E. "Local Politics and Local Economy". In *The Dynamics of Regional Development: The Philippines in East Asia*, edited by A. Balisacan and H. Hill, pp. 204–44. Quezon City: Ateneo de Manila University Press, 2007.

———. "Institutional Constraints on Philippine Growth". *Philippine Review of Economics* 48, no. 1 (2011): 71–124.

de Dios, E., and J. Williamson. "Deviant Behavior: A Century of Philippine Industrialization". UP School of Economics Discussion Paper 2013-03. 2013.

DepEd (Department of Education). *Philippine Education for All 2015 Plan of Action: An Assessment of Progress Made in Achieving the EFA Goals*. Pasig City: DepEd, 2014.

Diokno, B. "Reforming the Philippine Tax System: Lessons from Two Tax Reform Programs". *UP School of Economics Discussion Paper* 2005–02. 2005.

Fabella, R. "The Soft State, the Market and Governance". *Philippine Review of Economics* 37, no. 1 (2000): 1–11.

———. "Comprehensive Agrarian Reform Program and the Coase Theorem". UP School of Economics Discussion Paper 0302. 2003.

———. "Comprehensive Agrarian Reform Program (CARP): Time to Let Go". *Philippine Review of Economics* 51, no. 1 (2014): 1–18.

FEF (Foundation for Economic Freedom). "The Charter Change Issue: A Preliminary Paper Surveying the Evidence". Paper by the FEF Secretariat, 2012.

Friedrich Ebert Stiftung. "Reforming the Philippine Political System: Ideas and Initiatives, Debates and Dynamics". Paper by the Friedrich Ebert Stiftung, 2009.

Fukuyama, F. "What is Governance?" Center for Global Development Working Paper 314. 2013.

Ganchero, E., and P. Manapol. "Coco Technologies: Providing Livelihood Opportunities for Poor Coconut Farmers through Value-adding". GIM Case Study A012. New York: United Nations Development Programme, 2007.

Gloria, E., R. Mendoza, and S. Pena-Reyes. "An Analysis of Philippine Income Tax Reforms". Rizalino S. Navarro Policy Center for Competitiveness Working Paper 14-018. 2014.

Grindle, M., and J. Thomas. *Public Choices and Policy Change: The Political Economy of Reform in Developing Countries*. Maryland: The Johns Hopkins University Press, 1991.

Habito, C. *An Agenda for High and Inclusive Growth in the Philippines*. Mandaluyong City: ADB, 2010.

HDN (Human Development Network). *Philippines Human Development Report: Peace, Human Security and Human Development in the Philippines*. Quezon City: HDN, 2005.

Hutchcroft, P., and J. Rocamora. "Strong Demands and Weak Institutions: The Origins and Evolution of the Democratic Deficit in the Philippines". *Journal of East Asian Studies* 3 (2003): 259–92.

IBP (International Budget Partnership). "Open Budget Survey 2015: Philippines". 2015 <http://www.internationalbudget.org/wp-content/uploads/OBS2015-CS-Philippines-English.pdf>.

Llanto, G. "Reforming the BOT Law: A Call of the Times". PIDS Discussion Paper Series 2007-01. 2007*a*.

———. "Policy Reforms and Institutional Weaknesses: Closing the Gap". PIDS Discussion Paper Series 2007-07. 2007*b*.

———. "Fiscal Decentralization and Local Finance Reforms in the Philippines". PIDS Discussion Paper Series 2009-10. 2009.

———. "Toward an Effective Regulatory Management System". PIDS Discussion Paper Series 2015-32. 2015.

Llanto, G., A. Navarro, K. Detros, and M. Ortiz. "How Should We Move Forward in Customs Brokerage and Trade Facilitation?" PIDS Policy Notes 2014-01. January 2014.

Malaluan, N. "A Primer on the Freedom of Information Act. Right to Know, Right Now!" *Action for Economic Reforms*, 27 May 2009 <http://pcij.org/resources/nepo-malaluan-right-to-know-right-now.pdf>.

Manasan, R. "Local Public Finance in the Philippines: Lessons in Autonomy and Accountability". *Philippine Journal of Development* 32, no. 2 (2005): 32–102.

Medalla, E. "Trade and Industrial Policy Beyond 2000: An Assessment of the Philippine Economy". PIDS Discussion Paper Series 98-05. 1998.

————. "Philippine Competition Policy in Perspective". PIDS Discussion Paper Series 2002-25. 2002.

Medalla, F. "The Economic Impact of the Demographic Crisis: Its Implications on Public Policy". *Philippine Review of Economics* 41, no. 1 (2002): 33–43.

Mendoza, R., E. Beja, V. Venida, and D. Yap. "Inequality in Democracy: Insights from an Empirical Analysis of Political Dynasties in the 15th Philippine Congress". *Philippine Political Science Journal* 33, no. 2 (2012): 132–14.

Mendoza, R., E. Beja, J. Teehankee, A. La Viña, and M. Villamejor-Mendoza. *Building Inclusive Democracies in ASEAN.* Mandaluyong City: Anvil, 2015.

Mendoza, R.E. Gloria, and S. Pena-Reyes. "Recasting the Bureau of Customs as a Developmental Agency". Rizalino S. Navarro Policy Center for Competitiveness Working Paper 14-020. 2014.

Mendoza, R., and M. Melchor. "Economic Charter Change: Examining the Pros and Cons". Rizalino S. Navarro Policy Center for Competitiveness Working Paper 15-004. 2015.

Mendoza, R., and J. Ocampo. "Caught between Imperial Manila and the Provincial Dynasties: Towards a new Fiscal Federalism". Ateneo School of Government Working Paper 17-004. 2017.

Mendoza, R., and N. Thelen. "Innovations to Make Markets More Inclusive for the Poor". *Development Policy Review* 26, no. 4 (2008): 427–58.

Monsod, T., and S. Piza. "Time to Let Go of CARP? Not so Fast". UP School of Economics Discussion Paper 2014-03. 2014.

NEDA (National Economic and Development Authority). *Philippine Development Plan 2011–2016.* Pasig City: NEDA, 2011.

NITC (National Information Technology Council). "Government Information Systems Plan". Manila, 2000.

North, D. "The New Institutional Economics and Development". Washington University, 1993 <http://www2.econ.iastate.edu/tesfatsi/NewInstE.North.pdf>.

Nye, J. "Taking Institutions Seriously: Rethinking the Political Economy of Development in the Philippines". *Asian Development Review* 28, no. 1 (2011): 1–21.

Paqueo, V., A. Orbeta, L. Lanzona, and D. Dulay. "Labor Policy Analysis for Jobs Expansion and Development". PIDS Discussion Paper Series 2014–34. 2014.

Pernia, E. "Population Management, RH Law, and Inclusivity". UP School of Economics Discussion Paper 2014-09. 2014.

Pernia, E., and E. Pernia. "Population, Economic Growth, and Inclusivity". *International Journal of Philippine Science and Technology* 8, no. 1 (2015).

Pernia, E., S. Quimbo, J. Abrenica, R. Alonzo, A. Arcenas, A. Balisacan, D. Canlas et al. "Population, Poverty, Politics, and Reproductive Bill". UP School of Economics Discussion Paper 2011-01. 2011.

Quimbo, S., and X. Javier. "Rethinking the Taxation of Compensation Income in the Philippines. *Philippine Review of Economics* 52, no. 1 (2015): 1–22.

Reside, R. "Towards Rational Fiscal Incentives: Good Investments or Wasted Gifts?" Ateneo Economic Policy Reform and Advocacy Sector Fiscal Report 1. 2006.

———. "Can Fiscal Incentives Stimulate Regional Investment in the Philippines? An Update of Empirical Results". UP School of Economics Discussion Paper 0705. June 2007.

Rodrik, D. "Institutions for High-Quality Growth: What They Are and How to Acquire Them". National Bureau of Economic Research Working Paper 7450. 2000.

———. "Industrial Policy for the 21st Century". Harvard Kennedy School of Government Working Paper RWP04-047. 2004.

———. *One Economics, Many Recipes: Globalization, Institutions and Economic Growth*. Princeton, NJ: Princeton University Press, 2007.

Rodrik, D., and A. Subramanian. "The Primacy of Institutions". *Finance and Development*. June 2003 <https://www.imf.org/external/pubs/ft/fandd/2003/06/pdf/rodrik.pdf>.

Schiavo-Campo, S., and M. Judd. "The Mindanao Conflict in the Philippines: Roots, Costs, and Potential Peace Dividend". World Bank Social Development Papers 24. February 2005.

Sicat, G. "The Economic Argument for Constitutional Reform". UP School of Economics Discussion Paper 0512. 2005.

Solon, O., R. Fabella, and J. Capuno. "Is Local Development Good Politics? Local Development Expenditures and the Re-Election of Governors in the Philippines in the 1990s". *Asian Journal of Political Science* 17, no. 3 (2009): 265–84.

Teehankee, J. "And the Clans Play On". Philippine Center for Investigative Journalism. 2007 <http://pcij.org/stories/and-the-clans-play-on>.

Transparency International. "Corruption Perceptions Index". 2015 <http://www.transparency.org/research/cpi/>.

Usui, N. *Tax Reforms toward Fiscal Consolidation*. Mandaluyong City: ADB, 2011.

Vogel, I. "Review of the Use of 'Theory of Change' in International Development: Review Report". United Kingdom: Department for International Development, 2012.

World Bank. "Combating Corruption in the Philippines". World Bank Report 20369-PH. 2000.

————. "Improving Government Performance: Discipline, Efficiency, and Equity in Managing Public Resources". World Bank Report 24256-PH. 2003.

————. "Public Expenditure and Financial Accountability". World Bank Report 54584-PH. 2010.

————. *Philippines Development Report: Creating More and Better Jobs.* Manila, World Bank, 2013.

————. "Worldwide Governance Indicators". 2015 <http://info.worldbank.org/governance/wgi/index.aspx#home>.

World Economic Forum. *Global Competitive Report.* Geneva, various years.

Index